The American Fighting Man

THE

FIGHTING

The Macmillan Company **/** *New York*

Victor Hicken

AMERICAN
MAN

Collier-Macmillan Ltd. **/** *London*

The Macmillan Company, New York
Collier-Macmillan Canada Ltd., Toronto, Ontario

PRINTED IN THE UNITED STATES OF AMERICA

Contents

Foreword

MY INTEREST IN THE AMERICAN FIGHTING MAN began as far back as the 1930's when the United States still had a volunteer Army and Navy, and a volunteer Marine Corps. Many young men joined the services in those days simply because there was nothing else for them to do. Occasionally they came back on leave to visit their families, and were objects of wonder to every bright-eyed youngster in town. In those days the sailors wore the names of their vessels on black-strip bands around their caps. There was something eternally romantic about those titles—The U. S. S. *Pennsylvania,* the U. S. S. *Houston,* or the U. S. S. *Marblehead.* Army boys —the privates, that is—wore belted uniforms, well tailored, and they usually wore a string of metal bands won for marksmanship. The Marines always wore the brightly colored uniforms of the Corps. All of these boys—no matter what branch of service—were proud and swaggering, and just a little scornful of services other than their own.

The 1930's was just about the last decade of the old America. Memorial Day parades were really grand occasions. In my own small town the parades were led by an aging Spanish-American War veteran who rode a great brown horse. Then came the veterans of World War I; men who were in their early thirties. Lastly, and in an open touring car, came the one remaining Civil War veteran of the area. This gentleman was a bearded old patriarch who could still remember the fighting at Vicksburg, and who still, out of pride, wore a suit similar to his Union Army uniform every day of his life.

I do not mean to bewail the fact, but things are just not what they were years ago. The nation has become the world's leading power, and American boys, like Romans of old, man the walls of empire and attempt to keep the peace. Memorial Day is a day more for picknicking than parades; the reason being, I suppose, that our lives are too full of the housekeeping of empire for Americans to see much glory in it.

But that is the way history is. Perhaps someday the power of the United States will fade, just as Rome's and Britain's did. Then historians will write about the great American civilization, what it gave to the world, and how the idealism of its people uplifted an era. Old hates will be forgotten; old enmities will die; and writers will lament about the glories of the American past, when everything seemed to be well ordered and in good hands.

There is little written about the ordinary Roman soldier who marched with Caesar into Gaul, or who manned the walls of Hadrian. The British "Tommy," with all his qualities, is close enough in history for us to remember something of his role in maintaining *Pax Britannica*. Now someone must write of the American fighting man and his part in the growth of the American imperium. This I have attempted to do, sparing none of his faults, and emphasizing all of his virtues. In some ways, what follows is really a handbook on the American fighting man; in other ways it is a history. What I really intended to do was to write a tribute; simple, direct, and truthful.

No writer could attempt to do this without the help of others. Mr. Robert Markel of The Macmillan Company gave me the encouragement and advice to carry out the project. Librarians Balk, Wardell, and Huff of Western Illinois University gave great assistance in locating materials and information. The librarians of Knox College (Galesburg, Illinois), the University of Illinois, and the Illinois State Historical Library were extremely cooperative. Old friend Dr. Robert Allen of the Library of Congress gave me good advice. Mr. Don Daudelin, another friend, gave me access to his rather astounding collection of military history. Without the fine war letters of Professor Don Marshall, a colleague of twenty years or so, I would have been severely handicapped. William Carver of the Jewish War Veterans of the United States, and Kenneth A. Lohf of Special Collections, Columbia University, offered much assistance. Last but not least, Wilbur J. Nigh and Thomas E. Hohmann, both of the World War II Reference Branch, National Archives and Records Survey of the General Services Administration, were kind and helpful, and extremely patient.

More military histories will be written, because there will be more wars. This then is not a final summation on the American fighting man. I fervently hope, however, that the message this book carries is that the American people and their men in uniform represent something rather remarkable in history. I hope also to evoke thoughts of a great past and a valiant present. The fighting men of the United States are entitled to it.

V. H.

The American Fighting Man

1

The Military American:

His Wars and His Motivations

WAR CAN BE DEFINED IN A VARIETY OF WAYS. Grotius, centuries ago, claimed that it was a "condition of those contending by force. . . ." Only a few decades ago General Karl von Clausewitz argued that it was a simple "continuation of political intercourse, with a mixture of other means." A more recent scholar has written that war is a "legal condition which equally permits two or more hostile groups to carry on a conflict by armed force."[1]

Whatever the more acceptable definition of the word, it may be contended with great certainty that no national history is truly free of war. Switzerland, so often pointed to these days as a model of peaceful neutrality, merely gives the lie to its stormy past. Not only have the Swiss a military history, but they have long been regarded as among the best of all mercenary warriors. Of the three other traditionally neutral European nations, Sweden, Norway, and Belgium, only the first was able to escape involvement in the last two world wars.

As in the case of most of the nations of the West, it is in the American custom to regard peace as a normal state of affairs. The words "domestic peace and tranquillity" are written into sacred national documents, and almost every President has seen fit to use the word freely. President Truman, for instance, regarded the Korean War, publicly, as a "police action" designed to preserve the peace. President Lyndon Johnson, likewise, followed the same line in relation to the fighting in Vietnam, stating more than once that American troops were in that unhappy land in order to restore peace and stability.

Of the two words *war* and *peace,* war is more the fact of American history; peace is the euphemism. One writer has claimed that, during the history of the United States Army, American troops have taken part in approximately 9,000 battles and skirmishes and in 135 fighting sieges. Neither has the United States Navy been idle, engaging in fifteen fighting sieges, 1,131 clearly hostile encounters, and the capture of approximately 4,000 vessels of all types.[2] The third branch of the military service, the Marine Corps, was used to effect 180 landings of various types between the time of its formation and 1926. Some of these forays were partially ceremonial, some were designed to protect American property on foreign shores, but the greatest number involved a clear personal danger of one sort or another to the Americans involved.[3]

Most of these actions were not parts of what the generalist would call "wars"; that is, the declared and formal kind of conflict. It is, in fact, rather difficult to calculate the real number of wars in which Americans have truly taken part. Using the year 1607 as a base, one could conclude that American fighting men have seen action in twenty-two distinct major military contests up to the end of the Korean War. These would include such pre-Revolutionary wars as the Seven Years' War, and the War of the Austrian Succession; and a number of such lesser known post-1783 conflicts as the Franco-American Naval War, the Filipino Insurrection of 1899, and the Boxer Rebellion of 1900.[4]

Truly, if one uses only the simplest definition of war, a condition in which force is in effect, one must come to the conclusion that the American people have rarely seen a period when their men have not been off somewhere fighting an enemy—be it Indians, the people of some discontented island, or even other Americans. It is a matter of history, for instance, that Americans have not fought in Korea just once, but several times. The whole of the nineteenth century is filled with accounts of the use of force against the American Indian, while the twentieth century is filled with the actions of American fighting men in Asia and in the Caribbean.

The great tragedy is that, with the growing participation of the United States in world affairs during the last six decades, Americans have had to fight with increasing frequency. One historian has written that, in the fifty years following the Spanish-American War, only two of those years found the Marine Corps entirely free of combat duty. Some of the wars of this century that have involved Americans are passed over much too lightly by the military historian. Some seventy thousand American troops, for instance, were needed to quell the Filipinos at the turn of the century. Though scarcely considered a major conflict by many, the fighting in the Philippines was hard and bitter. In one incident on Samar, a little remindful of those of Vietnam sixty years later, an entire company of the Ninth U. S. Infantry was caught by guerrillas and killed. The abdomen of each soldier was ripped open and filled with jam in order to attract the flies.

There was retaliation of course. Shortly thereafter an American officer told his troops: "I want no prisoners. I wish you to burn and kill; the more you burn and kill, the better it will please me."[5] Yet, historically, this is one of those conflicts of American history more often placed in the category of the "nonwar."

One feature of the declared war is that it is seldom difficult to determine the number of casualties sustained by American fighting men in these conflicts. This is not so true of the lesser conflict— the "nonwar," the "police action," or the military expedition. The so-called Indian Wars are a notable example of this. History does show that over 100,000 American soldiers fought in these conflicts between 1870 and 1900, and that over 1,000 of them were killed in combat.[6] What it does not reveal are the number of pneumonia-ridden cavalrymen who died during the long forced marches, and were buried on the trail. Nor is it easy to trace down the number of ordinary soldiers who perished because of cold, want, or starvation, while serving in remote frontier posts in the eighteenth or nineteenth centuries.

One of the reasons for this is that Americans have rarely understood or stopped to analyze their own national character. The history of the nation has too often been written and read in order to confirm certain fundamental prejudices. One conceives of American history as filled with broad periods of peace; and so are the histories written, unmindful that the very nature of the American rise to greatness is the story of struggle against adversity.

Who was the first American fighting man? Discounting the Indians, he was very likely the first European who settled in the New World. One may be sure, for instance, that John Smith at Jamestown, or other settlers up at Plymouth, fired a few shots in anger at those who, two centuries later, would be called "hostiles."

The first war of any significance in the colonies was a dandy little fight between the settlers in Massachusetts and the Pequot Indians. Fought in 1637, it resulted in the virtual eradication of that particular enemy. From that time on, the Americans were almost constantly at war, either with the Redskins or with the French and their Indian allies. Never enormous in contemporary terms, the dangers of such frontier conflicts were such that the American pioneer considered his three most important possessions to be his gun, his axe, and his plow—in that order.

So great did the colonials regard the twin menaces of the French and the Indians that by 1730 every colony had a militia system in operation. Connecticut, for example, with only 100,000 inhabitants in 1739, had thirteen regiments of infantry militia. By 1774 the same colony had almost doubled the number.[7] Though the Connecticut Yankee was untrained in the niceties of more formalized warfare, he could and did fight hard on occasion. Every major colonial war found American militia in action, and though these men disliked stand-up warfare, much to the scorn of their British officers, they sometimes exhibited infinitely more battle wisdom than their commanders. One has only to recall the appropriate story about Daniel Boone's participation in Braddock's campaign into Pennsylvania. Boone, a wagoner, was so certain of disaster that, hours before it occurred, he hitched his reins so he might quickly disengage the horses from the wagon and escape. Braddock, had he lived, might have called it spineless cowardice. Boone, who did survive, often referred to it as the smartest thing he ever did.

If there was one lesson the British did absorb from Braddock's crushing defeat during the French and Indian War, it was that fighting in North America was infinitely different from that of Minden and Fontenoy in Europe. On the last-named battlefield, the British commander had shouted to his opponents: "Gentlemen of France, fire first!" Indians and French half-breeds needed no such invitation; they simply picked off the British officers one by one.

The result of this dark experience was a recognition that perhaps the American militia units, with their tendency to march light and to fight from cover, really had something after all. Thus, in December, 1755, various agents of the King began the recruitment of the first unit to be designed for special duty in the Americas. Officially approved by Parliament in 1756, the regiment was called the Royal Americans, or the Sixty-Second Regiment (later renumbered the Sixtieth Regiment). Fifty commissions were granted to the regiment, the actual commander of the unit being Colonel Henri Boquet, an able Swiss soldier who had served in Sardinia and in Holland.

The concepts involved in the establishment of the Royal Americans were greatly different from those hitherto practiced in the British army. First of all, many of the battalions were to be composed of recruits mainly from Pennsylvanians of German descent. The reasoning here was that these men would not only be sturdy fighters for Protestantism, but that their inclusion in the army would establish a base for support of the war in Quaker Pennsylvania.[8]

Second, the regiment was to be trained to fight and fire in open order, a method of combat much more suitable to the wilderness than the close order traditionally practiced. The men were equipped with the standard musket of the day, which weighed slightly over twelve pounds, sufficient lead to conduct a good fire fight, and a uniform more appropriate to the forests of North America. This last was indeed a radical departure from the time, when regiments went in for the brightest of reds and blues. The uniform of the Royal Americans was principally green, the only concession to sprightliness being the red garters to be worn on dress occasions.

By the end of 1756 the Royal Americans were considered among the best of His Majesty's Regiments in North America. Portions of the unit took part in the 1757 Louisberg campaign, while another battalion, which included James Fenimore Cooper's future father-in-law, was involved in a stiff fight at Fort William Henry. Other battalions fought at Ticonderoga, Niagara, Duquesne, and Quebec. In the last, the most important battle of the French and Indian War, the Second Battalion of the Royal Americans lost one-third of its complement, and it was while he was with this unit that General Wolfe was killed.

During the American Revolution the Royal Americans saw action in the British campaigns in the South. In general, however, the regiment served in a limited capacity; perhaps because, as the regimental historian has written, the soldiers had little heart for a fight between themselves and their fellow countrymen.

Following the end of the Revolution, the name of the unit was eventually changed to the King's Royal Rifle Corps. Under this title it has maintained a brilliant record, having at present more battle honors on its colors than any other regiment in the British army. One strange sequel to the story of the Royal American Regiment lies in the attachment it has retained with the land of its origin. Americans have served with honor with the King's Royal Rifles in both recent world wars. Seventeen Americans, some of them of Italian ancestry, fought with distinction with the unit in World War II, and four of them were killed.[9]

The foregoing brief history of the Royal American Regiment only serves to illustrate that America was a source of good fighting men long before the Revolution. Thus, it was natural that, when the colonies began the fight for independence, there was no initial trouble in raising a force to contend against the British. The real problem, as it turned out, was in persuading the men to stay on in the service. After all, no one could have imagined in 1775 the magnitude of the task the struggling colonies were undertaking.

As a prominent historian has written: "The Revolution is the longest war in which the United States has engaged, and it was, by the standards of the times and for the rebelling colonies, a stupendous military undertaking." The fight for independence lasted over eighty months, almost twice as long as the Civil War. Approximately 400,000 Americans enlisted at one time or another during the war, and when one considers that the national population of the period was two and a half million (perhaps one-fifth Negro), the number of fighting men produced is something to contemplate.[10] Even qualifying the figures by duplication of enlistments, the number of Americans who fought is still rather astounding. Add to this the Americans who fought for the British—at King's Mountain, for instance—and the estimated eighteen thousand privateers who operated against the British merchant fleet, and it is probable that the total of fighting Americans during the Revolution is equal to the American commitment to Vietnam in midsummer of 1966.

With the end of the Revolution in 1783, what existed of the American Navy disappeared completely, and the Army became virtually nonexistent. By 1790 the last named service consisted of a grand force of fifty-seven officers and 1,216 enlisted men, scarcely enough to put down a modern metropolitan riot. The American Indian came to the rescue of the Army once again, however, and the troubles in the Northwest Territory brought about a slight renaissance of that branch of the service. The Army, continuing to grow after 1800 because of the threat of Tecumseh, reached a total of ten thousand officers and men by 1810. By 1800 the United States Navy had also reemerged, having not only some of the swiftest and best designed ships on the high seas, but a naval complement of 5,400, and a Marine force of 525.[11]

Even so, when the War of 1812 began, no branch of the service was really ready. The Navy had too few ships, the Army was as poorly led as it would ever be, and the Marines were insufficient in number. Besides these handicaps, the War of 1812 was another of those conflicts in American military history concerning which the public was not sure that the national administration was right in its determination to fight.

It seems easy for present day historians to dwell upon the War of 1812 as one of the two conflicts in which American forces did not gain the decisive victory; the other being the Korean War. Perhaps this is because the total picture is seldom viewed. Actually the American fighting man of the period didn't do badly at all. Many battles were stubbornly contested engagements. General Emory Upton, a post-Civil War authority, asserted that the fight at Lundy's Lane was more costly in percentage of losses than any other American battle up to 1900. At New Orleans, General Andrew Jackson's men inflicted two thousand casualties upon the British, while suffering only seventy of their own. Too, what is generally forgotten about the war is the role privateers took in the fighting. Regarded by the British as "sea devils," these men took or destroyed some 1,600 merchant ships. By 1814, the cost of marine insurance covering even an Irish Sea crossing was prohibitive to all but the most prosperous British merchants.[12]

At the time of the Texas Revolution, the Army had increased in size from its turn-of-the-century complements. With the coming of the war with Mexico ten years later, the Regular Army was enlarged to 32,000, and 60,000 volunteer soldiers were brought into the service. The Navy, whose role in the war would be a limited one, enjoyed no significant increase in numbers except in relation to the Marine Corps. It may be noted here that, even though the feeling for the war with Mexico ran high in the United States, the total number of men participating in the conflict never once came close to American manpower statistics in the Revolutionary War.

There are, indeed, numerous misconceptions regarding the war with Mexico. First, the blame for the war does not, as many believe, rest entirely upon the United States; war fever in Mexico was equal to that of its northern neighbor. Second, the war was not, as many historians have been inclined to believe, a matter of David against Goliath. Mexico had a highly trained army in the early stages of the war, and its shock cavalry was European-trained and generally regarded as among the best in the world. All the geographical advantages lay with Mexico. It could fight the war on interior lines, while the United States had logistical and material problems of considerable magnitude.

Yet the small and usually outnumbered American armies never lost a battle, and the great wonder of modern military history should be Winfield Scott's campaign against Mexico City. With a force of six to ten thousand men, the Americans marched over 260 miles of rugged terrain, fought numerous battles, kept their supply lines open, and still had enough morale to police Mexico City once it had been taken. Thirteen years later it took Napoleon III's thirty thousand French regulars eighteen months to take the same city, and they did not do it without an almost disastrous check at Puebla. And a last tribute to the American fighting man of 1846–1848 is that battle deaths for the entire war totaled only 1,721; a credit to the sublime courage of the men involved and their leaders.[13]

After the Treaty of Guadalupe-Hidalgo the American Army was once again allowed to fall into a numerical decline. The entire force was reduced to ten thousand men, and was divided into eight regiments of infantry, four of artillery, two of dragoons, and one of mounted infantrymen. Though it was indeed small, the Army toughened to the tasks it was required to perform. It had to, because the number of men averaged out to one soldier for each 120 square miles west of the Mississippi.[14]

By the time of the attack on Camp Sumter in 1861, both the Army and the Navy consisted of good professional military men, who were commanded by competent officers. Truly, if these forces had been allowed to enter the Civil War intact, the Confederacy would have been so short-lived as to be almost a dream. But what happened was one of the real tragedies of history. While the Federal Army, from noncoms on down, remained loyal almost to a man, its more competent officers went South. The Navy, though less torn by such division, had quite another problem. Some of its officers, though excellent, were almost infirm. Many of these men were soon forced to resign, thus leaving the fleet with a loyal but traditionally very young enlisted complement, and a number of fairly inexperienced officers.[15]

It ought to be added that the Marine Corps barely reached five thousand men in the course of the war. Its use was truly limited, and it gained little glory in the conflict. Marine historians, as a matter of record, tend to skip blithely through that whole period of history that begins with the real accomplishments of the Corps at Chapultepec and ends with courageous activities of Marines in the Spanish-American War.

From any standpoint the Civil War was the most terrible struggle in American military history up to the time of the Pearl Harbor attack. The combined number of battle deaths for the Army, Navy, and Marine Corps approximated 140,000 men, and 94,000 more Americans were killed in the cause of the Confederacy. One has to look at total numbers, however. Though the number of deaths due to disease did decrease from 110 per thousand men in the Mexican War to 65 per thousand men in the Civil War (Federal forces), the very duration of the war caused great losses in this respect. The total number of deaths for the Federal Army alone was 364,511; a figure which is three times the number of American dead in World War I, seven times the number of deaths in the Korean War, and short by some 40,000 of the total American dead in World War II. And once again, in reminder, the figure 364,511 does not include Confederate deaths.[16]

The story of the Civil War has been well told. Because time has dimmed the horrors of the conflict, and because the struggle seems to have involved some quite elemental issues, a kind of mystique has grown up around the Americans who fought on both sides. What is strange is that it seems a little more appropriate and virtuous to write that a day at Gettysburg cost America more in lives than did Tarawa, and that a few minutes at Antietam may have equaled thirty days of fighting in Normandy. But what is always missing in any account is an understanding that the Civil War was a spasmodic kind of conflict, with major battles being fought when conditions of nature, supply, and spirit were just right. World Wars I and II, as well as the Korean War, were fought as almost continuous struggles—from trenches, mountain sides, aircraft, and ships. Indeed, the awfulness in World War II stands alone, for in that war the monthly average of battle deaths of Americans was 4,576, twice as many as the monthly average for the Civil War.[17]

The old cycle of decline returned to the fighting forces following the peace at Appomattox. The Army once again became a slender force of tough professionals, whose main task was the handling of the Indian problem. The Marine Corps suffered a slight decrease in size, and the Navy fell into a state of virtual disrepair; a condition in which it was to flounder until the Cleveland Administration in the 1880's. In that decade a naval building program was commenced, partially to draw off some of the treasury surplus of the time.

Thus, at the beginning of the War of 1898, the nation had a finely honed little Army of 25,000 officers and men, a tightly knit and thoroughly professional Marine Corps, and a new but rather poorly constructed fleet. During the four months of fighting with Spain, the Army grew to approximately 280,000 men, and the Navy was appropriately increased in size. The war itself was an exciting one, at least for the American public, and one in which the American fighting man behaved quite courageously and had a good deal of luck. The total battle deaths for the war seem ridiculously small, only 345 men; yet, in terms of monthly averages, they exceed the monthly human cost of the American Revolution and the War of 1812, and they equal to a man the monthly deaths of Americans in the Mexican War.[18]

As the United States has discovered, the real cost of the Spanish American War lay in its results. The nation came out of the war with a new Asian interest, the Philippines; a Caribbean responsibility in Puerto Rico; and demonstrated need for an Isthmian canal. The changes in American foreign policy that occurred because of these developments were highly significant. For forty-eight of the next fifty years the Marine Corps would be on combat duty somewhere—in Asia or the Caribbean. Three of the four major wars the United States would fight in the next sixty-five years would begin in Asia—partly as a result of the acquisition of the Philippines—and they would result in the killing and wounding of 450,000 American servicemen. Thus did that little war with Spain in 1898 have some far-reaching and significant effects.[19]

Despite the obvious fact that the nature of war had changed greatly in the previous seventeen years, the entrance of the United States into World War I found the armed forces in no state of preparedness. True, "be prepared" had been the highly publicized policy of the Wilson Administration, but the American Army was nothing less than a joke. It consisted of 92,000 good regulars, about 285,000 standard quality rifles, about five combat-ready airplanes, 550 antiquated artillery pieces, and enough ammunition for a nine-hour barrage. The Marine Corps, which had almost been put out of existence by interservice rivalry in the early 1900's, had recovered its political and military viability by 1917 and was a tough and dedicated outfit. The Navy, thanks to the new imperial responsibilities of the nation, was of good size and was equipped with a number of the new dreadnought class of battleship.[20]

The really great wonder of World War I is what American initiative and drive accomplished. A great army was raised, four million in all, and there were 800,000 men in the other branches of service. Half of the men wearing uniform managed to experience overseas service. By January, 1918, American doughboys and Marines were holding six miles of the Allied trenches in France. Seven months later they were in possession of fifty-five miles of trenches, and in October they held 101 miles of the line—almost twenty more than the British. These young men fought a bitter kind of war, suffering 54,000 battle deaths, 63,000 deaths from other causes, and 204,000 nonmortal wounds.[21] Short as the American participation in the war was, it involved so many new horrors for the ordinary fighting man that, despite the noble attempts to do so, a history which truly conveys the spirit of life in the trenches has never been written. Perhaps the reason for this lies in the words of the noted American medical officer of the war, Harvey Cushing. "Such was the war," he concluded."It was not a quadrille in a ballroom. Its interior history will not only never be written, its practicality, minutiae of deeds and passions, will never be suggested."[22]

There are some surprising misconceptions which abound concerning the great American effort of 1917 and 1918. Much of the nation's literary output in the 1920's was written around the horrors of the war, and in particular, about the effects of gas attacks. There was also a good deal put into print about the American conquest of disease in the trenches. With qualifications it can be said that both categories of writing suffered from poetic license. First of all, though over eighty thousand soldiers were affected by gas in some way, the actual number of deaths from this terrible weapon was slightly over two thousand. Second, the problem of the sick soldier was still a significant one. Disease accounted for 26 percent of the losses in the American Army, only 4 percent less than the comparable figure for the Russian army. At one time, November, 1918, over 190,000 American fighting men were in hospitals in France, most of them suffering from influenza and pneumonia.[23]

In the 1920's only the Navy was able to maintain a substantial portion of its numerical strength attained during the war. Indeed, it is a surprising fact that, even as late as 1939, the Navy plus the Marine Corps was almost as large as the Army in terms of personnel. The last-named branch of the service totaled only 190,000 in a period just after the Munich Agreement, and in the same year as the German invasion of Poland.

Yet, looking at the figures for the size of the American military forces in 1939, historians of the future will surely be amazed at the magnitude of the country's effort in the next six years. Such a national girding of the loins may never happen again, for the nature of global war changed quite radically after 1946. By 1945 the Army reached a size of 8,267,958 (it had been 189,839); the Navy climbed to 3,380,817 (it had been 125,202); and the Marine Corps totaled 474,-680 (it had been 19,432). Parenthetically, it also may be added that it was a fortunate circumstance the war came to an end when it did, for the bottom of the manpower barrel had been reached. Men with corrected club feet, or with only one eye, were being "selected" for limited duty at this stage of the struggle.[24]

If there is one common denominator for the Civil War, and for World Wars I and II, it is that the percentage of casualties per month increased with each month of the three conflicts. Grant's Petersburg campaign chewed up thousands of men in 1864 and 1865, and Lee's percentage losses at the same time were even higher than those of his enemy. In the Argonne Forest in 1918 the Americans suffered 120,000 casualties while taking only 1,550 square kilometers of territory; over 770 Americans per kilometer of ground taken. The highest casualty rates for World War II may be presented as two different figures: 59,000 per month for the last seven months of the fighting in Europe; and 12,750 per month during the American invasion of Okinawa, which came late in the war with Japan.[25]

The hue and cry for the quick dissolution of American military strength was an effective one after the final defeat of the Axis Powers. By 1950 the United States Army had shrunk to only 600,000, less than half the size of the Army during the Pearl Harbor attack. Something else of importance also had happened to that arm of the service. The caliber of garrison forces in the Far East was allowed to deteriorate, and laxity had crept into the officer corps. The equipment located in Japan and Korea was not only inadequate in quantity, but much of it was unworkable. Transport was in such bad shape that many trucks had to be towed in tandem, and such light tanks as were available were outmoded and unfit for duty. As for defensive equipment, there was an almost complete lack of anti-tank guns, and the "bazookas" with which each unit was equipped were leftover remnants from World War II. Thus, when the North Korean forces crossed the border into the South, they were faced by unsuitable South Korean and American defensive strength.

It is very likely that in no other war did the American fighting man meet with such ill luck. The Twenty-Fourth Infantry Division, substandard in numbers, was rushed into the fighting and was cut to pieces. Eventually Marine Corps units and some better Army regiments were brought in, and these not only stabilized on a defensive line, but were able to turn the tide of battle. The North Koreans were pushed back with a combination of brilliant strategy and heroic effort, and for one brief moment an astounding victory seemed to be at hand. Then thousands of Chinese "volunteers" were brought across the Yalu River, the Americans and other United Nations units found themselves once more facing a new and numerically superior foe, and the tide became outgoing again.[26]

Many have argued that the Korean War was not a victory for the American fighting men, basing their arguments on the fact that the Chinese were not driven back past the Yalu River. Yet history will show that, within the framework of war allowed to him by diplomacy and politics, the American combat man did everything that was asked of him. A line was established against the Chinese in 1951, and American search-and-destroy operations were causing tremendous casualties among the enemy ranks. In one such sweep in that year American forces killed or wounded 4,200 Chinese in eight days, losing only seventy men from their own ranks. The important statistic on the war is the final one, however. The Korean War cost the United States 142,000 casualties, and the North Koreans and the Chinese, an estimated one and a half million men.[27]

The great lessons of the Korean War were manifold. In essence they simply illustrate that an army can quickly become substandard in the quality of both equipment and men. As the 1950's rolled by, it became obvious that Army authorities were determined to emphasize the "selective" aspect of Selective Service. Great importance was placed on obtaining the best physical and mental specimens available. By 1966 it was possible to say not only that seven out of eight men in all of the services were volunteers, but that the remaining draftees were virtually handpicked out of the manpower pool. It was also possible to note that the Army had gone back to the building of *esprit de corps* in individual units, thus increasing the possibilities of pride in victory and anger in defeat among individual fighting men. These changes brought the Army in tune with the traditional pride of the sailor in his ship, and the *élan* and *esprit* of the Marine Corps.

The vastness of the American military commitment was also impressive by 1966. August of that year saw 365,000 Americans involved in the Vietnam struggle, 340,000 others stationed in European continental bases, 34,000 in Britain, and 4,000 in Iceland. And these figures do not include all the Naval and Marine Corps personnel in the service at that time, or American servicemen who were stationed in North America at that time.

It would be difficult, indeed, to provide figures on just how many American men have been enlisted on military rolls of one sort or another since 1607. In the two centuries following the American

Revolution, statistics were poorly kept at times. Guesses are sometimes necessary, however, and it is possible to estimate that around 35.7 million American fighting men saw military service between 1775 and 1965. The bulk of those men are still alive, approximately twenty-two million of them, and they include some six or seven survivors of the Indian Wars, a scattering of Spanish-American War veterans, a fairly large number of World War I fighting men, millions of veterans of World War II, and a vast number of individuals who wore the uniform after 1946. Thus is the nature of the *Pax Americana* which most of the rest of the world may criticize and yet enjoy. One out of every nine Americans in 1960 had lived to be able to relate his part in the creation of it. The millions who died in battle, or who have passed on since, are mute.[28]

There is no question that the great majority of Americans who have worn the military uniform have done so because the nation has demanded it of them by law. Yet patriotism is and always has been a factor in the battlefield motivation of the American fighting man.

One of the greatest misconceptions of the various nations that have engaged in war with America has been that the soldiers and sailors of that nation could not possibly fight with spirit because they are of a "mongrel" people, untied to the United States by blood, culture, and tradition. This assumption, when voiced by German and Japanese leaders in World War II, was just as ridiculous then as it must have sounded when asserted by British and French officers prior to 1783.

This mistake has always provided a peculiar advantage to the American fighting man, for in almost every war in which he has fought, his enemy has suffered from an early sense of overconfidence; the feeling that Americans could not possibly love their country enough to die for it. There are some who say that the turning point in the recent war with Japan came when, after the savage battle of Tarawa, the Japanese military suddenly realized that American Marines could die with great courage for a piece of real estate about which they knew nothing. What the Japanese really saw here was a later version of a characteristic noted by a French commander in the Seven Years' War, a decade before the Revolution. Americans may not look like fighters, he wrote, but given a reasonable goal they can charge like "devils."

Historians, who dearly love to play with numbers, often argue that American public sentiment during the Revolution was divided into three areas of thought. One-third of the people were for the Revolution, one-third were pro-British, and one-third were "neutral" on the side of the winner. Despite this easy generalization, it can truly be stated that the large majority of the American people were committed to one side or the other, and patriotism was a factor in the choice of their cause.

The fact is that many Americans chose to stay loyal to the British King out of a love for their country. It is not unreasonable to think that there were patriots of a kind who wanted to continue the tie with England. The great emotion felt by these people drove them not only to support the British forces whenever possible, but to supply to them American combat units. Evidence of the intensity of this spirit is to be found in the records of many of the Tory military units. One of them, for example, fought bitterly at King's Mountain, though the end result was defeat. There were many soldiers among the Revolutionary Army who claimed, even during the war, that they much preferred fighting the King's Regulars than American Tory soldiers.

Looking more intently at the Revolutionary soldier, however, one finds that he was a type of fighting man easily recognizable to the present-day American. He was, most of all, an independent sort; he disliked the outward signs of discipline, the marching, the commands, and the differences of rank; he was a practical and ambitious sort, impatient with foolishness, and ingenious in necessity. He was good humored in the face of adversity; and lastly, he *knew,* with certainty, that God was on his side.

The last characteristic was basic in the patriot fighting man. In some ways it exhibited itself in peculiar forms. One old soldier, fifty years beyond his participation in the Lexington and Concord fights, remembered that he fought so hard simply because the British were trying to take away liberties he had always enjoyed. Weeks before that famous episode the British had saturated the countryside with spies. Some of these, on their way back to Boston, stopped at a wayside inn, where they were served by a Negro girl. When, in attempting to gather information, they commented to her on the fine appearance of the land, she replied: "So it is, and we have got brave fellows to defend it."[29]

Documents and historical writings are filled with evidences of the pure patriotism of Revolutionary soldiers. Officers were often chosen by their men on the basis of their "love of liberty." An American militiaman, taking part in the siege of Boston early in the war, wrote concerning the British: "The Red Coated Philistines fired 31 cannon and 3 bums at the Sons of Liberty, who were building a parapet to secure themselves against the diabolical rage of the Parliamentary tools on Bunker Hill." And General Anthony Wayne commented after the Battle of Stony Point: "Our officers and men behaved like men who are determined to be free."[30]

"Liberty" as a patriotic goal was to the Revolution what "the Union forever" was to the Federal soldier of the Civil War. It was patriotism salted down with idealism. It was love of country mixed with principle. The British were positive in 1775 that Americans could never fight for such a quasi-abstraction, and there were even some Americans who were surprised when their countrymen did. "Was it credible," John Adams wrote, after viewing Continental troops, "that men who could get at home better living, more comfortable lodgings, more than double the wages, in safety, not exposed to the sicknesses of the camp, would bind themselves during the war."[31]

The strangeness of it all was that the lessons of the Revolution would soon be forgotten by would-be enemies of the United States, or even future American generals. American military men of every war since 1783 have complained about the lack of patriotism among their common soldiers; most often arguing that such men are just not as "good" as their fathers. Enemy generals have questioned the motives of American fighting men in every war after 1800. Yet British scholar Trevelyan discovered indelible traces of patriotism among Americans as early as the Revolution. "These men," he wrote, "entertained very definite notions about the cause which they had brought with them from their ploughs, from their dairies, and from the counters of their stores." And an American historian would just as succinctly say of the fighting American of 1776: "He was a humble instrument in a great cause; he profited by an opportunity that does not come in every generation."[32]

It is true that the motives which have inspired the individual American fighting men are as varied as human nature can conspire to make them. What made an Indiana boy walk one hundred miles in order to enlist for the war against Mexico? Was it unadultered patriotism or a desire for adventure? What caused thirty thousand Tennesseans to volunteer for the same war, when the quota for that state was only 2,800? Why did Westerners in 1861 flood the recruiting booths, and what made them walk scores of miles to join regiments of other states when their own state's quota was filled? To be sure, the reasons may have included ambition or love of adventure, but underlying all was the subtle call of the flag.[33]

The same can be said of 1898 and 1917. Recruiting posters, particularly in the early months of World War I, laid heavy emphasis on the patriotic motif. Invariably they were painted in the national colors, or they displayed the American flag. The underlying theme of the national effort was love of country. Thus, whether a draftee or volunteer, the American fighting man of 1917 and 1918 felt free to wear his patriotism on his sleeve. A Y.M.C.A. camp director noticed that the most popular songs among the troops in 1917 were "Over There" and "The Battle Hymn of the Republic." Without fail, he noticed, the reaction to the last song was an emotional one. The lines were solemnly and forcefully sung, as if the soldiers were attempting to evoke the great national past.

To the researcher, scrutinizing the dusty letters of the fighting men of World War I is a difficult and heartbreaking task, simply because of the real emotions that parade in step across the pages. Almost without exception, each new recruit writes of his love for the flag. He seldom refers to what the boys of Ohio or North Carolina will do to the enemy soldiers, as Civil War soldiers were inclined to do. The doughboy revels in his national pride. He becomes elementally sentimental, as did a 1918 American who wrote: "We must fight and fight for our rights of the flag of the Red, White and Blue." And he wrote such poetry as this:

> Yes, the hearts beat wild with joy
> When they look upon the flag
> And behold its colors bright
> O'er the homeland of the brave
> Let this emblem wave
> O'er all nations for the right.[34]

Such an unabashed patriotism was not quite so evident in the American fighting men of 1941. Few of these latter-day soldiers felt the call of the muse, and in fact, there were even some observers of the day who were worried about the seeming lack of good patriotic songs. "Where, in this war, is Mr. Zip-Zip-Zip?" asked a prominent historian in the midst of the conflict. Perhaps he had been too busy writing his book to take pause and listen.[35] By 1944 there was a host of patriotic songs ranging from "Remember Pearl Harbor," a piece of music hastily contrived after the big attack, to "Praise the Lord and Pass the Ammunition," a great favorite of the time. Every military camp rang to the sounds of "Anchors Aweigh," or similar specific service songs. And the unofficial national anthem during the entire war was Irving Berlin's "God Bless America."

But the World War II American was admittedly a far more silent fighting man than his predecessors. He was even inclined to greet overt patriotism with gestures of contempt. Yet in those unguarded moments when he wrote his loved ones, he could and did evince his love of *patrie*. "We're going to play for keeps so that 'Old Glory' will keep waving forever," a New York soldier wrote his parents in 1943. A sailor, fresh off the sunken carrier *Yorktown,* could write a real and fundamental meaning of his experience. "Deep down inside of me I've learned a lot. . . ." he confided to his parents. "My United States history has suddenly become quite clear. Washington, Hale, Grant and men who have served, and those who have died gloriously for our country—how easy it must have been for them to do as they did for such a great cause."[36]

For some American fighting men in World War II and in Korea, which followed, patriotism became inextricably entangled with other motivations and emotions. A few could say it very simply, like a Jewish soldier from New York City, who a week before his death, could write: "Private Gerald Herzfeld, in the service of a great country, for a great cause, for a great President." Other fighting men, particularly those who served in 1950 and 1951, could not be so direct. One American soldier in Korea, attempting to tie all his feelings together at the end of that conflict, wrote his parents:

I have a sense of pride for having served my country in two wars in the period of seven years—a claim that only a handful of millions of people who have lived in the U. S. in the past 175 years can make. It is demanding on your body and morale, but when successfully completed will always remain a point of pride. I don't want to be a "flag waver," but now that it is over . . . I'm not sorry I've been in Korea.[37]

The shade of difference between patriotism as a motivating force in the American fighting man and his basic national ideals can sometimes be so slight as to be almost indistinguishable. As has been illustrated, the American soldier of the Revolutionary period quite often got his love of liberty intermingled with his love for his land. In the War of 1812 the patriotic concept was an easily recognizable force in bringing an American to the colors. There was, in that war, much in the way of song and poetry about the flag and what it represented. Yet, when a soldier of 1814 sang "Hail Columbia, Happy Land," or when he read the lines of "The Star-Spangled Banner," he was clearly mixing pure patriotism with a few of the national ideals. The Confederate soldier of 1861 sang his "Dixie" and wrote home about "state sovereignty," while his opposite on the other side of the Rappahannock contended for "Old Glory" and "freedom."

The truth is that it is well-nigh impossible for the American fighting man to clearly separate his patriotism from his ideals. One must be sure of his ground in contending this point, however, for what the soldier sees as the ideals of the war may not conform with those of the propagandist. Modern social psychologists, turned loose on

World War II American soldiers, came to a conclusion that the idealism of the "Four Freedoms" was greatly subordinate to the realities of war in terms of major motivational forces.

It is quite easy to be misled by such surveys, however. One could probably argue with real conviction that few American fighting men of 1942 could name even one of the "Four Freedoms," but that is missing the point somewhat. The American Dream is difficult enough for the scholar to define, let alone the ordinary fighting men of a war; yet it is always there—in letters, diaries, or reminiscences of the common soldiers. A social worker, traveling through American military camps in 1917, found many soldiers who admitted that they lived in an "upside down" world and wished to put it right. A reporter of *L'Illustration,* a leading French publication, wrote that one of the first Yanks to land in 1917 had shouted: "I have come to fight all the kings." A France-bound American infantryman told another reporter in the same year that he was "fighting for the women and children of the world, and working toward that common end of 'making the world safe for democracy.'" And an Illinois private told his parents in 1918: "Now don't worry about us when we go across for a person don't die but once any how and if we do we will give our lives for a good cause."[38]

The fighting man of World War II was simultaneously both different from and alike to his predecessor of 1917. His patriotism was obviously more subdued; yet his idealism, though never strongly fortified with the concepts of the Atlantic Charter, could find a clear justification in the war. An American private, writing three months before his death in New Guinea, argued that "We are fighting for what appears to be the strongest hope for advancing the status of the individual man the world over." Another soldier, a sergeant in the South Pacific, expressed, as many did, his concern for the postwar world. "Maybe getting together with the rest of the world in a strong, determined organization won't work," he wrote. "Maybe we'll still have World War III. Maybe not. Down here a lot of us want to give the new way a chance."[39]

This idealistic concern for the world to come, the fear that there might be a future without freedom, struck deeper into the souls of

World War II American fighting men than many could realize. Looking backward, it seems that many such soldiers and sailors were anxious to set the world straight once and for all time. "I'd like to come home," a Midwestern sergeant wrote. "I won't deny that, but I wouldn't want to come home with the world in the sort of mess it is in. Maybe it will be possible for the next generation to get by without spending their lives and money for war, if so I won't regret these two Christmases away from you two and everything I love."[40]

There were times when the World War II American could write poignantly and expressively about the present and the future, and the sacrifices needed to achieve the ideals of the war. In 1943 an aviation cadet, writing a letter for his unborn child, crystallized the thoughts of many men of the day. "This fight we pursue is for you who will follow," he wrote, "for, in the winning of it, many of us will have lost all that gives to the world its savour. We want only, at the close of it, to return to whatever is left of the world we knew and finish out our time in peace." And a sailor, rescued from the sea during the Battle of Midway, wrote about his discovery of something special in the American Dream. "You can't beat men of that caliber," he commented about his fellow seamen. "It's so easy to do your job magnificently with the word 'Democracy' backing you up at all times. And it's just as easy and painless to die happily for that same word." He was a young man well prepared for the ultimate sacrifice, which he would eventually make.[41]

The United States is truly a nation of racial and ethnic minorities. Most of them have fulfilled the promise of the American Dream. There are still some who are called upon to fight in distant lands for a principle still unfulfilled in the land of their birth. So it has been with the American Negro. He fought in France in 1917 and 1918 in order to make the world, with the exception of his native soil, safe for democracy. He was brought into the service in World War II to fight for a freedom which he had never personally known.

Unfortunately, the American Negro of the past, handicapped by his inability to express himself, remains to a great extent a historical enigma. The hastily scribbled letter, found here and there, gives only vague clues to his feelings. Yet, one can sense in them the touch of idealism. The World War I Negro made occasional reference to making the world safe for democracy in every sense of the word. The same was true of the World War II American Negro fighting man. He always hoped that a little of the world's idealism would rub off on him. He *knew* that the world had to be a little better for him when he returned from the war. "Such things are all I have to think about," one World War II American Negro wrote, "that is, planning for the future."[42]

The American Jew, more literate, has always been caught up with the idealism of war. Even the Jewish Confederate soldier saw only the twin ideals of state sovereignty and freedom from Republican "tyranny" as goals of the Civil War. With a sort of strange contradiction to his own past, he found it easy to regard the Negro as a "nigger," and the Federal program of emancipation as unjust. The Federal Jewish soldier took quite a different tack. From the beginning he saw the true issue of the Civil War as the emancipation of the slave, and he fought quite bravely to achieve that goal.

The post-1900 Jewish fighting man presents a slightly different case. In many instances he was an escapee from the Russian and Polish *pogroms* of Europe. To be sure, the moment he set foot on American soil, his love of liberty and his desire for equality invariably became entangled with his sure knowledge that the achievement of these goals lay within the folds of the American flag. The Jewish-Americans of 1917 and 1918 took their love of the colors and the ideals of the war in equal doses, and thus the patriotism of the World War I Jew became intermingled with Wilsonian idealism.

There were similar instances in World War II. There was the German-Jewish soldier who broke down in tears when he was granted American citizenship. But World War II had, for the American Jew, some added implications. "I felt again it wasn't right for me to be safe behind the lines," wrote a Jewish soldier who had volunteered for front line duty. "I knew this meant fighting for me and my family because if Hitler won, my family . . . would certainly suffer more than the families of other soldiers who died in the fight."

For the American Jew who fought in Europe the war was touched with both idealism and realism; the last stemming from the sure knowledge that in victory lay the survival of the Jewish tradition. "In case I don't return," a young Jewish private wrote his parents in 1943, "I shall know I have not died in vain, but to make the world safe for all the Jerry Herzfelds that are to be born in the future." Another Jew in the same theater of war, shortly to be killed in front-line duty, wrote his family: "Mom, I want you to know that I asked for combat assignment. I did so for several reasons. One is that I had certain ideals within my own mind, for which I have often argued verbally. I didn't feel right to sit safely far behind the lines, while men were risking their lives for principles which I would fight for only with my lips."[43]

Idealism as a motivation for the American fighting man since 1946 has been obscured, to a large degree, by a lack of full public sympathy with the military goals of the United States. Contemporary war is harsh and demanding. Americans must serve in areas and for causes which are difficult to put into the standard framework of idealism. To confuse the issues, there were politicians who used the Korean War as a stepping stone to higher office, and there are ambitious or sincere public men who argue the rectitude of America's cause in Vietnam.

Yet, out of the very wellspring of American society there appears the natural optimism of the old American Dream. An American writer, noted for his keen perceptiveness and objectivity, quotes a young American in Vietnam as saying: "If I should have to give my life here so they [speaking of Americans] could have freedom—well, I know it would be one drop in the bucket, but it takes a lot of drops to do something, so it would be all right with me."

And a Saginaw, Michigan, soldier, killed in Vietnam several weeks after writing his wife, told her: "I'm not saying it will, but if anything should happen to me, don't ever believe or let someone tell you it was for nothing. . . . So if anyone ever tells you we don't belong in Viet Nam, let them read this, because it is written by a guy . . . who is as scared as any other GI, but still believes it's all worth it to help these people keep their country free."[44]

Mingled with the essential patriotism and idealism of the American fighting man is a deep-seated pride in the American way of life.

Time after time one finds this in the military tradition of the nation. That the national causes are just, and that God recognizes this fact of life, is written into America's anthems and hymns of patriotism. Justin Smith, whose history of the Mexican War is a classic, saw the same motivation among American fighting men in that conflict. It was a pride in the American system; an assurance, usually supported by first-hand observation, that other societies and other cultures had little to offer to man's eternal search for freedom and good will.

The doughboy of 1917 was no exception to this general rule. One observer, a military expert whose writings are excellent sources of information about America's participation in World War I, wrote about these men: "All were fighting to reach home and be free men again; freedom having a practical application for them. The longer they were in France, the more they felt they were fighting for America."[45]

GI's in World War II were quite often given incentive by the same emotions. "It is such a great thing we are fighting for and such a horrible thing we are fighting against. . . ." wrote an American boy in the early stages of the war. "Personally," another American fighting man wrote, "all I want is an opportunity to set foot on precious U. S. soil again." And a corporal in the China-Burma-India theater wrote his small son in 1943 that "freedom" was a basic issue in the war. What did "freedom" mean to this soldier? It was the "spirit and heritage gained by our forebears that made us the envy of the world because we did not believe in the dog-eat-dog principle of Europe and Asia." In one sentence an American fighting man was able to mix into one vision the patriotism, the idealism, and sense of social superiority of the common American soldier.[46]

Yet, there was a wide and understandable variance as to what that social and cultural superiority implied. Some soldiers, sailors, or Marines of World War II defined the rightness of the American cause in terms of decency and morality. Others saw it in more simple ways; an ice-cream soda after Sunday church services, or an evening with a best girl in the local dance spot. A good many thought of it in terms of the "old gang" back home. "One of the few reasons I want to successfully negotiate Jap bombs is to spend another week-end at Surf [Surf City, N. J.] with everybody talking at once," one World War II American wrote. Another, a private in the Army Air Corps, illustrated the occasional confusion experienced by the soldier in writing of the justice of his cause. He explained:

> I'm in here fighting for the things freedom stands for—our church bell ringing every Sunday, the truth on our radio and in our newspapers, our children going to school and learning something besides military tactics, everyone having the same privilege to get ahead, the gang on the corner doing and saying what they please, the Stars and Stripes waving in the office yard each day, all our competitive sports without worry of doing them Hitler's way, everyone happy because he is free and doesn't have to worry because of his race or creed, being able to have a car for cement dust to settle on.[47]

The sense of equality and freedom in American life—the feeling that the United States has achieved a peculiar destiny in the story of man—has been a continuing motivation among American fighting men since 1946. A soldier in Korea could mingle manifold meanings into a simple statement. "I don't necessarily believe in the big shots as individuals," he argued, "but there are a lot of people like me and you. I believe in them." Another, an American GI in Vietnam, is able to contend: "I want my kids to enjoy freedom as I have." How can one analyze these sentences without coming to a conclusion that the ordinary American fighting man, today or yesterday, is really extraordinary in the history of mankind? A European newsman may write snide satire on American naïveté, or an Asian may laugh at his natural optimism, but what both fail to understand is that the American has a meaningful confidence in his nation and its heritage. He is free, and he means to remain so.[48]

It is clear that, when one looks at the history of the American Republic, he comes to a conclusion that the American soldier or sailor is also motivated by an unusual sense of duty. One scarcely needs to add that the low pay for the ordinary private is, and always has been, insufficient inducement to follow the flag. The love of country or idealism should never be underestimated, as has been indicated, but one should realize that they act as prods to the American conscience. They create within the American soul a desire to make its individual contribution to the concept of freedom.

By the time of the Civil War, duty had become an easily recognizable spur to the fighting American. An Illinois farm boy tells his father in 1862 that he has decided to join a state regiment then being formed. The father replies: "Well, Leander, if you think it's your duty to go, I shall make no objection. But you're the only boy I now have at home big enough to work so I wish you'd put it off until we get the wheat sowed, and the corn gathered. Then, if you're still of the same mind, it'll be all right." To other young men of the day, the explanation of the call of duty to an anxious wife was much more difficult. "Dear wife in God's name what shall I do," pleaded a young married man, "stand out before the country as a perjured man as I think I would be and as some in our company and other companies are doing, or go when my oath and my country called." Though these are only instances on the Federal side, it must be added that duty, with all its qualifications of meanings, was significant also within the Confederate conscience.[49]

Even with the drafts that took place in the Civil War and World War I, there were thousands upon thousands of Americans who joined the fighting services because they felt a personal obligation. In each conflict—from 1861 to 1865, and from 1917 to 1918—the early patriotic or idealistic implications within this call to duty tended to wane, leaving most young warriors with the notion that there was simply a job to be done. Scores of Civil War writers have written about Pickett's charge at Gettysburg, or the Federal attacks at Petersburg, in terms of flaming emotion. Yet any real understanding of the impact of a continuing and brutal conflict tends to reveal such heroism as merely part of the accepted business of war.

The same was true about the enlistment and training of many of the men in World War I. "Everybody was doing it"; "I didn't want to be left out of the show"; "Seemed to be the only thing to do"; "Every decent chap ought to fight when his country is at war"; "Thought it would be a fine experience," were all comments heard by one observer in 1917. When the same individual visited American camps a few months later, he found "little exaltation of spirit and practically no spread-eagle patriotism"; the men were "calmly bent upon business."

World War II proved once and for all that Americans could die, as historian Dixon Wecter expressed it, "in cool blood for something he conceives to be his duty." Ernie Pyle, that slender poet of the foxhole, wrote a heartfelt comment along the same line. "They were American boys who by mere chance of fate had wound up with guns in their hands," he said, concerning the Normandy campaign, "sneaking up a death-laden street in a strange and shattered city in a faraway country in a driving rain. They were afraid, but it was beyond their power to quit. They had no choice. They were good boys."[50]

The unusual characteristic of the World War II enlisted man was that he was inclined to be a silent fighter. He made few charges on enemy trenches. He had no "Rebel yell," or "Union hurrah." Yet, he could be a great and infinite philosopher about duty. An air force soldier in Europe could write: "There is not the least doubt in my mind that this war is justified, and I have not the least remorse in having done what I consider to have been my duty." A noncom, stationed in Hawaii, admitted to his parents: "It's funny, but there are so many of us who actually know very little about the world affairs today. Why, well I suppose you could take it as being we're here to fight. . . ."

The most basic characteristic of the Marine Corps is its ability to train men with a special devotion to duty—the business of killing the enemy. "Hell," Robert Sherrod heard one Marine say before Tarawa, "if you don't stay out here and get shot at, somebody else will have to come out here and get shot at. Somebody's got to win the war. . . ." And another Marine, fresh from the bloody fighting at Guadalcanal, described his unit thusly: "There are not more than one or two in our whole outfit that even resemble what you might call worthless. They've taken a little bit of punishment, made sacrifices and laugh their way out with ease. . . . No professions of bravery or guts or anything similar. . . . It's a great feeling."[51]

Korea was, perhaps, the greatest of all trials for the American fighting man. Sent into the fighting poorly equipped, materially and psychologically, he found it very difficult to establish even a sense of duty early in the war. The late Marguerite Higgins wrote that she "saw young Americans turn and bolt in battle, or throw down their arms cursing their government for what they thought was embroilment in a hopeless cause." "Someone really gave old Harry [President Truman] the wrong dope on this war," one GI was quoted as saying. "He can find someone else to pin his medals on."

Even young officers in the early units committed to Korea lacked a will to fight. Troops left their machine guns without a struggle; indeed, some were not even trained to handle such a vital weapon. British and other United Nations observers reported that American troops, with the exception of the Marines, appeared to have no understanding of why they had been sent into that hilly and forbidding land. Truck drivers evidenced no sense of obligation to their fellow soldiers at the front; they appeared "disgusted and tired." One young officer, a veteran of two wars, who knew from experience what Americans could do, wrote:

> We are a literate nation proud of the Army that is the best informed in the world. Yet we field in Korea an Army that was ill-prepared psychologically for the task that faced it; and we continue to send to Korea men who did not see or could not see the reason that they should fight, under the banner of the United Nations, a war that is not a war.[52]

Much of the trouble in Korea can be explained by the fact that the early units sent into action were garrison soldiers, civilians at heart, whose training on the *Ginza* was poor preparation for Korea. As time went by, the Marines moved into the fighting, the excellent Twenty-Seventh ("Wolfhound") Regiment was thrown into battle, and the superbly equipped and trained air forces were used to great advantage.

Many of the later arrivals were reservists and draftees, normally looked down upon by the regulars, but they performed their tasks with that sense of duty necessary to good fighting men. After the first crisis at Pusan was passed, the American fighting man not only rallied but carried the battle to the enemy. There were even some who could see reasons for being in Korea. "I'm no hero," a Marine contended, "but if these people aren't stopped here on their own ground, we will have to share the thing which so many have died to prevent their loved ones from sharing—the sight of death in our own back yards, of women and children being victims of these people."

In some ways the performance of the American fighting man in Korea was nothing short of miraculous. Most of the men fought solely out of a sense of duty, and possibly pride. They fought while politicians back home told them that the war was useless, they sacrificed while friends back home enjoyed a general prosperity brought on by the war, they fought under military and political restraint, and they gave battle under some of the most miserable climatic conditions ever faced by American warriors.

All the while they suffered criticisms from the foreign and domestic press for not doing better than they did. Only a few, like Eric Sevareid, could see the nobility of their sacrifice. He would write in 1953 that the performance of the American in Korea "outmatches . . . the behavior of those who fought our wars of certainty and victory." "This is something new in the American Story," he concluded. "This is something to be recorded with respect and humility."[53]

The handicaps faced by Americans in Korea are matched somewhat by those presented to their present-day counterparts in Vietnam. Once again GI's and Marines are being told of the uselessness of their sacrifice. Once again politicians are using their agonies, victories, and defeats for personal gain. Once again the goals of the war seem dim and obscure.

If anything is different, it is the psychological and material preparedness of the soldiers in Vietnam. Richard Tregaskis noted this in a 1963 trip to that unhappy land. "Some people have World War I and some have World War II," one American was quoted as saying. "This is mine." Another American, an officer, told Tregaskis that he continued to lead missions even though he didn't have to, simply because "I wear the uniform and it's what I'm supposed to do."

Thus is the sense of duty felt ever so strongly by Americans in Vietnam. A man might question, as one did: "Why am I here? This is a war which doesn't involve America"—but most such doubts are overcome by what some would call *esprit de corps,* what others would call the notion of duty. "I don't have any grudge against them [the Viet Cong]," one young private told a reporter. "It's our job to do it, and it has to be done by somebody." And another soldier, asked about the depth of his patriotism, replied: "I have some patriotism. A hitch is a hitch, sure. But if I wasn't here, it might be my brother or one of my neighbors."[54]

So profound and strong is the sense of duty among American fighting men in Vietnam that even the most hardened and cynical observers come away convinced. "Anybody who wants to take a crack at the younger generation has me to fight," a veteran military observer has stated. "These guys are smarter and stronger. I think they've got a lot of dedication. . . . I've never seen soldiers fight like they do." Helicopter pilots in Vietnam have been described thus: "These boys aren't any more ready for death than anyone else. . . . Their whole attitude is that this is a job that has to be done." The same reporter, writing of the American fighting man in general, asserted: "I have never been more impressed at any time in my life with the courage and judgment and understanding and dedication and integrity of young men than I have been in this war. . . ." What is it that motivates these brave men? And again from the same correspondent:

The initial motivation is that these men simply will not let their comrades down. They know that their friends are being wounded and killed . . . they know what they are doing and why. They believe that it is right that they should be there to help these people [the Vietnamese] . . . these men have become fine, professional soldiers. . . . They are as good as the Americans of Revolutionary days or any men in all the wars we ever fought.[55]

It is not easy for Americans to hate. The old emotional intensities, which are easily aroused between the French and the Germans, or between the Russians and the Turks, are built on centuries of hate and distrust. Hatred of an enemy by an American fighting man is slowly baked in the cauldron of experience; it disappears, once a war is finished, as quickly as a fire without fuel.

In wars fought prior to the American Revolution, the American fighting man had enough Old World resentments left in him for hatred to be a common motivation in conflict. Many Americans were of Northern Irish descent, bitter enemies of Roman Catholicism and of anything that smacked of it. The same could be written about the German settlers in Pennsylvania. Thus was it possible for the British to raise militia units from such elements of the population in the periodic wars with the French.

Nor was it difficult to recruit from these same peoples during the American Revolution, or from New England Yankees, whose antipathies had been aroused by Parliamentary legislation. The great problem for the Continental authorities was keeping the men in uniform. Extended military duty was not a tradition of American life in 1776. The problems suffered by General Washington in this respect were compounded by the fact that portions of the colonial population were either unsympathetic to the Revolution, or unwilling to risk commitment to the cause.

On the other side of the coin, Washington did have some very effective pamphleteers working for the Revolution, the general support of the ministry, and a patriotic hard-line officer's corps. All of these were eventually able to impress the meaning of independence on most of the troops, and they came within a narrow margin of turning the war into a sort of holy crusade.

Among the many important factors that gave Americans the will to fight were the occasional atrocities attributed to His Majesty's Troops, and the general colonial propaganda successes relating to these incidents. Hessians, fighting for the British, were sometimes poorly behaved. They plundered farms and were involved in established instances of forcible rape. The same could be written of some of the regulars in old and famous British regiments. Unfortunately, for the cause of the King, the officers in command of the miscreants did not see the value of punishing them, but rather took the attitude that no less could be expected from good tough troops.

There followed, in the course of the war, numerous other incidents. Norfolk, in Virginia, and a number of New England coastal towns were sacked and burned by the British fleet. The massacre of American troops on the Waxhaws in South Carolina further added fuel to the flames of hatred. The Colonials had attempted to surrender after a close fire fight, but were met by a "no quarters" British charge. On top of this highly publicized incident came reports of a number of unchivalric offenses committed by Tory soldiers fighting for the British.

The result of these events, and the American propaganda concerning them, was that the attitudes of American troops stiffened. The original fear that untried militiamen had for the Hessians turned into bitter hate. There was an increasing desire for revenge, and patriot soldiers soon adopted a "no quarter" policy in respect to American Tories. Thus did hatred become a strong motivational factor in the American Revolution.

Because most Indian tribes had been allies of the British during the Revolution, and because of publicized Indian atrocities on the frontier, the American fighting man was probably at his best against that race in the years following the American Revolution up to 1815. True, there were Indian victories in the Northwest Territory in the 1790's, but slowly and surely the frontier was pushed westward to the tune of "A Good Indian Is a Dead Indian." The victory at Fallen Timbers, the crushing defeat of Tecumseh at Tippecanoe, and the smashing of the Indians on the Thames are examples of early American victories partially resulting from the hate factor.

The War of 1812 is not quite so easy to analyze in the same terms. This is partly because the genuine dislike of the British by New Englanders was balanced by a feeling that British-American commercial amicability was necessary to the prosperity of the region. Southern political leaders, to the contrary, found much they admired in the British; even though this attitude was balanced with their desire for expansion in the West. Only the Westerner could have a pure and unadulterated hatred for the British, for it was they whom he blamed for Indian troubles on the frontier. Unfortunately, for the Americans, there were not enough Westerners to tip the scales. Lastly, whatever early hatred of the British had been aroused was quickly dissipated by a generally inadequate military leadership.

It is likewise difficult to analyze hatred as a strong motivational factor in the Mexican War. Americans were the invaders here, and after the first flush of emotion inspired by "Remember the Alamo" (a battle fought about ten years previously), the conquering armies settled down to do a first rate and rather professional job of fighting. In fact, a perusal of reminiscences of veterans of that war indicates not so much a dislike for the "greaser," but rather an admiration for his way of life, the climate of his country, and his women.

Hatred was, of course, a prime motivation in the Civil War. In the early years it was probably true that the Federal soldier was less inspired in this manner than the Confederate. The latter tended to look upon the Yankee as an invader, the despoiler of his womanhood, the emancipator of an "inferior" race, and as the scum of the country ("mudsill" was the commonly used epithet).

The early Federal invaders of Tennessee and other parts of the South, on the contrary, tended to take the comparatively gentle attitude that the South was just a part of the nation that had gone astray and must be put straight. As the war progressed, however, this attitude changed. Thousands of rumors went through the Federal Armies in the West that Union sentries, stationed to protect homes and plantations in the South, were bushwhacked and mutilated. These stories, whether true or not, usually had the Federal soldier deprived of his ears, nose, and his private parts.

Later, the rumors passing the Federal ranks about the conditions in the Confederate prison at Andersonville tended to firm up the hatred of Yankee for Rebel. Yet conditions in Confederate prisons notwithstanding, it was probably the atrocity story that intensified the feeling of the Northern boy more than anything else, and planted the seed from which the tree would grow. Below is a paragraph, written by a western soldier in 1862, and showing what the future course of the war would be:

I begin to think the better way would be to utterly desolate *wherever we went and then it would not be necessary to leave a guard behind.* . . . I am heartily sick of seeing a constant detail of eight or ten men kept night and day around the dwelling of a man who is but 50 or 100 miles distant openly laboring for our destruction . . . if I had control when this army had marched through the Gulf States no land marks would be left to show the boundaries of town counties or states. . . .[56]

It is easy to see what happened during the Civil War in its late years. Hatred was fanned by propaganda on both sides—in the North, about atrocities and prison camps—in the South, about destruction and prison camps. In the end, one story piled on another until, on both sides, the war *had* to be fought to its long and bitter conclusion. Even after the war the easiest way to political success in the North was by way of the "bloody shirt." And here one is reminded about the hoary joke that, even as late as 1917, most Southerners didn't know that the phrase "damnyankee" was composed of two separate words.

The professional American fighting man is, by tradition, supposedly less inspired by hate than his volunteer counterpart. A professional army is what the United States had from 1865 to 1917 —with the exception of a small period in 1898. However, there were times when the professional soldier let hate rather than reason rule his emotions. There were needless massacres of Indians on several occasions by professional soldiers in the post-Civil War period. On other occasions Indian captives were tormented into attempting escape so that they might be killed. In the months following Custer's defeat on the Little Big Horn, the recruiting booths of the Army did a fine business in signing up "Custer avengers"; men who carried with them a most virulent hatred for the Indian.

It is probably safe to say that the hatred of the professional soldier for the Indian was far greater than that of the American fighting man for the Spanish in 1898. An examination of letters by ordinary American soldiers and sailors indicates no more than a normal dislike of the enemy in that short war. Navy hardtack was stamped with the words "Remember the Maine," and sailors of the U. S. Navy indicated a great desire to fight, but in comparison to other times and other places the antipathy of the American was lukewarm at the most, and temporary in every case. In fact, after the defeat of the Spanish in Cuba, the general attitude within the American Army and Navy was one of admiration for Spanish courage.

When treating with the factor of hatred in World War I, one is presented with the two faces of history. One side shows that in 1917 the largest non-British, white element in the United States was of Germanic origin. These people were among the best educated, best behaved, and culturally progressive in the nation. Thus in 1917 American soldiers found it quite difficult to conceive of Germans abroad as being different from those at home.

Perhaps, for this reason, there was no great rush on the part of Americans to volunteer for the services. Even the draft, when it was applied, sent more men to marriage bureaus than to the recruiting booths. In fact, it would be well here to illustrate by statistics that there was a small but undiminished reservoir of antiwar feeling in the United States throughout the entire conflict. There were, during the course of the World War I draft, some 337,649 draft evaders—11 percent of those called, and of these, approximately 160,000 were never apprehended by Federal authorities.

Even among some of the men who did not evade the draft, there was, in the beginning, a reluctance to hate the Germans. Within a few months, however, the excellent work of the Committee of Public Information, a propaganda agency headed by Mr. George Creel, brought about a radical change in opinions. The efforts of Creel were aided and abetted by a simple facet of human nature; the feeling of a man, once in uniform, that *his* war must have meaning—that it must have a purpose. Thus it came to be that American soldiers listened attentively while orators told them of the price of German "Kultur"; the mutilation of Belgian children and the rapings of French and Belgian women. The change of attitudes among the men was subtle but steady, and one private was able to assert after three months of steady indoctrination, "we're fighting Hell. . . ."[57]

There may have been some fear on the part of American authorities that these heavy doses of hate would not suffice once the soldier was brought to battle. This was a needless worry, however. The letters of the private soldier show that word variations of *Boche*—spelled *Bosh, boch,* or *bosch*—were more common than the word *German.* The word *hun* came into great usage. "We are going to finish the huns forever," an enlisted man of the 307th Field Artillery wrote. "I wish you could be here and see some of the fiendish things the huns have done. . . ." wrote another private. Thus did the American fighting man of 1917 learn to hate his enemy.[58]

In the twenty-three years that separated the two great world wars, American attitudes went through some interesting and radical changes. First of all, in the 1920's there was a general revulsion to war, and a feeling, common among intellectuals, that the sacrifices of World War I had been in vain. The most popular theme in the cinema and novels of the day was that which centered upon the futility of international conflict. An entire generation of American boys grew up with the conviction that the next European war should not involve the United States.

With the emergence of Hitler in the early 1930's, this attitude was put to a severe test. Though it was clear to most Americans that he was the personification of evil, the popular feeling was that, if he was ignored, the menace he represented would eventually fade. Even after the war broke out in 1939, and Congress reacted by passing a new draft law, there were many in the United States who vehemently argued a noninvolvement policy.

The Japanese attack on Pearl Harbor, far beyond the German attack on Russia, was probably the greatest mistake of the Axis partners after 1939. It brought into the war a massive industrial and military machine which was impelled by every motivation of war. It made it possible, and indeed fashionable, for every American to fight without a conscience. It made hate immediately acceptable, particularly as directed against the Japanese.

The American fighting man, from 1941 to 1945, held a bitter and unabiding contempt for the "Nip." Not only did he have to live down a little of the shame in the Pearl Harbor defeat, but the Japanese treatment of American prisoners taken in the Philippines was soon widely publicized. From Pearl Harbor on, it could be written of the American soldier, sailor, or Marine in the Pacific, that he was heroic, aggressive, capable of fighting against great odds, ingenious, and daring, even when equipped with inferior weapons of war.

He knew the Japanese were no easy foe, but hate carried him onward. "I feel that the war against Japan will be a lot tougher than any in the European theater," a Pacific area noncom wrote. "I came here to kill Japs," a wounded Tarawa Marine argued. "I didn't come here to be evacuated." "Oh boy. . . ," another Marine exclaimed, just prior to that island invasion. "I just want to spit in a dead Jap's face. Just open his mouth and let him have it." And of the Japanese soldier, an army private wrote: "Just give it to him in the guts and let him lay. . . . If you wait too long the little rat will let you have a volley of shots or a hand bomb."[59]

Though the American fighting man in 1941 was far less motivated by hate to fight the Germans than the Japanese, his attitude toward the former underwent a slow and imperceptible change. First of all, German infantry combat methods, seasoned into brutality by years of experience, came as a shock to the young Americans who fought in North Africa or Sicily. The American reverse at Kasserine Pass, and the German practice of heavy sniper fire, showed the newcomers to war that they had much to learn. And the GI resented such hard lessons being imposed upon him. "I want to go back and get those dirty Nazi bastards. . . ." one wounded American wrote after Kasserine Pass. "I want to show them we're not yellow." As for the snipers, by the end of the Normandy campaign of 1944, the Americans had so toughened, as Ernie Pyle noted, that they began to "shoot the sonsabitches" before "the time came for them to surrender."

A second factor in the growing hatred of Germans by American fighting men was the disclosure of battlefield atrocities by the enemy. The most significant of these was the massacre of seventy-one GI prisoners at Malmédy, during the Battle of the Bulge. There were others as well. A large number of prisoners from the 267th Special Reconnaissance Battalion were shot in Italy in 1944. In the same year forty-seven American, British, and Dutch fliers were killed at the Mauthausen Concentration Camp in Germany, mainly from beatings. And Hitler himself advocated the on-the-spot shooting of downed Allied pilots.[60]

Much of this information became well known to even the most ordinary American soldier, and he soon began to meet German soldiers with a toughness of his own. In October, 1944, a company of the 115th Infantry suffered almost total annihilation in a raid by German infantry near Aachen. On the following day the remainder of the First Battalion of the regiment conducted what amounted to a retaliatory assault on a nearby German town. After the village was captured, the torch was applied, and the Americans withdrew. "The smoke went straight up. . . ." stated one American after the assault. "It was a good day for burning buildings."

By early 1945 the bitterness felt by the 115th Regiment was commonly felt up and down the American line. An Indiana private wrote: "They [the Germans] live forever and breed like rabbits and everywhere they emigrate they remain a hard, foreign, un-assimilated element whose sole desire and ambition is to Germanize and brutalize the world into an exact replica of Germany." Another infantryman felt the same way, writing: "No German soldier deserves an ounce of respect in any form. Most anyone could sit down and write pages on the crimes of Hitler's soldiers and write true things beyond the realm of human imagination."[61]

Nor was such hatred to be found solely in the ranks of the ordinary soldiers. It went upward, figuratively and literally. "Personally I am now mad with the Germans. . . ." a bomber pilot wrote. "From now on I am going to try to kill them. . . ." And a general officer, a veteran of two wars against the Germans, wrote in December, 1944: "But slowly it's beginning to dawn on them that the only good German is a dead German—that the whole nation is solidly behind this thing. . . . The result is that we've killed more and [are] taking fewer prisoners."

The final clincher in the American military attitude toward his German opponent was the capture of a number of concentration camps. No soldier could walk through such valleys of death and not react with hate. "These camps held slave workers from other countries, and they did all the hardest and dirtiest work for the Germans. . . ." an army private told his parents. "I can now see more clearly than ever why I came over here." And another soldier, after visiting one such camp, wrote of his slow evolution of fighting spirit:

> I don't like army life, but for the first time I can wholeheartedly and honestly say that I'm glad I'm here doing a little bit to help stop these horrible atrocities. I don't tell you folks everything and I debated in my own mind for sometime about telling you this, and then decided if every grown American could realize what has really been happening here we could not help winning the right kind of peace as well as the war.[62]

The same slow development of hate in the American fighting man took place in the Korean War. "Undisciplined, untrained, unhating, they had come to battle," is one description of the American soldiers who attempted to slow the surge of North Koreans into the South. These young garrison soldiers were unprepared for the sight of death and violence.

Yet, within months, a battlefield maturity took place; partly brought about by enemy atrocities. Scores of American soldiers, their hands bound behind them, were shot out of hand by the triumphant Communists—their bodies to be discovered by resurgent Americans some time later. Some of the men had not even been allowed the dignity that ought to attend death. They had been castrated and burned before the final shots were fired. One does not have to ponder the reasons for a developing American ability to kill his Korean enemies without the slightest twinge of conscience. It was illustrated by the spirit shown by an American officer, who after reaching the top of another Korean hill, gleefully shouted to his men: "There are lots of them [the enemy], and you can kill them!"[63]

To all of the foregoing motivations which have impelled the American fighting man, one must add the call of adventure. Here is a lure which drew the rural Virginia or Carolina boy into the early colonial wars. It was the desire to see faraway places that drew many a young lad into the Continental Army during the Revolution. Privateering in the Revolution and the War of 1812 was an even more attractive call to adventure in those wars.

The Mexican War presented a real siren's call for American boys of the 1840's. Thousands of men volunteered for the army in 1846, because of the simple desire to be part of the romance of history, a desire to escape the dullness of the old home town, the possibility of winning honors, and the hope of impressing local girls. Few Americans, wrote the historian Justin Smith, thought of the death that might lie at the end of the adventure. Those who did viewed it as "something quick, unfelt amidst the excitement, and sweetened by the greatness of one's cause." How innocent were the Americans who responded to the call of "Ho, for the halls of the Montezumas!"

There was so much of the love of adventure left over from the Mexican War that it can be counted as one of the reasons for the great rush of volunteers to both sides in the Civil War. Bell I. Wiley, in his writings on the Civil War soldier, contends that the call of excitement and the lure of the romantic were two of the major motivations that brought young men to the colors in 1861. "On to Richmond," or "On to Washington," combined with the gaily martial aspect of rural towns, evoked many a mental image of Santa Anna fleeing before the gallant Americans, or of Zach Taylor standing firm before the Mexican onslaught at Buena Vista.[64]

Nor was the romanticism of the Civil War a quickly dying emotion. All the way into 1862 it lasted. One has only to view a few of the pictures of young men who submitted to omnipresent photographers of the age. These are innocent young men, who stand rigidly beside the bayoneted musket, or who pose with one hand inserted behind a jacket lapel in carefully posed Napoleonic casualness. Both positions were concessions to the Victorian concept that death, when met in places like Balaklava or Monterrey, was somehow glorious and clean.

Of the two soldiers, it is probable that the Confederate was slightly more serious in 1861 about the business of war than his enemy; perhaps because, generally speaking, he was less literate and had read less about the magnificent American victories in

Mexico. He was more inclined to let a victory or a defeat stand or fall for what it was; a characteristic the Federal soldier had to learn from experience. But, for both soldiers, the turning points of the war were Antietam and Shiloh. There romanticism died. Neither the South nor the North smiled after those terrible battles.

A comparable kind of early war romanticism was found in the United States during the first months of World War I. Among some of the volunteers and draftees of 1917 there was a zest and drive which was almost intoxicating; especially after the afore-mentioned George Creel had synthesized the ideals of the war. Amidst the falling confetti and martial music of the first few months of war, American boys could and did become groggy with it all. On one occasion in Chicago a battalion of soldiers found them-selves cheering almost everything which was said to them. A soldier who was there described it: "The speaker gave a heartrending ac-count of thousands of Poles being massacred, and thinking it was time to give another of our cheers, we yelled in unison 'Hurrah, Hurrah!' "

On the battlefield proper the same zest for adventure served the American fighting man well; at least until the terrible agonies of the Argonne Forest. At Saint-Mihiel, at Cantigny, and at Château-Thierry, doughboys charged with "exasperating energy . . . straight through to an objective. . . ." British and French advisors com-plained about the impulsive drive of American infantry; a censure they would completely reverse in the next war. Some American soldiers of 1917, stationed next to Australian units, were so anxious to fight that they borrowed hats from their favorite allies and un-officially fought with those soldiers.[65]

The American enthusiasm for action, slow to arouse in the be-ginning, was infectious. "My one ambition now is to be assigned to the overseas fleet," one sailor wrote his parents, "and I pray that the German fleet don't come out until I get there." Another seaman commented along the same line. "I want to see all there is to see of this war," he asserted. " 'Whole hog or none,' I want excitement."

One of the standard music hall jokes of 1917 indicates the novelty and excitement of the war in the American mind. So often quoted in letters home, it went: "English Tommies fight for their king and Italians fight for their queen, and Americans fight for souvenirs." Twenty-five years later another version would read: "The Japanese fight for Emperor and the Rising Sun, the Italians for Fascism and Mussolini, the Germans for Hitler and the Party, the British for the king—but the Americans fight for souvenirs and the hell of it."[66]

The doughboy of 1917 was basically an innocent abroad in the early months of the war. The GI of 1941, by comparison, held far fewer illusions about the romanticism of war; he knew guns could kill. After all, had he not been nurtured on such books as *All Quiet on the Western Front*?

Yet, with all his relatively studied knowledge of war, the World War II soldier was not immune to some of the excitement it offered. The famous "Merrill's Marauders" were, to a man, volunteers for extra-hazardous duty. The crack Ranger battalions were volunteer units which performed especially dangerous tasks. One such Ranger best described the sense of adventure that motivated these men. "There was just one thing about that kind of fighting," he stated, "by damn, it gave you a thrill. We never had to ask no questions about who was out front; we just started shooting. Hell, nobody wants to get killed . . . but it gave you a thrill, the way we fought."

The entire Marine Corps of World War II, with the exception of some draftees inducted late in the conflict, was composed entirely of volunteers. Training among these men was designed then, as it still is, to make the ordinary Marine restive when out of action, and deadly efficient when in combat. The early Marine brigades, especially those that fought at Guadalcanal and Tarawa, characteristically followed this pattern. "We've fought the Japs for water and cigarettes," wrote a Marine, casually, from Guadalcanal. "Often we have shot and ripped off a Jap's pack and canteen before he has the chance to fall." This is the spirit that has motivated Marines in several instances in the Vietnam fighting. One Marine's request for transfer into that combat area was explained this way: "He couldn't get there fast enough because he wanted to equal his brother's record."[67]

Of all the motivations that impel the American fighting man, the call to adventure is the most evanescent. It rarely survives the first bloody encounter; it never lasts beyond the first defeat. During the Revolutionary, Mexican, and Civil Wars, the numbers of deserters swelled after each battle. "On to Richmond," or "On to Washington" were enough to provoke roars of laughter among battle-tried veterans in the Federal and Confederate armies by 1864. More than one soldier had written home by this time stating that he had seen the "elephant" (war) and one experience was enough. Even in the Spanish-American War, the easiest of American conflicts, the sights of death brought an abrupt fading of the martial blue uniform. "Well, people can howl for war all they please," one fighting man of 1898 complained, "but after they have seen it I don't think they are anxious for it."

The same kind of reaction took place in the two world wars, and in Korea. "You people at home don't have the least idea what us boys have to go through," a doughboy of 1918 wrote. Another soldier, fresh from the triumph at Saint-Mihiel, admitted: "The more I see of this war the less desire I have to be a battlefield corpse." Ernie Pyle quoted an American infantryman of 1944 as saying: "Why don't you tell the folks back home what it is like? All they hear about is victories and a lot of glory stuff. They don't know that for every hundred yards we advance somebody gets killed." And an American soldier in Korea wrote in 1951: "Our offensive is ended—and we are getting ready to settle down for the winter—thank God! Perhaps they can get together and save the sacrifice of the lives of good American men. . . . Two wars in so few years have made me a firm believer in Peace."[68]

In a study of World War II American soldiers, which was published in 1949, a team of researchers attempted to establish a pattern of primary motivations as fighting men saw them. Of the men questioned, 39 percent stated that the desire to end the war was a major motivation in combat, 14 percent listed "solidarity with group" (what some would call *esprit de corps*) as the motive that kept them going, and 10 percent listed "thoughts of home and loved ones." The remainder of the 568 comments were scattered, percentagewise, among over a dozen possible motivations; not the least of which was "self-preservation."[69]

It would be ridiculous to assert that patriotism, idealism, the desire to preserve the aims of the American Dream, or duty are enough to carry a man's courage in battle. The above-cited study was a poll of men's attitudes after combat—not before, and most naturally not during battle. What it does not show is that all of the ordinary motivations may carry a man to the battlefield, but they do not necessarily make him stay there and fight well. Nor does it present any overwhelming evidence that, sooner or later, what really takes the place of patriotism or duty on the battlefield is the basic desire for survival.

Yet, in every American war one finds evidence of this elemental battlefield instinct. In the letters written by Civil War soldiers after battle, one finds common reference by the writer to taking care of "number one," the soldier himself. In some cases "number one" ran for survival; in others he stayed and fought for survival.

The great thing about survival as a motivational factor in battle is that, when used well, it becomes a tremendously effective combat emotion. The Marine Corps, rightfully so, teaches the art of survival as a unit concept. A Marine must fight well because, if all do as he does, the unit will survive. In World War I a great deal of the indoctrination of the infantrymen was built around the themes: "You must get him before he gets you," or "It's him or you, him or you, him or you."

The instinct for survival was equally strong in World War II and Korea, and it is evident in most battle accounts from Vietnam. There have, in fact, been times when the American fighting man in all of these wars could measure survival in terms of yards, hours, or minutes. At the end of a day of bitter fighting in Normandy a colonel and a private split a cup of coffee. The officer raised his cup, saying "To tomorrow"; the private replied, "Yes sir . . . to tomorrow." Not a decade later, reporters in Korea heard soldiers express the same prayer for survival in terms of "tomorrow."[70]

To the American soldier fighting in Korea, survival was not only measured in terms of getting down one hill and up the other, but it became the most acceptable motivation of the war. General Matthew Ridgeway, after taking over command of the Army in 1951, stated: "We are not interested in real estate. We are interested only in inflicting maximum casualties on the enemy with minimum losses to ourselves." That argument, according to the military historian, S. L. A. Marshall, "struck the right note to an Army which was already concluding that survival was the one unbeatable argument."[71]

Between the great wars the reasons young men have joined the American armed forces are significantly different from those offered in times of national peril. The boy who might have sought to evade the draft in 1918 because of his fear of danger, or the disinclination to work, might well have joined the Army in 1920 in order to escape the responsibilities of ordinary life. Conversely, the young man who may have rushed to the colors in 1861 because of patriotism might well have had nothing but scorn and low regard for the soldiers who composed the frontier units of 1870.

So varied have been the reasons for peacetime enlistments that they can be treated only in a general way. After 1800, for instance, the Navy had no difficulty filling its enlistment needs, simply because of the way of life that service offered. There was something vitally attractive about standing a deck watch beneath full sails, while the ship rushed silently over the sea. The Army could never offer anything quite the same in peacetime, except the loneliness of a remote frontier post.

In the period after 1845 both the Army and the Navy became havens for restless or unhappy Americans, as well as a sort of proving ground for newly arrived immigrants. Many of the former were young toughs who were counseled into the service by some local magistrate; many of the latter were Irish, German, or English boys, who found the services a good introduction to the West. In every branch of the service there was a variety of backgrounds that was astounding even for those days. One old cavalry officer, recalling the composition of his command, remembered "a bookkeeper, a farm boy, a dentist, and a blacksmith, a great many of position trying to gain a commission and a salesman ruined by drink, an ivory carver and a Bowery tough. . . ."[72] He might have added that there were many immigrant boys in the American uniform who had seen service with the British or Prussian armies.

What were the thoughts of these men as they presented themselves to the recruiting offices? Only by looking at a few of the reminiscences of that period does one obtain a partial answer to that question. In 1854 a penniless German immigrant enlisted in the Army. Here are his memories of that occasion:

> I did not know what to do. By chance I saw a flag hanging from a house and under it a sign. It was a notice that the United States wanted recruits for the army. This was my only resort if I did not wish to steal or beg. I went in. . . . I was bound to remain a soldier for five years, for clothes, lodging, and food, and eleven dollars a month.[73]

Twenty-one years later, another young boy, who eventually would fight on the Little Big Horn, made the same decision. He remembered it as follows: "I stopped and read it [the recruiting poster]. Half-heartedly, I went upstairs to the office, almost hoping I would be rejected." Taken in by the Army, he was immediately given his uniform, and then he carefully walked home by the back alleys because of the low esteem in which soldiers were held.

The Marine Corps found its recruits in quite the same manner as the Army. Several officers and enlisted men, wearing full dress, usually opened a recruiting office in some rural town. Then, as one old noncom remembered it, "the captain would get up on a dry-goods box . . . and make a speech to the crowd, telling them what a fine place the Marine Corps was for a man. . . . That's the way we got recruits in those days."[74]

After 1900 there was no longer even the lure of frontier life for a possible recruit. Yet the services could always get volunteers. Why? One ex-soldier remembered that his company, newly recruited in 1914, was composed of men who had joined the Army because they were jobless, or because they wished to escape a local sheriff. Some, he claimed, entered the service in order to escape a possible "shotgun" marriage in the old home town. Two years later, in 1916, another new recruit polled his company for answers to why each man had joined the Army. Some stated they were jobless; others gave the reason that they wanted to get "a crack at that fellow Villa." One new soldier answered: "If you'd see the town I came from you'd know. Deadest place in Georgia."

The novelist James Jones wrote an excellent portrayal of the pre-Pearl Harbor soldier in his book entitled *From Here to Eternity*. It is realistic and somehow frightening, but it is true. In fact, Jones' representation of the soldier of that period is almost applicable to the "peacetime" soldier of 1946. Most of these later volunteers were men who, with the end of the war, had a brief fling at civilian life. Unable to adjust, they quickly returned to uniform. One contemporary writer described them: "They were not intellectuals, they were not completely fired with patriotism or motivated by the draft. . . . A great many of them signed up for three squares and a sack."[75]

Perhaps something ought to be written about present-day American fighting men, since many of these fighting men are volunteers. From all indications one may say of them that they are probably better educated, better motivated, and better trained than any volunteer soldiers in American history. A partial reason for this lies in the recently developed American notion that service in the armed forces is an acceptable phase in the education of American manhood. *Esprit de corps* is high, mainly because of the efforts by military authorities to rebuild unit pride. Reenlistment is high, particularly among American Negroes, for the kind of equality many Negroes seek is best found in the various branches of the service.

There are only a few times when the historian is completely lucky. Occasionally, what he has in the way of information might be tied up in a neat little bundle. The human mind still defies generalization, however. No one expert can predict with certainty, or write with authority, about the way in which it might act, or has acted.

So it is when one treats with the motivations of the American fighting man. A biographer might write, as one has done, that he actually saw American soldiers smile in 1917 when they were handed a statement that told them they were fighting "the great battle for human freedom." But like that of the *Mona Lisa,* a smile can be as unrevealing as any other facial expression. Did those soldiers smile in agreement with the sense of the pamphlet, or were they indicating that they saw through the "ideals" of the war? The same question arises in relation to the Vietnam War. Does a soldier in that area tell a reporter what he really wants to say, or what he thinks the reporter wishes to hear?

This is the great problem the historian faces. At the very moment he decides that idealism has been a traditional motivation for the American fighting man, he discovers a study which argues that most of the enlisted men of 1943 could not name the "Four Freedoms." At just about the time the historian centers upon hate as an excellent emotional force in battle, he discovers a letter of an Indiana soldier of World War II which argues that German soldiers are "pretty much like the soldiers of any other army—flushed in triumph, bewildered by defeat."[76]

At the very instant the historian is certain that the call to adventure has motivated many an American fighting man, he finds the single thorn that pricks the balloon of his argument. Why, for instance, did soldiers volunteer for the extra hazardous duty of "Merrill's Marauders"? The answer, according to one such individual, reads as follows: "Most of us guys volunteered . . . because we figured we might get back to the States for training first. We had all been overseas 18 to 24 months at that time and we wanted to get home."[77]

The probable truth is that the American fighting man does what he does for a multitude of reasons—some of which jibe, some of which do not. It can be said that he does love his country; that he does have ideals, for he has been raised in an idealistic society; that he can hate, for that is a primary emotion; that he has fought for personal survival, for that is instinctive; and that he has fought out of a sense of duty, for humanity in general is always bound by obligations. As for the peacetime American soldier or sailor, he joined the services for equally complex reasons.

Among the various motivations that have impelled the American to fight, the ones that the old soldier usually recalls are the ones that are the most painless for him to remember. No American, years after some battlefield experience, likes to think that he killed without a reason, so it may be at this stage of his life that he evokes his memories of patriotism and idealism. No fifty-year-old American veteran likes to remember that he fought simply for "tomorrow." Remembered motivations are always more noble than that.

Thus it can be written that the real motivations of the American fighting man, historically speaking, are so varied, and so interrelated, that they are almost impossible to isolate, one to a man. Yet common observation tells the historian there is one generalization that can be made. Few Americans, long after their military service has ended, like to feel their sacrifices have been needless. Perhaps that is all to the good, for it allows one to say that no American, whatever his war, really died in vain.

2

The American Fighting Man:

As Seen by Allied

and Interested Observers

GOOD OBJECTIVE HISTORICAL ESTIMATES of the ability and qualities of the American fighting man are almost impossible to find. First of all, many accounts about early American soldiers or sailors were written by comparatively literate British, French, or German officers or observers, who because of class prejudices or distinctions, were inclined toward a jaundiced view. This is especially true in the case of the American Revolution, and immediately thereafter. The arrival of the United States into the family of nations implied an upthrust of "republicanism," which anyone with a consciousness of class naturally resented.

Second, no American was ever engaged in an official war outside of his own hemisphere until 1917; that is, with the exception of Manila Bay in 1898, and some lesser and earlier naval encounters. Consequently, the American fighting man was always judged by European observers in European terms. Whether these observers acted in an official or unofficial capacity, most of them were unable to understand that any conflict on the North American continent could not be fought in the same terms as war in Europe.

A prime example of European fallibility of military judgment when dealing in the North American frame of reference was the Mexican War, and in particular, General Winfield Scott's campaign to take Mexico City. This brilliantly led feat of arms, plus the casually hardened character of American soldiery, was far beyond European comprehension. Even the great Duke of Wellington failed to understand, crying "Scott is lost" when he heard that the American general had struck westward into the mountains from Vera Cruz.

A second example of European inability to understand the nature of North American war is provided in the American Civil War. In this instance, despite the fact that there were numerous European military "experts" on the scene, few of these men could immediately sense the meaning of the war or its innovational possibilities.

Third, the casual or experienced observer of American military practice has seldom remained uninfluenced by his predisposition toward Americans in general. Nor does he remain untainted by personal association with Americans in particular. The famous British Colonel James A. L. Fremantle was quickly won over to the Confederate viewpoint that Union soldiers were "mudsills" because it was from the Southern window that he observed the war. In World Wars I and II, French or British opinions, on both high and low levels, were profoundly influenced by the relationships which the European observers had with American personnel. Any British officer, enlisted man, or casual onlooker in World War II, whose poorer relatives had "chocolate bar" relationships with American fighting men, was necessarily affected by that circumstance. The same also could be said for the French in both world wars.

Fourth, but by no means last, it must be added that officially composed estimates of American fighting men by European observers are, to a large extent, still regarded as "confidential" information by defense departments of the various countries involved. It is far easier to find solid military analyses of Americans written by German generals in World Wars I and II than those composed by French or British military leaders in 1917 or 1942. Such an inference does not include reminiscences or biographies, which may be dangerously misleading because they are often written with the profit motive in mind.

Furthermore, it is true that foreign observations of the fighting American are peculiar to the era in which they are written. In each war the American presents a slightly different image to allies who fight alongside him, or to the "neutral" observer, who merely watches. This is understandable because war itself changes, as do the conditions under which nations become allied. Old hates may need modification; old friendships are renewed in differing ways. Yet, if one looks closely, he sees that many basic virtues and faults of the American fighting man, as seen by allied observers, may have changed but little in two hundred years. What does change are the conditions under which they are observed.

One such abrupt change took place during the American Revolution. Here the British Regular, who had always scoffed at the colonial militiaman in the past, had to fight the "cowards," the "rascals," and the "vermin," as one British officer called them. The French, who in prior years had sometimes viewed the colonial militia as respectable opponents, now found themselves in the peculiar position of acting as midwives to a "republic." Along with the French, as allies, came dozens of European mercenaries, to whom war was a profession. All these men—Von Steuben, De Kalb, Kosciusko, and Pulaski among them—were products of European military systems, and though they might have come to admire Americans in general, it is probable that their first measurement of revolutionary fighting abilities was against that which was contemporarily fashionable on the Continent.

Yet, what is surprising is that the opinions of outsiders who fought alongside the Americans underwent some subtle and yet perceptible changes. The French, for example, first regarded the ragged American Continentals as nothing more than mercenaries, who were led by a small group of well-meaning patriots. The hardships of the Americans, near nudity or ragged clothing being in evidence among them, were acceptable subjects of humor for French enlisted men and their officers. It was almost impossible for the latter to believe that these same Americans could have a cause for which they would die.

A turning point in such attitudes eventually was met, however.

A shipment of discarded French regimental uniforms was offered to the Americans, but the latter refused to wear them because they were *red*—a reminder of the hated color of the enemy. Such patriotic concern in the midst of grinding want served to convince many Frenchmen that their ragged allies were determined to have liberty, even though it meant considerable suffering.[1]

What, in the beginning, was a good-natured jesting on the part of the French toward the Americans now came to an end. The smiles were wiped away, and there began a virtual love affair between many of the younger French officers and their American counterparts. Everywhere, among foreign officers, there was a general admiration for the suffering American fighting man. The most convinced of these was Lafayette, who wrote that Americans were "inured to privation, more patient than Europeans," and that even the lowliest American soldier was skilled with his gun. To his dying day, Lafayette would feel that among the American forces that served under him was the greatest light infantry in the world. This was a sentiment which found some corroboration or agreement in the writings of the British Colonel Fremantle during the Civil War. To Fremantle the Confederate infantryman was among the greatest natural fighters in history.[2]

Two of the more astute foreign military observers during the American Revolution were Charles Armand Tuffin, the Marquis de la Rouène, who served as a colonel in Washington's army, and Baron Friedrich W. von Steuben, the grizzled German drillmaster of the American troops. Colonel Armand, like many of his French contemporaries, early in the war suffered from an occasional inability to probe the American soul. The personal obligation many Americans felt during the war was somewhat beyond him. During one hard period he wrote that the best of the American soldiers were "most affected by the perpetual denial of their wages"; yet in puzzlement he added, "they love and respect at the utmost the commander in chief. . . ."

At another time he added in a note to Washington: "I may assure your Excellency that the soldiers will all desert if they are not under the immediate command of the officer who enlisted them."

This again was a personal loyalty, which a Frenchman of the time could not understand.

Yet the same Colonel Armand wrote of the battlefield failings and virtues of the American fighting man with some instinctive insight. About the Continental cavalry he commented:

> We have never seen any of our squadrons *make* or *receive* a charge regularly—we have seen them in the field on many occasions which were favorable to them not attack and even retire with some disgrace from the field—not because they wanted bravery, God forbid me to say ever such a thing so much contrary to the experience I have of the Americans' courage, but merely because they did not know how to march off their grounds towards the enemy in presence of them, nor when arrived there how to form themselves and take their advantage in the attack . . . and it is a matter of fact that those who cannot form a regular attack have much less in their power to make an advantageous and even orderly retreat.[3]

Armand's observations that his Americans were sometimes unable to take advantage of victory strike a familiar chord. Some of the earlier Civil War battles were affected by the same American characteristic German intelligence reports of the World War I American fighting man also claimed that U. S. Army infantrymen were sometimes incapable of exploiting a victorious attack. And Armand's argument that Americans were untrained in the art of retreat was echoed by British observers of the U. S. Army during the Korean War.

Von Steuben, who was given the task of instructing the Continental Army in matters of discipline, also saw familiar virtues and weaknesses. The younger officers, he felt, failed to understand that the duties of command went beyond the battlefield to include the preservation of order in the camp. One finds similar complaints echoed throughout American military history down to the twentieth century.

Of the American fighting man himself, Von Steuben saw something that, perhaps, he himself did not quite understand. Yet his comment upon it stands as one of the shrewdest ever made on the

American soldier. "In the first place," he wrote to a European friend, "the genius of this nation is not in the least to be compared with that of the Prussians, Austrians or French. You say to your soldier, 'Do this;' and he doeth it; but I am obliged to say, 'This is the reason why you ought to do that,' and he does it." General William C. Westmoreland, two centuries later the commander of United States operations in Vietnam, hit almost upon the same personal characteristic when he described the American soldier:

> He is a man with a purpose. And when his Government sends him to Vietnam to perform a mission which he understands—and we have taken great pains to insure that he understands his mission and the role that he is expected to play—he puts his heart and soul into it, concentrates on the task at hand, and doesn't look over his shoulder.[4]

Just past the midpoint of the twentieth century one finds world opinion toward the United States to be divided into three areas. There is that segment of thought favorable to the United States because of what it appears to represent—freedom with affluence. There are many in the world community who resent America because of what it seems to have—power with affluence. And there are those in Europe, Asia, and elsewhere who try to be as objective as possible, and who weigh carefully America's role as a world power.

From the end of the American Revolution to post-World War II days there were likewise three groups of world opinion in respect to the United States. They included those who liked America because it seemed "the last best hope of the world"; there were those who attempted to view the rising young country with a scholarly objectivity; and there were those who disliked the United States because it represented a kind of republican success amidst a family of nations ruled by kings.

Unfortunately, in those years between 1776 and 1941, many of the individual foreign views of the American fighting man overwhelmingly reflect either a total admiration or a total dislike for the American system. The heart of the matter, the real fighting ability of Americans, is difficult to measure through such prejudiced opinions. There were many Europeans who felt, for instance, that Americans could not possibly fight well because "democracy" was no training ground for the military mind. There were still others who argued that the lack of national consciousness hurt Americans on the battlefield. German-Americans, Swedish-Americans, or Italian-Americans could not possibly be driven by a patriotic devotion to their adopted country.

European military thought, in particular, appeared to be dominated by such notions after the American War of 1812. It was further handicapped by a complete indifference to the logistical and manpower problems imposed upon Americans by the vast frontier. Furthermore, it was colored by the supposed inadequacies of the American fighting man during the War of 1812, and a failure to understand that it was the American himself who profited most by his mistakes in this conflict.

Such was the state of European thought at the time of the outbreak of the Mexican War. The same type of British mentality that sneered "Whoever reads an American book?" was the first to assume virulence toward the United States in 1846. The magazine, *Britannia,* for instance, referred to President Polk as a "backwoods" Napoleon, and the leader of one of the "weakest" powers in the world. Truly, the publication argued, the United States was a nation "fit for nothing but to fight Indians."

The fear of republican success dominated many other European newspapers. The London *Morning Herald* gloated that the United States was now involved in a hopeless war with no chance of victory, and the London *Times* predicted an American defeat after an "utterly uninteresting and inglorious" campaign. Parisian newspapers were split; understandably, since a republican revolution was about to begin in that city. Some royalist French journals argued that the Mexican War would be ruinous, fatal" to the United States, while republican papers applauded American drive and initiative.

Since many Mexican army units had been drilled along European lines, particularly the shock cavalry, the Mexican Lancers, many European "experts" quickly concluded that American professional and volunteer regiments stood no chance of victory. The Mexican correspondent of the London *Times* harped upon this theme constantly, almost as if he hoped the thought might provoke the deed. The moment the untrained Americans saw the dreaded Lancers, he argued, they would flee in terror.

In the early stages of the Mexican War, British military officials were quick to point up what they thought to be obvious deficiencies in the American fighting man. He could not march long distances, they contended. He did not have a "rapidity of movement" (Scott's campaign to take Mexico City took only six months). The American volunteer was careless, particularly about using contaminated water (this was true). American supply lines were poorly supported, and the Americans themselves were badly disciplined and would quickly offend the Mexican populace. The British minister to Texas agreed with all of these points, summarizing: "They [the Americans] could not resist artillery and cavalry in a Country suited to those arms, they are not amenable to discipline, they plunder the peasantry, they are without steadiness under reverses, they cannot march on foot."

The more success the Americans encountered in the war, the more virulent many British publications became. The victories at Monterrey and Buena Vista were considered to be ridiculously small encounters, for after all, the Americans had no money, no army, and no national purpose. Vera Cruz, Cerro Gordo, and Churubusco were merely products of the boasting of "Jonathan," nothing more. The Duke of Wellington's comment about the hopelessness of Scott's Mexico City venture was published and republished in scores of European journals. Finally, when Scott did capture the city, the same papers argued that now he had the tiger by the tail, and that he would never get out of Mexico alive.

Somehow, in spite of all of these arguments, the war was a brilliant victory for the American fighting man. If the British had looked carefully at how the Americans handled the Mexican Lancers, the "Charge of the Light Brigade" might never have happened. If Europeans in general had observed closely the behavior of the American officer corps, they would have seen something that might have shaken their own military systems. If every foreign observer had studied the entire war, they would have observed some very admirable qualities of the American fighting man.

This is not to say that there was no revision of military thought in Europe toward the success of the Americans. A Britisher in Mexico City would write home that "They [the Americans] are all and each of them heroes." Other British journalists and military men backtracked slightly, arguing that, after all, victory by the Americans was to be expected. Were they not Anglo-Saxons, just like the British?[5]

Still, with the signing of the Treaty of Guadalupe-Hidalgo, there remained in the European mind a residue of confusion regarding American fighting ability. American troops had been sloppy and undisciplined; yet they had conducted one of the great military campaigns of modern history. Europeans had seen Americans enter the war with an unbounded national enthusiasm, and yet the victors had taken far less Mexican property than European nations might have annexed at the time. American troops had marched over great distances with seemingly few recognizable motivations; yet their behavior in victory was comparatively "civilized." So good was it, in fact, that not a few Mexicans were anxious to have Scott stay on as monarch of the nation. Nor was every Mexican eye a dry one when, finally, the "gringos" marched out of Mexico City, never again to return.

The continuing mystique of the American Civil War is amazing. There are Civil War "buffs" in continental Europe, and in Great Britain, and there is even a "Civil War Roundtable" in Australia. American Civil War experts are in great demand at European universities as lecturers. The best known and admired American historical figure in Africa and Asia is most certainly Abraham Lincoln. In a more specific way, it can be said that Winston Churchill cut his teeth, figuratively speaking, on the legends of the Civil War. And the man who was one of Churchill's most bitter military problems in World War II, General Erwin Rommel, was an avid reader of the campaigns of Jackson, Lee, and Grant.

There are a number of reasons for the fascination the Civil War holds for the rest of the world. It represents, primarily, a triumph of good over evil. It was a sacrificial kind of war; a fire which was fed by the worst kind of hatred possible—the brotherly type. And it was the first American war to receive a great deal of attention from foreign military men and journalists; a circumstance that brought the tactics of the fighting at Fredericksburg, for instance, right into the dining rooms of Europe.

The list of foreign observers in the Civil War is not only long but intriguing. William H. Russell (known to Americans as "Bull Run" Russell) represented the London *Times*. Georges Clemenceau, the World War I premier of France, was the representative of *Le Temps* of Paris. Military "experts" came by the dozens; some as attachés, others as free-lance observers. Among the French military officers were such men as Colonel François DeChenal, Ernest Duvergier de Hauranne, the Marquis Adolphe de Chambrun, and some lesser figures. The British sent Lieutenant Colonel Henry Charles Fletcher and the later General Viscount Wolseley. Lieutenant Colonel James A. L. Fremantle spent some time among the Confederates as an unofficial observer. And there were a number of Germans—Heros Von Borcke, who served with Stuart's Confederate cavalry, and Otto Heusinger, who served with the Forty-First New York Infantry, being among them.

The writings of these men and others, in the war and post-war periods, tended to conform to a very simple pattern. During the time of the conflict virtually all of them viewed American tactics, strategy, and fighting qualities with a dubious eye. Fremantle thought that the Confederates were poor marchers, excellent shooters, and that they were lacking in discipline. Another Englishman, G. F. R. Henderson, later a British student of American Civil War tactics and strategy, echoed these sentiments when he wrote:

> The great fault of the American soldier in the early part of the war was that the obedience he rendered was based on intelligence rather than on habit. He did not resist authority when he considered its demands were reasonable, but when he thought those demands vexatious or unnecessary he remembered his birthright as a citizen of a free State, and refused compliance.[6]

Other supposed deficiencies were given considerable notice by European observers. Almost all of them felt that cavalry units on both sides were being misused. Neither the Federal nor Confederate armies, they argued, ever attempted to use cavalry as shock troops in direct charges on enemy works. This particular judgment is one to which European military experts clung—long after the British defeat at Sevastopol—and all the way down to World War I, when British cavalry attacked entrenched German machine gun positions. Even in World War II, Polish cavalry attempted to beat off German tank attacks.

Most European "experts" gave low marks to other aspects of Federal and Confederate warfare. The artillerymen on both sides did not have the snap and verve of their European counterparts, they felt, even though their marksmanship was surprisingly admirable, and despite the fact that Americans found a real application for rifled cannon. The same attachés and newsmen mocked the "mongrelization" of diverse nationalities that composed the Federal Army, though they were quick to point out the Anglo-Saxon makeup of the Confederate forces, especially if the observers were British. They were doubtful of Grant's qualities as a general, feeling him to be wasteful of men. They admired Lee because he was of a courtly and aristocratic background; everything that Grant was not. Sherman, they argued, lacked the knowledge of strategic concepts necessary to an eventual Union victory. In regard to the latter, it was the London *Spectator* that, in January, 1865, regarded Sherman's march to the sea as an event "calculated to make men who are not American hold their breath."[7]

There are many advantages in retrospect. In the years following the Civil War there was a complete reversal of form among these European observers. Many of these same men began to see the Civil War as the wave of the future in military terms, and in fact, some even began to romanticize certain aspects of the conflict. Heros Van Borcke, the German, and Colonel Fletcher, the Englishman, publicly acknowledged that the American use of cavalry as a disruptive weapon had its merits. American artillery practices came in for admiration on the part of the Germans, particularly the use of massed and rifled cannon. The development of trench warfare was duly noted, with Karl Bleibtreu, a German, accurately predicting that the next great war would be fought along these lines. American logistical and engineering capabilities, at first scorned by all, now were accorded universal praise.[8]

But what about the fighting Americans of the Civil War? Gradually but surely the European notions about the "mongrelized" Federal Army changed. Some, like the Marquis de Chambrun, argued that the endurance, fortitude, and courage of the Northern soldiers who served with Grant and Sherman were exceptional. Others, like Colonel Henderson, added to the aura of romance surrounding the outnumbered but heroic Confederate infantryman. As late as World War II the British expert Major-General J. F. C. Fuller contended that "the Confederate soldier was probably the finest individual fighter the world has ever seen."[9]

How were the Civil War leaders handled? Lord Charnwood, the British historian, was one of the first students of the Civil War to argue that Lincoln's strategic understanding of the war surpassed that of most of his generals. Jackson, the "Stonewall" of First Bull Run, became a historical *beau ideal* in British and German military circles. His strikes around the Union flanks fascinated such interesting young military officers as Erwin Rommel of World War II fame. Lee became widely recognized as a true genius in the war, and his nobility of sacrifice struck the romantic chord of European sentiment. Even poor Grant, denigrated at first, gained eventual recognition as a great general, and as the real innovator of modern trench warfare.

In view of the obvious abilities of Americans to endure the hardship and death of the Civil War, it seems fantastic that many European military experts should regard such qualities as peculiar only to the period between 1861 and 1865. Many foreign military historians soon returned to the standard portrayal of the contemporary American fighting man as an undisciplined, unkempt, crude, uncultured, and untrained citizen in uniform. These same experts failed to see the frontier American soldier of post-Civil War days for what he really was—a tough, seasoned, and hard-fighting professional, who, because of simple geography and nature, merely appeared more untutored alongside the more excellently caparisoned European military units.

Even the United States Navy did not escape such jibes. The fleet was, to most Europeans, filled with the castoffs and roughnecks of Europe—that word "mongrelized" again—and its ships appeared to lack the fine technical implementation of European design. When the Navy was rebuilt in the Cleveland Administration, the event went virtually unnoticed by European naval experts.

Thus was the situation in 1898, when the Spanish-American War began. Many foreign experts simply failed to recognize that the American Army, though small, was tough and well seasoned. They saw the Spanish fleet as being composed of faster vessels manned by sailors far better trained than the Americans. Furthermore, since the American fleet complement was composed of so many diverse nationalities, it seemed impossible for the U. S. Navy to fight for any national purpose.

Ridiculous as it seems today, there were many British and Continental observers who felt that American aggressiveness could never be backed by physical means. If the British fleet could wipe out the American Navy in a week, as many argued, the Spanish would take only a little while longer. Even Frederick T. Jane, the most noted British naval student of the day, forecast that the "meddling finger of Uncle Sam" would be burned. And when Dewey's fleet left the friendly confines of Hong Kong to fight the Spanish at Manila, there were scores of sympathetic gestures on the part of the many British who viewed the American venture as a doomed one.[10]

It was natural, then, that the foreign reactions to the American naval victories at Santiago and Manila Bay followed the lines of shock and amazement. "Mein Gott!" exclaimed a German naval attaché, upon hearing of the Santiago victory. "Sir, it is unheard of! I must go to inform my captain." Surprise in Britain was likewise revealing. It wasn't the gunnery or the communications that impressed the British in the battles. It was, in fact, a factor British seamen were always somewhat loathe to admit: the superiority of

American personnel. One Admiralty official was inspired to allow that Americans were "possessed of an intelligence and vigour which is not common in the British Isles . . . strength and endurance in their physical composition . . . courage . . . dash and initiative."[11]

A German observer saw the same qualities—hitherto strangely unnoticed or ignored. There was a stricter discipline in the U. S. Navy than one supposed; it was subtle but effective. There was pride, previously denied as a characteristic in Americans, and there was efficiency and drive. As far as the distribution of varied nationalities in the American fleet complement went, the German made a strange admission. It really made little difference, he noted, for the men were all "American"; they had excellent noncommissioned leadership, and the younger officers were superb.

Historians have, of late, written about the American military effort in 1898 with considerable levity. Yet one must place it in its time—a few years before the British fiasco in the Boer War, in the same decade as the crushing Italian defeat at the hands of the Ethiopians, and in a period of considerable European bungling in Africa and Asia. By comparison, then, the American Army in Cuba and Puerto Rico did exceptionally well. Military judgments were admittedly made in an unorthodox and daring way. The decision to land the American troops at Daiquirí, in Cuba, was arrived at on the spur of the moment. American troops were shuffled ashore, in haphazard fashion, along a desolate and disease-ridden shore. But as one of the German attachés present noted, the "Americans had good luck, as they always did. . . ." Perhaps there was more method than madness in the American decision to put ashore at Daiquirí, for even the Spanish had never expected a landing there.[12]

The comments of foreign observers traveling with American army units in Cuba were generally critical. Daiquirí was rashly chosen, they asserted; it was impossible to support an army logistically from this point. And the American advance inland was too unorthodox and casual. They further argued that the inland Spanish strong point at El Caney should have been reduced by artillery fire. This was not done, and the Americans moved against the fort, unsupported, and in a skirmish line.

Possibly to the mild disappointment of the European observers, who might have wanted to be proven right for a change, the Americans won going away. The drive inland to El Caney, and thence to Santiago, was successful; there was enough logistical support for the army; and at no time was American morale depressed by even the thought of defeat. There were blunders, of course; there are in every war. But these were overcome by what the French might have described as the *élan* of the American fighting man. A Manchester *Guardian* reporter saw this when he wrote: "The men in the trenches were like men out for a holiday; their chief characteristic was a habit of cheering on every possible occasion; they used to cheer when they went into the trenches, and cheer when they came out; they used to cheer when there was food, but also when there was no food."[13]

There was one military expert present: a German naval officer whose conclusions about the campaign were rather astute. The discipline of the Americans was quiescent rather than overt, he wrote, and it included a capacity to endure much hardship. The ordinary American fighting man, he noted, was "brave, too impetuous perhaps," and he concluded:

> I am probably not mistaken in the assumption that the good results attained by some of the volunteer regiments are partly due to the circumstance that outdoor sport is carried on with great zeal in the United States. . . . And if the volunteers further know how to handle their guns and are good marksmen, which is also included among their sports, they have very nearly all the qualities which the Americans require of their soldiers.[14]

If there was one impression from the War of 1898 which remained indelibly imprinted in the minds of foreign military observers, it was that American fighting men of that war were superb physical specimens, who were capable of great dash and endurance. One finds this sentiment broadly echoed through the years that preceded the beginning of World War I. "The United States Regular Army is one of unquestioned excellence in physique, discipline, and general military efficiency . . ." spoke a British major-general in the decade following the war with Spain. What such experts noted was probably quite true, for from whatever evidence there exists, one concludes that the Americans of 1898 (and indeed of the Civil War) were probably slightly taller and rangier than the doughboys of 1917.[15]

When the United States entered World War I, the same physical characteristic was looked for and duly noted by French, British, or other Allied observers. When the first American troops came ashore in France, their lack of parade expertise was dimmed by the obvious physical fitness which they possessed. The size of the men, their trim physiques, and their open alertness contrasted broadly with the squat solidity of the French and the wiry smallness of the British soldier of 1917.

General Ferdinand Foch, later the supreme commander of all Allied troops in France and a man with a good military eye, remembered the early American arrivals like this:

They made an excellent impression. We were impressed by the height of the men, by their well-fitting uniforms, by their physical development and poise, by their splendid health and vigour. If their gait lacked something of suppleness, this defect was compensated by the accuracy and precision of movement altogether remarkable.[16]

It should be understood that these early American troops were, by circumstance, taller and sturdier than the draftees who would later follow. Yet first impressions are always important, and the French press gave wide notice to the obvious physical differences between the Yanks and their allies. One Gallic reporter, after watching the Seventy-First Infantry Regiment march in New York in 1917, asserted: "They were marching in perfect order, like a professional regiment, and their equipment was splendid and brand new. Their khaki uniforms and felt hats made them look very much like the first Australian regiments which arrived in France in 1914." Another, representing *L'Illustration,* was struck by the "quasi-religious" seriousness of American troops who arrived at Saint-Nazaire in 1917. "These young men with their lithe and muscled bodies," he wrote, "their smooth faces and springy steps, resembled players on the gridiron but did not in the least evoke our heavy, unkempt and untidy *poilus*."[17]

General Pershing, who was to command these same men along the Western front, viewed the early American soldiers with a more critical eye. They seemed to be of a lesser quality than the men of '98, and he was slightly abashed because they were composed only partly of Regulars. "The untrained, awkward appearance of this unit, which was regarded by the French officers as representing our Regular Army," he would later lament, "could not have escaped their critical observation."

Perhaps what Pershing really saw was not just more raw material for the meat grinder at the front, but untrained men who would ultimately be forced to establish the reputation of the American fighting man in Europe. Pershing was indeed a proud man, but not too proud to realize that there were many aspects of the new trench warfare about which his men were unlearned. He asked for French and British instructors for his troops, and he got them; along with a lot of assumptions that, since instructors were needed, the Americans were totally ignorant about what war was like. The instruction was painfully administered to the doughboy, who like every intelligent officer all the way up to the straight-backed Pershing, knew something that the French and British didn't know—and that was that the nature of the war had to change, or the war would never be won. The war simply had to get out of the trenches, or the dream of victory was a delusion.[18]

Still, the notion that the Americans were totally ignorant about the art of war became an *idée fixe* with both the French and the British. The first American experience with the *Chauchat*, the French automatic rifle, brought guffaws from French instructors—whose smiles were quickly frozen when the doughboys adjusted range and distance and began hitting the centers of the targets. A similar event, on a much higher level, occurred in front of a Congressional visiting party. General Henri Pétain, the French hero of Verdun, was asked in the presence of American officers about the training of American soldiers. According to a veteran American officer who was present,

Pétain "gave one of those nice little shrugs of the shoulder and nods of the head which indicated that in his opinion there was much to be desired in the matter of training."[19]

While the French were condescending in their early views of the doughboy, the British were much more generous. A British officer, after his first look at the Americans, wrote: "The physique, bearing and conduct of the American troops created a very favorable impression, while all the ranks showed great eagerness and aptitude to learn. . . ."

Marshal Douglas Haig, the commander of British forces in France, confided to his wife about the Americans: "I have been seeing a good deal of Americans lately, and I must say, speaking from my own experience, our idea of what American men are like was quite wrong! . . . Personally, I am finding the American men connected with the U. S. A. Forces very much like our own officers. I need give them no higher recommendations."[20]

Haig's earliest misconceptions and Pétain's tactlessness were not missed by the Americans. United States Regular Army officers, in particular, felt themselves to be no novices in the art of war, and in fact, they had history on their side to prove it. In the one hundred years prior to World War I, 1814 to 1914, the United States had experienced far more of the suffering and success of war than had either the French or the British. They also knew that they had much to learn, and that they had the drive and initiative war demands. An American surgeon who had served with the British before donning the American uniform found himself surprised with the hurried atmosphere in American camps. "What would they say to this at the British C. C. S.?" he commented on the American practice of predawn reveille. As far as the British military instructors were concerned, Americans had their own quiet opinions. "If they had succeeded in Britishizing us Americans," an American soldier wrote after the lifting of censorship in 1919, "the war would be going on today."[21]

And for the French, the American fighting man soon lost the glow of interallied fraternalism. The constant French complaints about the awkwardness of American staff relationships came to mean nothing at all when United States troops were faced with shortages of arms and equipment created by French bureaucracy and inefficiency. The most ordinary of doughboys was struck by the Gallic inability to get things done; they called it "backwardness." Even Pershing lost what the French would call his *sang-froid*. Writing to Secretary of War Newton Baker, he complained:

> The morale of the Allies is low and association with them has had a bad effect upon our men. . . . The fact is that our officers and men are far and away superior to the tired Europeans. High officers of the Allies have often dropped derogatory remarks about our poorly trained staff and high commanders, which our men have stood as long as they can.[22]

The earliest appearance of American troops in the trenches brought differing reactions from the Allies. It had been Pershing's wish that his men should be slowly introduced to battle; consequently American units were brought into "quiet" sectors of the front. In these areas there existed tacit agreements between the Germans and such units as the Fifty-Ninth French Regiment that there should be no more shooting than necessary. French and German troops washed their clothing in full view of each other, and there were no snipers placed anywhere along the line.

Now the Americans were here, however, and they not only wished to "see the Boche," but to "kill the Boche." Old German sergeants, sitting peacefully in the sun while smoking their pipes, were sent into eternity by eager American farm boys. The Germans retaliated, puzzled at the sudden activity on the other side, and soon these portions of the line were active with raids and counterraids.

The reemergence of this kind of fighting upset the men of the Fifty-Ninth French. "When one labours for four years in Artois, at Verdun, and other bad sectors," some French soldiers complained, "and one has the good fortune to find a quiet and wooded spot, what bad luck to see some brainless men 'excite the sector.'" Another French soldier, writing a decade later, would recall of the Americans: "It was noticeable that every time an American division appeared at the front line to gain experience in what had been considered a 'quiet zone' the calmness sought for was immediately broken up and the sector at once became animated; the foe was kept constantly on his mettle."[23]

In May, 1918, the Germans achieved a real tactical surprise. Toward the end of the month they smashed through a tired French defense and reached the Marne, thirty-seven miles from Paris. Pétain, forgetting his earlier impressions of the Americans, asked for and got two divisions from Pershing in order to help stem the tide. They were the Second and Third Divisions; both of them were partly Regular Army. The Second also included a Marine brigade. The Marne crossings were held, mainly by the heroism of these men, the Château-Thierry road to Paris was secured, and Belleau Wood was retaken by the Marines. Previously, in the Somme salient, a sharp victory at Cantigny had been won by the American First Division. Truly, the three American divisions had not only saved Paris, but in saving Paris they had saved France.

How did these new troops look to the Allies? From a technical standpoint there were numerous surprises. American artillery support, to the amazement of French liaison officers, provided a progressive curtain of fire before any advance. The American infantry was a further revelation. Some French, right down to the moment of the fighting on the Marne, had feared that the Americans might bolt before the Germans. The opposite occurred; the Americans fought with a sharpness and aggressiveness the French had so often desired in their own troops, but did not have. "American infantry showed itself skilled in maneuvering," a French communiqué stated. "The courage of officers and men approached recklessness. . . . The courage of the combatant troops is equaled only by the superb coolness of some of their medical corps who, in a perfect hail of bullets, gave aid to the wounded."[24]

Now there was praise of the Americans everywhere. Suddenly, in the words of various Allied reports, the United States troops were magnificently "aggressive," they had a "real technical skill," the Marines were "very high class" fighters, and the Americans in general were "amazing." The very British Marshal Haig noted in his diary that "Foch was in good form. He was pleased with Italian situation and with the fighting qualities of the American Divisions. . . ." And Haig, like Foch and a dozen other Allied generals, suddenly decided that he too wanted more Americans along his portion of the front. Only Pétain put in a discordant note, arguing that Americans were too "prone to forward rushes, disinclined to stay in trenches. . . ."25

With the halting of the German offensive, the public lionization of the Americans began. Marines were halted on the streets by Parisians who hailed them as saviors of the city. "Everyone hears of the bravery and 'flair' of our boys," a young American of the Second Division wrote, "and an American can get just about what he wants now." Some French officers now decided to take a closer look at the doughboy, to see what made him tick. They concluded that the outstanding characteristics of American fighting men were "national pride and a strong spirit of independence . . ."; the only danger to the Allies lay in a possible failure to allow for these "idiosyncrasies of American mentality."26

It was at this very moment of the war that the honest and dignified American General Tasker H. Bliss wrote a bit of solid fatherly advice to his commander, General Pershing. "It occurred to me," Bliss told Pershing, "that it would be a good thing to quietly put on record such statements. . . . There may be a tendency a year or so from now to minimize the credit which at the moment they gave to our troops. . . ." Bliss was wiser than he could ever have supposed.27

In July, 1918, the Second Battle of the Marne began, with elements of the American Third Division, particularly the Thirty-Eighth Infantry, behaving with exceptional courage. When the Germans were finally halted, the Aisne-Marne Allied counteroffensive began, with eight American divisions taking part near Soissons and on the Vesle and Aisne rivers. There were, in all, approximately 300,000 American troops involved in this fighting.

In September the Saint-Mihiel salient was reduced by three American and one French corps. After the astounding success here, the Meuse-Argonne offensive began, involving mainly American troops. This last drive, carried out against strong and easily defended German positions, cost the Americans dearly. Progress of the attacking forces was slowed by wooded ravines, barbed-wire entrenchments, hidden machine-gun emplacements, and logistical handicaps.

The impressions on the French by all of this fighting were varied, and ranged from sheer admiration to critical doubt. The "Rock of the Marne" Regiment, the Thirty-Eighth, came in for praise from all quarters for its performance against the Germans in the Champagne-Marne German offensive. A French officer liaisoned to this unit wrote that the Americans were "quite equal to our own best troops. . . . Having received orders to hold on at any cost they got killed only after having accounted for at least three times as many as the enemy. . . ." While the Thirty-Eighth was regarded as "first-class," other regiments in the same battle, those in the American Third, Twenty-Eighth, and Forty-Second Divisions, elicited such phrases as "perfect . . . calm under bombardment . . . great endurance . . . tenacious. . . ." And in all American regiments, rifle accuracy was regarded as phenomenal.[28]

The French saw Americans in much the same way at Soissons. "Most of us were amazed by the displays on the part of Americans of what they call, I believe, hustle," a French officer asserted. Of wounded Americans during the Soissons fight, a French soldier noted: "They endured everything without a groan or a grimace. They even jested. . . . They sang in chorus. They were unhappy only when they could not move." The comment was reminiscent of one made of Confederate soldiers by a Federal officer during the Civil War. "Their great characteristic is their stoical manliness"; he had written, "they never beg or whimper, or complain. . . ."[29]

There were some French criticisms by late 1918, however. French prisoners complained to German captors that Americans were trying to take credit for all the fighting. French attachés and higher officers continued to complain of poor American staff work, pointing to the fact that an American Marine unit had fought for forty-eight hours without water. There were too many American casualties, the French claimed, and these were caused by too much "ardour," too much of a desire for hand-to-hand fighting, the persistence of "rush" and "go" in the American units, and decisions to attack without necessary machine-gun support.

Still, the ease by which the Americans reduced the Saint-Mihiel salient shocked the Allies, from generals down to the ordinary soldiers. Foch came to describe the action as a "master stroke, which had a far-reaching moral effect upon the German Staff and rank and file." Even the dubious Pétain reacted, ordering a French mission to visit the newly won area in order to discover the American secret of attack. No unusual conclusions were arrived at by the visiting French, except that perhaps the long legs of the Americans had allowed for an easy penetration of barbed-wire entanglements.[30]

As Pershing would note a decade later, the French mission overlooked the more obvious reasons for the American success at Saint-Mihiel—the expert use of wire cutters and bangalore torpedoes, and sheer drive. The last—something the French might have described a few years earlier as the doctrine of "attack, attack, and attack"—was something that even some Americans could not explain. "The French didn't think we could go through the Germans but we did," a young American soldier wrote. "When I get home I'll be scared to go uptown."[31]

The British, from the moment of the American declaration of war in 1917, had requested that American troops be sent to their own sectors so "their fine fighting qualities" might be used effectively. Some American divisions were assigned to Haig's command, but by August, 1918, these had been withdrawn by Pershing to another front; an act Haig never forgave. His anger at losing his American troops was not dissimilar to that of General Orde Wingate in Burma in World War II, when that British officer had American troops taken from him. "What will History say regarding this action of the Americans leaving the British zone of operations when the *decisive battle* of the war is at its height. . . ." Haig asked of the silent pages of his diary.[32]

While they were with the British, however, the Americans came under close scrutiny. A London *Times* reporter noted that the Americans fought with a "gripping earnestness and an intense desire to get to close quarters with the enemy." A British officer, after seeing Americans close up in 1918, wrote: "The pride of the race is very strong. The Americans are earnest serious people, even the private soldiers, who have nothing of the devil-may-care light heartedness of our men. They have come here to do or die and are as keen as mustard but still very serious and quiet about it all."[33]

British officers were on hand when American units drove hard at the Hindenburg Line near Saint-Quentin. "Your Yanks are crazy. . . ." one of them later observed. "Your troops went through their own barrage and entered the town of Brancourt twenty minutes ahead. . . . I tell you, the Yanks are crazy." An Illinois soldier was told the same by a British noncom. "You blighters acted like Jerry was stringing you and afore we knew it," the latter stated, "you took the lead so bloody quick we had to come up close behind you—you didn't need any schoolin'." And a British officer, who walked across the captured field at Saint-Quentin, wrote: "American dead lay in long orderly lines, a tribute to the high spirit and splendid courage with which they had advanced to certain death." How remindful those lines are of the scenes at Gettysburg during the Civil War, or of Iwo Jima in World War II![34]

The American triumph at Saint-Mihiel was as much a shock to the British as to the French. It was true that the Germans had previously prepared a withdrawal from the salient, and that they were caught in a quick roll-up, but still the vigor of the American assault was impressive. "Even if the opposition was not of very high quality," a British staff officer wrote at the time, "the question whether the Americans can conduct a great operation has been decidedly answered in the affirmative. . . ." The same officer, after inspecting the captured German trenches at Saint-Mihiel, added some subtle praise for the attackers:

Good dug-outs and bomb-proofs, and a daedalus of trenches. The American dead here are not yet touched and lie as they fell, with all their arms and equipment still on them. The first dead man I saw was a drafted man called Roy Bassett of the 366th Infantry. The trenches were filled with unexploded shells, grenades, mustard-gas remains, and devilments of all sorts, compelling us to go warily.[35]

Of all of the Allied troops, the most favored by the Americans were those from Australia and New Zealand—the Anzacs. The affection of the Americans for these men was returned by the admiration for the Yanks by the other. Aussies, fighting alongside the American Thirty-Third Division, claimed that they had never seen such "determined ferocity" in any soldiers. "You'll do us, Yanks," an Australian soldier was quoted as saying, "but you're a bit rough!" And an American of the First Division wrote home in July, 1918, that he liked the Anzacs the best of all. "They are more like us than any other of our allies," he concluded.[36]

As has been indicated previously, there were some criticisms of American troops by French or British officers during the war, but they were mostly of an official variety—statements of Allied liaison officers, or guarded comments by Allied general officers. Haig, for example, reputedly was told by an Australian officer in September, 1918, concerning the American fighting man: "all are very ignorant but most keen and quick, and never have to be told a thing twice." A French officer complained that Americans were "much less disciplined than is safe for them . . . they rush into the firing line because that is their temperament . . . they are obeying an impulse." A British general saw the Americans as being wasteful of equipment, as "poor horsemasters," and neglectful of staff detail for smaller needs. And, he added, there was too much "passing the buck" to lower echelon commands.[37]

With the end of the war, and from the safe distance of retrospect, a general criticism of Americans became rather fashionable. The French General Mangin's war communiqué that the Americans had captured Château-Thierry almost joyously was quickly forgotten. Pétain's temporary enthusiasm for Americans was quickly replaced by his original prejudice, and even Foch got in some fairly good licks against his former allies.[38]

The criticisms usually followed the line that American losses were too severe, and that American troops had done well only because they had fought with overwhelming strength against a foe weakened by previously persistent British and French pressure. Americans, they argued, were too reckless and too inexperienced, too "prone to forward rushes," and unable to stand the rigors of trench warfare. As late as the 1950's a French military historian, writing about the

Second Battle of the Marne, could scarcely bring himself to mention the 300,000 Americans who took part in that battle. To him it had been purely a French victory. Old Tasker Bliss had been right when he had reminded Pershing to keep the record straight for the sake of posterity.

There were even times when the writing of the events of the war by French or British historians ceased to be anything but vindictive and insulting. Below is an account of the performance of the men of the Ninety-Second Negro American Division as written in the *London Times History of the War:*

> They [the Germans] merely lit up the forest with Very flares and lights, fired occasional shells into where they thought the niggers were and made occasional night raids. With the aid of a few gas alarms they soon had the niggers contemplating the murkiness of the forest with staring eyes and gaping mouths. Under white officers the niggers might have fought off the fear of realities and the fear of superstition, but the black officers were black the same as themselves, and therefore to their minds as ignorant and as helpless as themselves.[39]

The numbers do show that American losses during the brief participation of the United States in the war were severe. Considering, however, the fact that American troops occupied a tremendous section of the front by the end of the war, and that Pershing took the war out of the trenches, the heavy casualties are partly explainable. As for the performance of American units—perhaps even that of the Ninety-Second Negro Division—it ought to be added that the Americans experienced no fiasco such as that at the Dardanelles, that no Americans had mutinied as parts of the French army had done during the war, and that there had been nothing like the squandering of British lives on the Somme, or the French at Verdun. Americans had fought brilliantly during the war. They saved the French from possible disaster in 1918, and they managed, by sheer effort, to lift the war off base. Perhaps nothing more needs to be said.

A great part of what is remembered about war is what people

wish to remember. From the end of World War I there existed, in the European military mind, a set of rather fixed ideas of what American fighting men were like; and these remained solidly established until well into 1942. They included such notions as that the United States had a fairly competent navy; a better navy than the Japanese, but a poorer fleet than the British. Because of the excellent fight the Marine Corps had put up at Belleau Wood, and because of the widespread publicity about the Corps, most Europeans tended to regard these men as elite American shock troops.

The U. S. Army, though given occasional credit for its service to France, was most often written out of the history of the war, or almost out of it, by European military historians. Forgotten were the heartbreaking sacrifices of American soldiers on the Marne, or in the assaults upon the Hindenburg Line.

The problem was that such men as Haig, who had strong predispositions to regard Americans as crude colonials, never really had changed their opinions. Perhaps it was that American tourists of the 1920's, who flooded London and Paris, served to reestablish the image of the brash American; or perhaps it was that some American writers had tended to overstate American contributions to the winning of the war, leaving out due references to sacrifices made by the British and French. Whatever the cause, European military opinion once again returned to arguments that the American fighting man was crude, unlearned, undisciplined, unpredictable, and lacking in staying power.

Then came World War II in 1939. French officials, watching Nazi legions flood around the edge of the Maginot Line, pleaded for American assistance. Winston Churchill, given the task of saving Britain from Hitler, quickly realized that he could not accomplish that job without American assistance. The Japanese attack upon Pearl Harbor relieved Churchill of his anxieties, and soon American troops were on their way to the British Isles.

Once various elements of the American Army had landed in Northern Ireland, Scotland, and England, the old pattern of European superiority toward the American fighting man reasserted itself.

Though no important American officers had argued otherwise, British military officials complained that the ordinary GI was spiritually or physically unready for battle. During midsummer of 1942 Churchill and a number of British general officers viewed American parachute drops and live ammunition drills. To Churchill, ever cognizant of American opinion, they were "impressive and convincing." British officers who were present concluded that putting "such troops against continental troops would be murder." Churchill's reply was a wiser one. "They are wonderful material and will learn very quickly," he argued.

Churchill, along with higher American leaders, recognized that battle experience could only be gained in battle. One could not learn it at Fort Leonard Wood in the Ozark hills, or at Fort Benning in Georgia. Yet there were some British generals who could never quite respect the virtue of patience. Truly, if virtue existed in any quantity, it was among the Americans who came to regard the supercilious attitude of many British officers as one of the unavoidable penalites of war.

There were some American generals who could not hold a check rein on their anger, as Pershing had done several decades earlier. Generals Bradley, Patton, and Stilwell complained about the British habit of looking down their noses (a common phrase among Americans at the time). Bradley, in particular, was irked by British arguments that the Americans were "unlettered in the intricate art of combat," and that American field troops carried too much equipment.[40]

As more and more Americans piled into Britain, there were many in the British army who joked privately and publicly about the "pink" trousers of American officers, and the constant saluting of American enlisted men. The American writer John Dos Passos found during his travels that younger British officers looked upon American soldiers with a certain "scorn." "They couldn't help thinking of us as usurpers of the Empire that was their birthright," was Dos Passos' contention. An American prisoner-of-war, in Japan, ran up against the same British attitude. He wrote:

. . . the English merchant marine officers were stuffy, ridiculously aloof, and supercilious characters . . . there was nothing more amusing than a Limey officer looking down his long nose at a "half savage" Yank whom he considered his inferior. We had pretty thick skins, but those characters used to bug us by ridiculing everything American from Red Cross gear to Baseball, and they never missed an opportunity to point out the real and imaginary deficiencies of our speech, mores, and manners. And while they always tried to disguise their sarcastic jibes as bright, sophisticated humor, they were never able to bring it off as such.[41]

The roots of the occasional trouble between the British and Americans lay deep, and they were grown partly in American as well as British preconceptions. Almost every American soldier who traveled to Britain on British troopships complained too loudly about the food he was served, and how it was cooked. On the more crowded transports out of Boston or New York there were two meals a day, both usually composed of boiled fish. As Ernie Pyle was to point out later, both the crowding and the meals indeed were bad, but these conditions were unavoidable.

Even in an officer's relations with his men there were broad differences between the American and British tradition. British officers carried class distinctions over into the army and the navy; each had his "batman," and each maintained that any intimacy with enlisted men only served to bring trouble. The American combat officer made no special effort to insure the gulf between himself and his men, particularly in the field. Veteran Marine officers in the Pacific slept out on the decks of troop transports along with their men. Front-line American combat officers stood in the same "chow" lines as enlisted men. An excellent example of the basic difference between British and American armed forces in this respect occurred in Italy. There, an American officer was reprimanded by British lieutenants for drinking tea with enlisted men. "It just isn't done in *our* army," a British officer complained.[42]

After the American setback at Kasserine Pass in North Africa in 1943 there was general unrest between British and American soldiers up and down the ranks. Though the British were inclined to blame the defeat on American inexperience, the real causes included poor leadership in the field, General Montgomery's slowness in moving against the Germans from another direction, and the thinness of American manpower and equipment. The last had partially resulted from the fact that hundreds of new Sherman tanks had been sent to the British Eighth Army, leaving the Americans with insufficient firepower to counter any German offense.

Still, Kasserine Pass was no overwhelming victory for Rommel. The Americans eventually fought him off, and he was forced into retreat. Unfortunately for the cause of the Allies, however, there were some higher echelon British who quickly forgot their own earlier defeats at Tobruk, Crete, and Norway and took occasions after Kasserine to rub it in to the Americans. General H. R. L. G. Alexander, the senior British commander in the Middle East, generally regarded with respect by the Americans, reputedly got in some good licks about the physical and mental softness, as well as the discipline and efficiency of the newly blooded troops. "You know . . . " he supposedly said to Hanson Baldwin, the American military historian, "your chaps talk a good bit—often derisively—about our 'old-school tie,' but it has demonstrated its worth in war."[43]

Most Americans could take Alexander in measured doses, but Montgomery was something else, indeed. That salty general never knew how to offer advice, and he always appeared to Americans to be measuring the publicity value for himself of any proposed military action. When Montgomery, with a flourish, offered to send military advisers to help the Americans, the latter swallowed their pride and waited their chance. Not long afterward, Montgomery ran into trouble in the Tunisian hills, whereupon the American command quickly returned the offer of military advice.

The truth about Kasserine Pass, and the whole American experience in North Africa, is that the Americans may have lacked in men and materials for the fight, and there may have been some mental unreadiness for war; but all in all, there was no lack of courage. Rommel saw this, and while the British were criticizing American inexperience and inefficiency, he kept notes on the organizational and fighting abilities of his new opponents. Churchill, perhaps re-membering the unexpected British collapse in North Africa some months earlier, saw the event at Kasserine for what it was. "They are brave but not seasoned troops," was his description of the Amer-ican soldiers, "who will not hesitate to learn from defeat, and who will improve themselves by suffering until all their strongest martial qualities have come to the front."

A most telling estimate of American courage came from an un-named British general, who after the fighting at Kasserine Pass, inspected the overrun American lines. As he saw the dead young Americans, still in their foxholes and still clutching their rifles, all he could utter was "Brave men. Brave men!" Perhaps it was Ernie Pyle who best described the Americans in North Africa. "I saw them in battle and afterward and there was nothing wrong with the Ameri-can soldier," he wrote. "His fighting spirit was good. His morale was okay. The deeper he got into a fight the more of a fighting man he became."[44]

As the war rolled on, there was a constant but irritating dispute between the Americans and British over the credit for victories, and the blame for defeats. The Americans felt that Sicily was taken mainly by their efforts, but complained that Montgomery had taken the lion's share of the publicity of victory. General George Patton's constant argument, that it was he who had licked the crack Hermann Göring Division in that fighting, finally forced Alexander to write Churchill that the Americans had done a "grand job of work" in the winning of the island.[45]

A similar dispute arose in December, 1944, when Hitler gambled all, with a surprise attack through the Ardennes Forest. The initial stages of the assault were highly successful, and German armor and men smashed a broad hole in the thin American lines. But American troops resisted bravely at such places as Saint-Vith and Bastogne, creating islands of resistance which, particularly in the case of Bastogne, the Germans could not crack. Eventually, Patton's Third Army, and the American First Army, reduced the German salient, and the Battle of the Bulge was written into history as an American victory.

Unfortunately, the publicity-conscious Montgomery could not resist the lure of headlines, and created an impression that it was he who had provided the plan of victory, and that it was British troops who had created the situation for the German defeat. The reactions of all American troops, plus those of Generals Patton and Bradley, were so violent that Churchill was constrained to state the truth before the House of Commons. The fact, said the Prime Minister, was that the Americans had done virtually all of the fighting at the Bulge, and that they had lost sixty to eighty men for every British soldier who was a casualty of the battle.[46]

The war-long contest between the British and Americans over news releases was not really significant in reducing the chances of victory in Europe, but it was needlessly irritating. American pilots complained that purely American air raids were announced by the BBC as "allied raids," whereas British forays into Germany were duly recognized. "We don't get U. S. papers," complained an American pilot in England, "but do understand that credit on our first raid has been misplaced." Again, Generals Patton and Bradley were miffed when, after having pushed American troops across the Rhine at Remagen, the BBC announced thirty-six hours later that Montgomery had crossed the great river in force.

By 1945 the attitudes of the British and Americans towards each other were fixed. Most Americans felt that, although they had done over 50 percent of the fighting, they had received only a 50 percent break on the headlines. Whether so or not, it was certainly true that American efforts elsewhere in the world received scant attention from the British. It was never quite understood by the latter that the United States was the only one of the three major Allied powers that was fighting a full-scale war on two fronts. American losses at Tarawa, for example, received a "good deal of monocle-type sneering from a safe distance" by the British. Guadalcanal, Buna, the Coral Sea, and Midway were never really understood by the British public.[47]

Only an occasional British leader would recognize that the American thrust toward Myitkyina in Burma was a "brilliant feat of arms," or that "the bravery and self-devotion of the American airmen and sailors and the nerve and skill of their leaders" had shocked the souls of Japanese Samurai. Even Churchill's view was occasionally ambivalent. At the very time when the United States was struggling to turn the tide in the Southwest Pacific, he feared that Australia would become too aware that it was the Americans who were saving them. To counter this, he pondered the possibility of sending R. A. F. squadrons to that continent; their places in England to be taken by U. S. A. F. squadrons brought in from Asia. "It is my duty to preserve good will between Mother Country and this vast continent of Australia. . . ." was his rationalization.[48]

Throughout the war there were certain aspects of the American military effort the British simply did not admire. The British felt, in particular, that the Americans placed too much confidence in long daylight bombing attacks against Germany. They were correct in this until the U. S. A. F. came up with two excellent long distance fighters which provided bomber protection. The British reluctantly admitted American ingenuity in the war, but claimed that it was they who had dreamed up many of the various devices first. They felt, particularly in regard to landing craft crews, that the American Navy sent insufficiently trained men to Britain. In this they were correct.

The one side of war the British never really grasped, and the Americans did, was that of logistical support. Constantly, the British underestimated the American fighting man's ability to move men and supplies at great speeds over long distances and under bad conditions. In North Africa the Americans were able to supply twice the number of men planned under British estimates. During the Battle of Salerno it was the courageous and industrious American landing ship operations that saved the entire Allied effort there. After this beach was secured, Prime Minister Churchill singled out logistics as a "work in which the Americans excelled. . . ."[49]

Even Montgomery, in his postwar story of the European campaign, recognized the ability of the Americans to supply advance units. Using the editorial "our" in describing the American pincer to close the Falaise pocket, he wrote: "Very great credit is due to the American administrative machine, greatly assisted by rapidly

developed air supply arrangements, for the outstanding administrative improvisation and ingenuity which enabled us to continue
offensive operations on our southern flank." About the Battle of
the Rhineland, and the American redeployment of troops, he added:

> It was in fact achieved remarkably quickly. Some of the United
> States divisions had to move over very long distances using ap-
> palling roads and tracks in the worst possible weather, but they
> got into position on time and gave an excellent example of the
> truly remarkable mobility of American units when regrouping.[50]

Perhaps what the British never really understood was that the
magic in American logistical support was really a result of hard
work on the part of the American fighting man. Given a goal, he
proved time and again that he could work night and day at his
task. He was the one who kept the famed Red Ball Express rolling
through France under all conditions. He was the one who flew aircraft in the worst possible weather over the Hump to China. He
was the individual who, to the amazement of Australian bystanders,
had damaged locomotives back in motion within hours after taking
Philippine railroads. The ordinary reaction of Allied observers to
such efforts was exemplified by an envious reaction at this last
accomplishment. "Oh you Yanks. . . . You're always at it," was
the sputtered exclamation.

World War II is now a quarter of a century past, and time has
not helped in a true assessment of the events of those years. How
did the British really view the American fighting man in that war,
for example? The military expert Major General J. F. C. Fuller,
writing for an American magazine, saw him as less tough but far
more flexible and technologically capable than the Russian soldier.
The indomitable Montgomery, in his story of the war, described
Americans: "I saw them constantly and got to know them well.
The American is a brave fighting man, steady under fire, and he has
that tenacity in battle which stamps the first class soldier." Cyril
Falls, another British military writer, wrote as follows: "The Americans possessed great aptitudes for modern warfare. They analyzed

it scientifically. In some respects their minds moved more quickly to their objective than did those of the British because they were rather more imaginative and more at home in the realm of industrial mechanics. . . ."[51]

Though the British were the principal allies of the Americans in the war, it must not be forgotten that Chinese and French soldiers fought alongside the GI's, and that the Russians came into occasional contact with the fighting American. Unfortunately, in these cases, little is available in the way of written information relative to the viewpoints of such soldiers concerning Americans.

The Russian viewpoint as an ally was exceedingly vague. Reputedly, Stalin told the Japanese diplomat, Matsuoka, April, 1941: "The Japanese Army is very strong. . . . The United States is probably building a large navy, but it will prove of no effect in the end as it does not have the spiritual strength of the Japanese Navy." The Russian dictator's later resentment about the failure of the British and Americans to launch a second front is better known. And in one specific instance, a special Russian mission to Italy came to understand quite well the handicaps American troops faced in fighting their way up the boot of that country.

If there was anything that was tangible in Russian notions about the United States, it concerned the organizational ability of American capitalism. Even at the end of the war, when the Russian propaganda machine quickly adopted the Nazi line concerning Americans, the economic strength of the United States was admitted. John Dos Passos, after a postwar visit to East Germany, wrote: "They [the Russians] spoke of Americans as barbarous children. They admitted that we had been able to build up an effective industrial organization and that our industrial organization had won the war for us."[52]

The French view of the American war effort was likewise vague. Many French never quite forgave the American attack on the French fleet in North Africa, and, as most historians realize, relationships on the higher levels of command were seldom amicable between the French and the Americans. A little of this was seen occasionally on the lowest levels. The French in North Africa, for example, considered American troops there to be totally undisciplined. "Our boys sang in the streets," wrote Ernie Pyle, "unbuttoned their shirt collars, laughed and shouted, and forgot to salute. A lot of Algerians misinterpreted this as inefficiency."[53]

One of the basic difficulties between the French and the Americans was a failure on the part of both sides to recognize the real accomplishments of the other. France, to General de Gaulle and others, was and is the center of European culture, and these Frenchmen resented being assigned a secondary role in the war. France, to the American fighting man, might have been the cradle of Western civilization, but these were the same people who had needed help in two world wars.

Thus were individual incidents magnified on both sides. A group of drunken GI's climbing the Eiffel Tower almost became an international incident. American soldiers, in general, were regarded by the French as gullible, naive, and uncultured; despite the fact that few French families, other than those of the lower class, attempted to understand the GI. Here one is reminded of the story of a young American private who visited a small French church in 1945. When the priest, attempting to be facetious, asked the boy who his favorite composers were, the cleric was met with the reply that Bach was preferred, with the French composers coming second. The priest was so surprised, he invited the young American to have a drink of his best cognac. "That was the first and the *last* brandy that I'll ever drink," one truly naive American wrote. "Gosh, it was strong."[54]

Post-World War II views of the American fighting man have been clouded by the residue of irritations left over after 1945, and by a multitude of developments taking place since that time. The United States emerged from the war as the richest and most industrially advanced nation on the face of the earth. Its efforts to help less fortunate nations were accepted, but always with some resentment. The goals of American foreign policy, first in Korea and then in Vietnam, did not always meet with the approval of the European intellectual community; that group which always resorts to quick criticism and grudging praise. These inflections of thought were bound to affect almost every delineation of the American fighting man.

During the Korean War British newspapers, forgetting that they had sent only picked units into the conflict, were exceedingly sharp in the attacks upon U. S. Army training. In the early stages of the fighting, when poorly equipped American garrison troops were struggling to stem the tide of Communist aggression, British and French journalists inferred a lack of tenacity and courage on the part of the American soldier. Eventually, but only after French and British troops were thrown into the conflict, it was much easier for correspondents from those countries to recognize the obstacles under which American troops had fought.

The following picture of the American soldier in Korea emerged from the conclusions of European observers. He had, they said, "intelligence, physique, doggedness and an amazing ability to endure adversity with grace." What he lacked, the same experts stated, was training in the "art of retreat," and a reluctance to take casualties for his "own good." Then, too, there was too much concern for the amenities of life. Tanks had been held up for beer trucks, and entire movements were slowed because of an unwillingness of commanders to inflict hardships on their men.[55]

The most favorable impressions in Korea were made by the Marine Corps. These troops, said a British newsman, were "well trained and physically toughened, the NCO's were hard, and the officers looked like officers. They wore badges of rank proudly, and the men reacted accordingly. Regimental spirit was tangible. . . ." Another Britisher, a military observer at the Pusan perimeter, cabled home:

> The situation is critical and Miryank may be lost. The enemy have driven a division-sized salient across the Naktong. More will cross the river tonight. If Miryank is lost Taegu becomes untenable and we will be faced with a withdrawal from Korea. I am heartened that the Marine Brigade will move against the Naktong salient tomorrow. They are faced with impossible odds, and I have no valid reason to substantiate it, but I have the feeling they will halt the enemy.

I realize my expression of hope is unsound, but these Marines have the swagger, confidence and hardness that must have been in Stonewall Jackson's Army of the Shenandoah. They reminded me of the Coldstreams at Dunkerque. Upon this thin line of reasoning, I cling to the hope of victory.[56]

Very likely, this was the first instance in which this particular observer had seen the U. S. Marines in action; the Corps not having taken part in the European campaigns of World War II. One is inclined to view the implied criticism of U. S. Army garrison troops as being rather harsh, especially in view of the sacrifices those men had already made. Other Army regiments were eventually brought in—the famed "Wolfhound" Regiment, for example—and these proved that the American Army could continue to be proud of its heritage. As Major General Fuller put it: "The United States has nothing to be alarmed about concerning the courage and grit of the individual American soldier. . . . I strongly disagree with those newspaper critics in Britain who suggested differently."[57]

The difficulties of obtaining objective foreign criticism of the American soldier in Korea were basically the same as are presently experienced in relation to Vietnam. The European intellectual community opposes the war; Asians, when far removed from the Chinese problem, are critical. A French newspaperman describes Americans in Vietnam as being trigger-happy, naive, or erratic. According to him, they shoot anything that moves—"buffaloes, peasants, chickens. . . ."[58] Almost nowhere does one find praise of American courage in the valley of the Ia Drang, or in the skies over North Vietnam.

Sifting out whatever objectivity can be found, one comes to the conclusion that many foreign observers feel that American tactics are too aggressive in Vietnam, that there is too much concentration on the importance of airpower and firepower, and that American infantrymen are untrained in the tactics of night attack and infiltration. Overlooked is the partial success of the Americans in a place where the French failed, and the fact that large American troop concentrations are still maintained for the defense of Europe.

In all of the comments of allied and friendly observers there appear certain common denominations of opinion. In virtually every conflict the American is viewed as a courageous individual soldier. He is ingenious and clever at improvisation. To the great surprise of many foreigners, he is able to endure adversity with more grace than expected. He fights stubbornly and well.

Yet there are contradictions. Most observers through the ages have viewed the American fighting man as too undisciplined and untrained; that is, until he is observed at closer range. They contend that, in World War II, he saluted too little in North Africa; too much in Britain. Further contradictions include criticisms of confusion in staff work as opposed to real American logistical accomplishments; that the Yank is a product of mixed cultural backgrounds, but that he has a "pride" of race and a deadly seriousness about the business of war. He is naive and gullible, and yet he is accused of too much national sensitivity. In one war he is too aggressive on the field; in another he is too lacking in drive.

In the end one must rest his case concerning the fighting American upon the actions and comments of men who were in a position to know. Lafayette regarded his Americans as the best troops he had ever seen. Henderson, Wolseley, Von Borcke, and Fuller—all students of the American Civil War—argued that the American fighting man was equal to, or better than, any in the world. Marshal Haig was angry to the core when his American divisions were taken from him in 1918. Old Foch knew that the same war was near an end when American divisions had proven themselves on the Marne. Orde Wingate flew into a fit of temper when he lost the command of American troops in World War II. Even Montgomery managed to crank out a few favorable words for the American fighting man after World War II. On these bits and pieces of evidence, and against the indisputable facts of history, the occasionally uttered criticisms of the fighting American by his erstwhile allies tend to carry little weight.

3

The American Fighting Man:

Through the Sights of a Gun

IN THE SENSE THAT ENGLAND FELL BEFORE William the Conqueror, or France before Hitler, the American people have never been beaten by outsiders at war. There were some narrow escapes, the American Revolution and the War of 1812, but the remainder of America's conflicts have resulted in clear victories. In the Civil War, which pitted brother against brother, it took four years of unrelenting struggle for the numerically and materially superior Federal armies to defeat the South. It can be generalized, therefore, that either the American fighting man has been gifted with extraordinary good luck—many said this was the case in 1898—or that he is deceptively plucky and courageous in his struggles against his country's enemies.

It is a strange fact, however, that the American fighting man has not always seemed formidable to his enemies. The attitudes of the nation's opposition have seemed as varied as the wind, and oddly enough, these notions are sometimes as naive and unsophisticated as Americans themselves are often accused of being. One is reminded here of the remarks of Germans who watched the first GI's march across the Rhine in World War II. How could *those* troops beat the

Wehrmacht? They seemed so sloppy, so undisciplined, and so unmilitary. Yet, they were the apparent victors.

The education, or reeducation, of America's opponents in war has been a periodic one. No one can really tell when the first such instance occurred. Perhaps it was when American militiamen, scorned and ridiculed by British regulars, were allowed to take the field against the French during the Colonial Wars. There are incidents which are barely seen through the mists of history. In 1755, for instance, a French unit of regulars took on a Massachusetts militia regiment, confident in their commander's assurances that they were fighting "the worst troops on the face of the earth." By nightfall the same French officer was a prisoner of the colonials, and had already admitted that the Americans fought like "good boys" in the morning, "like men" at noon, and like "devils" in the afternoon.[1]

To the British, the colonial still remained a dubious factor in warfare. The Redcoat regarded the American as the man who had fought behind trees during Braddock's defeat; a cowardly course of action while British troops were being slaughtered in the open. The early American fighting man was the same individual who disdained, and sometimes laughed at, the restraints of discipline. He was rough, uncultured, inclined to fight at his own convenience, and determined only when victory was possible.

But then the views of the British had a few variances, too. There was a British general who felt that the American was "an effeminate thing, very unfit for and very impatient of war." There was a British admiral of the same period who wrote: "As to what you hear of their taking arms, it is mere bullying and will go no further than words. Whenever it comes to blows, he that can run the fastest will think himself best off . . . they are numerous, but a mere mob without order or discipline and are very awkward in handling their arms."[2]

Such views were quite common among the class-bound officers who held what amounted to sinecures in the British army. Indeed, the overconfidence of the British was the greatest single weapon the colonials had at their disposal during the Revolution. The events at Lexington and Concord did bring some modification of outlook, but the change was slight. Lord Percy, who commanded British Regulars about Boston, once described the American militia as making a "despicable appearance as soldiers." After the sad retreat along the stone walls of the Boston countryside from Concord, he toned down his verdict of the fighting American somewhat. Now he called them "sly, artful, hypocritical rascals, cruel and cowards." They were also men who could meet death with fortitude and courage if the need arose.[3]

Percy's inevitable reassessment of the colonial is typical of the historical pattern of America's enemies. The rebels who fought at Concord, he wrote, were not an "irregular mob . . . for many of them concealed themselves in houses and advanced within 10 yds to fire at me & other officers, tho' they were morally certain of being put to death themselves in an instant." "For my part," he concluded, "I never believed . . . they wd . . . have had the perseverance I found in them yesterday."

A British captain, younger than Percy, was equally surprised at the American resistance in New England. He wrote:

The rebels, you know, have a long time been making preparations as if to frighten us, though we always imagined they were too great cowards ever to presume to do it; but though they are the most absolute cowards on the face of the earth, yet they are just now worked up to such a degree of enthusiasm and madness that they are easily persuaded the Lord is to assist them in whatever they undertake, and that they must be invincible. . . .[4]

The Battle of Bunker Hill and the siege of Boston added further evidence of the unforeseen quality of American fighting men. The coolness of the defenders in the earliest of these events came as a shock. One American sharpshooter, handed rifles by two or three loaders, was able to pick off twenty or more British officers before he was overrun. "Damn the rebels," wrote one of the survivors of the charge, "they would not flinch. . . ." It had been far worse than the more gentlemanly fight at Minden in Belgium a decade or so earlier,[5] he concluded.

In looking back at the siege of Boston, it seems as if the British had never really understood American temperament during the long years of colonial rule. How had such undisciplined mobs captured Fort Ticonderoga? How had they managed to drag the heavy cannon from that place to the hills overlooking Boston? And where did they learn to fire them with such accuracy? The astonishment of one British officer is hereby noted. "The Rebel Army is not brave . . ." he wrote, concerning the siege, "but it is agreed on all hands that their artillery officers are at least the equal to our own. In the number of shells they threw last night, not above three failed."[6]

Shortly after the lessons administered to the British at Boston, the English attempted another landing at Charleston, South Carolina. Here the local patriots had erected Fort Moultrie and gave the British the fight of their lives. A British officer wrote that the "artillery of the *Yankies* was admirably well served, their works admirably constructed, and we had not a single deserter [from the Americans] for three weeks."

Another Britisher described the American action at Charleston like this: "The Provincials reserved their fire until the shipping were advanced within point-blank shot; their artillery was surprisingly well served. . . . This will not be believed when it is first reported in England. I can scarcely believe what I myself saw on that day. . . ."[7]

Washington's success at Boston was only the opening gambit in what was to be the longest war in American history. The Rebel cause was sporadically successful, and the great general's difficulties in outfitting and holding together an army are well known. Much of the fighting in the ensuing years was between British Regulars and American militia or Continentals, both of which the British saw under a different light in each engagement. At Long Island a British soldier wrote that his opponents were the "poorest mean scoundrels that ever surely pretended to the dignity of Rebellion." To him the famed Virginia riflemen were good fighters only when trapped. There were even some British officers who argued, after Long Island, that the Rebel menace was finished, and that the conquering British regulars would soon "return covered with American laurels. . . ."

The great turning point of the war was the American victory near Saratoga, New York. Here the combined British and Hessian forces were not only outmaneuvered but outfought, and the image of the American fighting man established here was to hold to some degree for the next century. The enemy was, according to some of the British during the Saratoga campaign, wholly unpredictable. There were times when he scampered off into the woods when faced with a numerically equal opponent. There were still other times when individual American riflemen moved to within eight paces of Hessian cannon in order to pick off the cannoneers. Natural cover was greatly used, with American snipers hovering on the British flanks to pick off stragglers. Most adept were these sharpshooters in hitting the officers. Burgoyne, who commanded the British expedition, wrote that Americans "placed themselves in high trees in the rear of their own lines, and there was seldom a minute's interval of smoke, in any part of the line, without officers being taken off by a single shot."[8]

When the Battle of Saratoga was over, and the British and the Hessians got their first real glimpse of their tormentors, there were some mild revelations. The Americans, though wearing no uniforms during the surrender ceremonies, behaved with surprising discipline. The lines of brown-clothed victors were straight and silent. As individuals they appeard to one Hessian soldier to be "so slender, so handsome, so sinewy." They were larger physically than the beaten troops. The same Hessian would write later that the Americans were far more fitted for military life than he had previously supposed. Truly, it was "no joke to oppose them . . . they can coldbloodedly draw a bead on any one."[9]

What disturbed the British more than anything else in the Revolutionary War was the American practice of ignoring the protocol of traditional warfare. It wasn't quite right, British regulars argued, that men should stand behind stone walls and shoot at their enemies from such a great distance. Even worse, to British notions, was the practice of shooting at officers who were, theoretically, gentle-men and not entitled to such sudden and inglorious death.

The rifle itself was a weapon deserving nothing but contempt, according to the British. It had a merited accuracy at long distances, but the British "Brown Bess" musket could be loaded more quickly, and still be fitted with a bayonet. British technique, in some cases later in the war, was to allow the Americans to fire a rifle volley and then attack with bayonet before the defenders had a chance to reload. This procedure worked well in the open, or at least when the British could catch the Americans on spacious grounds. In the way of war, however, the Americans soon devised a retirement maneuver for use when they were employing rifles; that of having one-half of the force fire a rifle volley and retire to the rear, while a second half waited with loaded muskets for the expected British bayonet assault.

Despite American victories now and then, there remained within the British army and in British ruling circles an element that looked upon the Revolutionaries as rude, undisciplined, depraved, dirty, and unkempt "banditti." As these people saw it, the American forces were composed of the outcasts of British prisons, Northern Irish, and Pennsylvania Germans. A British officer, early in the war, concluded that two regular British regiments could whip the entire Massachusetts militia, for the latter was nothing more than a "mere mob." Western Americans were regarded as being "more savage than Indians. . . ." They traveled, according to one Britisher, "two hundred miles through the woods, never keeping any road or path, guided by the sun by day and stars by night. . . ." And the Earl of Sandwich, far away in London, looked upon Americans as fol-lows:

> They are raw, undisciplined, cowardly men. I wish instead of forty or fifty thousand of these *brave* fellows they would produce in the field at least two hundred thousand; the more the better, the easier would be the conquest; if they did not run away, they would starve themselves into compliance with our measures. . . . Believe me, my Lords, the very sound of a cannon would carry them off . . . as fast as their feet could carry them.[10]

Most of the immediately foregoing comments are those of men who were either far removed from the American scene, or whose experiences in the colonies had been limited. Among the British who really understood Americans, there was an occasional early sentiment that the task of putting down the revolution would not be easy. Horace Walpole, son of the famous Sir Robert, was quick to perceive that Bunker Hill and the American Quebec campaign showed a spirit and enthusiasm which would soon be supplemented with means and ability. The great Edmund Burke argued that the Americans were more literate and liberty-loving than Englishmen supposed. Both Walpole and Burke, however, were lights that glowed as pinpricks midst a darkly unsophisticated British public attitude.[11]

In the wilds of America, or along the byways of New York, New Jersey, or the Carolinas, the British soldier who understood the American temperament was more forearmed than he could have supposed. Some British officers, even of general rank, recognized that the "zeal and enthusiasm" of the enemy, plus a certain "military spirit," meant trouble for the British. One of the King's officers, a little lower in rank, came to admit: "We have, indeed, learned one melancholy truth, which is, that the Americans, if they were equally well commanded, are full as good soldiers as ours."[12]

Hessian soldiers, after the Battle of Trenton, and some British, after Stony Point, became converts to the principle that Americans could fight. Even the American militia, despised as it was, came in for occasional praise from the enemy. And on the sea, the American privateer, part of the elite among fighting Americans, was feared and hated. These men, sometimes out of sheer nerve and the zest for war, occasionally took on and defeated regular British naval vessels.

It should be understood about the American Revolution that not all the British modified their opinions of the American fighting man. There were many whose class and background would not allow an admission that they had been fought to a standstill by self-trained and casual troops. After all, the art of warfare was supposedly a gentleman's vocation, and by British definition, there were few such individuals in America. Even Cornwallis, struck down by this complex, refused to take part in the surrender ceremonies at Yorktown. Yet, by this same strange contradiction, Washington could become a hero to the British. He was, on form alone, a gentleman of class, and was therefore entitled to a page or two of British history.

The United States, in 1812, was far removed from the troubles of Europe. Britain, fighting for her life against Napoleon, could scarcely do anything else but to view her troubles with her former colonies as a secondary issue. Her navy, already steeped in the myth of Nelson, scorned the small American fleet; and her army, tautly trained in the Wellington tradition, considered the American fighting man as little less than a subject for humor.

Thus it was when the United States went to war with Great Britain in 1812. Disdainful English newspapers wrote that "the contemptible flag of the United States would be swept from the ocean," its "arsenals would be reduced to heaps of ruins," and the American merchant marine would be quickly captured. What these English writers did not know was the quality of the small United States Navy, or the ability of its men. They merely assumed that no American shipyard could turn out anything to equal British naval construction, and that American seamen, lacking a national drive, could not fight on the level of the British tar.[13]

Those small but swift American vessels—the *Constitution,* the *United States,* the *Constellation,* and others—were therefore scorned by the British press. The first, which would eventually earn the name "Old Ironsides" from its crew, was dismissed as a "bundle of pine boards." It was a "bundle" that was finely put together, however. Within a short time it had won a surprising number of victories, and had sent a tremor through British commercial and shipping companies.

How had it all happened? The British press now searched for explanations, and came up with some interesting reversals of form. H. M. S. *Guerriere,* originally described as a model of perfect British seamanship, was now considered to be "an old worn-out frigate," much in the need of refitting; especially after its defeat by the *Constitution.* And when "Old Ironsides" defeated H. M. S. *Java,* the American ships suddenly grew in size. It was obvious that the frigates were really "seventy-fours [guns] in disguise."

Though the form and speed of the small American fleet had surprised the British, the elemental shock came from the complement on board the little ships. The shooting, the seamanship, and the drive of the Americans was unexpected. How could it happen that British ships were beaten by a "piece of striped bunting flying at the mast-head of a few fir-built frigates manned by bastards and outlaws?" "It is not merely that an English frigate has been taken . . ." commented the London *Times,* "but that it has been taken by a new enemy, an enemy unaccustomed to such triumphs, and likely to be rendered insolent and confident by them."[14]

There were too few *Constitutions* on the side of the American cause during the war, however; in fact, there was too little of almost everything. The general officers were untrained, the militia system broke down, and though much of the manpower was excellent, it was misused in fruitless offensive efforts directed toward Canada. The result, generally speaking, was a weakening of the image of the American fighting man in the eyes of the contemporary British army, and among many who would later become wartime enemies of the United States.

Unfortunately, the greatest American land victory came much too late to affect the course of European thought along different lines. The British repulse at New Orleans, fought after the signing of the peace treaty, was achieved strictly by American courage and ingenuity. A surviving British officer of that bloody struggle, one of the few left to record his feelings, wrote that Americans showed a "firmness and resolution," and that they "never for an instant wavered or quitted their entrenchment." But it was all too tardy, and the real victory won by Andrew Jackson at New Orleans was not in the field, but in providing for the American general a springboard to the White House.[15]

The implications of New Orleans were therefore lost in a strange peculiarity of history. Thirty-one years later, at the opening stages of the Mexican War, Santa Anna and other Mexican generals predicted that the course of that conflict would follow the precedent of the War of 1812. Americans, they argued, were committing national suicide. Mexican cavalry, artillery, and infantry, all European trained, were so superior that "it would be an injustice not to recognize the fact. . . ." And as a famous Japanese admiral may have done one hundred years later, Santa Anna indicated that he might just have to dictate the terms of peace from the steps of the White House.

The remainder of Mexican public opinion in 1845 followed Santa Anna's line of reasoning. The American Navy, so said Mexican public officials, was manned by undisciplined and incapable sailors. The U. S. Regular Army was regarded as weak, overburdened with frontier duties, and poorly trained. Any volunteer soldiers raised for such an army would be "totally unfit to operate beyond their frontiers." The last was a throwback to the War of 1812, when volunteer militia did refuse, in some cases, to cross the Canadian frontier.

Most Mexican self-assurances were directed at the American fighting man, however. The officers lacked a single will, so said the Mexicans, the men were without national spirit, the American camps were unsanitarily maintained, the infantry was undisciplined, the cavalry lacked shock-troop training, and the general marksmanship of Americans was poor. It was further contended that, since many of the American enlisted men were Irish Catholics, a large part of the American Army might be seduced from the ranks by promises of reward or appeals to religious prejudice. With these notions it is little wonder that the Mexican General Méjia issued a pronouncement in which he stated about the Americans: "Those adventurers cannot withstand the bayonet charge of our foot, nor a cavalry charge with the lance."[16]

Mexican intelligence about the Americans was only partly right. There would be considerable illness in the American camps. There were some deserters from the American cause: Catholics who formed up the San Patricio Battalion of the Mexican army. And there was some lack of discipline in the ranks.

These faults did not really affect the course of fighting, however. As the Americans won battle after battle, and as they moved deeper and deeper into Mexico, it appeared to most Mexicans that the

Americans were incredibly brave. A real turning point in the war came when Santa Anna placed his hopes in stopping Scott at Cerro Gordo, where the Americans faced an almost vertical climb against an entrenched foe. The Mexican leaders thought their position here to be invulnerable, and many young Americans, such as U. S. Grant and Robert E. Lee, agreed with them.

Yet, with a great deal of cursing and shouting, the shabbily dressed North Americans climbed the hill, seeming to "despise death," as a Mexican onlooker would write. There was no skulking among the men, no flinching, and no cowardice. An American officer wrote later that, when the hum of Mexican bullets seemed loudest, and when death "talks more familiarly face to face, the men seemed to rise above every terror." It is little wonder that when the American troops finally entered Mexico City a few weeks later, the inhabitants of that place marveled at their accomplishments.[17]

The achievement of Scott in taking Mexico City caused a slight reassessment of the American fighting man throughout the world. Among the Mexicans there was created a complex about the United States and Americans which is still a subtle and underriding one, and exceedingly difficult to define. In Europe there was a general shaking of the notion that Americans were cowards, but a confirmation of the idea that Americans were given to poor discipline, sloppiness, and unsoldierly behavior.

The greatest effect of the war was upon the Americans themselves. It was broadly understood that the regular and volunteer troops had won a rather unusual victory against great odds, and a highly colored romanticism came to envelop the history of the fighting against Santa Anna. It was the heroic vision of this war that pervaded the Union at the moment of disunion. Young men, impressed with the popular lithographs of Mexicans fleeing before brave young Americans, rushed to join the armies of both sides. Officers, young and old, and with no experience in leading troops in battle, dreamed of being the Scott or Taylor of the new day. Such illusions were to quickly vanish upon the sight of stiffening battlefield corpses, leaving Federals and Confederates alike with more soberly thought out estimates of their opposition.

And what were these estimates? First of all, it must be realized that there were almost as many measurements of the enemy's fighting ability as there were soldiers. Each man in each army came to some individual conclusions. Still, there came into existence some general notions—some about certain enemy regiments, certain enemy armies, or even about enemy soldiers from specific states.

In brief they followed this pattern. The Federal soldiers of the East, specifically those of the Army of the Potomac, had high respect for Confederate soldiers of the Army of Northern Virginia. A similar high level of admiration for the Potomac troops was not returned by Lee's men. There was a general sentiment that some Irish regiments of McClellan's army were good, but that German and "Yankee" troopers lacked a zest for battle.[18]

The situation was slightly reversed in the West. The Federal Armies of the Tennessee and the Cumberland were highly regarded by their Confederate opposites. Western Federals, it seemed to their opponents, fought with tenacity and courage. On the other side the generally accepted idea was that the Confederates were brave, clever, and aggressive—but not unbeatable. It was probably this Western Federal confidence of eventual victory that allowed Grant to take Vicksburg, despite the initial numerical superiority of the Confederate defensive forces in the early phase of that campaign. It was the same drive and confidence that carried Sherman into Georgia and beyond.

The American Civil War was a momentously tragic event, and yet it represents, historically speaking, the real blooming of the martial American spirit. The traditions of Grant, Lee, Jackson, and Sherman became the traditions of the American Army. The solid emotional impact of Farragut and Semmes became the core of the American naval spirit. Europeans, in a general sense, continued to ignore the great changes which had occurred, however, continuing to contend that Americans were good only for fighting Indians. One might add that such understatement was indeed fortunate for the United States in general, for it was only well into the twentieth century that the world discovered the true merit of the American fighting man.

Thus it was when the United States declared war on Spain in 1898. Most Americans knew they could not lose; most Europeans felt the Yankees could not win. In the minds of the former it was a match between the historical shadows of Grant and Lee and another nation of "greasers." In the Spanish mind it was a match between the conquistadores and the discarded riff-raff of Europe.

Most Spanish opinion in 1898 was directed against the United States Navy, for it was obvious to any military expert of the time that a battle between the two fleets would decide the course of the war. Thousands of items relating to the quality of the American ships and the crews that manned them appeared in Spanish newspapers, most of them derogatory in tone. The Madrid *Herald* editorialized that "as soon as fire is opened the crews of the American ships will commence to desert, since we all know that among them are people of all nationalities. . . ." It was contended that the Spanish navy was vastly superior to the American Navy, and that the Latins would teach the ruffian Americans "a salutary lesson for the future." Throughout the length and breadth of Spain there were assurances that the United States was in for its comeuppance.[19]

Among the Spanish officialdom there was an inclination to swallow these reassurances. A Spanish government official, writing an impatient letter to the ill-fated Admiral Cervera, asserted: "In your estimate you do not count for anything the effect of homogeneous troops, well trained and disciplined, as against the United States crews of hirelings (mercenaria). . . ." The Spanish governor of the Philippines issued a manifesto claiming that "the North American people, composed of all the social excrescences, have exhausted our patience and provoked war with their perfidious machinations. . . ." A Spanish military official, also in the Philippines, pronounced: "A squadron manned by foreigners, possessing neither instruction nor discipline, is preparing to come to this archipelago with the ruffianly intention of robbing us of all that means life, honor, and liberty. . . ."[20]

There were some sensible voices to be heard amidst this cacophony of Spanish overconfidence, but they were all too few. A Madrid newspaper reminded the Madrilenos that the American Navy was practiced, efficient, and fit. "The Americans are constantly making voyages in all seas with their vessels," the paper pointed out, "so that they have a trained personnel for the machinery." A Spanish officer of a lower rank pointed out that the American Navy was a good one; it was well drilled and well manned. And lastly, Admiral Cervera, who would lose to the Americans at Santiago, wrote of the Americans: "As for the crews, I do not know them, but I may say that the crews that defeated our predecessors at Trafalgar had been recruited in the same way."[21]

The actual fighting in Cuba, the Philippines, and Puerto Rico proved the complete unsophistication of Spanish, and indeed of most European military thought. Dewey's attack on Manila Bay was aggressive and determined. The American blockade at Santiago was effective. The American Army, wherever it fought, acted with courage and restraint. For the next decade, Europeans searched for easy explanations of the American victories, finally coming up with the conclusion that the good fortune of the winner was the answer.

The Spanish knew differently, however. They realized that it took more than luck to get Dewey into Manila Bay, and more than good fortune to capture Santiago. The prewar Spanish slogan, *Los Americanos tienen canones pero no corazones,* was inevitably amended to "The Americans have no cannons, but by God, what a stomach they have for fighting." This last was a reference to the American assault on El Caney without artillery preparation, a move that prompted the defenders to admit that the Yankees fought with a "truly admirable courage and spirit," and that they had rushed "with veritable fury upon the city."[22]

The entrance of the United States into the first great war of the twentieth century unveiled an American fighting man who was deeply immersed in the traditions of his military past. Washington, Scott, Grant, Lee, Sherman, Jackson, and all the rest were all part of a prideful history. The American Navy, fresh from the triumphs at Manila and Santiago, had not only built a new fleet since 1898, but had raised the standards of its training. The Marine Corps, almost crushed by Congressional opposition during the early 1900's, had not only proven its right to existence, but had set about to build an *esprit de corps* among its men which was almost unparalleled in history.

As has been noted previously, however, British and French officers in 1917 were too quick to overlook the American past. They adopted an insularity about American military methods which was almost incomprehensible. Without the real proof of battlefield performance, the Allied attitude toward the American fighting man was based upon the notion that he could not possibly fight well until he was well seasoned with European instruction.

On balance, the Allied and German attitudes toward Americans were approximately equal in their implications. German military leaders were no more or no less knowledgeable about Americans than Foch, Pétain, Haig, and the rest. They did operate on five early assumptions, however. These were: The Americans could not get enough troops over in time to save the French; the American will to fight was not strong enough to beat the Germans; technologically, the Americans were inferior; the American morale could not be sustained in the trenches; and the Americans would not take over much of the fighting. In every instance the German officers were wrong.

After the first actual military experiences with American troops, there was a mélange of reports emerging from the soldiers, intelligence officers, and generals of the Western front. These, mixed with American intelligence reports on German opinions at the end of the war, and with the writings of German generals, give a fairly good picture of the American fighting man as seen through the sights of a rifle.

It would be impossible to treat with the German opinions of each American division in the conflict. One must restrict himself to specific references. The American First Division, fleshed out with volunteer soldiers, was involved in the brisk and surprising victory at Cantigny. The doughboy was, to the opposing Germans, far more experienced than they had been led to believe. He was cooler and more aggressive under fire than could ever have been expected.

"We did not believe that within five years," a captured German said of the Cantigny fight, "the Americans could develop a division such as the First."[23]

A real blow to German morale occurred with the performance of the American Second and Third Divisions. The Second was composed partly of Marines and Army Regulars. The Third was a mixture of Regulars and volunteers. And how both divisions fought along the Marne crossings, at Château-Thierry, and at Belleau Wood in 1918! A German intelligence report on the Second read:

This division must be considered as a very good one, perhaps even as a shock unit. The material of the rank and file is very good indeed. They are healthy, physically well-developed men from eighteen to twenty-eight years of age. Their morale is inexhaustible, and they are embued with the spirit of implicit confidence. Significant are the words of one prisoner: "Kill or get killed." All of the attacks in Belleau Wood in July were executed briskly and without hesitation. Their nerves are still strong and they are well fed.

Of the Marines, the Germans had this to say:

The Marines are considered a sort of elite Corps, designed to go into action outside the United States. The high percentage of Marksmen, Sharpshooters, and Expert Riflemen, as perceived among our prisoners, allows a conclusion to be drawn as to the quality of the training in rifle marksmanship that the Marines receive. The prisoners are mostly members of the better class, and they consider their membership in the Marine Corps to be something of an honor. They proudly resent any attempts to place their regiments on a par with other infantry regiments. . . .[24]

Similar German reports were written concerning other U. S. Divisions. The Third was considered to be first class and vigorous; the Twenty-Sixth was reported as having *élan* and toughness; and the Thirty-Third was rated a top American unit. The Forty-Second, the "Rainbow Division," likewise was given excellent marks by the enemy. And the Eighty-Ninth, strictly draftee in makeup, was recorded as a "good American Shock Division, which undertakes many strong patrol movements."[25]

German line officers who faced Americans across the scarred surface of France came to similar conclusions, but there was an added attempt to rationalize German failures. The defeat at Cantigny was hard to take, for it was hoped that American morale could be smashed with some early German victories. When the American First collapsed that hope, however, many German officers felt that the enemy success was less due to *élan* than to German confusion. This, at least, made a good temporary excuse.

The American performance during the Ludendorff offensives of 1918 forced the Germans to focus on the Yankee problem, however. "If there are more like you," said a German prisoner, "then the game is up." Another German said to his American captors: "We have fought the Canadians and the Australians, but you fellows are rougher."

During the fighting in the Aisne-Marne triangle in 1918, German line officers were profoundly impressed with the accurate rifle and artillery fire of the doughboys, and by their willingness to close with the bayonet. There also seemed to be an unsuspected tenacity among the Americans. "Isolated Americans, lying flat in the field," reported a German prisoner, "caused us very heavy casualties." And an officer of the crack German Grenadiers stated: "We were very much impressed by the conduct of the American troops, who showed great bravery and a great deal of skill in the use of the terrain."[26]

Few Germans expected their new enemies, men who were so far from home, to exhibit such a readiness to fight to the death. There were times when even the most common German soldier could admire this characteristic. On one occasion a fifteen-man American patrol, cut off by the Germans, fought to the death rather than surrender. Above the mass grave of these men a German soldier placed a sign which read *15 Tapfere Amerikaner*—15 brave Americans.[27]

Certain aspects of American military training amazed the Germans. American artillery fire was exceedingly heavy and accurate. Time after time one reads that the German trench soldiers feared it more than anything else. They blamed it for the shortage of food and water in the front lines, and they blamed it for the destruction of communication lines. During the Saint-Mihiel attack, a German headquarters' report stated that the "Americans fired with great precision, not only on our first lines but also on our rear communications."

The American ability with machine guns was a further revelation. After the successful American assault on the Saint-Mihiel salient, German officers concluded that the doughboys spent much time "on these instruments which they possess in great number." Furthermore, the Americans fired the rapid-fire guns at anything that moved— German personnel, enemy patrols, and enemy airplanes. A German report on the Meuse-Argonne fighting read: "They [the Americans] would immediately open fire with guns and machine guns against any flyers within range. According to the prisoners, this kind of fighting appeals to them primarily as sport."

That fighting could represent a sporting challenge had never occurred to the Germans. They could never quite understand the savagery of the American attacks, the sheer firepower, and the bayonet work. There were some who came to the conclusion that Americans, particularly the Marines, fortified their courage with liquor before attacking. A thoroughly beaten German prisoner taken at Belleau Wood indicated such a sentiment. Pointing to a leather-neck, he exclaimed: "Vin rouge, vin blanc, beaucoup vin."[28]

The whole image of the American fighting man of 1918 was further confused by American prisoners taken by the Germans. "Why are you fighting the Germans," was the usual question asked of the doughboys. "We kill or get killed," was the ordinary answer. Beyond this the prisoners were exceedingly reticent. Time and again they indicated no interest in the Allied objectives in the war. What were their motivations? Duty, patriotism, and adventure were the common replies. Why did they fight Germany when they had German names? Well, the usual reply went, we are not Germans, or Polish, or Hungarian—we are American. To say the least, it was all beyond Teutonic comprehension.

On the higher echelons of German command there were some

interesting conclusions about the Americans. General Ludendorff was greatly upset by the show the doughboys put on at Saint-Mihiel, and complained that they simply could not be that good. As shall be shown, however, Ludendorff had an overwhelming distaste for Americans; a frame of mind he held through the remainder of the war and beyond. "The Americans must not be rated too highly," he wrote in the fall of 1918. "They are pretty dangerous, but up to the present we have beaten them back."

Not all German generals were like Ludendorff, however. General Max von Gallwitz considered the American fighting man as a superb physical specimen with energy and fortitude. The American flyers were brave to the point of recklessness. "I never expected such speedy developments," he wrote during the war, "The Americans are becoming dangerous."[29]

Nothing can be so descriptive as the very words of the people who make history, or of the very soldiers who fight the wars. Here below are a collection of statements concerning the fighting American of 1917 and 1918—written or spoken by their German opponents—gathered by American intelligence and other agencies in the months or years following the end of the war.

Replacement, armament, and equipment of the American troops are good. Their training is still insufficient. Notwithstanding this fact, the first American unit employed in the front line, against a German attack, behaved very well. It is to be expected that the American soldier, after additional training and war experience, will amount to a formidable opponent. [*German High Command*]

In general, the fighting value of the American divisions, considering their limited war experience and insufficient training, must be considered as good. When on the defensive, even the youngest troops gave a good account of themselves. The American soldier proves himself brave, strong, and skillful. Casualties do not daunt him. . . . In judging the fighting value of the American soldier, it must be taken into consideration that, until now, only such units have been encountered as must be termed crack troops. [*German High Command*]

I fought in campaigns against the Russian Army, the Serbian Army, the Roumanian Army, the British Army, the French Army and the American Army. All told in this war I have participated in more than 80 battles. I have found your American Army the most honorable of all our enemies. You have also been the bravest of our enemies and in fact the only ones who have attacked us seriously in this year's battles. [*Chief of Staff—Third German Army, 1918*]

Three Russians, used by the Germans as workmen, escaping to the Americans, stated: "We have seen numerous French, Italian, and British prisoners, but no Americans. The Germans fear the Americans more than any other enemy forces on the front. [*American Intelligence, 1918*]

I did not meet the Americans on the battlefields but I have talked with the German soldiers who did. These soldiers were against the Rainbow Division near VERDUN and said they don't want any more such fighting as they encountered there. The Americans were always advancing and acted more like wild men than soldiers. [*Statement of German, 1919*]

Bauer is a butcher who was with the German heavy artillery for three years. Referring to enemy artillery he said the French was the most accurate and could throw shells where they wanted. . . . It was difficult to choose between the French and American infantry; there was however, a difference in the way they fought. The French would not advance unless sure of gaining their objectives while the American infantry would dash in regardless of all obstacles and that while they gained their objectives they would often do so with a heavy loss of life. [*American Intelligence, 1919*]

The troops, Weller says, soon recognized that the American soldier was a brave and worthy opponent, that he advanced rapidly with little regard for cover and was daring in his night patrolling. [*American Intelligence, 1918*]

His experiences on the Eastern front caused him to say that the Russians were the poorest soldiers. . . . The real fighters were the

British, French and Americans on the Western front. Oberlander stated that in his opinion England had the best infantry, the American artillery was the most accurate, and the American aeroplanes the most feared. He considered the achievements of the American airmen wonderful, considering the length of time they had in the field. [*American Intelligence, 1919*]

His opinion of the American soldier is very high. In this attack [Saint-Mihiel] the artillery fire was very accurate and very heavy and the advance of the infantry was in good formation and irresistible. He thinks the American soldier does not look as well on the road or in camp as in the field but likes our discipline very much because of the greater freedom given the men. He thinks that individually the German soldier is not as good a fighter as the American. [*American Intelligence, 1918*]

He said Bois de Belleau was well known in Germany. He also said they had never before met such a sudden shock and deadly machine gun and rifle fire, and that most of their losses were from the above mentioned arms. They came to Chateau-Thierry with a company strength of one hundred and fifty men and had lost only two per cent until they met the Americans the first of June . . . when relieved the 10th of June . . . [they] had only thirty men left in his company. . . . [*American Intelligence, 1919*][30]

During the 1920's there was a tendency for a reassessment of the war among German military circles. Ludendorff, in particular, fell victim to the racist notions of the rising German demagogue, Adolf Hitler, and grasped at any rationalization for the 1918 defeat. By 1930 he was claiming that Saint-Mihiel was possible as an American victory only because the Germans were withdrawing from the salient anyway. He makes no reference to the American verve and zest in Pershing's first real offensive. As far as the total defeat was concerned, Ludendorff argued that the accomplishments of the German army had been undermined by a "Jewish conspiracy" on the home front. Even the American prisoners taken in the war, he contended, failed to realize that they had been willing victims of "international Jewish money-lending capitalists."

Again one finds the old European myth intertwined amidst Ludendorff's review of the war. American soldiers were a "mongrelized" mob—many of them being Poles and Russians who had been "pressed into American uniforms." They were untrained, sometimes "stubborn and skillful," but soon exhausted of their "valour and good nerves." They lacked the "sweeping impetus of patriotic exaltation," so said Ludendorff, mainly because the war had been forced on them by "Jews, initiated Freemasons, and Jesuits. . . ."

When one gets right down to it, Ludendorff almost included all Americans by this last generalization.[31]

There were other postwar German reminiscences which were untainted by Ludendorff's spiteful and twisted opinions. Crown Prince William, who had commanded many German troops during the war, and who had nothing to gain by his praise of the American fighting man, argued a decade later that two American divisions saved France from destruction in 1918. General Walther Reinhardt, a German General Staff officer, admitted that the Americans had changed the course of the war. In Reinhardt's opinion the Americans had brought a new and needed impetus to the Allied cause. This German officer harked back to a quotation of Frederick the Great in order to describe American troops. "They may not look so good," the Prussian ruler had once said of a military unit, "but hell, how they can fight!"[32]

The Japanese attack upon Pearl Harbor, December, 1941, was the greatest strategical error commited by either side in World War II. Though it is true that the immediate results were spectacular, the smashing of the American Pacific fleet stimulated the United States to the greatest military effort in its history.

Japanese planning for the attack was not done overnight. It was the product of over twenty years of naval indoctrination and effort, and of army encouragement and propaganda. The early Japanese strategy—as dictated by the tradition of the country—was to lull the enemy into overconfidence, and to create in the Japanese mind the idea that Westerners could be beaten. Why did the United States need such a big navy, a Japanese admiral had asked in the mid-1930's? "Without a big navy, it would feel no inconvenience . . ." he asserted. "How happy the world would be if the United States did not have so big a navy!" And prior to Japan's entry into the war, an army publicist stated: "In point of mentality, Japanese are rather superior to Americans."[33]

Japanese military thought by 1941 was a strange admixture of opinions. Thinking in Japanese military circles on the eve of Pearl Harbor was truly not as monolithic as one might suppose; there were many who warned against fighting the United States. Yet, even among the defeatists there was a peculiar self-delusion—a strain of Japanese historical romanticism and mysticism which brought them to feel that Japanese success was inevitable.

In the very center of the Japanese High Command was the spot where this self-delusion held greatest sway. Hideki Tojo, the army general who became dictator in 1941, argued that America did not have the spirit for war, that there were German-Americans who would not fight against Germany, and that labor troubles in the United States would cut production to a minimum. Matsuoka, the Japanese diplomat who made a pre-attack tour of Europe, was totally ignored when he presented warnings to the Imperial Government from other Axis capitals against the attack.

The problem in Tokyo seems to have been that nobody really wanted to make a firm stand on the issue of war, excepting the hard-line militarists. There were some, like one high Japanese official, who politely pointed out that Japan had enough spiritual power to win a war against the United States, but little enough of the required material power. There were a few Japanese naval officials who opposed the war, but didn't have the courage to face down the more radical elements in the Japanese capital. Politicians, like Prince Konoye, nervously circled the issue of war and merely asked for more time.[34]

The planning for the strike at Pearl Harbor was done by Rear Admiral Takijiro Onishi, under the general supervision of the great sea-lord Admiral Isoroku Yamamoto. The latter was, by 1941, more than a living legend in the Japanese navy. He *was* the navy. It is indeed surprising, in view of his premonitions against such an attack, that he didn't exercise more restraint within the government.

What did Yamamoto really think about the Americans? First, it should be noted that he had spent some time in the United States, and that he was well versed on the character of its people. Despite the fact that he was once reputed to have said that he looked "forward to dictating peace to the United States in the White House," his ideas concerning his future enemy were well thought through. In answer to a question on Japan's chances for victory against the United States, he was reputed to have said: "I can raise havoc with them for one year or at most eighteen months. After that I can give no one any guarantees." In reply to the question: "Don't you think our gallant navy will win?" his reply was: "No, I do not." Another source quotes him as saying:

> If you tell me that it is necessary that we fight, then in the first six months to a year of war against the U. S. and England, I will run wild, and I will show you an uninterrupted succession of victories; but I must also tell you that, should the war be prolonged for two or three years, I have no confidence in our ultimate victory.[35]

Yamamoto's pessimistic outlook in case of a prolonged war was based upon two fears. The first was a wholesome respect for the American Navy; the second was an abiding respect for American economic production. Most of the men surrounding Yamamoto also realized that Pearl Harbor, even if successful, was only the opening move in a great Pacific naval chess game—with Japan's real chances lying in a successful island-to-island defense from Australia northward. Few Japanese officials felt that the American people would sue for an early peace; all argued that retaliation might be swift and savage. To the Japanese who pointed to the hardness of Japan's mighty army, and the quality of the nation's navy, Yamamoto replied:

> Most people think Americans love luxury and that their culture is shallow and meaningless. It is a mistake to regard the Americans as luxury-loving and weak. I can tell you Americans are full of the spirit of justice, fight and adventure. Also their thinking is

very advanced and scientific. Lindbergh's solo crossing of the Atlantic is the sort of valiant act which is normal for them. Do not
forget American industry is much more developed than ours—
and unlike us they have all the oil they want. Japan cannot beat
America. Therefore she should not fight America.[36]

Despite the strange Oriental contradiction in the man, Yamamoto's plan of strategy called for a quick strike at Pearl Harbor,
and a coordinated invasion of the Philippines, Malaya, and the
East Indies.

The success of the great assault was beyond the wildest dreams
of almost every Japanese citizen. Nineteen American ships were
sunk or damaged at Pearl Harbor (eight of them battleships), 200
planes were destroyed or damaged, and 3,800 American fighting
men were killed or wounded. The East Indies and Malaya were
taken easily, but the Philippines presented a harder problem. The
Filipino Scouts plus American military personnel held out there
until the following May, when Corregidor finally surrendered. The
defeats on Bataan and elsewhere did not really end the fighting
in the Philippines, however, and in a sense they were never conquered by the Japanese. To the very moment when American troops
returned, there were large portions of the islands that remained
under American and Filipino guerrilla control.

The total effect of the skein of victories upon the Japanese public
was galvanic, and as shall be seen, rather fortunate for the United
States. The concept of innate Western superiority was probably
ended forever—all over Asia—but in Japan it was replaced by an
overwhelming confidence which could only lead to disaster. Marshal
Koichi Kido, watching the sun rise over a building in Tokyo,
would translate the event into a symbol of the "destiny of this
country. . . ." A Japanese naval captain, broadcasting on Radio
Tokyo, announced: "I might add that the Imperial Navy would
like to hold a review off New York Harbor. Could anything be as
grand as a naval review off New York Harbor and formal entry
into London?" Only Yamamoto remained querulous about the
astounding success of Japan, writing:

This war will give us much trouble in the future. The fact that we have had a small success at Pearl Harbor is nothing. The fact that we have succeeded so easily has pleased people. Personally I do not think it is a good thing to whip up propaganda to encourage the nation. People should think things over and realize how serious the situation is.[37]

The innocence that pervaded Japan in 1941 is understandable, for a great deal of naïveté had dominated American thinking to the very moment of the Pearl Harbor attack. Up to the day that the bombs fell on the U. S. S. *Arizona,* Secretary of the Navy Frank Knox was handing out pronouncements that the fleet was prepared for every contingency. Furthermore, many Americans had contended, Japanese planes were made in toy factories, Japanese torpedoes were fabricated in jerry-built factories, and Japanese pilots were simply not up to the American standard.[38]

Yet, if the Japanese lacked a real knowledge of American character, and the Americans were foolish enough to suppose that Japanese pilots could not shoot straight, it must be added that Germanic misinformation about the United States was equal to, or in excess of, that of any of the powers that would oppose the United States.

Hitler was the main contributor here. His knowledge of the United States was not only based upon wrongful myths, but much of it came from the twisted logic of General Ludendorff, a man who could never bring himself to admit to the quality of the World War I American soldier.

Therefore, Hitler's prewar notions of the United States were filled with monumental errors. He had nothing but contempt for the American military. The United States was a weak nation—too "mongrelized" to be effective in war. To the Japanese he expressed the opinion that the "German soldier naturally ranks high above the Americans"—a comment echoed by equally unlearned underlings, who argued that "the United States would undoubtedly try to avoid meeting German troops. . . ." Hitler's concept of the American fighting man was placed in the Ludendorff framework. The American soldiers were "nothing but a bunch of rowdies. They can't stick in a crisis. They have absolutely no ideals."[39]

Belying the reputed thoroughness of the German mind, Hitler and his associates had little real knowledge of the American military or productive potential. Some of these men did not even know the population of the United States, thinking it to be over 200 million; hence providing a ready explanation for previous United States military successes. All of them followed Hitler's argument, that the United States *could* raise an army, but that German submarines and airpower would prevent any American landings in any part of Europe. As far as industrial production was concerned, such claims were nothing but "typical American exaggerations, propaganda and bluff." Even fat Hermann Göring would repeat such nonsense, arguing that the United States could produce nothing but fairly excellent razor blades.[40]

Unfortunately for the Axis powers, much of what Hitler and Tojo believed was supported by secret German reports on American military strength. There were, in those pre-Pearl Harbor days, few modifying influences on the German leader. There was an occasion when he was shown some aerial views of New York City, and he was profoundly impressed by the "enormous vitality and power radiated by those buildings. . . ." But it was a brief glimmering of reality, soon to be demolished by the events of December 7, 1941.[41]

The effects of the Japanese success on that day were felt around the world. Hitler was thoroughly impressed, and a sand castle of Japanese overconfidence was quickly constructed. A Japanese sailor wrote in his diary: "What will the people at home think when they hear the news? Won't they be excited? I see them clapping their hands and shouting with joy, "We will teach the Anglo-Saxon scoundrels a lesson!' " He was right. The people did go wild; so much so that they forgot the real meaning of Pearl Harbor.

And Japanese propaganda helped them to forget. "The degenerated spirit of the crews of the American fleet could do nothing but offer their warships as excellent targets . . ." concluded a Japanese magazine, "it was not a match for the heroic fighting spirit of Nippon naval men." American "braggadocio" had been defeated, concluded the Japan *Times and Advertiser:* "Only a few weeks ago they were boasting that the United States could finish off Japan in three months. Today these same Americans are trembling in their shoes and they have every reason to do so." A Japanese radio commentator in 1942 saw America as "a white grave" of "inordinate ambitions of world domination." And from a Japanese admiral came an argument which could easily be understood by Hitler. "The United States is a patch quilt of heterogenous [*sic*] population, lacking in national consciousness . . ." he stated. "Once it is deprived of its slender hopes of victory, the country will be thrown into confusion and restlessness."[42]

As the fighting in Bataan went on through the early months of 1942, a certain note pervaded Japanese propaganda about the American fighting man. The Americans, it seemed, lacked the stomach for battle. They suffered from numerous psychological problems. They had "mental derangements," a "morbid fear," they suffered from "bomb-phobia," they were astounded at the iron nerves of Japanese soldiers, they were "cry-babies," they were "untrained and undisciplined," and their favorite phrase was OHIO (over the hill in October).[43]

As far as battle techniques were concerned, the Japanese did admit that their enemies had a certain proficiency in mortars and artillery. Japanese soldiers, they contended, were far superior in night-fighting, and much more patient and enduring. Many Japanese news reports stressed the concept that the American Army was filled with "unwieldy masses of raw conscripts, armed only with paper weapons." The Americans were simply "boy amateurs fresh from short summer training courses . . ." they concluded.[44]

Beneath this facade of self-assurance, however, there was an undercurrent of worry, but it existed among a few higher Japanese civilian and military officials. Some Japanese officers, prior to the war, had even feared that the American military might conceive of a tunnel to Japan under the Bering Sea. Now, after Pearl Harbor, there was a gnawing notion that somehow, and in some way, the Americans would think of a method by which they could bomb Tokyo and even the Imperial Palace itself.

These were vague concerns, however. There was such a general Japanese euphoria relative to the war in 1941 and 1942 that it quickly redounded to the American advantage. It expressed itself in various ways on all levels of the Japanese military machine; but whatever the shape it assumed, it was simply an unmerited over-confidence. During the fighting in New Britain, for example, heavy losses were incurred when the heavy-footedness of the Japanese infantry revealed its position to American artillery. Japanese officers were killed while carrying maps and important information, which not only revealed the course of the campaign, but the plans for the future.

The sudden Japanese superiority complex affected every branch of their military force. Every time an American submarine under attack released debris to the surface, Japanese destroyers sailed blithely away to claim another sinking. By the end of the war the Japanse navy had claimed 468 sinkings of American subs; yet the real American losses only totaled forty-eight.[45]

After the Battle of Midway, and the American island-hopping campaign from Australia northward, the tone of Japanese military thought underwent gradual change. One of the few Japanese prisoners taken at Bougainville, after seeing the massive power of the American armada, even offered to seduce other Japanese to desert. "With our ancient ideas . . ." he exclaimed, "how can we expect to win over the arms possessed by the civilized and world-prominent country of America?"

Tarawa was a further blow to Japanese ideology, not so much because of the American firepower exhibited there, but because of the inexorable onslaught of the U. S. Marines, who contrary to Oriental concepts of the American fighting man, kept coming in waves against Japanese positions. When the island finally fell, the Japanese newspaper *Yomiuri* fought hard for a rationalization. "As in judo," it editorialized, "let the enemy push and push. Then at the end we shall make use of his strength to throw him over."

A Japanese document captured early in the war made the following claim about the American fighting man. "If he once gains self-confidence he becomes over-bold," it contended, "but if anyone opposes him he becomes radically less aggressive at once." Though the statement had been written about Americans, it was essentially more correctly descriptive of the Japanese. As Guadalcanal, Midway, Tarawa, and Buna were written into the pages of American military history, it was the Japanese who became "radically less aggressive."

What the American victories at these places did was destroy the Japanese hopes for not only a quick but an eventual victory. The capture of Saipan added further woes, for the Japanese General Staff had declared the island to be "absolutely invincible." The mood of the Japanese public now underwent a radical change. American prisoners in Japan began to receive slightly better treatment, and even Tojo admitted the seriousness of the situation to the people.[46]

The remainder of the war against Japan was filled with violent but decisive explosions of conflict. Iwo Jima was taken by the Marines with heavy casualties and great courage on both sides. Okinawa was won with sheer drive and logistical skill, and by the ability of the U. S. Navy to absorb heavy damage from Japanese suicide planes. The total American capacity for war had far outstripped the Japanese code of *Bushido*. The German surrender, and the success of the atomic bombs on Hiroshima and Nagasaki, speeded the Japanese decision to haul down the Rising Sun in surrender.

German attitudes toward the American fighting man were varied according to time, place, the individual German who was involved, and his intent. On the lower levels of German soldiery, the statements expressed about Americans reflected the *esprit de corps* of the unit from which the soldiers came, or even the very conditions under which those soldiers fought.

Generally speaking, the German private had a high respect for American Rangers, American paratroopers, American artillery, and American air power. He usually felt that German infantry was more aggressive, and that American Negro soldiers in Italy gave a poor performance. He was astounded by the comparative ease of the German breakthrough in the Ardennes Forest late in the war, but he was shocked by the quick recovery of Americans in the Bulge and their persistence at Bastogne.

More specifically, many Germans were quick to assert that Americans lacked experience in North Africa, though not bravery. American artillery was, from the time of Kasserine Pass, a respected element in the war. By the time of Saint-Lô—during the Normandy fighting—German reports from the front lines laid great stress on the accuracy of the big American guns. They were destroying German troops far to the rear as well as in the hedgerows.

American paratroopers during the Normandy invasion impressed the Germans with their aggressiveness under adverse conditions, and their adaptability to defense. It is rather surprising, indeed, to read that German commanders in Normandy were complaining that their own high losses were due to the "inexperience" of German soldiers as compared to the Americans. One prisoner taken by the Americans during the fighting here had a different complaint. The Americans, he said, were "unethical" in their night fighting. "You Americans!" he exclaimed. "The way you fight! This is not war! This is madness!"[47]

Above all, the ordinary German soldiers feared American fire-power more than anything else—whether it came from land-based batteries, the U. S. Navy, or from the air. Later, after the war, they would say that it was foolishness to waste bombs and shells the way Americans had. During the war, however, there was a plenitude of reports from the front which complained of barrages as "never seen before," and of bomber support never before experienced in such quantity or quality. Not even the vaunted "superiority of German infantrymen" was allowed to prevail.

What the front line German soldier saw in the American was entirely different from that which was seen by Hitler or the German propaganda machine, or even the retrospective view of the post-war German. The Nazi dictator, having failed in his promise to stop the Americans on the Normandy beaches, wore a different mantle after the Patton breakthrough into France. The blame really rested on his generals, he contended, but anyway, the "more Americans" racing from extended supply lines "the better."

By the time of the Ardennes breakthrough his tone had somewhat moderated. He spoke of possibilities rather than assurities, as he said: "If we succeed, then we shall smash up half the enemy front, and then we'll see what happens. I do not believe . . . the enemy will be able to stand up to the forty-five German divisions we will have available by that time."[48]

As indicated previously, Hitler's views of the American fighting man were highly colored by what Ludendorff had told him. Though he had never fought against Americans in 1918, the dictator once told a Nazi official that World War I Americans were not nearly as good as the French or British, and that they had run "straight into the line of fire, like young rabbits." They were not "soldierly," he asserted, and they had much of the "wise guy" in them. Such sentiments were echoed by the German propagandist, Joseph Goebbels, when he wrote in his diary in 1943:

These American boys are human material that can in no way stand comparison with our people. One has the impression of dealing with a herd of savages. The Americans are coming to Europe with a spiritual emptiness that really makes you shake your head. They are uneducated and don't know anything. For instance, they ask whether Bavaria belongs to Germany and similar things. One can imagine what would happen to Europe if this dilettantism could spread unchallenged. But we, after all, will have something to say about that. . . .[49]

German radio and press propaganda followed the lines established by Hitler and Goebbels. Early in the war it claimed that German strength would keep Americans from even reaching Great Britain. Having been proved wrong on that, it proceeded to attack the fighting spirit of the American soldier. The GI, it said, was poorly led, inclined to braggadocio, disinclined to take risks unless there was a profit motive, and brutal. Furthermore, so said German propaganda, the Americans were in the war in order to take over the British Empire.

A strong theme throughout Berlin radio broadcasts and the state-controlled newspapers was that the United States was a nation without a true culture, and that it hadn't produced a single distinguished author, artist, general, or statesman in its entire history. Later, when the war began to go against Germany, there was a grudging admission that Americans, particularly those with German names, had "all qualities of the natural fighter . . . and considerable technical gifts." But, so went the conclusion, they were still no match for the true Nordic.[50]

On the higher levels of the German military one finds numerous contradictions to German propaganda of the period, and to the post-World War II German picture of the American. It may be true to say that in World War I the politicians feared the Americans while the German generals scoffed at them. In World War II the situation in Germany was entirely reversed. Hitler did the scoffing then, while his generals quickly recognized America's importance in the war.

The first real clash between German and American troops took place at Kasserine Pass in North Africa. Here, a sudden attack by Rommel caught the untried GI's off guard, and smashed them back with some losses. Alexander and other British generals were quick to claim that the battle proved American troops were physically and mentally soft. Rommel's point of view was different, and so were those of his subordinates. One of the latter would write that the Germans accomplished very little at Kasserine and Sbeitla because the "Americans offered strong resistance." Rommel, himself, wrote that American soldiers were "green," but that they fought with great stubbornness.

The important aspect of Rommel's conclusions was that he never lived to see them published; perhaps he never even wrote them with that prospect in mind. His praise, therefore, was not bought by the promise of postwar book sales in America. The "Desert Fox" felt the Americans had "excellent qualities." Their infantry did not flee before the Afrika Korps, the American artillery and mortar fire was extremely accurate, and the tanks were well handled.

Alexander had criticized the organization of American troops. Rommel thought it to be exceptional. He wrote: "The Americans were fantastically well equipped and we had a lot to learn from them organizationally. One particularly striking feature was the standardization of their vehicles and spare parts." For a German, Rommel was admitting a great deal.

Here is Rommel on the American fighting man after Kasserine Pass:

> Although it was true that the American troops could not yet be compared with the veteran troops of the Eighth Army, yet they made up for their lack of experience by their far better and more plentiful equipment and their tactically more flexible command. . . . The tactical conduct of the enemy's defence had been first class. They had recovered very quickly after the first shock and had soon succeeded in damming up our advance by grouping their reserves to defend the passes and other suitable points.

Here is Rommel on the Americans after Normandy:

> What was astonishing was the speed with which the Americans adapted themselves to modern warfare. In this they were assisted by their extraordinary sense for the practical and material and by their complete lack of regard for tradition and worthless theories. An intellect directed to practical ends, initiative and the urge for material wealth have combined to make America, economically, the strongest power in the world.[51]

Contemporary views by other German generals tended to substantiate and support Rommel. In almost every case there was praise for American fighter and bomber pilots. The aggressiveness of the former hurt the Germans badly on every part of the front. In 1944 General Adolf Galland, the chief of German fighter operations, reported: "The standard of the Americans is extraordinarily high." And as for the bomber crews, it was generally felt that the daytime bombing proved the willingness of Americans to suffer a higher casualty rate in the air than any other power.

Of the infantry, it was generally conceded during the war that the Americans were much less reckless than the Russians. Yet, after the Battle of the Bulge there was a widespread admiration among

German officers for the "aggressive defence" of the Americans at Bastogne, and for the American ability to take "set-backs and then recover."

The American handling of tanks likewise came in for praise. The American Fourth Armored Division, on the basis of its "outstanding tank attack . . . over ideal terrain" at Singling, was marked by Lieutenant General Fritz Bayerlein as one of the "best divisions in the American Army." The Seventh Armored, which fought at Saint-Vith, and the Tenth Armored, which fought at Bastogne, received similar accolades.[52]

World War II, like every war in history, has been the subject of retrospective reassessment. Autobiographies of various generals have placed the blame for losses on others, and have gathered the laurels of victories into the hands of the writers. British historians have argued that it was the early sacrifices of their nation that paved the way to victory. Russian historians have contended that it was the heroism of the Russian soldier at Stalingrad that turned the tide of the war. American historians have argued that without American help neither Britain nor Russia could have lasted. German generals, and some Japanese military leaders, have written official assessments of Allied victories and defeats; or they have produced books for commercial distribution.

On the official side of the ledger one can find little assessment of the war by the Japanese. What does exist are a few reminiscences, some of them well written, by former officers of the Japanese military. In general these writings are fair; their only fault lying in an unfortunate but characteristic overstatement. Strangely enough, the same overstatement is to be found in the few translated Japanese official documents available to this writer.

The loss of the war was a tremendous physical and psychological blow to the Empire of Japan. The huge merchant marine of the country was destroyed, entire cities had been leveled, the navy was gone, and an entire culture was torn from its base. The Japanese acceptance of defeat was no easier for the losers to take than it would have been if the situation had been reversed. A Japanese official taking part in the surrender aboard the U. S. S. *Missouri* wrote:

> I looked up and saw painted on the wall nearby several miniature Rising Suns, our flag, evidently corresponding to the planes and submarines shot down or sunk by the gun crews of the battleship. As I tried to count these marks a lump rose in my throat and tears quickly gathered in my eyes, flooding them. I could hardly bear the sight.[53]

The few Japanese reminiscences which do exist are from the medium level of command—flight leaders in particular. While not admitting American courage or bravery—this was expected of any fighting man by the Japanese—these recollections do indicate what the Japanese admired in the fighting American. But this is done rather incidentally and in an Oriental manner, in which one sees, by inference, a picture of the victor. A former Japanese flyer wrote: "Vital to every battle is the indefinable element we term aggressiveness, or spirit, or *esprit de corps;* whatever it is, the Americans had it." From another Japanese reminiscence came these words: "Opportunistic but lacking a spirit of daring and independence, we are wont to place reliance on others and to truckle to superiors. Our want of rationality often leads us to confuse desire and reality, and thus to do things without careful planning." From the foregoing, one may conclude that the American fighting man had all those qualities the Japanese lacked.[54]

German officers who were asked to write critical observations of Americans after the war were not at all reticent about expressing their views, or even about retouching the wartime portrait of the American fighting man. Fair in some cases, their critiques are to a greater extent prone to illogical and contradictory reasoning. Moreover, they are at odds with the facts of the war. For these reasons it is probably best to merely present segments of these opinions as they apply to aspects of the American military effort. The campaign described in the commentaries is listed at the end of each comment.

ON AMERICAN AIRMEN

The enemy had full mastery of the air, and behaved so arrogantly and boldly, especially at dusk, that the low-flying planes were often shot down by infantry weapons, or caught their wings in the tree tops and crashed. [*Normandy*]

A commitment of bomber squadrons and non-stop activity of fighter bombers on such a scale had never been seen before. [*Normandy*]

ON AMERICAN INFANTRY

It [weakness] is typical of the stamina of an American soldier and his lack of experience, when enemy planes are making an attack on his positions. The commitment of several close support airplanes in the sector of the 352 Inf. Div. . . . led to a panic in the camp of the enemy. [*Normandy campaign*]

Moreover, the American attacks were successful only when the sluggish (moving slowly without conviction or desire) American infantry was preceded by a solid wall of armor. In many cases when it had not sufficient tank support, the infantry was thrown back by us without much difficulty. The almost wasteful, in our opinion, use of armored forces was dictated by the American High Command in order to avoid placing an excessive burden on the infantry, which was the weakest factor in the battle, and to keep losses to a minimum. [*Normandy*]

The American soldier is a perfectly armed, uniformed and experienced soldier. Nevertheless, he is full of complaints and demands; he is seldom satisfied. My observation showed that he fights not for an ideal, but because of a desire for adventure. . . . He is the exact opposite of what I saw of the Russian soldiers on Lake Ladoga, near Velikie Luki, in the Carpathians, and in other places. [*Italy*]

He is intelligent, courageous on the defensive, and persistent on the offensive. These qualities he has acquired from boxing. He is afraid of engagements at dusk and at night. During the day he starts fighting rather late, about eight or nine in the morning, and discontinues the activity early in the evening. . . . As a guard the American soldier is a glaring example of carelessness: he often lets enemy patrols pass by in the hope that other stronger posts will stop and neutralize them. [*Italy*]

A strong artillery and mortar fire, lasting about one hour, prepared the advance. The infantry, however, advanced very slowly and cautiously, and at times came to a complete halt under our machine-gun fire. [*St. Omer Region—translated from Russian*]

It may perhaps not be completely correct to assert that it probably *was* the inability to go forward to the attack with courage and bravery, which was the cause of the enemy's operation plan not being executed. . . . If such a plan cannot be fulfilled, then the American soldier begins very soon to lose interest in the actual fighting, and his thoughts will be in his far distant homeland. [*Normandy*]

The ground reconnaissance of the enemy was limited; it was not sufficiently active, although it could have been conducted with larger forces had there been stronger artillery support, especially at nightfall or in the early morning hours. Americans lacked combat experience; there was an absence of perseverance among the subordinate officers, and a desire to show their material superiority. [*Italy*]

However, in spite of this wealth of material, the American soldier fought unwillingly. There were several cases in 1942, when separate groups of Americans prematurely laid down their arms, showing no desire to break through and emerge from an encirclement. . . . The American soldier fights more bravely and fiercely in a unit than individually. After capturing ground, the Americans immediately organized a defense. The counterattacks launched by us a few hours later often ended in failure. [*N. Africa*. Author's note: Despite Hitler's order to fight to the death, an entire German army was captured in N. Africa]

Troop security is bad, especially after dark. . . . The reconnaissance was not sufficiently organized; there were too many defects in its execution. Night time was not utilized for engagements. All ground enagagements were discontinued at nightfall, and the Americans "went home." . . . The terrain was used rather well. The infantry quickly passed from the attack to the defense. No initiative whatever could be observed. The command, "Forward, charge the enemy" was unknown to the Americans. . . . There were no surprise movements. [*Scheldt Estuary fighting.* These notes were summarized for the Russian Army.]

ON AMERICAN TANKS

Tanks were committed in large number; however, they all took cover as they were met by a powerfire of antitank guns. [*Scheldt Estuary*]

The Americans placed a particular stress on the use of tanks and aviation, which are well coordinated in combat. [*N. Africa*]

ON AMERICAN ARTILLERY

The artillery fire of the heavy guns was well-adjusted. We believed that the Americans had at their disposal a good and fast radio reconnaissance, as our observation points were very often subject to a strong and continuous fire the moment they were established. [*General observation*]

One could often see, for instance, that the Americans expended a great deal of ammunition on all sectors, paying no attention to the fact that they were not occupied by us. [*Italy*]

ON AMERICAN PARATROOPERS

In spite of being isolated, they continued to fight stubbornly under the protection of fences and bushes against every target that appeared, whether it was one soldier, a group of soldiers, wagons, or anything else. They inflicted considerable losses on us, until we finally succeeded in liquidating them in separate encounters. [*Normandy*]

ON AMERICAN PRISONERS

They were strong, brave, and impetuous men with rather unsoldierly behavior and a dissatisfied expression. The impression they made on us was that they were fighting not because of their convictions but for the money they got out of it, carrying out orders in a sober and businesslike manner. According to the statements by the American infantry prisoners, the paratroopers and airborne troops which had landed, were recruited for the most part from gangsters. [*On paratroops captured in Normandy*]

Some of the American war prisoners made a curious impression. They were incommunicative and complained of the personal risk to which each participant in the European War was subjected. They refused to make statements concerning the causes of the war, its connection with the world economy, the aims of the war, etc. One could deduct from the conversations with the American PWs that the Americans depended too much upon their abundant material resources, which were supposed to overwhelm the enemy. "We infantrymen will not attack while the enemy machine guns rattle." The Americans did not hurry, since they were sure that time was on their side. [*German officer's summary for the Russians*]

ON THE REASONS FOR LOSING THE WAR

I personally saw thousands of men returning from their furloughs waiting for transportation first to Bologna, and then to Florence, while they were badly needed at the front. [*The use of Allied airpower*]

It can, therefore, not be wide off the mark, to assert that the enemy would have found himself in a predicament against an adversary equally strong in material, a predicament, which, in spite of his physical training and—it may well be—in spite of his spiritually better preparation in the field of propaganda, would not have brought him the successes which began to take shape on the 13 June, 1944.

Any soldier knows that he must be defeated by sheer weight of material, if he has none himself with which to put up a fight against a superior enemy.[55]

The contradictions within the above statements, and against the facts of history, are wide and varied. American infantrymen are accused of panicking at the sight of German planes in Normandy. This was supposedly "typical" of the American soldier. Yet it was during the same campaign that another German officer wrote of his own troops: "Low-flying planes appeared unexpectedly above the treetops and forced us to run for cover." In another instance, American infantrymen are accused of a lack of "conviction or desire." Within the same statement the German officer writes of his attempts to gather a German infantry force: "These I collected at the assembly points, together with those who tried to *evade* the fighting [*author's italics*]."

In one instance a German officer states that the American infantryman would not have "possessed the offensive spirit and combat enthusiasm" were it not for his material superiority. This is a constant complaint; the argument that always the German soldier was outweighed by the obvious material superiority of the Americans. Such contentions are partly true but one must recall that the German victories against Poland, Norway, Denmark, Belgium, and France resulted from the same disparity of material equipment. The military critic who attempts to remain objective must remember that logistics, material equipment, and numerical superiority are all part of what a nation can expect to face in war.

In regard to German criticisms of the lack of American initiative in Normandy and elsewhere, one senses a certain disappointment that American troops did not attack solid German positions frontally, and without artillery and tank support. One German officer, after criticizing the American attempt to consolidate positions in Normandy, finally concludes his statement with the admission that it was the American *"adherence to his original plan,"* plus the brilliance of the Patton breakthrough that brought victory to the Allies. Another German general officer, perhaps less resentful of defeat, described the American use of tanks, artillery, and infantry as "fast and ruthless," but absolutely necessary in modern warfare.[56]

This is not to claim that many of the German criticisms were invalid. There were poorer American infantry divisions, just as there were admittedly poorer German infantry divisions, and they may well have been slow to advance. Americans were very likely to be careless because of their material superiority in Europe—just as the

Japanese became careless in the Pacific. Americans may have thrown down their arms on occasion without a fight—just as did the Germans in North Africa, Sicily, and in Europe—but there were occasions when, at Bastogne and elsewhere, they fought to a bitter conclusion. Americans may have appeared to be chronic complainers to the Germans, but that is in the nature of American individualism—and furthermore, the records show far fewer American deserters than German. Americans may well have been unmethodical at times, but it was a German force that left the Remagen bridge undestroyed—and it was the Americans who took quick advantage of the omission.

It is not an easy thing to compare fighting men in modern times. It is the opinion of one former British officer that the Japanese soldier was the toughest and guttiest World War II soldier. General Franz Halder, the one-time German chief of staff, rated the British soldier, the American, the French, and the Russians, in that order, according to their fighting abilities. But Halder was talking to a British writer when he made that postwar judgment.[57] Rommel, as indicated previously, felt that the Americans had brought an entirely new dimension to warfare. Japanese general officers have made few postwar observations on the fighting qualities of Americans, simply because few who fought directly against the Americans survived the war.

All in all, the great lesson to be gained from World War II was that war did not mean one man fighting from behind a tree against another. It meant air power striking at faraway objectives, or at clumps of hidden defenders; it meant banks of artillery throwing out stupendous barrages; it meant minutely planned air and sea landings on islands or beaches; it meant that war involved total effort. Göring had failed to see this when he remarked early in the war: "The Americans only know how to make razor blades." Rommel showed perceptiveness when he answered: "We could do with some of those razor blades, Herr Reichsmarschall."[58]

The difference between Rommel and Göring is that the latter was as lacking in knowledge as his *Fuehrer* about the Americans, while Rommel had read a little of American history. Surely, the "Desert Fox," somewhere in his study on the American Civil War, had come across Nathan B. Forrest's comment to the effect that victory in war was a matter of getting there the "fustest with the mostest." Unsoldierly as Forrest's analysis might have sounded to most German ears, that was what World War II was all about.

Within a year after the defeat of the Axis powers, the powerful American Army was demobilized, and much of the Navy was "mothballed." The arms budget for the Truman Administration continued to spiral downward by the year, despite the contradictory and blanketlike pledges to be found in American foreign policy. Perhaps it was assumed that the "bomb," the destructive power of atomic energy, was enough of a real deterrent to enemy aggression. This grand illusion was destroyed by the sudden Communist attack upon South Korea in 1950.

The drive of North Korean troops toward Seoul and to the southwest in 1950 was amazingly successful. Inexperienced and underequipped South Korean troops were unable to stem the tide, and green American troops, fed into the struggle as soon as they arrived, also fell back to the Pusan perimeter.

At this stage of the fighting, the attitude of the enemy was similar to that of the Japanese almost nine years earlier. They were winning. The South Koreans and the Americans were losing. Losers were to be regarded only with contempt. Both Republic of Korea soldiers and Americans were sometimes killed upon their capture, or were taken to the rear under conditions much worse than the famous Bataan "death march" of World War II.

The unfortunate characteristic of the early Korean fighting was that most of the American troops who were thrown piecemeal into the war were simply unready for the conditions or horrors the war brought upon them. They were mostly young boys who had become used to comparatively easy duty in Japan, and though they fought bravely in most cases, they did not inspire fear in the hearts of the enemy. As a captured North Korean officer so aptly phrased it to an American reporter: "Your countrymen will be defeated by a longing for a hot shower."[59]

As tougher American troops were brought into the perimeter, the

North Korean notion of the American fighting man underwent some change. Hitherto successful Communist tank attacks were thrown back by sheer heroism. The U. S. Marines, also brought into the fighting at Pusan, helped to reverse the course of the war by going on the offensive.

It was clear to both Communist and "neutral" observers by 1951 that the elite fighting force of the United Nations side was the U. S. Marine Corps. Great attempts were made to cut Marine battalions to pieces; the idea being that once the "leathernecks" were beaten, the remainder of the American Army would fold. These usually failed, however, mainly because of the bravery and tactical superiority of the Marines. Midway through the Korean War, a captured enemy major expressed his feelings about the Marines: "Panic sweeps my men when they see the Marines with yellow leggings coming at them."

When the Chinese Communists entered the war at the very end of 1950, the Marines continued to be the center of attention for the enemy. It was generally felt in China that "America was but a 'paper tiger . . .' " which would quickly fall, once various elite corps were beaten. Even the Marines, they contended, were "monsters" and "fascist stalwarts" who would "quickly lose their combat fervour" when they were faced with a worthy foe.

Thus, as the Chinese flooded across the Yalu River, the First Marine Division and various army units were singled out for special attention. Cut off near the Chochin Reservoir far to the north, outnumbered by the Chinese by six to one, and under the worst climatic conditions, the Marines fell back to the nearby port of Hungnam. At this point of the fighting, the Peking radio announced: "The annihilation of the United States First Marine Division is only a matter of time."[60]

Not only did the Marines get out, but they did so brilliantly and with relatively few casualties. Furthermore, they had tied down sufficient Chinese and North Korean forces to allow for a consolidation of American and United Nations troops in the South. By the end of January, 1951, the Chinese offensive had not only lost its strength, but the Communists were forced to go on the defensive. Indeed, there are many military experts who argue that, had armistice talks not intervened, the Americans and their allies were on the verge of completely routing the Communist forces.

Whatever arguments might arise over the latter decision, it might well be contended that the nature of present fighting in Vietnam has been modified because of the experience of Korea. North Vietnamese troops are sent into South Vietnam, not as the Chinese in Korea in 1950, but they are filtered through the jungles and along the heavily bombed supply routes from the North. Once at their destination, they join with local Viet Cong to fight Americans under conditions as grueling and cruel as those in any war.

From what little one can discover about North Vietnam—the battlefield opponent of the American fighting man in the mid-1960's —the attitudes of the North Vietnamese soldier are varied. He has a great regard for American firepower, and for special troops such as those of the Marines and air cavalry. He fears ordinary American infantry a little less, feeling that they are cautious and slow. He respects the use of helicopters and air power. How does he compare the Americans to the French? There is little to compare, he claims, for the Americans are much better.[61]

On the official level North Vietnamese propaganda follows the standard line relative to the American soldier. It asserts that the motto of the Americans is to "Kill all, destroy all, burn all." It contends that the Americans have used poison gas, and that their treatment of civilian populations is bad. "American soldiers committed unprecedented atrocities," says one North Vietnamese writer, "they herded the people at gun-point and massacred them, they killed children before the eyes of their parents, they raped and then killed women, they destroyed and burned down villages, schools, pagodas and temples."

Just as Russian authorities in Germany tended to adopt Nazi propaganda approaches concerning Americans in 1945, the North Vietnamese sound at times much like the Japanese in 1942. A Communist leaflet distributed in South Vietnamese villages in 1963 described Americans like this: "They say that they are allies but indeed they are masters, they think that they are civilizers, proud of the white race and look at our people with despising eyes." And

General Vo Nguyen Giap, the commander of North Vietnamese armed forces, makes noises much like Radio Tokyo back in 1943 when he says: "Due to the unjust character of its war, the U. S. expeditionary corps is fighting without an ideal and hence has low morale." Giap, far away from the battlefield in Hanoi, credits the American fighting man with the following faults—he throws "away weapons and ammunition when withdrawing," and he is "afraid of dense forest, sun, wind, malaria. . . ."[62]

The similarity between the propaganda of World War II and present Communist propaganda regarding Americans is sometimes startling. The Nazis felt the paratroopers who were dropped in Normandy were former "gangsters." To the present-day Soviet citizen, the American fighting man is pictured as having similar characteristics. The famous Green Berets are a collection of "picked cutthroats." The American infantry soldier is portrayed as a "present-day barbarian wearing American military uniforms and sowing death and destruction. . . ." The Marine Corps is described as a special force which is designed to quash "popular movements." The "Leathernecks," so says Russian propaganda, are "reliable people," mostly "men of Anglo-Saxon origin," who search for an easy way to make a living.[63]

How do the Russians regard the training of the American soldier, that is, in propaganda terms? The answer is, a composite of ways, one sometimes wholly contradictable to the other. According to the Russians the American television character Batman is a means by which American character is fashioned to the notion that killing can be done "elegantly." Another Russian writer sees the *Playboy* philosophy as being important. It makes of American men "obedient tools" who are permitted to do anything—"to kill, to rape, etc." *Pravda* argues that American soldiers are taught to be aggressive; they are "brainwashed" in the barracks to act "completely without scruples."[64]

American military technology, while admired by the Russians, comes in for severe criticism. Guam-based B-52's, used in the bombing of the Viet Cong, are given much space in Russian newspapers. These planes, say the Russians, are piloted by Texans and Oklahomans, men who have been unsuccessful in their own country, and who represent "all the worst that American imperialism has engendered." The bomber crews are further described as follows:

> They have been taught how to drop nuclear bombs. Now their job is to drop mere "hunks of iron" and how can one fail to appreciate the modesty of these fellows? "I like the regular bombing raids," said one of them, "more than the training nuclear raid." For this "intellectual" it is better to kill with a mere bomb than to fling training nuclear bombs to no use.[65]

One arm of the American defense forces which comes in for a surprising amount of Soviet attention is the United States Navy. Much was written about the accidental sinking of the American nuclear submarine, the U. S. S. *Thresher*. The naval expert of *Izvestia* explained that tragedy, as well as all other accidents in the American fleet, as follows: "Shortcomings in design and equipment led to the loss of the American atomic sub Thresher in April, 1963. They are also common to other American atomic subs, which are being built in an atmosphere of military hysteria."

Unfortunately, concludes the same writer, all of these could be avoided if the U. S. Navy were not so aggressively inclined. The desire of the American admirals to use their carrier fleet, and the innate aggressiveness of the Marine Corps, were the real factors in bringing the United States into the Vietnamese War, concludes the writer.[66]

From the British in the American Revolution to the present-day Chinese and Russian Communists, there are threads of history regarding the American fighting man; common denominators which fit equally each period of the past. First of all, Americans are, and have been, regarded by their enemies as undisciplined, untrained, unprincipled, and unready for the horrors of war. Second, it has been generally assumed by America's opponents that Americans, for some strange reason, are incapable of sustained and hard warfare over a long period of time. Third, the enemies of the United States have always taken the approach that with one good defeat—an object lesson, so to speak—the American fighting man will simply fold his tent and go home.

None of these assumptions has been correct. The discipline of the American, always appearing to be outrageous to friend and enemy alike, is much more subtle and firm than is supposed. The casualness of the American to the needs of war and the officer-enlisted man relationship are never quite understood by those on the other side of the line. Perhaps the answer to this lies in the fact that Americans are loyal by instinct rather than by discipline, and really need less of the outward manifestations or organization than do other peoples.

Whatever the reasons for the failure of America's enemies to understand American men, the situation has invariably led to the ultimate advantage of the United States. Hitler, who had no firsthand experience with American fighting men, could speak glibly of their rabbitlike characteristics. In this frame of mind he could plan the Ardennes offensive of World War II, which was at first successful, but then ended in a disastrous German defeat. He could not have known that American troops, most of them inexperienced, would fight as they did. One is reminded here of a Belgian Fascist's description of some dead American boys in that battle.

> I came upon a trench on the western summit of Saint-Vith. In it were dead young Americans, lined up just as they had been when they were alive and with their cheeks still pink from good food and exposure to fresh air. . . . The trench was full, because every one had stuck to his post, in spite of the wave of fifty or a hundred tanks that had swept up on them, leaving tracks which I could still see in the snow.[67]

How like this description is Ernie Pyle's picture of dead American boys at Kasserine Pass, or the comments by British generals on American troops in World War I. These comments—all of them—indicate mild surprise that good, strong, healthy American boys, far from home, could fight to the death under such terrible handicaps.

The various misunderstandings of the American boy, as advantageous as they sometimes are to the national cause, are nevertheless galling, simply because they fly into the face of history. Time and again the enemy assumes that Americans will not fight because they are a "mongrelized" people, without ideals, and without the necessary sense of patriotism. Even the Russian argument that the present Marine Corps is an "Anglo-Saxon" force is wonderfully funny, and yet irritating, because it simply ignores the fact that Italian-Americans have long gone into the Corps because of its basic appeal, that some of the Marine heroes of Guadalcanal were Jewish, and that Polish and even Russian-Americans are legendary figures among the "leathernecks."

Another enemy contention, which Americans may find interesting, is that which concerns the use of infantry. In World War I American infantrymen were considered, by German defenders, far too reckless and too daring. In World War II, they were accused by German officers of being too cautious. Such criticisms lead one to believe that enemy opinions, particularly pronounced after defeat, might well be discounted.

The fact of the matter is that enemy estimates of the fighting qualities of Americans have been, and are, far more unsophisticated than one can ever imagine. American infantrymen in World War I had the dash and *élan* that every foreign army wished to have: American infantrymen in World War II had a knowledge and understanding of technology which allowed them to understand that a bomb was better for clearing a hedgerow than a rifle.

As far as drive and initiative are concerned, there is no war in United States history wherein the Americans have not shown these qualities. Washington's raid on Trenton, the forays of the *Constitution* in the War of 1812, Jackson and Sherman in the Civil War, the doughboys at Saint-Mihiel, and the GI at Saint-Lô are examples of these characteristics. The other side of the coin—the willingness of Americans to dig in and hold—has been shown at Bunker Hill, Petersburg in Virginia, the Battles of the Marne in 1918, and Bataan and Bastogne in World War II.

If ignorance on the part of the enemy, or potential enemies, of the great American military tradition is the price of victory, then let it be so. The rewards of victory are far more acceptable than the bliss of military tradition—that is, to Americans at least.

4

A Nameless Face in History

To paraphrase an old french aphorism, a nation changes and yet remains the same. The character, the culture, and the spirit of a people are blunted and shaped by time, almost as is a mountain by the centuries. Yet the basic material remains solid. Only the surface is changed.

So it is with the American fighting man. He is different from the old soldier of 1850, and yet he is the same. As indicated previously, what his friends and enemies have liked or disliked in the fighting American may only be modifications from age to age. How the American fighting man sees himself, how he looks at his service to the nation, and the very impact of that service on his own inner self, may be but slightly different from what they were fifty or one hundred years ago. A military tradition, once set, becomes increasingly difficult to reshape.

What the fighting American has been and is, physically, also seems firmly fixed as a fact of history. Only through the eyes of the contemporary beholder does the image undergo change. A British officer, recruiting for the Royal Americans in the South in 1756, thought the hundred or so new recruits he had taken in Virginia were totally unfit. That same officer would probably have agreed with the local authorities of the Virginia colony that the would-be soldiers were the "most dastardly and inactive mortals" ever to wear the uniform. Parenthetically, it might be added that a little more than a century later, the grandsons of these same men became the finest infantry on the face of the earth.[1]

The most notable Lord Loudoun, the commander of the Royal Americans, was not a unique figure in history. Washington complained constantly about the quality of the recruits sent to him from New England. American officers during the War of 1812 were positive that the men of that conflict were not up to the standards of the Revolution. Many an officer of the Civil War who had established a previous war record in Mexico grumbled that his men were not up to the quality of 1846. An old Army officer of 1898 complained that the 220,000 volunteers of that year were most disappointing. And an American general in 1917 wrote about the doughboy: "It was plain to us who have known the American Regulars for years that they [the volunteers] were not up to the standard, say of '98. . . ."

Even the fighting Americans of the last twenty-five years have not escaped censure. An American commander in Australia, before the attack on Tarawa, was quoted as saying: "I'm afraid the Americans of this generation are not the same kind of Americans who fought the last war." General Patton, comparing the GI of 1942 to the doughboy, stated: "We've pampered and confused our youth. . . . Now we've got to try to make them attack and kill. God help the United States!"

Even the American soldiers of Korea and Vietnam have failed to fit the retrospective image of every old campaigner. The contemporary American fighting man has been accused as lacking in motivation, hardiness, and will. But as stated previously, these are but the views of the contemporary beholder. One is inclined to answer with the statement "Go tell it to the Marines"; particularly those who have fought in the two most recent American military campaigns.[2]

The bedrock of fact is not difficult to find. The Revolutionary American fighting man appeared to the enemy as a tall and rangy man, capable of enduring great hardship. The hard core of Washington's Army was tough and rugged, and it became more dedicated as the war continued. And once the conflict ended, these old Continentals seemed to live forever, almost in vindication of their resilience. Here one is reminded of a Joseph Warner, who had served with distinction in a Virginia company. Far past middle age, but tired of living in Virginia, he moved to Ohio in 1802. A few years later, at the age of one hundred, he moved to Illinois. Two years later he still attended church every Sunday, even though in the winter he could only reach the building by crawling across a frozen creek on two icy poles. How could Washington have lost with such men in the service?[3]

The American frontier Army after 1830 was composed of some of the finest physical material available anywhere. The reason for this lay in the fact that, since Congress was quite penurious in its financial support of the Army, the military authorities were forced to be very selective in the choice of men. The Dragoons, especially, were an elite physical group. Virtually all of these men were well over five feet, eight inches in height. Many of them were over six feet tall, and weighed over two hundred pounds.

The armies of the Civil War were the first in American history to consist of very large numbers of men. The Federal Army was also the first to keep substantial data on the physical qualities of the recruits. This development was not so much because of improvements in military medicine, but it stemmed from a growing realization on the part of authorities that statistics were of real importance. Despite this fact, the physical examinations of 1861 were virtually worthless, because most of the regimental physicians knew little more about the inside of the human anatomy than an ordinary village druggist. One Illinois soldier later described his own physical examination as little more than "two or three 'love taps' on the chest." He did not even have to remove his clothes. Thus, the fact that women very often sneaked into the ranks is not surprising. One girl, listed as Private Albert D. J. Cashier of the Ninety-Fifth Illinois, not only served through the war, but fought at Brice's Crossroads, Spring Hill, and Franklin.[4]

Because of the improved keeping of records, especially on the Union side, more is known about the Civil War fighting man than any other Americans previously in the service of the nation. As far as the various branches of service were concerned, there were basic differences in the men. Sailors were generally younger than soldiers, and they were probably physically smaller. The Confederates, from what can be gleaned out of their scanty records, were younger than their Northern opponents. Western soldiers of the Federal Army were taller and more muscular than Yanks who came from the East, or the soldiers of the Confederacy.

Looking at the Federal Army alone, one finds that about 98 percent of these soldiers were in the eighteen to forty-five age category; the average age for July, 1862 being 25.10. As the war progressed, the average age moved upward somewhat, being 26.32 in May, 1865. Such figures, though presented here, must be considered carefully, however. Many young men added years to their age in order to enlist; older men sliced off a few in order to qualify. Nevertheless, as Bell I. Wiley points out, the Federal Army was a "youthful" force, which had a "priceless core of ruggedness, optimism and resilience. . . ."[5]

The Indian Wars of the 1870's and 1880's brought the American Army to a fine edge of physical excellence. The rebuilding of the U. S. Navy and the Marine Corps also allowed for the establishment in those forces of standards unequaled in the rest of the world. By 1898, therefore, it was generally conceded that, from a physical standpoint, the American fighting man had a broad edge on the ordinary Russian, British, or German soldier. Though the volunteers of 1898 failed to equal the height and physical strength of the Regulars in all branches of the American service, it has been assumed by some military historians that the American fighting man of that year was not to be equaled in physical appearance for several decades to follow.

The very nature of World War I brought some interesting contradictions in the physical characteristics of the American fighting man. The Regulars and early volunteers for the services in 1917 tended to follow the 1898 pattern; they were rangy and muscular.

Those who volunteered from the West, particularly in the Dakotas, were taller than Eastern volunteers, perhaps because of immigration of Mediterranean types into New England and New York. Many of the early volunteers were college graduates. At one time in Camp Devens, Massachusetts, there were as many as 695 college men in uniform.[6]

All in all, the earliest American arrivals in France in 1917 thoroughly impressed Allied staff officers. They were obviously taller than the French soldier, more solid than the British, and seemingly more alert than Italian fighting men.

With the application of draft quotas, and the continuing growth of statistical information, a picture of the normal American fighting man in World War I emerged. The average height of registrants for the draft in the two years of the war was five feet, seven and one-half inches. The average height of those who actually served in the armed forces was five feet, seven and seven-tenths inches. The average fighting American for 1917–1918 weighed approximately 140 pounds. Once again it can be assumed that the Marines were taller and heavier than Army enlisted men, while American naval personnel, though equal in height, probably weighed less than the ordinary doughboy.

It is sometimes argued that the American of World War I was shorter by a fraction than the ordinary Civil War soldier. In considering this judgment, however, one must remember that virtually all Federal and Confederate soldiers were volunteers, while the majority of World War I American fighters were draftees. Among the 2,510,-000 men examined in the first year of United States participation in the First World War, only 29.1 percent were rejected on physical grounds, which carries an implication that standards were not very high. The leading states in the percentage of draft rejections were California, Connecticut, and Louisiana, proving little, if anything, about the quality of material from certain sections of the country.

The standards for service rejection were virtually eliminated as the war progressed into 1918. Dr. Harvey Cushing, the eminent Army surgeon, noted in his journal that 250 from one division alone were sent to his hospital for reexamination. These men, mostly from

New York City, suffered from a number of defects, including hammer toes, hemorrhoids, hernia, varicocele, tuberculosis, and heart disease. One of the soldiers of this division, the Seventy-Seventh, weighed only ninety pounds; less than the pack he was expected to carry. Another, a Swede, had such a bad case of mitral stenosis that he was unable to run without collapsing.[7]

The keeping of statistics in World War II approached the ideal. The draft was in operation long before Pearl Harbor day, and this allowed medical authorities to perfect statistical procedures by the time of the great war effort of 1943. Once again the figures are varied and interesting, but require close interpretation. According to information researched by one authority, the average height of registrants for the first two years of the draft was exactly equal to that of the recruits for World War I, which offers some sort of a surprise.

The standards for induction were considerably higher in the early years of World War II, however. From November, 1940, to November, 1941, 50 percent of those called by draft boards were rejected for various reasons. By 1942, after four million men had been called into the Army, it was written that the average American soldier was approximately five feet, eight inches; he weighed 144 pounds; his chest was 33¼ inches; and his waistline was 31 inches. Furthermore, the average GI of 1942 had brown hair, a light complexion, and was twenty-one years of age.

Statistics were even used to cite differences between draft recruits from various regions of the country, as well as between various branches of the armed forces. Soldiers from the South, for instance, had larger feet, while privates from New England were thicker about the middle. Infantry combat soldiers were shorter and lighter than the average for all services. Further indication that the infantry did not get the better types is shown in the fact that, in terms of education and intelligence, the infantryman ranked lower on the scale than all other branches of the service. Also, because of the number of volunteers present in the air forces, the Navy, and the Marines, these more selective types tended to be stronger both mentally and physically than the ordinary footslogger.[8]

A study of American enlisted men in March, 1943, showed these characteristics. Of the enlistees, 42 percent were in the twenty to twenty-four age bracket, 54 percent had a high school or college education, 90 percent were white, 8 percent were Negro, 61 percent came from the North, 29 percent came from the South, and 10 percent of the men came from the West.

The inclusion of the men from special units in the statistics makes an obvious difference. Frederick Lewis Allen, who gives no source for his information, states that the men who were available for the service in 1941 and 1942 averaged sixty-eight and one-tenth inches, and weighed 152 pounds. The key word in the previous sentence is *available,* which indicates that Allen may have included Marines, sailors, air force candidates, and special service forces. A later study, one done in the 1950's, gives the average height of the World War II American inductee as about sixty-eight and four-tenths inches, and his weight as about 150 pounds. These figures naturally include those who were inducted into the Marines and the Navy in the last few years of the war.[9]

Despite the complaints of such generals as Stilwell and Patton, the World War II American fighting man had been well toughened by the years of depression which preceded the Pearl Harbor attack. Whether it called for a fourteen-mile march over the Owen Stanley range in New Guinea, or the arduous Stilwell strike into Burma, the GI usually was up to the task required. The ordinary infantryman may have adjusted to his conditions in differing ways—cursing in the "torrential obscenities of Eastern city men," or in the "simpler and more profound" manner of the Westerner—but the end result was that he met his difficulties with an admirable stoicism.[10]

Though it is usually accepted that Marines were normally physically superior to Army infantry, and that air forces pilots were among the mental elite of American fighting men, it is not generally known that the Navy had its own internal gradations of quality. Battleships and aircraft carriers were alloted men of superior training and background, and American sub crews were composed of picked volunteers. On the other end of the scale were the men who made up the crews of the various landing craft. Some of these individuals were sailors who were unwanted by the so-called "fighting ships" of the fleet. Others were men who had served time in naval brigs about the country, semi-illiterate mountain boys, or refugees from the city streets. In one specific case, a member of an LST crew, a patricide, had been sent into the service by a gentle judge. Within three weeks at sea he suffered a nervous breakdown on the bridge of his ship.

To command such men, the Navy produced officers through special training programs at such universities as Notre Dame, Columbia, and Northwestern. The midshipmen who sped through these 120-day courses were college graduates in most cases, and in most cases, were totally unacquainted with the sea. The wonder of it all was that they did so well under combat conditions; taking their ships into beaches under heavy fire, or living under such terrible conditions when not in combat that it stretched their utmost fortitude.

The latest figures on the American fighting man indicate a continued growth in average size. The primary reason for this is that, for some years, the Selective Service has been quite selective, indeed. The inductee for 1958 was approximately a half inch taller and seven pounds heavier than the World War II draftee. White recruits for 1958 averaged sixty-eight and nine-tenths inches tall, and weighed 158.4 pounds. Negro recruits for the same period averaged sixty-eight and eight-tenths inches tall, and weighed 155 pounds.

As for sectional differences it may be said that the highest percentages of draft rejections for physical reasons in 1964 were found in Hawaii, Massachusetts, Montana, Oregon, Utah, Vermont, and Washington. The states having the highest percentages of disqualifications for mental reasons were Alabama, Arkansas, Georgia, Louisiana, Mississippi, South Carolina, and Tennessee.[11]

At the close of World War II, General George C. Marshall concluded that the best American soldiers were those in the eighteen to twenty-year-old age bracket. These, according to General Marshall, were the most daring, the most hardy, and the most aggressive. Not every important American military authority has agreed with General Marshall on the age factor; in fact, there were some who claimed that the American Army in Korea in 1950 was too young. Nevertheless, virtually every American military officer has tended to follow Marshall's allusion to aggressiveness as a most important element in battle. And most would argue that the American fighting man has always been endowed with more than his share of that characteristic.[12]

The facts of history bear out this contention. The Continental Army did well during the American Revolution, considering the circumstances, but its war was wisely fought along Fabian lines. The most aggressive phase of the American war effort during the Revolutionary period was carried out by the privateers. The descendants of these men probably do not qualify for membership in the Daughters of the American Revolution; indeed, in that day, privateers were not even considered as part of the Continental Navy.

Yet there was seldom any trouble in 1776, and in years thereafter, in outfitting and complementing the ships that were to privateer on the Atlantic. One nineteenth-century American historian concluded that the states were able to keep more men in privateering than in the Army or militia. Massachusetts alone outfitted six hundred ships for privateering purposes, and Salem, in that state, had fifty-nine such vessels at sea at one time.

The achievements of American privateers in the Revolution were rather spectacular. They took three thousand prizes during the war, and even attacked British naval vessels on occasion. The powder used in the Montgomery-Arnold expedition against Quebec was captured by privateers, and some of the mortars used in the siege of Boston were taken from captured British vessels. Supplies taken in the depredations by the privateers were used to outfit the French fleet in Boston later in the war.[13]

The derring-do of the privateer was similarly exhibited in the War of 1812. In terms of aggressiveness and success, these men far exceeded the achievements of the American land soldier. The small privateer *Saucy Jack* ranged up and down the American coast during the entire war, and on one occasion chased two heavier British vessels at the same time. The *Kemp,* sailing out of Baltimore, captured eight enemy prizes at one time, but had to let four go because it didn't have enough men to man the vessels. There were an estimated 250 American privateers in all, and these reputedly captured or destroyed close to 1,600 British vessels. So aggressive were they that British maritime insurance went as high as thirteen guineas per 100 pounds of cargo value for an Irish Sea crossing.[14]

Aggressiveness was part of the taproot of American military tradition by the time of the Mexican War. In a general way the characteristic was typified by a New York *Morning News* editorial of 1846, which said of the annexation of Texas: "Who's the next customer, California or Canada?"

The American Army that invaded Mexico was young and adventuresome. It was composed mainly of old American stock—tall and rangy—but appropriately seasoned with newly arrived Irish and German immigrants. And it was tough! There was almost constant quarreling between the regiments of various states when the Mexicans were not around to fight, and on some occasions live ammunition was even issued to the troops for these internecine encounters.

The aggressiveness of these same Americans became a major factor in each victory of the war. At Contreras, for instance, the Mexicans were entrenched with five thousand infantry, two thousand cavalry, and twenty-three artillery pieces. The American force consisted of only fifteen hundred men, and had no cavalry and artillery. By a vigorous charge, which took only seventeen minutes "by the watch," the Americans sent the defenders racing to the rear.

The same situation existed at Cerro Gordo. Here the Americans had eight thousand men; the Mexicans more than twelve thousand. The Mexican position was atop a precipitous hill and well fortified. Seeming to "despise death" in the eyes of one Mexican observer, the Americans climbed the hill, routed the defenders, and captured three thousand of their troops. Near Churubusco, some time later, six thousand Americans attacked a defending force of fifteen thousand and won another startling victory. Part of this attack was carried over a "wet ditch," probably a small drainage canal, with a brisk bayonet charge.[15]

The aggressiveness that was such a major factor in the Mexican War was an even stronger characteristic of the fighting American in the Civil War. Daring and enterprising raids were conducted into enemy territory by such Confederate leaders as Forrest, Morgan, and

Stuart. Union cavalry under Grierson and Wilson likewise made extended invasions of hostile country to cut Confederate communications and to destroy transportation facilities.

The real aggressiveness in the Civil War was on the battlefield, however. Battles were fought close-up with muzzle-loading rifles, and hand-to-hand fighting was often the result. The traditional picture of the war is far more romantic than it truly was; legend has obscured, or at least dimmed, the bitterness of conflict. Yet there is enough left of the truth to show that the American fighting men on both sides carried the national fighting spirit to the limits of fiction. "Now come on, you d----d blue bellied yankees," shouted young Confederate soldiers at Fort Donelson, "we are ready for you now." During a lull in the fighting at Corinth, a Federal picket ran to within eighty yards of the opposing trenches and sang *The Star Spangled Banner*. At Chickamauga, a Federal and a Confederate soldier struggled over a flag until one managed to sever the hand of the other with his sword.[16]

Though death was omnipresent in the Civil War, the aggressiveness of the common soldier was never quite stilled. A Federal officer wrote in January, 1862: "I am urging that as soon as we get a couple more Regts we float up the Cumberland some night and take 2 forts for breakfast." Months later, after Fort Donelson and Shiloh, the same officer told his wife of the boredom of the Corinth campaign. "I think Darling I shall enjoy a battle if we have one," he stated, "I do indeed." The fighting at Stone's River was so bitter that the dead were found frozen into aggressive postures; a common result of hard-fought battles. Years later, during the Second Battle of Ypres, British soldiers were found in similar positions. And in World War II, American soldiers died at Kasserine Pass and in the Ardennes with their rifles in firing position, or with grenades in their hands.

One could write endlessly about the Civil War; indeed, some have. But some stories of that conflict are so exemplary of the American fighting man that they must be told and retold. A private soldier, sitting with a friend during the Battle of Atlanta, saw his companion hit by a direct shot through the head. "He fell across my lap . . ."

the private wrote, "and his brains and blood ran into my haversack, spoiling my rations. So I took his." Another private, writing of his colonel's attempts to get rear-line duty for the regiment, complained: "The majority of them [the men] had much rather be in active service, endure marching and fight battles than to stay here."

The desire for victory on the part of the Civil War soldier existed to the very end of the conflict. "They 'can't whip' this army," a Federal soldier wrote about Sherman's invasion of Georgia, "it's 'too big to be whipped.'" Lee's soldiers pleaded with their commander to continue the fight at Appomattox. Some Confederates were so unwilling to accept defeat that they fled to Mexico, Brazil, and even to Egypt.[17]

Thus did the Confederate and Federal aggressiveness in the Civil War set the pattern for the War of 1898. The American naval battles at Manila Bay and Santiago, and the Army campaign in Cuba, were partially the products of what was now a basic tenet of American character: the notion that it was far better to win or be whipped in someone else's backyard than in one's own. The risky march to San Juan Hill was conceived with no consideration of defeat whatever. Southerners and Northerners alike, now clothed in the same uniforms, vigorously assaulted the incline as American tradition dictated. One private wrote: "You lose all feeling; you fear nothing; all you think about is getting a shot at the Spaniards. . . . It seemed strange to me . . . how a man could go into battle and not fear death. . . ." And when the charge was stopped momentarily by an enemy Gatling gun, there was a young officer who cried: "Come on—come on, you fellows! . . . Come on—we can't stop here!" How similar to this exhortation would be those uttered forty-six years later at Omaha Beach![18]

American aggressiveness in World War I brought differing reactions from those who viewed it first hand. The French were surprised. The British credited it to inexperience. The Germans were afraid of it. And the Americans felt that it was part of their tradition.

A closer look at the various results of the impetuousness of the doughboy reveals some interesting insights. During the first attack by the Americans in front-line areas, participating French and

British soldiers were left far behind. In time the American fighting man complained about the backwardness and the inefficiency of both Allies. The Allies, on the other hand, argued that doughboys pressed forward so fast that they bypassed German strong points which should have been cleaned up right then.

As far as the fear of the German soldier for the American in 1917 was concerned, there is some basis for this contention. A French officer, observing the Yanks, wrote: "He arrived a born soldier. . . . I think the Germans are afraid of him." Rumor spread behind the German lines that it didn't pay to fight well against the Americans; for they seldom allowed the Germans to surrender after putting up a stiff fight. One American regimental history, that of the "Rainbow Division," substantiates this possibility by claiming that its men "fought to kill," and that few prisoners were usually taken. Indeed, the facts on the "Rainbow Division" show that, for the amount of fighting the regiment did, very few prisoners were taken.[19]

Various reminiscences and letters of the men themselves prove that the doughboy was indeed aggressive. General Pershing, years later, recalled that American divisions in training in France could hardly be kept away from the front. Another officer would later write: "The men were prepared in the red blood that coursed young arteries, in their litheness and their pride and will to 'go to it.'" General James G. Harbord, commander of the Second Division (a composite Marine and Army Regular unit), remembered a number of incidents along the same line. A sergeant major, acting as a typist, left his desk behind the lines near Belleau Wood, just because he wanted to get into some of the fighting. Harbord also recalled some assaults by the Second along the Marne, near Château-Thierry, in which the Americans left the French far behind in their attack. Remembering his men as they returned from the front, he wrote: "No doubt in their minds as to their ability to whip the Germans. Their whole independent attitude, the very swagger of their march, the snatches of conversations we could hear as they swung past, proclaimed them a victorious division."[20]

The very interrelationship of such units as the Second Division inspired further aggressiveness in the doughboy. Dr. Harvey Cushing saw it as a jealous competitiveness between the Army soldier and the Marine private. In the fighting about Vaux in 1918, the Army complained that it had been cited in the fighting only twice, while the Marines had received three citations. To balance the score, the authorities were virtually forced to allow the Regulars a chance to equal the heroism of the Marines; which they did. As humorous as Cushing's journal notation might appear today, it does not equal a story told by Floyd Gibbons, the "Ernie Pyle" of World War I. During the fighting along the Marne, some men of the Twenty-Sixth Division had brought back a German machine gun. What were the Germans doing while the Yanks had taken the gun, an officer asked. "Why, sir," replied one of the soldiers, "they weren't doing anything. They were dead."[21]

What did the private soldier of 1917–1918 have to say about his own aggressive drive? Plenty, for the doughboy was a sentimental, prolific, and unabashed writer of long letters. A sampling of correspondence during the hard fighting of 1918 tells the story. A young officer writes home to tell the story of a German-American private who crawled up to the German parapet during a mission, listened for awhile, and then sauntered back through "no-man's land" to his own trenches. A private writes of the pride he has in his machine gun, and how he is going to provide "wooden overcoats [coffins] for the Hienies [*sic*]. . . ." A soldier of the 307th Field Artillery writes that soon "we are going to finish the Huns forever. . . ."[22]

One would suppose that such aggressiveness might be diminished by the heavy casualties of late 1918. Not so! A private wrote in September that it was almost impossible to hold the Yanks back. Another complained: "I don't think I would sleep very well if I didn't have a lot of noise [shelling] for that is what rocks one to sleep." A fellow infantryman partially agreed, writing: "For my part I'd rather be right up in front because back here [in the rear] nothing but the "big babies" [shells] can reach me. . . ." And a last complained about rear-line duty, writing: "Only when I'm up amongst the guns is it worthwhile, because then there is lots of excitement."[23]

The aggressiveness of the American fighting man in World War II has been given altogether too little credit for the winning of that conflict. Yet this personal and national characteristic was seen in every theater and phase of the fighting. The United States Navy, after Midway, carried the war to the Japanese doorstep. American submarines, manned by picked crews, ranged far at sea to destroy the Japanese merchant fleet, and in doing so they performed seemingly improbable feats. A "pigboat" sailor, in the middle of the war, bragged that he ate his Christmas dinner "laying under the water alongside of Corregidor." By June of 1945 American subs were in the Yellow Sea and the Sea of Japan. One, the U. S. S. *Barb,* even landed a party on Honshu, and it managed to blow up a bridge and a train. Shades of the privateers of earlier days![24]

The air forces of all three major services were spectacularly aggressive. In his first letter home after the Pearl Harbor attack, an air corps officer wrote to his parents: "We don't have to wait any more. . . . I've waited around fourteen years preparing myself for this war—and, believe me, I'm ready." Marine pilots on Guadalcanal, some time later, were impatiently aggressive. "Tojo is apparently catching his breath," complained an American pilot on the island. "Some of the lads fear more than anything that they will get a furlough before a Jap plane."

As the war with Japan moved on, and as American planes gained a numerical and technological superiority, American pilots scorned enemy opposition. The Japanese antiaircraft, so said one flier, "can't hit a kite on a string." On an American B-29 flying from Saipan to raid Tokyo, the crew actually broke down and cried when the plane was forced to return to base because of engine trouble. "God damn the engines! God damn the engines! God damn the engines!" was the bitter complaint of the pilots.[25]

With all the postwar rewriting of the history of the war, only a few British or German writers have changed their wartime estimates of American flying prowess. The facts would not allow them to do so. American fliers were exceedingly aggressive and daring in all phases of combat. An American pilot in North Africa, expressing the thrill of combat patrol, wrote: "Feeling all victorious, I dived and strafed everything that came in front of me. . . . Maybe I'm a bit cold-blooded, or maybe I'm still young enough to enjoy it. It just takes five to be classed as an ace in this day and age." A Yank pilot, arriving at his home base in England after a raid, reported to his superior: "I spotted an airdrome. Nobody else knows where it is. Let's gas up and give it a bounce. It won't be dark until 8 o'clock." And an American bomber pilot told Ernie Pyle that his greatest thrill was when he "accidentally hit a barracks full of German troops and killed hundreds of them." Truly, in their own way, these men were the Griersons, Forrests, and Morgans of a latter day.[26]

The aggressiveness of the Americans in the Pacific theater of war needed very little encouragement. The perfidy of the Japanese attack on Pearl Harbor, and a natural racial antagonism, which had developed before and after that attack, brought the Pacific fighting down to elementals. American pride had been hurt as well. "They caught us with our pants down," an American GI wrote from Hawaii, "but don't worry, it won't happen again." Another fighting man, an American officer, would later describe his attitude toward the Japanese as follows: "We conceived of the Japanese as a pestilence that infected the land." So deep was the aggressive antagonism of the Marine Corps to the Japanese that in the mid-1960's one former Marine refused to participate in a joint Japanese-American ceremony honoring the Iwo Jima dead.[27]

To really understand how Americans felt toward the Japanese during the war, one must resort to the words and actions of the fighting men themselves. An American sergeant exulted in the kind of training he received in Hawaii; writing to his parents: "You know the kind of stuff, how to kill a guy quietly and cleanly, how to prevent a person from choking you, kicking you, or knocking you down, how to break bones, poke out eyes, break ear drums, etc." An American on Guadalcanal was cruelly facetious when he wrote the home folks about the downing of a Japanese pilot. "The pilot was brown on all sides," he exclaimed, "and ready for the A-1 Sauce!" An Indiana corporal who fought on Okinawa described the art of killing as follows: "In another way it is like hunting at home.

When you shoot a rabbit, the guy out of the group that shoots it gets it. Well, here when you get a Nip he is yours. That is, anything in his pocket you want."[28]

Nowhere else in the war did fighting become so close and so intense as in the Pacific. From jungle hollows Japanese infantrymen shouted: "American soldier will die tonight. Prepare to die, Yank-eee!" From his foxhole an American Marine answered: "Tojo eats——!" These were the moments when the ordinary American fighting man occasionally lost his usual and comparative equanimity. A sergeant in New Georgia, having lost all his men on a patrol, went berserk and killed all the Japanese in one trench with a grenade and a knife. An American infantryman in one island invasion completely forgot himself and stood erect with his carbine to take a Japanese *banzai* charge. In Burma a group of Merrill's Marauders caught a truckload of Japanese in the open and shot or bayoneted all of them. In still another instance in Burma it was reputed that a Marauder had gotten to a helpless Japanese prisoner and slit his throat. And at Iwo Jima more than one Marine was found dead in the crouched position of attack. It was Stone's River all over again.[29]

The language of the American fighting man during a *banzai* attack was, to say the least, infinitely more colorful than that of the GI in Europe. In Burma the Marauders were forced to take a Japanese assault near the bank of a river. One American boy, whose machine gun's cooler jacket was damaged, fired his weapon until his hands were burned. So intense was the combat that words came in an acidlike fluidity. "Come and get some more of it," shouted the Americans, "you yellow sons-of-bitches. . . . Get those bastards! Get those bastards! Oh, Jesus, that did it!" How remindful are these phrases of the words of a Jewish-American fighting man who fought elsewhere in the Pacific! Running out of cartridges, he cried: "Jesus Christ! Get some more ammo up here!"[30]

The true story of the aggressiveness of the American fighting man in the Pacific can best be told with statistics, however. Consider, for instance, the record of the American First Cavalry Division, which fought through the Philippines. In the Leyte-Samar phase of the fighting, the division killed Japanese troops on every day of the campaign from 20 October, 1944, to 4 January, 1945. Japanese dead for the period totaled 5,937, while the First Cavalry lost only 241. In the Luzon campaign, the division killed 14,114 Japanese, while losing only 680 of its own.

One last statistic about the Pacific theater treats with the number of prisoners taken by each side. Allied forces, mainly the Americans, captured 37,000 Japanese in the war. Americans captured by the enemy, including the large numbers taken on Bataan and Corregidor, came to only 16,000. A comparison of these figures, plus the battle deaths inflicted by the First Cavalry, truly indicate that the GI carried the war to the Japanese.[31]

One interesting aspect of the fighting in Europe is that U. S. Army historical authorities valiantly attempted to make on-the-spot descriptions of various phases of the struggle against the Nazis. A general reading of this information shows, as indicated previously, that the battle language of the European theater GI was infinitely more stilted than that of his Pacific comrade. The historical records also reveal that the European GI was a slightly different type of soldier from his World War I predecessor. This variance was to the extent that the later fighting American was more methodically aggressive and less affected by *élan* than the doughboy. As one World War II historian put it: "Our soldiers tend to fight silently."

The language and the behavior of these men, as shown by historical record, bears out these contentions. During the Carentan Causeway battle of the Normandy campaign, a soldier was heard to say of the Germans: "Well, let's keep firing at the dirty devils." A modern television scriptwriter would reject such a phrase immediately. In the same struggle an American infantryman was heard to say to another: "Did you know today is Sunday?" The answer was "Jesus Christ, why didn't somebody tell me?" Such battle exchanges bear just a little resemblance to the searing language of U. S. Marines on Guadalcanal.[32]

Still, in many ways, the fighting in Italy, France, and Germany was harder than combat in the Pacific because it demanded much more in continual courage and devotion; much more in endurance and determination. There were few towns or cities to be taken in the Pacific; while the war in Europe consisted of capturing one town after another. One never really knew where the Germans might make a stand. In December, 1944, for instance, a few Germans decided to fight for the little town of Enchenberg in France. American soldiers of the Forty-Fourth Division were forced to slide along the walls of the town, and to hammer down each door while shouting "Kommen Sie aus." And when the Germans didn't come out, the GI's had to go in and get them.[33]

Like the Pacific theater, the war in Europe forced Americans to perform deeds of violence which their mental processes sometimes refused to record. In Normandy five Germans who were manning a machine-gun position were killed in an American bayonet charge. Yet none of the attackers could remember the circumstances of the assault in immediately recorded interviews. The reason was simple. Bayonets, to the mind of the GI, were the most horrible instrument in his arsenal, and he could not bring himself to admit using them.[34]

Because of the bitterness of the fighting in France and Italy, there were other moments when the American fighting man forgot the accepted ethics of war. In Sicily it was not uncommon for soldiers of the crack Hermann Göring Division to fake a surrender, and then to open fire on exposed Americans. After several instances of this the Americans began to take revenge. One story had an American infantryman pulling a little "Malmédy" by machine-gunning thirty-six German prisoners. What little salvation there was in this episode came when the men who committed the atrocity were severely punished by Army authorities. The Germans did not do likewise after Malmédy, however.

One of the troubles Americans faced in Europe was that the Germans were tough and determined fighters, who were infinitely more clever at warfare than the Japanese. During the Carentan Causeway fight in 1944 the struggle became so emotional that advancing American infantrymen killed outright four Germans who came out of the hedgerows to surrender. In the Enchenberg fighting, a member of the Forty-Fourth Division shot and killed a young German boy who had hidden himself under a blanket. Another

German was flushed out of a cellar in the same fight and killed by a GI because, as he put it, "prisoners are too much trouble when you're fighting." And in the last month of the war a story went around the U. S. Ninth Army that a German prisoner who had refused to talk had been taken out and shot.[35]

The fact of the matter in World War II was that the American fighting man, aggressive by nature, learned to apply his own methods to the varying conditions of Europe. Most German prisoners, as shall be shown later, were exceedingly well treated. Some were unfortunately shot in close combat because other Germans had failed to follow what Americans considered to be the established rules of war. Nor were all Americans the "silent" fighters of historical record. The 115th Infantry of the Twenty-Ninth Division once went through a hedgerow in Confederate fashion by firing from the hip and giving loud whoops. "Yelling keeps heart in our men . . ." was the explanation of the officer-in-charge. "Our prisoners said it scared the piss out of them."

Killing soon became an unavoidable condition of war to the European GI. An American, by 1945, could casually write his mother: "I sorta settled a little score I had with them when I got inside [a church]. I went up in the top of the steeple and spotted twenty of the dirty —— down below me. I had a field day." And on another occasion some members of an American airborne unit who were landed off target had difficulty with one of their own men who suffered from a mental aberration. Only the arrival of British infantrymen nearby saved the unbalanced GI from being killed by his comrades.[36]

A post-World War II military study has attempted to prove the point that not all of the American soldiers were equally aggressive; that only part of the members in each unit carried the fight to the enemy. This is not an astounding revelation, for it has been true in every war. American World War II officers were quite aware of this, and took advantage of it to form special task units in many infantry regiments. Certain individuals were chosen from the tough First Marine Division to form a special force called the "Alamo Scouts." In the Bougainville fighting, a special American infantry unit called the "Tigers" was formed. Members were rewarded with ten cents for every twelve Japanese killed and with beer for prisoners taken. A special force known as "Carlson's Raiders" was formed from what some would call the world's most elite fighting force— the Marine Corps. Its slogan, "Gung Ho," became a rather permanent phrase in the American language.[37]

In every theater of war, special units were organized by American forces. The U. S. Ninth Army formed a unit called "The Raiders," in which the volunteers had "wonderful times." "There were 16 of us," a member of the unit wrote. "We had a tent to ourselves, extra clothing, all automatic weapons . . . and once went two miles in front of our lines." Even Merrill's Marauders, strictly conceived as a volunteer unit, had its "Dead End Kids." They killed Japanese infantry by the dozens. "Those little bastards must think we're amateurs at this jungle-fighting stuff," growled one "Dead-Ender," ". . . *Banzai* charges might have terrified the civilians at Singapore, but they're nothing but good, moving target practice for us." After one long hard day of killing in Burma, it was reputed that a tired Marauder stood up and shouted into the jungle: "Come on, you little bastards. Come and get your lead!" No wonder the nearby Chinese infantrymen under Stilwell's command were somewhat frightened by the sheer aggressiveness of the Americans![38]

A good many sociomilitary studies have been done since the end of World War II. One argues that only a quarter of the American infantry actively fired their weapons, and that 1 percent of the American fighter pilots accounted for 30 to 40 percent of enemy aircraft. Another, based upon surveys done during the war, asserts that in January, 1944, 49 percent of white enlisted men in the United States wished to be in combat overseas; that Americans stationed in Panama, where there was no fighting, were the least happy of all American troops; and that Yanks who were stationed in Alaska were least satisfied with their contribution to the war.[39]

Whatever these studies attempt to prove, they fail to dislodge the historical fact that World War II American fighting men—in the Army, Navy, or Marines—carried the war to the enemy almost from the beginning. The worst insult to any man in the service of his country after 1941 was to call him a "U. S. O. soldier." Even rear-line duties were sometimes disliked. As one American GI auto mechanic put it: "I would rather fight than sit here on my fanny and see that trucks are kept clean after driving through mud."[40]

The quick dismantling of the American Army after World War II was tragic in more than one way. The more aggressive types left the Army quickly, found civilian jobs, and successfully fought their way into the business and professional world. There were others who briefly tried the rigors of civilian life, but being less able, or perhaps less aggressive, returned to the gentler life of post-World War II soldiering.

This was the type of army that was thrown into the breach in order to stop the 1950 Communist assault on South Korea. As pointed out previously, it did its best, but was cut to pieces. Only the arrival of more professional Army and Marine units, plus the high quality of Naval and Air Force units, brought the North Koreans to a halt on the Pusan perimeter.

The Marines, particularly, continued to display an aggressiveness which had marked the action of United States forces in World War II. There was a slight but marked difference in performance, however. While the Marine of Guadalcanal or elsewhere had picked his way silently through the jungle, the leatherneck of 1950 fought a different kind of fight. He was a shouter; a throwback to the "Rebs" of 1862 or the Indian fighters of 1870. Other than this, he was the same old purple-prosed killer. "I'm one Army guy who feels the more Marines I have around the better I like it," wrote General Mark Clark, who commanded American forces in Korea for some time. "Marines are men rarin' to go, men with their tails up." A marine expressed it in a different way. "We have to train men so we can tell them to go forward and draw enemy fire," he said, "and we're not going to reward them with a 72-hour pass."[41]

Fortunately, the aggressiveness displayed by the Marine Corps in Korea was contagious. Sailors left their landing craft at Inchon in order to carry a rifle for awhile. The Army, with better trained units coming into the fight, picked up the challenge as well. By

1951 an American magazine could report about the American GI: "Bravery is rarely lacking. At the fighting level, the skill of U. S. armed forces is unquestioned." Added to this is the simple truth that, by 1951, the American soldier was infinitely more aggressive than most of his United Nations allies, many of whom represented picked battalions.[42]

The metamorphosis of the American fighting man in Korea presents an interesting picture. He began the war as an unmotivated and rather disinterested mercenary. The longer the war ran, the greater became his professionalism and his desire for total victory. The last change was eventually muted into a bitter frustration. As one soldier expressed it:

> I can't see why we keep trying to fool ourselves—this is a war and we might as well act like it is a war. If it takes an army of a million men in Korea to get it over, then let's send a million men. . . . This uncertainty from day to day as to whether the Chinese are going to declare war is getting my goat—and I for one am ready to say "Get out of Korea or face the U. S. and the A-Bomb." In a world where force seems to be the only thing that is respected, let's give them force and see what happens.[43]

Denied the use of the "bomb," the American fighting man in Korea relied on his traditional weapons—his firepower, his air power, and his native aggressiveness. "I'm no barracks-parade-ground marine," complained one American. "I'm a Cherokee Indian and I'm happiest being miserable with my men up in those mountains." An Army boy wrote to his parents: "The Regiment got credit for killing 16 Chinese yesterday and of that total my platoon was responsible for 12! That made my men pretty proud of themselves." The same soldier, a college instructor "on leave," further told his parents: "I'm not saying this to boost your morale, but my men are *anxious* to get back to the front! That shows you what a difference 1500 yards will make. . . . I won't say that I'd rather be in Korea than teaching school, but Korea isn't half as bad as I had pictured it."[44]

The struggle in Korea was a strange twilight war, and yet it affected the United States in so many ways; politically, historically, and in social terms. There were times when it stripped bare the American soul. Negro fought alongside white against the Oriental. Generals' sons were lost in battle with the sons of Tennessee farmers. Even the Commanding General of the Eighth Army, General Van Fleet, lost a son on a B-26 bombing raid.

Yet, in the end, when the Chinese finally stopped blowing their bugles, and the North Koreans ceased shouting the few English obscenities they knew, the indomitable American will to win still remained. Over one portion of the now quiet battlefield came the strains of "The Marine Hymn," begun by a solitary private and taken up by other members of the Corps. Less than one hundred years earlier, a part of the Army of the Cumberland had grudgingly left the battlefield at Chickamauga singing "The Battle Hymn of the Republic."[45]

Thus is the basic characteristic of the American fighting man still present. It is an aggressive will to win, and despite the occasional eulogies written for it by contemporary commentators, it lies deep within the soul of the nation. In 1959 William S. White, regretting the death of the "old army," wrote:

There are many things—[these men were] often short in their grades in the intelligence tests; nearly always deplorable in their manners and morals in captured towns; dirty and sometimes surlily so, and without a touch of glamor. They have also been the only fighting men who ever gave a human quality to warfare. It was their duty to kill other men in a nastily personal way—with bullet, bayonet, or club.[46]

As Mark Twain might have said it, White was a little premature in his announcement of the death of the "old army." It is really still around, and doing quite well in Vietnam. As an old soldier, now in the rice paddies of that country, put it:

Here, you're hit hard and fast. There's no time not to fight back. Our boys fight like cats and dogs. Real scrappy. I'd just as soon have the kids of today with me as those of World War II or Korea.

They're not better-trained, they're the same kind of kids; but they really know how to follow orders, dig in and fight.[47]

While aggressiveness may be defined as a social characteristic of a people, it might also be added that this very facet of American society has its own way of expressing itself in times of stress. In war these expressions are called techniques. Some of these, as shall be shown, have remained wholly unchanged throughout the long history of the American fighting man. Others, wholly or in part, have undergone modifications from age to age.

The gun—musket or rifle—has been the most important single military weapon of the last two hundred years. The British won the Battle of Waterloo because they handled their muskets more ably than the French. Again, on the field at Mons in World War I, the British temporarily stopped the German army with the accurate rifle fire of the "old contemptibles." In Korea and Vietnam, despite the importance of air power, the infantry has still remained as the "queen of battles."

The rifle has always had a special significance in American military history. Until 1900 at least, a rifle was considered by most Americans as part of the household furniture. A usual gift to a rural American boy of the nineteenth century was a new rifle. Even in the twentieth century the collecting of guns, old and new, has approached and possibly exceeded the popularity of philately.

Marksmanship has always been a special pride of the American fighting man. During the formation of the Royal Americans in the 1750's, it was the aim of the British to create a corps with a special expertise in this skill. The rifle was adopted along with the musket, and attempts were made to teach the men to load and fire with speed while lying prone.

It is probable that the British chose the rifle as a significant weapon for the Royal Americans because the colonists were well used to it. Hunting, a major means of acquiring food in North America, required a rifle rather than a musket. Furthermore, the skill of the Pennsylvania-German gunsmiths had provided the so-called "Kentucky long rifle," a hunting piece with extraordinary accuracy at great distances.

By the time of the American Revolution, it can be said that the marksmanship of the ordinary American militiaman exceeded that of the ordinary British Regular. During the British retreat from Concord, American militia inflicted heavy casualties upon the enemy with both musket and rifle. The bright uniforms of the British, and the stone walls that lined the countryside, made perfect conditions for the application of colonial rifle accuracy.

The same was true in certain other battles of the Revolution. American riflemen at Bunker Hill decimated the officer complement of the British Regulars by well-directed fire. One American was seen to kill twenty field officers of the enemy before he was overrun by the Grenadiers of the Royal Welsh Fusiliers. The Battle of Saratoga was won partly by American ability with the rifle. Time after time Burgoyne, who commanded the British forces during the campaign, complained that he was losing his best officers and men to the American rifle.[48] One of the British generals here was killed at a distance of three hundred yards by an American rifleman named Timothy Murphy. In another instance, a British soldier was killed at 250 yards, even though only half his head was showing above the parapet. At Cowpens, another American victory, Morgan's Riflemen destroyed British battlefield leadership by killing or wounding virtually every enemy officer within sight.[49]

In the War of 1812, and in the Mexican War, there were similar instances in which American riflemen won the day. At the Battle of New Orleans, Jackson's sharpshooters almost destroyed the attacking British force while American losses in the same encounter were very small. American marksmanship was brilliant throughout the war with Mexico, with Mexican Lancers and infantry being picked off before they could reach entrenched American positions.

The Civil War was fought in widely varying conditions. Some battles were conducted along the lines of simplest strategy; one parallel line opposing another. Others, such as Shiloh or Chickamauga, were struggles in wooded areas, and the outcomes of these

were determined less by marksmanship than by waves of infantrymen outflanking the opposition. The siege at Petersburg was trench
warfare in its earliest version, and though it offered some opportunity for the sharpshooter, the battle really represented the movement of mass against mass.

Still, rifle ability was an underlying factor in many engagements
of the war. In its early stages the Confederate soldier was easily
superior to his enemy, in both the accuracy and the reloading of
his weapon. In time, however, the Federal soldier not only came
to equal the "butternut" infantrymen in these aspects of rifle warfare, but he was able to add a dimension to the direction of the
war. This was the sheer amount of firepower. Not only did the
Federal Armies have more guns because they had more men, but
by adding repeating rifles, Spencers and Henrys, to their mounted
cavalry, they gained an added advantage. These factors, plus an
increasing will to win on the part of the Federal Armies, eventually
determined the outcome of the conflict.

The Americans entered into the War of 1898 with at least one
disadvantage. The Army had failed to convert from the old black
powder cartridge to smokeless powder; something the Spanish had
done some time before. Yet American Regulars and many of the
American volunteer units were much more skilled in handling their
weapons than the Spanish soldiers. Foreign observers were quick
to report to their home governments that the American infantryman was expert with a rifle; a technique most of them attributed
to the remaining frontier conditions on the North American
continent.

During the preliminary stages of the training of the doughboy
in World War I, General Pershing laid much emphasis on the use
of the rifle and the bayonet. Though French advisors objected
strenuously to these methods of training, feeling the use of mortars
and grenades to be much more important, they were among the
first to congratulate the Americans when their methods proved
effective. At Belleau Wood, for instance, the French were quite
impressed with the use of the rifle and bayonet by the Marines,
and even the Germans somewhat feared to oppose the Yanks be-

cause of their willingness to come to close quarters. In some World War I battles, those on the Marne in July, 1918, and at Saint-Mihiel in the fall of the same year, American riflemen inflicted heavy casualties upon the Germans. Some of the old Regulars as well as a few of the volunteers were fantastic in their shooting accomplishments. The well-remembered Sergeant York applied his practice with the squirrel gun to the trenches, and became a legend in the war. And a young lieutenant, writing to his parents, described the work of his noncom in September, 1918: "Sergeant Pigman saved the lives of a lot of us and I hope to get the D. S. M. for him. He shot eight Huns himself with his rifle and blew the brains out of every one—right through the head every time."[50]

Rifle marksmanship, though still important in World War II, lost some of its significance to an increasing dependence on artillery fire and air power. Yet there are instances that show the ordinary American had not lost any of his legendary skill. In North Africa a Ranger sharpshooter was able to silence a German machine-gun nest at 1,350 yards by using a telescopic sight. Another Ranger was able to bring down a low-flying German fighter plane in the same theater with a burst from an automatic rifle. Later in the war, in Germany, an army sergeant was able to pick off close to twenty Germans from an observation tower on the outskirts of a town.

In the Pacific theater the marksmanship of the Americans was excellent; it had to be. An American soldier on Bougainville managed to shoot thirty-five Japanese infantrymen during an enemy attack. Another picked off nine charging Japanese with twelve shots. "Just took my time," he said, "kept cool and, damn, I got them." A Marauder in Burma, while on patrol near Shaduzup, amazed an officer by killing an enemy sentry at eighty yards "without seeming to take aim."[51]

Despite these excellent samples of marksmanship, rifle training of the American fighting man has somewhat declined in the last fifty years; that is, with the exception of the Marines or special Army units. By mid-1966 a major American news magazine was able to report that only 14 percent of the new recruits taken into the Army were given concentrated training on the firing of weapons. In Vietnam officers have complained that some men spend so much time tinkering with their rifles that they will not fire when emergencies arise. But the war in Vietnam, as wars sometimes do, has brought an emphasis on basic essentials. In December, 1966, the Army announced that it would now attempt to teach GI's to fire from the hip. And on the battlefield, where training really counts, more than one American platoon has decided that its patrol point-man ought to be equipped with a rapid-fire shotgun.[52]

The traditional ability with the rifle served early to influence the American capacity to use artillery effectively. From the very beginning one finds a respect on the part of the enemy for the accuracy of American artillery. British Regulars at Boston and Charleston were amazed at the methodical handling of the cannons by the "provincials." The Americans made much use of seamen in land artillery during the War of 1812, and with excellent results. The field artillery of Taylor and Scott in Mexico was superb. In one instance an American artillery unit not only stopped a Mexican advance, but it trundled its cannon behind horses and proceeded to pursue the retreating enemy.

American artillery came into its own in the Civil War. Naval cannon saved the Federal forces at Shiloh when they had been driven to the bank of the Tennessee River. At Stone's River the Federal forces handled their cannon like "playthings" and helped to win a dubious victory. The handling of the Federal cannon at Gettysburg blunted Pickett's charge before it reached the famous stone fence. At Petersburg and elsewhere Federal armies refined the use of rifled cannon, mortars, and siege guns to a standard unequaled elsewhere in the world.

The accuracy of American artillery and naval fire in the Spanish-American War, though colorfully publicized, was actually overrated. The number of hits by the U. S. Navy at Santiago has been variously estimated at from 119 to 286 out of 9,500 shots fired. One source claims that hits from the main United States naval batteries at Santiago amounted to only forty-two out of 1,300 attempts. Even American land batteries were really inaccurate. El Caney was attacked without artillery support, and at San Juan Hill, artillery fire served to confuse the Americans as much as the Spanish.

The real story about United States naval and land heavy gunfire in 1898 brought about some important and significant renovations in the decade that followed. It could be said that by 1908, the U. S. Navy had the best shooting fleet in the world. The Army, likewise, had adjusted itself to changing times, and had proceeded to lay heavier stress on the training of artillery.[53]

Thus, when the United States went into World War I, the American fighting man had some proficiency in the contemporary use of heavy guns. In the early stages of America's effort in the fighting, an attempt was made by the Army to develop techniques in calibration and in progressive curtain-fire. The results astonished both the French and the Germans. A French liaison officer with the American Second and Third Divisions reported that the artillery along the Marne was fired with great accuracy, skill, and vigor. A German soldier who had fought on every section in the war claimed that "American Artillery was the most accurate. . . ." Other German reports indicated that the big American guns were "right on target," and that the artillery fire was "very accurate and very heavy. . . ."[54]

The lessons taught by the use of artillery were well learned by the American Army in World War I. They were quickly applied in World War II. Early Japanese intelligence reports indicated a high respect for the United States big guns; a feeling that was heightened when the American Navy began to use the battleship as a moving artillery platform in support of beach landings. At Kwajalein, for example, the combined naval and air bombardment left a capsule version of the First World War's Verdun. There were no Japanese buildings left, and no trees. The island was a wasteland of shell holes. By the time of Okinawa, Japanese military leaders realized they could not contend with naval gunfire support, and drew their forces inland to meet the Americans. Yet, even here there were times when battleship fire helped to turn the tide. The U. S. S. *Tennessee* killed over one hundred Japanese infantrymen with a series of salvos in a single incident. On another occasion, during a mass Japanese assault of American lines, both naval gunfire support and land based artillery decimated three battalions of Japanese, and caused a fourth to disappear without a trace.[55]

American land artillery in the Pacific also had an occasional moment to itself. At Bougainville extremely proficient mortarmen laid 4.2 shells only twenty-five yards ahead of an advancing line; a high degree of accuracy to say the least. At Villaba, in the Leyte campaign, the Seventh Regiment of the First Cavalry Division called for artillery support so close that it blew the helmets off American troopers. During *Galahad,* the operation involving Merrill's Marauders, the Americans had only a few artillery pieces, but used them so effectively that the Japanese were much demoralized.[56]

On the other side of the globe American artillerymen and naval gunfire teams really showed to an advantage. German officers were amazed at the volume and accuracy of artillery fire and assumed that the Americans had developed a new and fast radio reconnaissance. Ernie Pyle wrote that, during the invasion of North Africa, Rommel's army feared American artillery more than anything else in the Allied arsenal. This is supported by a letter of a young American officer after the savage fighting at Hill 609. "Our artillery was deadly awful," he told his parents, "and the German prisoners which we captured said that they had never seen anything like it, and most of them had come directly from the Russian front."[57]

American artillery was once again fantastic during the Normandy invasion. Ernie Pyle writes of a German officer-prisoner, who said to his captors: "I know you're going to kill me, but before you do would you let me see that automatic artillery of yours?" Rommel credited much of the American success in Normandy to naval gunfire support, while other German officers in that fighting complained that they could get neither troops nor supplies to the front because of massive American artillery bombardments.[58]

A crucial turning point in the Battle of the Bulge was reached when American artillery was able to smash attacking waves of German troops. An American private lived through those terrible days to be able to write his mother that the "wonderful support" of the big guns had stopped the enemy. "How we did it I don't know," he concluded, "but we held our own and gave those Huns back triple what they threw at us." Later the same artillery support was instrumental in the Rhine crossing. General Eisenhower would describe the barrage there as a "real drumfire." And toward the end of the war General Marshall summarized the accomplishments of American artillery by writing: "We believe that our use of massed heavy artillery fire was far more effective than the German techniques and clearly outclassed the Japanese."[59]

Massive artillery barrages were also a feature of the Korean War. On occasion American artillery was called upon to fire point-blank into an onrushing tide of North Korean soldiers. After one massive artillery barrage against Chinese Communist positions in Korea, American observers were able to count almost five thousand enemy corpses.

As in Korea, American artillery has been used at point-blank range against Viet Cong attacks or enemy positions. It has been reported from time to time that the elusive enemy in South Vietnam fears artillery far more than air attacks, mainly because no warning is given before the shells begin to land.[60]

The uses of the rifle and artillery in the art of war have remained essentially unchanged over the years. Other techniques of war have changed. Cavalry, which the American Army developed as its striking force in war, played roles of varying importance in the American Revolution, the Mexican War, and the Civil War. The employment of the horse soldier as a means to destroy enemy communications in the Civil War was strictly an American innovation. During the Indian Wars that followed, the Army Cavalry became the most romanticized branch of the military service. So much glory did it carve out for itself that some American generals absolutely refused to accept the demise of the horse as an instrument of war. Pershing, who commanded Americans in France in World War I, was an old cavalry officer. And as late as 1941 a book, which carried a foreword by Hanson W. Baldwin, contained this statement: "Cavalry today carries on its long and honorable tradition of usefulness. Its work is as diversified as that of any other part of the

Army, and it still demands the daring and ingenuity of the old days. Methods of warfare change, but the need for a strong, up-to-date Cavalry doesn't."[61]

World War II finally ended the role of the horse soldier in battle, however. What he had done back in the days of Custer was now taken over by other innovations. The tank, an invention of World War I, assumed the role of the shock-cavalry of an earlier day. And the air forces displaced cavalry as a strike force designed to disrupt communications and to scout enemy positions.

The American fighting man did have some experience with tanks during World War I. These were French Renaults, which because of their lack of speed and maneuverability, really served to slow the powerful drive of the energetic American infantry. During the 1920's, while old generals dreamed of the return of the horse, little was done to improve the tank. In practice maneuvers held prior to Pearl Harbor day, many Regular units were forced to simulate tanks with trucks—ordinary vehicles with the large word "tank" written across them.

Once American industry was turned loose on tank production, however, much of this deficiency was eliminated. Some of the early tanks that were developed, the General Grant for instance, lacked the armor and muzzle-velocity necessary for modern warfare. The General Sherman, built and modified to meet most of the conditions to be found in World War II, proved to be a very effective workhorse of the new cavalry.

Two newly developed techniques of conflict tended to make Americans much more advanced in mechanized war than any other nation involved in the struggle. First, the Americans learned early that strike coordination between tanks and airplanes made both machines more deadly. Second, the Americans were the quickest to absorb the lesson that one could not wage mechanized war with tanks alone. Communications, logistical supply, replacement, and repair were all part of the new *blitzkrieg;* a bit of knowledge of which Hitler was unaware when he sent his tank columns into Russia. As Major-General Fuller, the British military theoretician put it, the Americans were the first to become "spanner-minded."

The word "spanner" is British for the good old "monkey-wrench."[62]

The use of the airplane as support for the tank was only one of the uses to which Americans put air power in World War II. Actually, by 1941, Americans were well acquainted with the importance of the airplane. During their brief participation in World War I, American pilots had brought down 753 enemy planes and seventy-one balloons, and had established a reputation for daring and aggressiveness which was well deserved. Unfortunately, however, American aircraft design fell far behind American aerial strategy after 1939, and United States pilots were handicapped by cumbersome and overrated planes, which were completely unequal to the Japanese "Zero." Only the extra skill and courage of the American pilots at Midway, for instance, brought victory over the Japanese in that conflict.

Soon the P-38 "Lightning" was developed, however, and it was capable of achieving higher altitudes than any of the Japanese planes. Eventually the famous "Thunderbolt" came off the drawing-boards, as well as the "Mustang," and American Army Air Force pilots found themselves flying the best mass-produced airplanes of the war. Naval aircraft also improved spectacularly from 1941 to 1945.

The great variety of planes produced by American industry after 1941—the "Fortresses," "Liberators," "Corsairs," etc.—allowed for an application of differing techniques to each theater of war. The "Thunderbolts" were great ground-support planes. When used in Normandy along with the "Mustang," they paralyzed rail and road transport to the German front. The heavy armorplate on the American planes gave pilots an extra sense of security when attacking enemy positions, and sometimes the machines were flown so close to the ground that front line American infantrymen could feel the propwash as they flew by them.

American planes were used so effectively during Patton's race into France that the American right flank needed no other support than that given from the air. As one German general was forced to report in July, 1944: "Yesterday's heavy fighting was successful for the enemy only because he paralyzed all our movements by employing fighter-bombers on an unprecedented scale. . . ."[63]

American pilots, no matter which plane they flew, were quickly able to adapt themselves to the prevailing conditions of each theater of war. The "Thunderbolts," which were not nearly so maneuverable as British or German fighter planes, needed a special touch to bring success against the enemy. The Americans achieved it. One unit, the Fifty-Sixth Fighter Group, was able to claim 1,006 German planes destroyed by the end of the war, with only 128 losses of its own.[64] Even the high-flying but less maneuverable "Lightning" found its place. American pilots soon learned to fly these high above Japanese formations, and to pounce upon the enemy with single passes. It was by this very procedure that Japanese Admiral Yamamoto was shot down by "Lightning" pilots in the Pacific.

Following the end of World War II, the American air forces continued their mastery of differing techniques. The "siege" of Berlin by the Russians in the late 1940's was met and defeated by the skillful operation of the Berlin Air Lift. Later, in 1950, the American airplane and its usually well-trained pilot performed fantastic feats in the name of the United Nations. Young Navy pilots, flying with their large landing flaps down, cruised slowly down Korean rail lines at night to find supply trains. Marine and Air Force pilots flew their jets or "Mustangs" like arrows in order to mark enemy positions to American artillery.

In the air outnumbered American planes met Russian-built MIG's, which were flown by a variety of nationalities, and virtually drove them from the sky. At one period, in the latter stages of the war, the hot American fliers were shooting down enemy planes at a ratio of fifty-five to one.[65]

Air power in Vietnam has also given American forces an extra edge. B-52's flying from Guam and Thailand have blasted Viet Cong jungle positions. Low-flying American jets and prop planes have acted as mobile artillery by dropping napalm or bombs in advance of GI patrols. The newest American technique in air power, however, is the use of the helicopter. These machines, plus their daring pilots, have given the infantryman a kind of mobility hitherto undreamed of. Indeed, the helicopter has reversed the course of the war in Vietnam.

None of the foregoing techniques—the use of the rifle, mechanized warfare, the effectiveness of American artillery, or air power— could ever exist were it not for the American ability to produce logistical solutions. American ability in this area existed as early as the Revolutionary War. One of the great feats of that conflict was the hauling of captured British cannon over the snow and ice from Ticonderoga to Boston.

In the Mexican War, American supply and organization was spectacular for the 1840's, and on one occasion it allowed one American unit to cover thirty-five miles in twenty-four hours. German observers in 1861 were amazed at the logistical and engineering accomplishments of the Federal Army. In a specific instance, U. S. Army engineers produced a railroad bridge 414 feet long in forty hours. This was an astounding performance when one considers that American engineers were thought to have achieved a miracle in World War II when they built a prefabricated Treadway bridge across the Rhine in ten hours.

American logistical and engineering accomplishments in World War II were a source of unending surprise for friend and enemy alike. The British constantly underestimated American capacities in these respects; and Germans, while admiring them from the other side of the battlefield, never learned the secret of these American successes. The U. S. Navy saved the Allied landing force at Salerno by bringing five thousand tons of supplies to the beach each day. At Normandy, the Americans averaged thirty thousand tons and thirty thousand troops ashore for each day of the first few months after the landing. Following the American breakout at Saint-Lô, the famed "Red Ball Express," an American transportation system, moved 410,000 tons of material to keep the Patton drive going.

The moving of troops and supplies was only part of the work of American planners in World War II. Experts developed the famous "C" and "K" rations, which despite the constant complaints from soldiers, were two of the more ingenious American contributions to the war. Preloaded trucks, the fueling of ships at sea, the efficient use of the newly invented fork-truck, the repair facilities for mechanized equipment, and prefabricated airstrips were further results of imaginative planning. Bridge building equipment produced by Americans allowed GI engineers to build five bridges in all across the Rhine, three of them over 3,000 feet long; all five of them built in an average construction time of nine days and one hour.[66]

One of the developments of American logistical and engineering planning was an imaginative use of amphibious vessels to supply captured beaches. Small "ships" with alphabetical names—LCVP's, LCM's, LCT's, LST's—were built in American shipyards in a minimum amount of time. The smallest of these lacked in comforts of any kind. They were manned by inexperienced boys and officers whose bravery was sometimes credited by onlookers to their relative inexperience. These men took their landing craft into the beaches of Salerno and Anzio under heavy fire. They floundered at times, but got their men and cargoes into the hell of Omaha Beach in Normandy. They stayed with the Marines at Tarawa until the island was secured, and supplied American land forces at Iwo Jima and Okinawa.

The same logistical abilities have served the United States well in Korea and Vietnam. The Inchon landing, the "left hook" behind the Communist forces in South Korea, was accomplished by methods learned in World War II. And American maintenance and supply in Vietnam have left little to be desired. Even on Thanksgiving and Christmas days in 1967, troops in far-off jungle positions received their specially prepared dinners on time.

Though the Germans and Japanese never really solved the inner secret of the American logistical effort, the key to such success was plain for anyone to see. It has been, and still is, the willingness of the American fighting man to sacrifice and to work hard over long stretches of time. The hauling of the cannon from Ticonderoga was done through sheer effort. The beaverlike activity of the Americans in the Civil War was noted by almost every foreign observer, and immediately forgotten by all. The British in World War I could never quite comprehend the intense American desire to get on with the war until it was won.

Ernie Pyle saw it in World War II, however, when he wrote that American sailors really worked to keep their ships mechanically operative in the Italian invasions. Others saw it at Tarawa, where Seabees, rather than take the time to remove hastily buried Marines, simply built airstrips over shallow graves. On Iwo Jima, American engineers, working day and night, built a road to the top of Mount Suribachi in two weeks; a task that the Japanese had been working on for twenty years. During the same invasion each of fifty-five Sherman tanks of one Marine unit were knocked out of action three times; yet all were kept in the fight by hard-working mechanics. On an unnamed Pacific island, construction battalions worked for two weeks on their own time to provide a jungle theater for American fighting men.

Similar feats were achieved in Burma. The capacity of the Bengal-Assam railroad was doubled by American engineers, despite the intense heat of the Brahmaputra valley. United States Army pilots flew the "hump" into China, and kept Allied units supplied in Burma as well. Such deeds were sometimes accomplished on very short notice, by men yellowed by Atabrine, who drove trucks composed of cannibalized parts, or by pilots who were only a year or two away from the Iowa prairies and college proms.[67]

No less sacrifice has been asked of Americans in Korea or Vietnam. In both places airports were carved out of river plains or jungle, and airplanes have been flown under the worst conditions in order to keep troops on the battle line. In the retreat (or advance as the Marines would have it) from the Chochin Reservoir in North Korea, the cold was met and conquered. Opposite conditions in Vietnam, the monsoon seasons and the jungles, have been overcome by the American ability to contrive and to work hard.

The common denominator of victory in each American war is the fighting American. Though he has a nameless face in history, the circumstances of battle have given him a number of aliases. He was the *gringo* of the Mexican War, and the *Johnny Reb* and *Billy Yank* of the Civil War. Every veteran of the Spanish-American War thought of himself as a *roughrider*. He was the *doughboy* of World War I, and the *GI* of World War II. From time to time he has been called a *gob,* a *leatherneck,* a *hayfoot,* a *foot-slogger,* a *mac,* and just plain *joe.*

Different as are the names and appearance, though, he is basically the same now as he was a century ago. He even bears a passing resemblance to his predecessor of two hundred years ago. To friend and enemy alike he has always seemed the sturdy fighter, and a man gifted with some very admirable physical and mental qualities. He has never lacked in ingenuity or the surprise factor. Most times with astounding success, on occasion with little, he has always attempted to carry the war to his enemy. He is aggressive, hard-working, amazingly adaptable, capable of great endurance, at times unpredictable, and he never likes defeat. In other words, he is a winner.

5

The Nature of the Man

THE GROWTH IN THE TRADITION of the professional American fighting man was a slow but progressive one. Yet, it can be said that by 1800 the career soldier was common in the services. Such individuals were seldom native-born Americans, but they were veterans of foreign armies, or immigrants who saw in the American Army a chance for integration into the life of the growing country. There are many instances in which some of these men became old soldiers, indeed. One Englishman, who joined the Army in 1805, finally terminated his military career in 1862. Another, an Irishman, who enlisted in 1822, stayed in uniform until 1864. Though similar information is not available on the U. S. Navy, it might be assumed that enlisted men were even more inclined to stay in service for longer periods than those in the Army.[1]

Through the long history of the U. S. Army and Navy, all the way down to the draft in World War I, the pattern of the ordinary enlisted man rarely changed. The men who joined the services in time of peace rarely did so for the honor of wearing the uniform, or for the pay involved. They were, in general, recently arrived immigrants, men who were seeking adventure, or Americans who had found that civilian life carried too many responsibilities. They came from all walks of life, and from varied backgrounds. In 1853, for example, an enlisted man on trial for striking his noncom, astounded his officers with his literate and eloquent speech in his own behalf. Doubtlessly, concluded one observer, this was a man who had joined the army in a "fit of disgust at some moral or social delinquency on his part."[2]

By 1860 many of the enlisted personnel in the Army were of German and Irish backgrounds. When the war came in 1861, these were the men who stayed loyal to the Union, while many of their American-born officers took off the blue and put on the grey. With the end of the war the Army and the Navy returned to the older pattern; their enlisted complement once again consisting of native-born Americans who wished to avoid the problems of civilian life and foreigners who saw the services as a best way of being introduced to the country. One Regular Army soldier of the Indian Wars noted that the Irish were the main immigrant group in the frontier army, while many other soldiers came from Germany, England, Canada, Scotland, and France. In recording similar information about various cavalry units during this period, the same writer also noted that each company of one particular regiment contained at least one or two well-educated men. In 1883, for instance, a Third Cavalry company had an excellent Bible student as one of its enlistees. In C Troop of the Eighth Cavalry in 1890, there was a Harvard graduate, and in the Tenth Cavalry (a Negro unit) in 1888, there was a former schoolteacher.[3]

As shall be shown below, the rude mixture of the educated and uneducated among American professional fighting men was true down to 1940, and at specific times since the end of World War II. After World War I, for instance, it was not unusual for high school or college graduates to join the Army or the Navy simply because there was nothing else for them to do. And it is certainly true that the supply of enlisted men for the services varied in accordance with conditions of prosperity and depression, particularly in the 1930's.

The hardships endured by both Army and Navy Regulars in

the nineteenth century were enormous when viewed alongside those of later years. Regular naval complements, when at sea in the early 1800's, rarely had a warmed meal; their diet consisted principally of hardtack and liquor. The old *Constitution,* when tied to the dock, did have a small cooking facility which could be used. It consisted of a single large pot, hung from a chain, and warmed by charcoal embers resting on an iron plate in the hold.

The sufferings of the American frontier army were more severe at times than those of the Navy, but fortunately the effects of such stresses were broken by post-duty, which offered some small relief. Quite often there were long marches, however, and those were extremely difficult to endure. In a long march from Fort Gibson in the 1830's, only 190 men out of the 500 who started were fit for duty at the end of the campaign. One hundred horses broke down under the strain, and many men were carried on travois for the last two-hundred miles.[4]

Another long campaign, by Dragoons in the late 1840's, traveled over 1,500 miles. At the end of that same year one such soldier estimated that he had ridden over 3,100 miles during the summer. These forays into the plains served to toughen both men and horses. One old Dragoon, recalling the quality of his comrades years later, wrote: "Two or three horses were changed by the quartermaster, some shoeing done, a little replenishing of clothing, and in a week we were ready for the field again."[5]

The ruggedness of the American Regular Army, having saved the country in its war with Mexico, became a well-rooted service tradition. In the 1850's, just prior to the Civil War, a German immigrant soldier in the West wrote:

The pay of the soldiers is not bad, but the hardships in the United States army are greater than in any other. Our Company, for instance, during the past year journeyed almost 3,000 miles—2,400 afoot and 600 by water—while during the last four years it was over 7,500 miles, and hardly 1,500 by water.[6]

In the post-Civil War period the difficulties faced by the American frontier army were increased manifold. The vastness of the territory to be covered or policed, the general attitude of the American public toward the Army in both the East and the West, the occasional difficulty in raising recruits, and the small number of men allowed to the Army by its slender budget, placed extraordinary hardships before the officers and men. The Regular rose to the challenge, however, developing a toughness and resolution unequalled elsewhere in the world.

Examples of these characteristics are not difficult to find. During the Sioux campaign of 1868 an American soldier, wounded in the thigh with a bullet lodged near the femoral artery, used his own razor to cut out the projectile. In the Sioux campaign of 1876 the men carried only hardtack and bacon. They slept in gulleys washed by pouring rain. Horses collapsed from sheer exhaustion. Some men marched with swollen or bloody feet until they collapsed. Most had to wear their boots through the entire march because they feared they could not get into them again if they once took them off their feet. One newspaper correspondent who covered the campaign wrote: "An American army can stand without much growling or the slightest approach to mutiny more than any other troops upon this earth." The four hundred Congressional Medals of Honor awarded to the Army during this period were scant compensation for the hardships suffered.[7]

The pay for the ordinary soldier in the years past, though equal to or better than most other armies in the world, seems inconceivable by modern standards. In 1792 the private received eight dollars as bounty for enlistment, and three dollars a month while in rank. In the 1840's an infantry soldier received seven dollars a month (one dollar retained until expiration of enlistment) while mounted privates received eight dollars a month. During most of the Civil War, the pay for a white private soldier was thirteen dollars a month. By 1916 an enlisted private was given fifteen dollars a month, a corporal received twenty-one dollars, and a sergeant thirty dollars a month. One sergeant, who left the Army in 1916 after having served twenty-eight years, was retired on $67.50 a month. Prior to Pearl Harbor the ordinary Army private started his military career at twenty-one dollars a month. A master-sergeant in 1941 made $126.00 a month.[8]

Extra allowances available to the American fighting man in the 1800's offered little inducement to enlistment. Before the War of 1812 the ordinary private was given a minimum of clothing and one blanket. Army diet in that day consisted mainly of meat, flour, and whiskey; vegetables being left to each private's ability to garden or to forage. In 1803 the Army's total yearly allowance for clothing was $29.66; the private had to buy all necessaries beyond that amount. The Army also gave each private a "junk bottle" in which to keep his liquor.

Medical supplies on the ordinary post consisted of opium, quinine, herb medicines, calomel, some crude surgical instruments, and penis syringes. The equipment was no better on naval vessels. The *Constitution's* operating table was just that; an ordinary wooden table on which the various saws, crude cutting tools, and straps were laid out. With the exception of anesthesia, the improvement in military medicine through the nineteenth century to the end of the Civil War was very slight. After that time military hospitals did function with a slightly better understanding of the necessity of sanitation.[9]

All in all, the rewards for the professional American fighting man have been astoundingly small for the sacrifices which he has made. During the late nineteenth century the American press hailed the exploits of the British "Tommy" in India, and condemned the American frontier army for unfair treatment of the American Indian. America's frontier soldiers were regarded, even by the people they were directly protecting, as uncouth and unworthy individuals. A prostitute who catered to Army trade was considered the lowest of the low. In seaport areas it was reputedly not uncommon to see signs on business houses which read: "Sailors and dogs not allowed."

Until 1941 the reaction of the American public to the death of an American professional fighting man was always predictable. The death of Custer's men was a subject for public sympathy only because of a peculiar romantic aura which surrounded the fight.

Otherwise, single or multiple deaths in the line of duty received little public attention. Even before World War II the American public attitude toward the professional soldier or sailor was that these were "rugged mercenaries" who knew what they were getting into when they volunteered. If they were killed, it was their own tough luck. When Hitler's submarines damaged the U. S. S. *Kearny* and sunk the U. S. S. *Reuben James,* both destroyers, the public reaction was slight. The parents of a Gillespie, Illinois, sailor, killed in the *Kearny* incident, were the recipients of taunting phone calls and letters. As Robert Sherwood wrote: "There was a sort of tacit understanding among Americans that nobody was to get excited if ships were sunk by U-boats, because that's what got us into the war the other time."[10]

In the case of Vietnam, the death of approximately thirty thousand American fighting men by the end of 1968 has been relatively calmly received by the general public. Anti-war demonstrations have to a great extent been anti-draft demonstrations, and these have been participated in by young people who have managed to evade service by attendance in college. And, as in the instance of the *Kearny* sailor, wives and relatives of many men killed in Vietnam have received malicious telephone calls and letters. The temper of these anonymous contacts is such as to condemn the deceased for their participation in the war, and to indicate that the unfortunate men had no business being in Vietnam in the first place.

It is not uncommon for the death of an American fighting man to receive no attention at all; not even from his immediate family. In World War I, the burial commission of the U. S. Army sent out 75,000 letters to families of deceased soldiers, inquiring for advice on the disposition of identified bodies. Over forty thousand families wanted their boys to remain in French soil, nineteen thousand wanted the bodies brought back home, but for the remainder there were no answers at all. A precedent to this was an earlier practice by the frontier army of burying the ordinary private in a makeshift cemetery with a headstone carrying the simple words "Soldier buried here." Even in more recent days, since the beginning of the Vietnam War, there have been several cases of unclaimed bodies. One, a soldier named John F. Barzan, was eventually buried in a Long Island National Cemetery when no family claims were made for the body.[11]

It is true, historically speaking, that when the United States becomes involved in a national struggle necessitating a call for great numbers of volunteers or draftees, the attitude of the American public quickly changes. The scorned soldier of 1855 became the hero of 1861. Nothing was too good for the volunteer on both sides. Once the war ended, the old attitude returned; the professional fighting man became, once again, scorned and unloved. In World War I only the draft brought the American public to look upon the fighting American as "our boy." The Chicago *Tribune* editorialized:

> It is with an unashamed emotion that we think of Pershing's men. They are our first sacrifices. The regular soldier—the confession now humiliates that nation—has never been close to the affections of the American people. He has been respected for efficiency and used. He has done his work well, and, we believe, cheerfully. But there has been no fondness in the nation for him.[12]

Such sentiments were short-lived, however. The doughboy returned to find a sudden reversal from the adoration of 1917. Even the three great heroes of the war—Sergeant Alvin York, Sergeant Sam Woodfill, and Major Charles Whittlesey—were either demeaned or quickly forgotten by the public. Whittlesey, accused by some of having misled the famed "lost battalion" of the Argonne, disappeared off a Caribbean-bound vessel, apparently a suicide. Woodfill, a gallant and little publicized Regular, left the army to become an Indiana farmer; remembered by Pershing but forgotten by the public. York, a draftee soldier, received the greatest publicity of the three, but died a penniless dirt farmer. How well they might have counseled Ira Hayes, an Indian hero of the Marine invasion of Iwo Jima, or "Machine Gun" Charles E. Kelly, the one-man battalion of the American Army in Europe in World War II! Both of these men lived out the remainder of their short lives as unhappy and perhaps tormented men.[13]

Despite the glories of World War II, and the Korean War, the American public still generally regards the military career as one to be shunned. A poll taken in 1955 among male teenagers indicated that the armed services ranked fourteenth among the preferred professions; even behind that of bookkeeping and mail carrying. During the Vietnam War college enrollments have been swelled by men seeking to delay service with the Army, and in at least one case, parents of draftable boys have been accused of using devious means to circumvent calls from a draft board. Yet the strange paradox of it all is the attitude of the American public toward generals or admirals who seek political careers. Washington, Grant, and Eisenhower were prominent generals who have occupied the White House. Pierce, Garfield, and Theodore Roosevelt attained a measure of fame while in the military. Dozens of other military officers have received solid political support for the Presidency.[14]

From all of this one would suspect that professional American fighting men, the Regulars, might be lacking in pride. Actually, the reverse has always existed. The Regular has perpetually demeaned the volunteer, sometimes with reason, and sometimes without. The *esprit* of the Regular goes deep into American military tradition. Washington made much of the dependability of the Continentals, and the unpredictability of the militia. Military historians have always stressed the poor quality of militia or volunteer units in the War of 1812. Some of their conclusions ought to be reconsidered, however. The truth about the War of 1812 was that the British and Canadians had as high a percentage of volunteer militia as the Americans, but that the British officer corps was of a much higher quality.

A Regular officer's reminiscences about the quality of volunteer militia is hardly a dependable source upon which the historian can rely. Lieutenant G. G. Meade, writing of the volunteer in the Mexican War, claimed that the volunteers were a "set of Goths and Vandals, without discipline. . . ." Meade and other officers felt that the Civil War volunteer was poor; that is, in 1861. Four years later the same generals were contending that their victorious troops were not really volunteers, but men whose experience had somehow metamorphosed them into regular soldiers. Such reasoning makes little sense.[15]

In 1917 Pershing's attitude toward the volunteer soldier was a mixed one. He wrote in his autobiography that he was somewhat embarrassed at the awkward appearance of the first American troops in France, and attributed their faults to the fact that many of the men were volunteers. Marines and Army Regulars sometimes ragged drafted men unmercifully in the early stages of the war. "Don't worry about the fighting, little doughboy. . . ," a Marine supposedly told a drafted soldier on the front line. "This is a tray forte sector. If you don't get killed the first eight days, the orders is to shoot you for loafing." There were even times during the conflict when Pershing had to moderate the deleterious influence of Regular Army officers and men. When it was all said and done, and the war was over, nothing irked the Army Regular more than to hear Sergeant York referred to as the great hero of the war. To the professional, and to Pershing, the "greatest soldier in the A.E.F." was a Regular, Sergeant Sam Woodfill, and not York. The case of Woodfill was a matter of Regular Army pride; a characteristic the professional American fighting man has always had.[16]

The Navy and Marines, by their very nature, escaped the eternal conflict of volunteer and Regular; at least until 1943. Both of these services were proud of this fact, arguing that a nation couldn't have a battleship "commanded by a man who had only been first mate of a lake steamer, or a skipper of an oyster-pungy in the Chesapeake, and with a crew that had been jumbled together from all over the country. . . ." Even the Army, after 1918, regained its professional pride as soon as possible. By April, 1919, a private soldier was able to write: "You see Uncle it is a great thing to be a United States Regular soldier because they are very much different from the Home guards. In a way Uncle we get the best and have the best of there all over here."[17]

Despite the prideful contempt of Regular toward volunteer or draftee, there is much evidence to indicate that citizen-soldiers have added much to the military tradition of the nation. Most militiamen in the American Revolution, rightfully so, felt that some of the ancient practices carried on by the Continentals were stupid. Some officers insisted that their men powder their hair on special occasions. The only thing available for this was flour, which sometimes became so wet that the appearance of the men often became ludicrous. As far as the actual fighting in the Revolution was concerned, the militia did extremely well at Cowpens, at King's Mountain, and in New Jersey, where in 1780, five thousand of these "summer soldiers" saved Washington's army.

The militia also had its moments during the War of 1812. While militiamen admittedly fought poorly at Bladensburg, they saved Fort McHenry. In the Battle of New Orleans, Jackson had only eight hundred Regulars out of his total force of five thousand men, and won a sharp victory. In most cases where the militia showed poorly, the fault really lay with the available leadership or with state regulations forbidding the militia to fight outside states in which it was raised.

The Civil War was a volunteer's war, despite the insistence of some that it was the professional soldier (Grant, Sherman, Sheridan, etc.) who really won it. The armies of both sides were mainly raised from men who had never before worn the uniform. As far as military leadership was concerned, it might as well be added that there were some excellent "political" generals on both sides: Logan, for instance, in the Union Army, and Forrest in the Confederate Army. There were also some extremely poor "professional" generals: Buell and Pope in the Federal Army as examples, and Bragg on the Confederate side.

In World War I the draftee came into his own. The great demand for troops, along with the shortage of Regulars on all levels, necessitated the creation of divisions composed almost entirely of drafted men. As would be expected, some of them were good divisions; others were not. A great deal depended upon the kind of leadership such divisions received. Many of the draftees were foreign born, others came from the hills of the South, and thousands came from the city streets. One Regular's reaction to the new men read: "When I saw them piling off the train . . . the undisciplined sons of undisciplined people, I wondered what they would do to us. They had not been in camp a day before I knew that they were going to play the game."

The attitude of the World War I draftee soon became such

that he considered himself no different than the Regular. In some cases the Regulars reciprocated. A junior officer from Illinois, writing to his sister in 1917, was proud to boast that he was accepted without distinction by the West Pointers of his division. Many of the early draftees and volunteers were of such high quality, physically and mentally, that in these characteristics they exceeded the Regulars. This helped to pave the way for a general acceptance of the draftee in 1918.[18]

Throughout World War II, either in the Army, the Navy, or the Marines, there was some occasional static between the Regulars and the draftees. The Army, the first of the services to accept the draftees, was also the first to show the irritations between professional and citizen soldiers. A young Texas volunteer who enlisted on Pearl Harbor day was severely criticized by his sergeant for fainting during a drill. "How can we win the war with these babies," the noncom complained. The boy, whose name was Audie Murphy, became America's most decorated soldier by the end of World War II. An Air Cadet, writing home, stated: "At Sheppard Field the G.I. privates and sergeants and all tried to make us feel that we were the lowest type person in the army." A study of complaints by U. S. enlisted men in World War II turned up these comments: "I consider the Army tradition bigoted and medieval, utterly out of keeping with our democratic ideals"; "The American Army is the most blunderingly successful Army in the World"; and "My own officers are more interested in women and other things than the job we have to do."[19]

For the first time the U. S. Navy also felt the impact of large numbers of draftees and wartime volunteers. The relationship between professionals and volunteers, particularly among officers of the lower ranks, was not always good. The peak number of naval officers during the war was 310,000, of which only 10,000 were Annapolis men. These 10,000 made their presence known, however; many of the reservist volunteers feeling that the Annapolis men operated as a solid but effective clique. Yet much of the talent in the Navy was in the reservist element. Most of these young Reservist officers were not only better educated, but they were specialists of a type the service needed. Indeed, approximately 98 percent of all United States naval radar officers by 1945 had never been near Annapolis, and because of their bitter feelings toward "trade school officers," the Navy was forced to beg them to stay in the service at the end of the war.[20]

The key to the early dissatisfaction of the draftee with the concepts of the Regular or professional fighting man was education. In the Navy most of the products of V-7 Midshipmen Schools were more liberally educated than young officers out of Annapolis. In some cases, men with college degrees served under old and uneducated "mustangs," who had been jumped to lieutenant grade rank on the basis of service. The Army had the same problem. An early survey of one army division after Pearl Harbor showed that its sergeants had the lowest education of all soldiers in the entire division, with one-third of them not having any school beyond the grammar school level. Of the privates (mostly drafted soldiers), 35 percent had finished high school, while only 27 percent of the sergeants had done so.

The contrast between the character of the old Regular and the new draftee was of an abrasive nature. The better educated the common soldier, the less he thought of close-order drill, surprise inspections, and "spit and polish." He saw the war, instead, in what he considered essentials—realistic training, the study of weapons of war, and a recognition of the basic strengths of his enemy. The difference between the draftee and the Regular is best expressed by one of the earlier studies of the U. S. Army in World War II. It reads:

> The Regular Army enlisted man was a youth of less than average education, to whom the security of pay, low as it was, and the routines of Army life appealed more than the competitive struggle of civilian life. By self-selection he was not the kind of man who would be particularly critical of an institution characterized by authoritarian controls. He might get in trouble, of course—there were problems of drunkenness, venereal disease, and AWOL. But he would be more likely than the kind of new citizen-soldier to accept the Army's traditional forms as right.[21]

In the long run, what the draftee needed was a little of the Regular's notion of discipline, and what the Regular needed was the more imaginative and better educated mental processes of the draftee. When one is left without the other, that is in the modern American military machine, the nation suffers. When both qualities are missing, the country is really in trouble.

This last development is really what happened in the early days of the Korean War. Not only had better educated types left the Army after 1946, but the Army abandoned some of its traditional standards of discipline. The old powers of the noncoms had been undermined. The Army, in order to get volunteers, resorted to degrading forms of publicity. By 1950, therefore, certain units in the Far East consisted of nothing more than modern forms of the old "bounty" soldiers of Revolutionary days.

As the draft was speeded up after 1950, and as reserve units were called up, the weaknesses of the Korean War Regular were further exposed. A young reserve officer writes shortly after his recall in 1950:

The Army is much different than it was before! Very rapidly I am learning to dislike *Regular Army* officers. The peace time regular army officer is nothing more than a bloodsucker in my estimation. By that I mean that he is overimpressed with himself, conceited, and thinks that the entire U. S. should exist for the benefit of the regular army officers. . . . Luckily there are so many reserves at Fort Riley that the Regular officers are in a minority. The reserves hang together and say, "To hell with the Regulars. . . ." I suppose I could be hanged for writing the previous paragraph, but the Regular Army is the laughing stock for the Reserves. I think when I get out I'll run for political office on the platform "A kick in the ass for every Regular!" At least 1,000,000 people would vote for me.

After a year's combat in Korea, the same officer wrote:

From what I've seen the caliber of man you get from the draft is better than the regular army soldier. That is as you might expect.

All of my NCO's except the platoon sergeant are draftees, but they are good. Most of them don't realize the power they have got—but they are learning.[22]

A military expert, writing on the effect of the draftee and reserve on the Korean War, stated:

The American soldier and officer who held the line in late 1952 and early 1953 was yet another breed from the man who had gone into Korea, who had fought during the massive battles of 1951, or who had watched the front during the second Korean winter.[23]

The American Army learned its lessons in Korea—from the Marines, who had maintained their standards, and from its own mistakes. Training was improved. Most Regulars were forced to meet higher standards. The military advisers and American troops who have been sent into Vietnam have been of excellent quality. Yet, as can be supposed, there are the occasional exceptions. It has been reported that out of four advisers sent to one Vietnamese unit—all Regulars—one was too old for arduous duties, one was a drinker and a woman chaser, and a third had a heart attack.

Discipline in the American armed forces, and the reaction of the fighting man to it, has always posed problems to the officers and commanders of American units. To a great extent this has been because of the very character of the individual American. He has considered his individual freedom as his most important gift, and from generation to generation has fought against ceding it to military authority.

Even back in the time of the Royal Americans, discipline and desertion were the twin problems of the regiment's commanders. In 1756 thirty Royal Americans deserted, the main causes being the enticements of freedoms found among the general population of the country. Indeed, in some cases, when deserters were found, they were sometimes rescued by sympathetic mobs and carried off in triumph. A year later, while in Pennsylvania, many of the German enlistees in the Royal Americans deserted to take up homes with the German farmers of that colony. Out of the fifty such deserters, eighteen were eventually recovered, and four were hanged.[24]

Discipline in the Continental Army was poor in the beginning, principally because of the leveling spirit that pervaded the whole country. The soldiers saw no reason to salute men they had known all their lives; there were too few uniforms available to inspire pride, and the privates honestly saw no reason to stay in camp when not on duty. Even when in camp, many off-duty soldiers felt no compulsion to adhere to regulations.

The Revolutionary militia was even worse. Their short-term enlistments gave them the confidence to defy authority, even when administered by the highest officers. "Sixty untrained militia are all the artillerymen in the Fort," wrote a distraught lieutenant colonel to Washington, "the provisions are almost out. The Militia refuse obedience to Captain Treat, and have underwent no sort of training." And Washington, himself, would write of these men: They "come in you cannot tell how; go, you cannot tell when; and act, you cannot tell where; consume your Provisions, exhaust your Stores; and leave you at last in a critical moment."[25]

Desertion was thus quite common among the Revolutionary forces. The hardships the men were called upon to endure, the inadequate and undependable pay, the recruitment of deserters from foreign armies, and the prevalence of unworthy officers were some of the reasons that caused enlistees to run away. Yet, in spite of all, Washington was reluctant to severely punish offenders. Among some one thousand penalties for desertion after October, 1776, about 70 percent called for light flogging. The remainder involved light fines or imprisonment.

Between 1800 and 1860 the disciplinary and desertion problems in the American armed forces differed as to time and place. There was great difficulty getting militia units to conform in the War of 1812. Desertion posed a major handicap to commanders on important posts. During the Mexican War some of the volunteers looted and behaved badly. Discipline varied from post to post, and from commander to commander. Under West Pointers or Annapolis men, it was strong and severe. Under volunteer officers it was often lacking.

Furthermore, there was some desertion in the war with Mexico. Some deserted from the Navy, which numbered only about eight thousand, because of the attractiveness of some Mexican cities as opposed to shipboard life. In the Army there were many German and Irish Catholics who, lured by promises of land and by religious factors, deserted to fight in the San Patricio Battalion for Mexico. Approximately four dozen of these were eventually caught and hanged.[26]

The peacetime frontier army also had its problems with discipline and desertion. The long marches, plus the low regard in which the public held the services, caused some 1,251 desertions in 1830. A frontier military doctor of 1852 wrote that each payday brought desertions on his post. These men, according to the physician, were "nearly all foreigners" who took off for Texas as soon as they had accumulated enough pay.[27]

Discipline during the Civil War was generally quite rigorous. Offenders were punished in a variety of ways. Some were drummed out of camp, some were hung by their thumbs, others were given the "Buck and Gag" treatment, and not a few were shot after appropriate trials. Bell I. Wiley, quoting War Department figures, indicates that there were 267 executions in the Union Army alone; 141 of these being for desertion.

Despite these impressive figures, however, desertion from both sides was never quite halted by the principle of execution. Indeed, the numbers of men who really deserted during the Civil War may never be known, partially because of the thin line of distinction between the case of a soldier who merely went home because of his principles concerning slavery, and the real act of desertion. Wiley quotes figures for a short period in 1863 which exemplify the nature of the problem in the Army of the Potomac. Some 592 men were tried for the offense of desertion, but only 291 were found guilty. Another prime example of the difficulty of understanding the desertion rate for the Civil War involves an Illinois regiment. Recruited from the southern part of the state, it reacted violently to Lincoln's emancipation policy and simply went home. The regiment was eventually disbanded, but none of the men was punished.[28]

By the 1890's the generally good discipline of the Navy had declined, while that of the Army had improved. It has been estimated that in the decade which preceded the Spanish-American War, desertions in the U. S. Navy ran from 9 to 17 percent of total personnel. Few men reenlisted in this service, mainly because of the lack of comfort on the heavy and unventilated ships.[29]

The record of the Army was much better, however. The morale of these Regulars was extremely high, and the behavior of the men was excellent. During the Spanish-American War the Fifth Corps, numbering twenty thousand men, most of whom were Regulars, established a spectacular record of not having a single court-martial.[30]

Discipline in the First World War differed from unit to unit. The earlier divisions, composed of Regulars and volunteers, performed and behaved generally well. Some draft divisions were made up of immigrants who could barely speak English, and of lower-class American types, and from these there was some trouble. There were also times when some Regular units kicked up trouble. In August of 1917 about one hundred soldiers of the Twenty-Fourth Infantry (Negro) rioted near Houston, Texas, causing a good deal of trouble. There were a few instances of Marines who shot off their own toes to avoid going into action. Altogether, however, there were only eleven executions of American fighting men in World War I; all for murder or rape. The complete lack of executions for desertion shows an increasing leniency among military authorities toward that misdemeanor.[31]

Despite the generally good record of American fighting men in World War II, on occasion the discipline either became lax, or failed completely. In North Africa, early in the war, General Patton was forced to lay out heavier disciplinary punishment for carelessness in dress and saluting. Enlisted men and officers alike were fined if they were found not wearing the protective helmet. On the other side of the world the men of Merrill's Marauders, after having been withdrawn from the Myitkyina fight, fell into a state of complete indiscipline. Men refused to salute, and there was a good deal of drinking and disorder in the rest camp set up for the unit.[32]

Considering the number of men who wore the uniform in World War II, there were very few real desertions. One writer states that about forty thousand men "bugged out" in the entire war. Of these, 2,854 were tried by general court-martial; forty-nine of them received the death sentence; but only one execution was ever realized. From the records available the picture of the deserter becomes quite clear. Only 1.5 of every thousand college-educated enlisted men was accused of desertion. Among those enlisted men having only a grade school education, the figure rises to 7.9 per thousand.[33]

Even in World War II, however, the line between real desertion and simple absence-without-leave remained a thin and indistinct one. Yet, the similarities in the character of both real deserters and AWOL's stand out clearly. The better educated types rarely went AWOL; the more poorly educated had a greater inclination to do so. One study, published before the end of the war, indicated that mental deficiencies or disorders caused 63 percent of the AWOL's, while the rest were brought about by military or domestic maladjustment. In a case study of one hundred AWOL's, Army officials found that only forty-three had been raised by both parents; seven had been raised in well-furnished homes; fifty had not been raised in homes having radios, refrigerators, or automobiles; twenty-five were mentally defective, the average IQ for all one hundred was 81.5; sixty-four were alcoholics, eighty-three had been AWOL before; and most of them were married.[34]

There was a real discipline problem in the early days of the Korean War. Many of the American soldiers immediately "bugged out" when their officers were killed. Sergeants and other noncoms could not enforce discipline, and officers were ignored. Told to take a Chinese gun position, one American soldier was reputed to have said: "You want it, you go take it, Lieutenant." Another soldier's reply was: "Take it, and shove it up your ass." Discipline among some American troops in Korean prison camps, as shall be shown later, failed to meet desirable standards.[35]

Desertion figures in the Korean War show some strange contradictions, however. Prior to the opening of the conflict, the rate of desertion in the Army was six per month per ten thousand troops. In the first year of the war, the rate dropped to 3.5 only to rise again after the beginning of the truce talks at Panmunjom. By January, 1953, however, it was still well under the World War II desertion rate of forty-five per ten thousand per month.

AWOL figures for the Korean War showed an average of 140 per month per ten thousand men. Prior to the conflict it had been 168 per month per ten thousand. In January, 1953, it was estimated that twenty thousand soldiers vanished each month, while seventeen thousand returned. From where did the real deserters come? Mainly the Army, which listed 11,000 from the start of the conflict to January, 1953. The Air Force listed 851, the Navy admitted 1,242, and only 697 Marines were said to have deserted.[36]

Though the Army has generally taken the lead in disciplinary problems, a fact partially explainable by the broad use of the draft for that particular service, the Navy and the Marines have had some troubles of this sort. After the famous Platoon 71 Case in the mid-1950's, involving the court-martial of Sergeant Matthew C. McKeon for overzealous disciplinary training, three of the members of that unit went AWOL, one Marine deserted, another was placed in the brig, and still another was charged with violation of discipline. In 1958 Hanson Baldwin wrote that the Navy recorded 48,000 courts-martial annually, and that 11 percent of the strength of the service received disciplinary action in a single year.[37]

What about U. S. troops in the Vietnam War? Though no figures have been published on desertion in this struggle, one can refer to the comments of General Westmoreland, who states: "There have been very few cases of this indeed, although there have been some. But, percentagewise, the number of offenses of that sort has been negligible."[38]

Despite the impression that may be left by figures on desertion, the American fighting man has never been as badly behaved as some have implied. Nor has he ever professed to be the model of good behavior. And he has never been a reliable candidate for membership in a temperance society. He has been, and is, like any other fighting man on the face of the earth in his drinking and social habits.

Before the Revolution, British officers argued Americans were unfit for the military service because most young men cared for nothing but drinking and gambling. During Washington's time drinking in the Continental Army was so common—each man being allowed so much liquor per day—that generals and subordinate officers gave up any attempts to control it. Drinking in the Continental Navy was likewise encouraged by the daily allotment, though it must be added that the liquor was probably safer to drink than kegwater, and it undoubtedly added some solace to the lonely weeks at sea.

During the 1830's the whiskey ration for the frontier soldier was one gill a day, but this was usually supplemented by purchases that could easily be made outside the gates of any fort. Service in the frontier establishment was so devoid of refinements, women, or entertainment, that it was not unusual for one-fifth of the men of any fort to be confined at any one time for drunkenness alone.

Liquor flowed freely during the Mexican War. Corpus Christi, for example, was the scene of daily drunken brawls between the volunteers from various states. Officers who attempted temperance campaigns were successful only on the surface. Men signed pledge cards and then went off to the nearest bar to celebrate the event.

The problem of drinking in the West became a significant one in the 1850's. The further men were removed from civilization, the greater the temptation to drink. Officers fell victim to the habit. Whole battalions went on binges. A liquor store at Fort Riley was taken over by armed and drunken soldiers in the early 1850's. One German, newly recruited into the Army, was moved to comment: "The greater part of the army consists of men who either do not care to work, or who, because of being addicted to drink, cannot find employment." Nor was the Navy immune to the difficulties caused by drinking. In 1858 the men of the U. S. S. *Powhatan* tangled with some equally drunken sailors from H. M. S. *Highflyer* and there was, until British troops arrived, a real brawl between the two groups of men. After soldiers came on the scene, however, the sailors of both navies joined forces to fight the common enemy.[39]

Drinking was a major problem for both sides in the Civil War. Among Confederate troops the attempts of general officers to curtail consumption of liquor met with little success. Richmond, Savannah, and other Southern cities were occasionally torn up by rioting groups of drunken Confederate soldiers. If there was anything unusual about "Johnny Reb," it was in the ingenuity he displayed in making alcoholic beverages from almost anything available—blackberries, apples, rhubarb, or dandelions.

Liquor posed some difficulties among the Union forces as well, and with an occasional Federal general or two. The Irish troops, who made up much of the Army of the Potomac, were hearty drinkers. They celebrated weddings, funerals, birthdays, victories, and defeats with whiskey. In the West, Federal German regiments, particularly those raised in the Peoria, Illinois, region, were the envy of other units, for they were always well supplied with beer. Federal Army work units were usually sent to their tasks with the usual refreshments on hand. As one Western private wrote: "Our Company, as did all the rest, drawed a bucket full of Whiskey and each mess got a quart, and it revived us up sure."

Later in the war, when it became more difficult to get volunteers, recruiting officers filled their quotas by filling up prospects. A young man, writing to Governor Yates of Illinois in 1863, complained that he had been given all he "could hold" by a recruiting officer, and had awakened the next day to find himself in the Army.[40]

As with the Confederates, the Northern troops were frequently precipitated into violence by drinking. The well-lubricated Eighteenth Illinois, in 1861, hanged a private for murder after a drumhead court-martial. "All parties felt that they had performed a virtuous act," a shocked Eastern visitor noted. In the same year the soldiers of the Eighth Illinois tore up a small town saloon because of an indiscrete comment by the bartender. A minstrel show, entertaining the troops at Birds Point, Missouri, turned into a riot when drunken troops took over the show. The Eighty-Second and Ninety-First

Illinois Regiments had a free-for-all in 1862 following a friendly gathering over a barrel of beer. Quincy and Centralia in Illinois, St. Louis, and an occasional southern town were subjected to damages because of drunken riots. When Lee finally surrendered, many regiments simply went wild. Men of the XIV Corps of the Federal Army, after emptying the whiskey from their canteens, filled them with gunpowder and set off some frightening explosions. But there was one poor Western soldier who didn't have it so good. "No one at these headquarters got drunk," was his complaint. "Care Why? Nary a drop of whiskey!"[41]

The gradual growth of the temperance movement in the United States after 1870 brought about some rather paradoxical situations within the armed forces. Much of the Army, and a good portion of the Navy, was made up of foreigners—Irish, Germans, Swedes, etc.—and drinking in the lower ranks of these services was very heavy. Among the officer corps, however, temperance made a good deal of headway, and in many military camps or stations, drinking was forbidden. This did not solve the problem, as one might guess, for the soldiers or sailors either bought the liquor outside, or made their own. The whole situation grew so contradictory that by 1899 the Secretary of War advised that facilities for drinking should be provided by the Army in order to stop the soldiers from imbibing in "vile resorts."

Drinking in the First World War was part and parcel of the trench warfare of the conflict. "Glor-ree-us, Glor-ree-us!" soldiers sang as they entered the trenches. "One keg of beer for the four of us." In the rear, soldiers and Marines found such a plenitude of liquor that it was almost impossible to abstain. "Booze and girls are both plentiful over here. . . ." one private wrote. "I have tried to carry myself just as straight in the army as I did before I was drafted." Others did not resist so hard. An American soldier involved in the Siberian expedition in 1919 wrote: "Three fourths or more of the men here never drank a drop in their lives before they came to Siberia but they sure came down the pole and fell off the water wagon, and they are drunk every pay day. . . ."[42]

In one small way, however, World War I was just a little bit different from most American wars. In the Civil War, Federal troops had celebrated the end of the fighting by drinking everything they could find. In World War II the news of peace brought similar reactions; the crew of one naval vessel had only one man who was sober and available for duty on that occasion. The horrors of World War I brought a more subdued response. As Mark Sullivan described it:

At the armistice hour there was no demonstration by shouting, slapping each other on the back, dancing, and tossing of hats. When the noise of battle ceased there was a restful peace that passeth man's understanding and his ability to describe; there was no hilarity or jubilation. Among the Germans opposite there was considerable shouting, singing, beating of drums, and blowing of bugles, all up and down the line—a remarkable contrast to the actions of American troops.[43]

The GI of World War II was exceedingly inventive in methods for producing liquor. In the Navy the standard method was to concoct a fermented beverage out of raisins and pineapple juice, or anything else which was available, and to place the liquid in the ship's refrigerator. Once the water in the container had frozen, it was removed, leaving an extremely powerful drink. Marines and soldiers on isolated islands condensed the alcohol out of hair tonics for their "jungle juice," or if they were more fortunate, they drank captured Japanese beer or rice wine.

But the need for invention occurred only in special circumstances. Officer's clubs and bars for enlisted men supplied the normal desires of most men. Ships carried large supplies of American beer which were made available to shore parties. Troops in Europe, especially those in Italy, "liberated" substantial quantities of wine, which they often carried in their canteens instead of water.

As in the Civil War, explosions of violence sometimes resulted from an overconsumption of liquor. The end of basic training often brought on celebrations which had sorry conclusions. "I'm going to blow every nickel. . . ." stated one soldier at the finish of his training period. "Then I got to line up a few hot dates. That ought to take care of the fifty."[44] The "hot dates" were sometimes prostitutes, or girls who would "jackroll" the soldier once he had drunk himself into oblivion.

Overseas the explosions were unpredictable and always wild. Pilots in England were inclined to drinking bouts that ended in physical dares or fights. Thunderbolt fliers, drunk, sometimes amused themselves by firing their pistols into the ceiling. In Burma in 1943 the Marauders celebrated Christmas by firing tracers and magnesium flares throughout the camp. Officers sent out to put down the drunken riot found their men "dancing about like satyrs, firing revolvers into the sky." During the Leyte-Samar campaign in 1944, the Second Brigade of the First Cavalry Division so upset the commanding general with their wild behavior that he called brigade headquarters to settle the situation. "Jeeze, General," replied a lone sergeant on duty, "it's New Years Eve, ain't it?" The general, finding himself at a loss to reply to this logic, hung up the phone and went to bed.[45]

On the occasion of the false rumors of victory over Japan, many island garrisons, as well as those on ships offshore, abandoned all pretext of discipline. One LST, off Saipan, was manned almost entirely by a drunken crew. Several officers passed out for days, and the officer-of-the-deck fell overboard. Ship's crews fired signal flares at nearby vessels, and in some cases, captains opened their beer lockers. On Okinawa the violence of the false victory celebration was so great that scores of men were killed or injured.

In the Korean War much of the liquor problem was handled by "rest and recreation" furloughs in Japan. Invariably, however, each soldier returning to the front from Tokyo brought back substantial quantities of liquor for friends in his company. In Vietnam the sale of liquor, much of it obtained from blackmarket supplies, has become a major industry of the country. Saigon and Danang, both of which have concentrations of United States servicemen, have large numbers of bars, some of which cater to white Americans, and some of which cater to American Negro soldiers. As in other wars there is occasional violence in Vietnam. Some have had a racial overtone, and have merely involved American soldiers. Others, such as the fight between American servicemen and Japanese sailors in Vietnam in 1963, have simply resulted from too much liquor being available.[46]

It is to be recognized that life in the service unites elements from all classes of society. Most American fighting men behave as one would expect young and healthy males to act. As in the service of any country, however, there are always some Americans who, because of their background, reflect badly upon the uniform of their country.

Liquor is only one of the troubles that all military authorities must handle. So is gambling, an age-old concomitant of military life. Gambling was common among Revolutionary soldiers. In the war with Mexico, such games as Old Sledge, chuck-a-luck, and poker were very popular with soldiers. One Federal soldier of the Civil War wrote that he couldn't sleep because of the continuous gaming that went on in his tent. Another told his wife that "card playing and swaring" were the two main occupations of his regiment. As in the Federal Army, the main games of chance among the Confederates were poker, chuck-a-luck, raffling, faro, euchre, and keno.

In the Spanish-American War, pitching pennies was a great pastime of soldiers. The Western soldiers of that conflict generally played stud poker; the Eastern troops played draw poker. Craps, a game highly popular among Negro regiments, rapidly spread throughout the Army as one of the most popular forms of gambling. In World War I, gambling was so widespread that many officers became sincerely concerned about the state of American morality. Soldiers rolled "the bones" night and day, they sometimes cut for high card at $500 a wager, and one sergeant was reputed to have sent home $8,000 which he had made from gambling. Harvey Cushing, the famed Army physician, wrote: "I've confessed before that we were a blasphemous and a thieving army thus this gambling business never came home to me acutely as on this voyage home. If it's as widespread as these young men admit, I'm not sure but that wine and women are less serious evils."[47]

Cushing should have been well aware of the fact that gambling, and all that went with it, were old problems to the fighting services. Washington constantly warned his officers against vice and immorality during the Revolution. In the Army before 1812 there were rumors that many officers kept stables of prostitutes available to their men, and that even General Anthony Wayne took a mistress with him on his campaigns. Near frontier posts there were many Indian women who could be purchased for a mere trifle.[48]

Prostitution flourished wherever the American Army campaigned in Mexico in 1847. During the Civil War women became such a problem to Army authorities that in Memphis, for example, the prostitutes were shipped out of town *en masse*. The Confederates had the same problems. Bell I. Wiley states that records show that in July, 1861, there were 17.8 new cases of gonorrhea and 3.8 new cases of syphilis reported for each thousand men of certain Confederate regiments. The Tenth Alabama, which reported to Richmond with a mean strength of 1,063 in the summer of 1861, reported sixty-two new cases of gonorrhea and six of syphilis for the month of July in that same year.[49]

As far as the Spanish-American War was concerned, the war was virtually over before the prostitutes had time to gather their own forces. At every large Army camp thereafter, however, prostitutes could be found in large numbers. A large "red-light" district in East St. Louis served the soldiers stationed at Jefferson Barracks in St. Louis prior to 1917, and to the time of the closing of the base. During the 1916 campaign against Pancho Villa, prostitution was to be found on both sides of the border—in Columbus, New Mexico, or in the Mexican border towns. In Mexico the women lived in unsanitary shacks and catered to long lines of waiting soldiers. One Mexican woman admitted to having served as many as sixty American soldiers on one night, forty on the next, with fifty customers being the normal nightly business.[50]

Mankind's oldest business flourished as never before in the First World War. In the United States large prostitution centers were to be found in Deming, New Mexico; El Paso, Waco, San Antonio, in Texas; Jacksonville, Florida; Savannah, Charleston, and Columbia, in South Carolina; and in Montgomery, Alabama. In France the mademoiselles were plentiful and inexpensive.

The sex problem in World War II followed traditional as well as newer patterns for the American fighting man. In Honolulu, where prostitution was driven underground, "massage parlors" drew long cordons of men. Here the prostitutes were quite often Filipino or Japanese by national background. In some cases strange and romantic liaisons grew between these women and some American soldiers. One young Midwesterner even found himself invited to meet the husband of the girl he had been dating for several months.

In World War II, the Korean War, and Vietnam, as shall be shown in a succeeding chapter, sexual habits of the American fighting man were moved out of the traditional arenas of houses of prostitution, and into different types of relationships. The well-paid and well-dressed American soldier in Europe, plus the poor economic conditions and the shortage of civilian men, allowed for liaisons which were based on convenience. British, French, and German women became kept mistresses to many rear area soldiers during World War II. In Korea the practice of maintaining a mistress became an accepted notion. In Vietnam, the American habit of supporting a monogamous but somewhat expensive relationship with local women has partially upset the economic and social structure of the country.

It has always been true of the American fighting man that, since the development of the modern mail system, he has spent much of his time writing letters. Some of these were to members of his immediate family; a great many more have been just to girls. The Civil War soldier carried on a correspondence with any girl willing to reciprocate. To his friends in other regiments, he very often wrote about his feminine acquaintances. "I found the sweetest girl here that ever man look at. . . ." a Federal soldier wrote from Savannah. "I swear I was never so bewitched before." Another Federal soldier, replying to a friend's letter about sexual conquests, stated: "I see you are as great a women's man as ever. Instead of soldiering having altered the tendency of your mind from women

I see you are still prone to go in raptures about the beauty of the feminine sex."[51]

Some American fighting men were no different in World Wars I and II. A Peoria, Illinois, soldier wrote to 150 different women in 1918, and his wife typed the letters. Robert Sherrod, en route to Tarawa in World War II, saw Marines writing to four or five New Zealand girls in one day. One LCT sailor maintained two common law wives in Mississippi, and wrote identical letters to both. Almost every single man, and a good many married ones, kept correspondence with more than two women.[52]

The letters of fighting men to wives always include a good deal of sexual reference. A Federal soldier, complaining that he had vacated his tent to accommodate a friend and his wife, wrote his own spouse: "Never mind I am going to see my woman some day & then maybe Ill make him vacate." Shocked by the appearance of one wife in his camp, a Union soldier wrote to his wife: "But it seems as though she might stand it without being knocked up for 9 mos longer."[53]

Almost every American fighting man informs his wife by mail about the hardships of sexual deprivation. A Federal soldier in the South wrote his wife that he had seen so few women that he would "freeze to the first one" he came into contact with. A doughboy of World War I warned his wife: "Take a long look at the floor, Martha, because when I get home, you aren't going to see anything but the ceiling for a long, long time!" A dive bomber pilot, writing from Guadalcanal in World War II, argued that all the men in his outfit wanted to get home and "raise damn good hell with their wives. . . ." And a soldier in Italy, writing poignantly to his wife, admitted: "I sometimes feel a little ashamed at the way I long to come home to you."[54]

What the armed forces allow the serviceman to do with his life is probably most likely in the direction of his natural inclinations. A college boy, raised with high moral standards, is likely to behave no worse in uniform than out of it. Another type, brought up in an atmosphere of laxity, is also likely to be lax in his behavior in service. A really small percentage of American soldiers in any one period, or in any one war, fell victim to venereal disease, or made a practice of drinking themselves into unconsciousness while on leave. A Negro soldier of World War II wrote that, despite the occasional drinking among his comrades, he was "too much of a conscientious sentimentalist to participate in a lot of their reckless ways of living." A white American soldier in China in the same conflict admitted that his first taste of strong liquor had come from the hands of a Catholic priest. General Patton, who probably made fewer allowances for bad behavior on the part of his soldiers than most other general officers, once stated: "All our soldiers do not drink like beasts. In fact, the lack of drinking in our Army is remarkable."[55]

What does take place in the character of the young American fighting man is a good deal of maturation. The young boy merely acts the part of a man until he really does become one. In World War II the young man inducted into the service usually did two things upon first donning the uniform. If he had not smoked before, he bought a pack of cigarettes: "Old soldiers" always smoked, he usually concluded. Second, he purchased as many ribbons as he thought he might be entitled to wear, and occasionally more than that. These he flaunted, that is until he found that real veterans of conflict seldom wore their ribbons while on leave.

Another evidence of maturation comes with the adoption of military jargon. Desiccated potatoes to the Civil War soldier were *desecrated* potatoes. In World War I salmon was called *goldfish,* canned beef was called *monkey meat,* coffee was *java,* stew was *deep Sea,* and meat balls covered with dough were called *hash with overcoats.* In World War II the various army rations, as well as that old Navy standby, chipped beef on toast, had various but unprintable names.

When there has not been an established military jargon for particular situations or practices, the American fighting man has provided them. The World War I equivalent of SNAFU (situation normal, all fouled up) was GOK (God only knows). The doughboy was SOL (soldier out of luck); the GI was FUBAR (fouled up beyond all recall). The GI "sacked out"; the doughboy performed FTD duty, which literally translated was "feeding the dog." The American Marine in Vietnam doesn't shoot the enemy; he "zaps" him.

A World War II study of American fighting men indicated that most soldiers and sailors were as tame in their behavior as could be expected. For those stationed in Britain, life was a bit livelier; most men saving their money for possible weekends in London. More than one-half the men questioned went to church, only 37 percent drank liquor while off duty, many fighting men liked to spend off-duty time listening to dance music or news on the radio or reading.[56]

These findings are well supported by evidence. Americans, wherever they were stationed, generally listened to Armed Forces Radio. A young officer with Merrill's Marauders wrote of listening to an American station while crossing a six-thousand-foot pass in Burma. "That night," he stated, "was one of those rare times when we were able to pick up a program of good music from a U. S. Army station in Australia. It included Marian Anderson singing 'My Heart at Thy Sweet Voice,' the spiritual 'Heaven,' and the Largo from Xerxes." Annual football classics, such as the Army-Navy game, were listened to avidly by ordinary soldiers and seamen.

Many soldiers in World War II owned small phonographs. A CBI soldier, belying the common charge that Americans were uncultured and crude, once wrote of having purchased records of the "Nutcracker Suite," "Vaise Triste" by Sibelius, the "1812 Overture," and the "Tocata and Fugue in D Minor" by Bach. Many American soldiers stationed in England were proud collectors of Glenn Miller and Benny Goodman records, and also boosted the sales of recordings by their favorite British singer, Vera Lynn.

From the Civil War to the present most American fighting men have been fairly active readers; thanks to the growth of public education. Federal soldiers, from 1861 to 1865, were partial to newspapers and tracts; the latter being either of a religious or military nature. *Uncle Tom's Cabin* was widely read by the Yankee soldier, as were more adventurous stories such as *Masked Batteries, The True Story of Lucknow,* and *The Soldier's Talisman.* Some

Confederate soldiers, as did their Federal enemies, delved into heavier stuff—Thiers' *French Revolution,* Swift's *Gulliver's Travels,* and Dumas' *Count of Monte Cristo.* Magazines and books of poetry found ready acceptance on both sides of the battleline.[57]

Among the professional American fighting men from 1865 to 1917, there was always a goodly number of individuals who read anything upon which they could lay their hands. Newspapers were particularly prized in the West because of their relative scarcity. Naval men, who had access to bookstores in larger ports, read a variety of materials. A sailor aboard the U. S. S. *Buffalo* in 1911 wrote in his diary that he had read a good many of Scott's works, Thackeray's *Vanity Fair,* and a book entitled *How to Know Architecture.* A few months later, while his ship was docked in Japan, he read a book called *Characteristics of China.* During midsummer the same sailor ordered from New York a number of books on mathematics, nautical science, naval architecture, shipbuilding, mechanical drawing, and chemistry. This young man was only an ordinary seaman; not an officer.[58]

The World War I doughboy evidenced less concern for reading than any American soldier for some generations. The ratlike existence in the trenches did not lend itself to books, and furthermore many of the young men were immigrant Americans, who while possibly literate, could scarcely be expected to be interested in the great literature of the day. Magazines were popular, however, as were newspapers. Not only could they be read, but they offered further utility in the trenches.

The American fighting man of World War II was a determined reader. Each naval vessel had it own library, and books that were bought by sailors themselves were passed from hand to hand. Magazines, such as *Life* and *Time,* found a ready home on shipboard. GI's and Marines read whenever they could, and usually from camp libraries or from literature sent from home. *Yank* and *Stars and Stripes,* both service publications, were popular.

All in all, reading in World War II, as would be expected, ranged from high level literature to the grossest type. Sex plots were prized literary possessions, as was the most crass pornography. So were pulp publications. "The boys all like to read the comics you send," wrote one GI to his aunt. Some men held to higher forms of literature. One soldier advised his family that he had read all of Shakespeare and Hemingway since his induction into the service. A young naval officer was able to complete a Ph.D. dissertation in economics for a New York university while at sea. Some men just read anything they could find. An Illinois soldier wrote:

Spend a lot of my time reading. I belong to the Book of the Month Club & special service sends pocket size editions over. Some of the boys get all kinds of magazines & I've spent an enjoyable evening with Good Housekeeping believe it or not. Even memorized some of the recipes for future reference.[59]

For the American of the Korean and Vietnam wars, life was and is much the same. "Hurry up and wait" was the GI's sarcastic reference to life in World War II, and it hasn't changed much since. Reading is the great eraser of time and place. "Yesterday I spent a leisurely day reading a book. . . ." an American in Korea wrote. "It was quite interesting and enabled me to lay around while my men were working. . . ." The American soldier in Vietnam is very likely a more diligent reader than his predecessors. He illustrates the importance of reading materials.[60]

Through the years it has become traditional for United States military officials to bring entertainment to military camps and bases. Movies were popular with the doughboys of World War I. Their showing in World War II was greatly anticipated and enjoyed by men in every theater of war. Live entertainment is now also a tradition. The comedian Bob Hope has brought laughter to fighting men in three different wars. USO entertainers have played to packed audiences from the beginning of World War II to the present. Nor is a Hollywood sex symbol necessary in order to pack a base showhouse. The Metropolitan Opera soprano Lili Pons played to large audiences in Iran in World War II. Yehudi Menuhin, the violinist, drew big crowds in Panama, and the Shakespearian actor Maurice Evans successfully played *Macbeth* in the Pacific.

THE REVOLUTIONARY WAR: Uniforms shown include the Third
Pennsylvania Regiment, the Second South Carolina Regiment,
Washington's Guard, the Eleventh Virginia and the Maryland Riflemen.
(*U.S. War Department General Staff photograph*)

UNION SAILORS: Aboard the gunboat *Mendota* during the Civil War. Note the wide representation of races and nationalities. Color was no bar to a rating at this time. (*U.S. Signal Corps photograph*)

INFANTRYMEN: A company of the Third U.S. Infantry Regiment, Fort Larned, 1867. The picture indicates little change in dress uniform and drill practices from the Civil War period.
(*Kansas State Historical Society, Topeka, photograph*)

INDIAN SCOUTS: Captain Taylor's Indian Scouts, Pine Ridge Agency, South Dakota, in the 1880's. These fighting men apparently lived in the tepees to the rear. The word "notet" is a misspelling of "noted."
(*Nebraska State Historical Society photograph*)

NEGRO SOLDIERS: Soldiers of the Twenty-Fifth Infantry Regiment stationed at Fort Snelling, Minnesota, in the 1880's. (*U.S. Signal Corps photograph*)

DRESS REVIEW: Troop A, Twelfth Cavalry, Fort Robinson, 1907. Personnel of the U.S. Army were of a high quality at the turn of the century. (*Nebraska State Historical Society photograph*)

THE MARINES: A machine gun crew of World War I in France during the winter of 1917–1918. (*U.S. Defense Department photograph*)

DOUGHBOYS: A 37mm Howitzer crew in action against German positions. Once again, the GI proved himself a tough, resilient and resourceful opponent. (*U.S. Defense Department photograph*)

THE SILENT SERVICE: Submariners are a special breed. Here, American sailors in World War II bunk alongside hulking torpedoes.
(*U.S. Navy Department photograph*)

TENACITY: Pfc. James R. Kennedy of the Twenty-Sixth Regiment, First Division, aims at a sniper who wounded him a few moments before (note bullet hole) in World War II action inside Germany.
(*U.S. Army photograph*)

BACK FOR A REST: Marines on Saipan come back for some rest after twenty straight days of slugging it out with their Japanese foes. (*U.S. Defense Department photograph*)

SANSEI: Japanese-American infantrymen of the 100th Infantry Battalion moving up to the front in the Velletri area of Italy in May of 1944. (*U.S. Army photograph*)

DRAWING A BEAD: A Marine on Okinawa lines up a sniper in the sights of his tommy gun and prepares to move forward. (*U.S. Marine Corps photograph*)

P.O.W.: Pfc. Truman A. Franklin was captured by the Germans and forced to work at slave camps. He survived on a daily diet of one-sixth of a loaf of bread and potato-peeling soup. Here he enjoys a chocolate bar after being liberated. His weight was down to 100 lbs. (*U.S. Army photograph*)

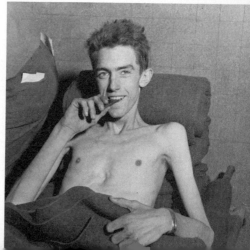

SURVIVORS: These just-liberated GIs are soldiers, sailors and marines captured on Bataan and Corregidor, left behind by retreating Japanese when U.S. troops entered Manila. (*U.S. Army photograph*)

THEY HELD OUT: These released American prisoners refused to die in captivity, despite brutal beatings, forced marches and almost no medical care. Here they await transfer to a hospital. (*U.S. Army photograph*)

MERRILL'S MARAUDERS: American GIs and Kachins of Burma formed this fighting team during World War II. This was one of the outstanding "special combat forces" organized. (*U.S. Army photograph*)

ON THE FIRING LINE: Battling for a ridge on Okinawa, these Marines show the toughness and aggressiveness that the GI is famous for. (*U.S. Defense Department photograph*)

HOUSE TO HOUSE: Two infantrymen move through the rubble of Ludwigshafen, Germany, searching the remains for German snipers. This ferreting operation is one of the most dangerous assignments of war. (*U.S. Army photograph*)

INCHING UP IWO: A team of GIs on Iwo Jima prepares to move forward. In one of the bloodiest and most hard-fought operations in the history of warfare, American GIs distinguished themselves for their valor and determination against a well-entrenched and stubborn foe. (*U.S. Defense Department photograph*)

TAKING FIVE: Leathernecks of the Seventh Marines catch a few moments of rest during their heroic breakout from Chosin, Korea, during the winter of 1950.
(*U.S. Defense Department photograph*)

COMRADESHIP: A radioman comforts a buddy who broke down after surviving a battle in which nearly all of his platoon was wiped out. The conditions in Vietnam, both physical and psychological, have been some of the most difficult ever faced by American soldiers.
(*U.S. Army photograph*)

AMERICAN INGENUITY: Two Army chaplains conduct a baptismal service by immersion in Vietnam. The GI has long had a reputation for adapting, and this is nowhere so evident as in Vietnam. (*U.S. Army photograph*)

READY TO FIRE: A machine-gunner and his assistant get ready to go into action. Note the names on the helmets. (*U.S. Defense Department photograph*)

TAKING THE HIGH GROUND: Marines move up a rugged slope as they take on North Vietnamese regulars. These men made heavy contact with a well-fortified enemy armed with automatic weapons. The landscape and type of action reminded some veterans of action at Tarawa in World War II. (*U.S. Defense Department photograph*)

TOUGH CONDITIONS: Fire team members of a Marine company wade through a waist-high stream roofed over by dense jungle just south of the Demilitarized Zone in some of the most savage and difficult fighting ever demanded of American GIs. (*U.S. Defense Department photograph*)

PAUSE FOR PRAYER: Paratroopers of the 173rd Airborne Brigade pause for religious services in front of a redwood and brick chapel they built in their "spare time" at Bien Hoa, Vietnam. (*U.S. Army photograph*)

Actually, the presentation of live entertainment for American fighting men goes back to the Civil War. The well-known Lombard troupe entertained Federal troops at Vicksburg. The famous Hutchinson family gave performances to troops in the East. Minstrel shows, plays, and glee clubs were occasionally visited upon Billy Yank and Johnny Reb. Dances and cotillions were popular with officers on both sides.

The American fighting man, with time on his hands, has resorted to a variety of ways to fight boredom. The sutler of an earlier day, the ship's store and post-exchange of more recent times, have always been seductive to the wallet. A professional soldier of the 1850's wrote: "The rations are not touched. The men live on dainties until their money is gone. Then they are not satisfied. As regards myself, I must confess that I have not saved a cent. . . ." How familiar this must sound to an aging veteran of World War II![61]

Athletic activities have likewise been popular with the camp-bound soldier or sailor. Baseball, quoits, foot races, broad jumping, and wrestling were common in Civil War camps. World War I military authorities encouraged baseball, and every camp sponsored boxing programs. In World War II, basketball, baseball, and touch or tackle football were the most popular of sports; though there were other games, which found willing participants. "We play volleyball two or three times a week," wrote one GI in Italy. Within three days of the Normandy landing there was an almost continuous soccer-football game between British and American sailors on the mine-laden Omaha Beach.[62]

From early days to the present the loneliness of nights in camp or at sea has been lightened by music. The American fighting man has, by nature, a love of music. The Mexican word *gringo* is reputed to have come from the American soldier's predilection for the song "Green Grows the Laurel" in 1846. Confederate and Federal soldiers were great singers in the Civil War. "John Brown," "Old Hundred," "Home Sweet Home," "Come Where My Love Lies Dreaming," and "Johnny Fill Up the Bowl" were songs of the night for Billy Yank. They allowed for close harmony about the campfire. "When Johnny Comes Marching Home," and "The

Battle Cry of Freedom" were songs for the road. During the fighting in the Wilderness in 1864, and in the Federal withdrawal from Chickamauga, the final Yankee taunt to the victorious enemy was:

> We'll rally round the flag,
> Boys, we'll rally once again,
> Shouting the battle-cry of Freedom.

As in any war, songs crossed Civil War battle lines without difficulty. The "Bonnie Blue Flag" had both Confederate and Federal versions. "Home Sweet Home" was popular with the Southerners, as was the "Just Before the Battle, Mother." "Lorena," a beautiful and sentimental ballad, and "All Quiet Along the Potomac Tonight" were fireside songs for Johnny Reb. "Dixie" and "My Maryland" were battlefield songs of the Confederate Army.

In the Spanish-American War the songs of the American fighting man were not dissimilar from those of the Civil War period. Soldiers of any period are likely to have a collection of tunes ranging from the rollicking to the sentimental, and from the proud to the profane. "The Banks of the Wabash," "Sweet Marie," and "I Don't Like No Cheap Man" illustrate the variety indulged in by the 1898 soldier. By far and away the most popular song of the day was "There'll Be a Hot Time in the Old Town Tonight," which "Mr. Dooley," the most quotable humorist of the day, described as the "new national anthem."[63]

Most of the popular songs of World War I were rousers. "Good Morning, Mr. Zip, Zip, Zip" was a modified dance tune, which had numerous camp versions. George M. Cohan's "Over There" was a well-used marching song, which inspired a delightful parody starting with the words: "Underwear, underwear." The "Mademoiselle From Armentières" spawned hundreds of verses—most of them unprintable.

The doughboy was a singing throwback to his Civil War grandfather. He sang everywhere, and all the time. Singing coaches, professional stage people, were placed in camps to encourage vocal exercise. The men sang in the trenches, in the camps, in theaters, and on the streets. "You have probably heard of Uncle Sam's singing army. . . ." wrote an Illinois soldier. "I have seen troops embarking, regiment after regiment, all singing." A young Army officer wrote of the singing "problem" at sea:

> After we got out of hearing of the Docks and no lights lit at all as there were liable to be Submarines laying in waiting for us most any old place it was not necessary to repeat the orders for a day or so as every man on the ship had a funny feeling including myself as I never did think I would make good feed for the Fishes but as the time wore on the men got careless and it was necessary to keep after them to keep the quiet especially at night as they liked to sing. . . .[64]

Singing in World War II was usually heard only in the training camps. Young air cadets, stationed in colleges about the country, almost always sang as they marched from one building to another. Naval midshipmen at Notre Dame, Northwestern, and Columbia followed the same practice. Marines, while in boot camp, were drilled in the traditional songs of the Corps.

Many of the songs were service-connected. The Air Force, the Navy, the Marine Corps, and parts of the Army were partial to their own hymns or "fight" songs. "Remember Pearl Harbor" was one "civilian" song which enjoyed early popularity with American fighting men. "God Bless America," the traditional "Battle Hymn of the Republic" (Southerners sang their own version), and "The Yellow Rose of Texas" were well-established songs of the war.

By 1944, however, most of the services had settled upon certain original, adapted, or adopted songs. The infantry developed a cadence-chant, which was usually led by the most expert "chanter," and which started with the words "Sound off." These choruses, some not of the parlor variety, were quite similar to the old Zouave chants of the Civil War.

There was not a great deal of singing in the Pacific during World War II. The conflict there simply did not lend itself to music. In Europe, however, the story was different. If there was ever a campfire song in this conflict, it was the German "Lili Marlene," which like Civil War songs, crossed the battle lines. There was also a highly popular British ditty—very bawdy, and usually sung on the streets at night by British girls and American soldiers—which had as its chorus: "Roll me over, lay me down, and do it again."[65]

There was little singing in Korea, and few songs came out of that conflict. Occasionally a "hillbilly" song like "Heartbreak Hill" gained a modicum of popularity, but nothing like that of the doughboy's "Over There." The same has been true of Vietnam, which has produced one mildly popular song about the "Green Berets." If there is a reason for the paucity of singing in the two most recent wars, it may lie in the establishment of the Armed Forces Radio Service. These radio stations, plus the easy availability of radio receivers, negates the need for group singing.

Yet, to say that there was no singing at all in Korea, and that none has existed in Vietnam, is wrong. The "cadence chant" of the infantry was and is still popular. The Marines, when escaping from the Chochin Reservoir trap in Korea, marched out singing the "Marine Hymn." S. L. A. Marshall, writing of the Eighth Army in Korea, stated: "But I have heard them singing as they moved along in single file on either side of the road carrying their fighting baggage and sometimes their barracks bags, for lack of any other transport." And more recently Richard Tregaskis has written of listening to American pilots in Vietnam singing such songs as "The Jolly Coachman" and "I Want to Go Home."[66]

Though outward forms may have changed, the need of the American fighting man for music has not. This is a basic factor in military life. One may suspect that no fighting man can do without music; it uplifts the spirit, or it evokes memories of home. In one sense the same may be said about "leave" or "liberty." One may be sure that no military force could survive without allowing the soldier to escape from the confines of military life every so often. Here again the outward forms may change—"leave" is now called "rest and recuperation," or "R and R"—but the behavior of the ordinary American while away from camp has not.

It can be safe to say that, historically speaking, the American fighting man on leave has sought the kind of society he might have sought on Saturday night in his own home town. The one exception may come in the realm of sexual behavior, which is doubtlessly affected by conditions of war or peace. The possibility of sexual contacts may be seriously increased, as in Europe in World Wars I and II, or as in Japan and Korea during the Korean War. Otherwise, just where the on-leave soldier or sailor eats, or the entertainment he seeks, is determined by his environmental background and by the natural maturation of each man.

Up to the beginning of World War II, when America remained predominantly rural, many American boys had never been away from home before donning the uniform. During the Civil War many a Western boy had seen nothing but the prairies of his own country before his enlistment; a factor that helped to determine his behavior while on leave. "I saw for the first time the sky and water meet," a young Union soldier, destined to be killed at Missionary Ridge, wrote after he had seen Chicago. Such wide-eyed responses were not peculiar to that war only. A young sailor of World War I, after having seen New York City for the first time, wrote: "I wouldn't mind living in New York City. It sure is a lively place, and there are skyscrapers and lively girls here." A World War II Navy veteran remembers his first view of the same great city from a New Jersey dock. He had heard the phrase "Bagdad on the Hudson" before, but now it made sense. To this young boy, who had never seen a city larger than twenty thousand, New York appeared as the enchanted city.[67]

Generally speaking, the American fighting man is as well behaved as can be expected while away from camp; though it must be added that the kind of entertainment he seeks on his first liberty may differ considerably from that of his last. Federal soldiers of the Civil War, off-duty for their first time, usually sought out Sanitary Commission hostels where they wrote letters or played dominoes or cards. Later, as the armies moved into the South, their horizons broadened. Western soldiers on their first visit to New Orleans went sightseeing in the French Quarter, visited Lake Pontchartrain, and visited a statue of Henry Clay. The second visit to New Orleans was broken up by a call at the barber shop, where each soldier got the "works," and by a meal at one of the better restaurants. A third visit included a theatrical performance, and perhaps a girl-hunting expedition into the French Quarter.

This subtle change in the life of each American fighting man is best described by a professional soldier of the pre-World War I period. His earliest excursions into town invariably ended in establishments operated by the Y.M.C.A., the Salvation Army, or the Knights of Columbus. Later he sought out the dime-a-dance halls. "Anyhow, it was a little different from the Y.M.C.A., where everything was cut and dried for you," he wrote. "Here you were on your own and not obligated to anyone—you paid for your fun." Such desires to be free from restraint are buried deeply in the American soldier. A World War II private, writing his parents that he wished to stay at a hotel during his visit to them, explained: "I just want a lot of night freedom for a change. . . ."

For many American fighting men in recent wars the happiest accident that could happen on any leave was to come into contact with hospitable foreign or American families. During World War I it was the custom of some British families to invite American soldiers to meals. Other such meetings were accidental. A 1918 American soldier wrote: "Bill and I craving to get away from the city jumped on a trolley, jumping off at a small county town. We met some very hospitable people, who have entertained us wonderfully each time we go to see them."[68]

Visits to French families in World War I were arranged through slightly different circumstances. Quite often doughboys would "adopt" a French family, supply them with canned goods, and pay occasional visits to the family circle. In other instances, familial contacts were made when a French girl brought her new American boyfriend home.

In World War II the pattern was similar. The British made rather exceptional efforts to get to know Americans. British volunteers worked in Red Cross hostels. GI's were invited to spend Sundays with British families. The girl-boy relationship likewise inspired familial contacts. The last was also true with the French after 1944; though in general, French families were inclined to view American soldiers as merely another brand of soldier with which they had to contend.

Despite occasional leaves, or sports, or recreational facilities, life in the service is, for the most part, filled with a rather routine existence. This is traditionally so, and probably accounts for the great masses of letters the American fighting man is accustomed to writing. And it was just as true in frontier days as today. A soldier wrote in the 1850's: "We are experiencing the most favorable side of soldiering now; it is either a very lazy tedious sort of life, or else one that demands the last ounce of physical strength. . . ." Of his comrades the same soldier explained: "Others entertain themselves with continual chatter, one telling the others what he claims to have experienced—truth or falsehood, it matters not, so long as the story entertains."

Much of the time of the Civil War soldier was spent in winter quarters, or in preparing for campaigns to come. Polishing weapons, pressing clothes, writing letters, playing cards, or just talking helped to pass the time. Among Federal soldiers and Confederate alike, there was considerable griping about everything—general officers, food, living conditions, Negroes, and the two governments. The routine was fixed and usually unvarying. As an Illinois soldier described it: roll call was followed by a breakfast of bread, meat, and coffee; then followed a two-hour drill; a short time was allotted to mending and fixing; the noon meal consisted of bread, meat, and potatoes; and then there was more drill. The only relief, to this young soldier, was the Sunday appearance of "plenty of preaching preachers," and an occasional chance to go into the nearest town in search of entertainment.[69]

Despite the Hollywood-inspired romanticism surrounding America's frontier army, life for a soldier in those far-off posts was interminably dull. Commenced by a bugle call in the morning, it was filled with little but tedium until the last note of "taps" echoed off the desert plains. Nor was the life of the pre-World War I professional sailor any different. Following are a group of excerpts from the diary of a 1912 fleet enlisted man:

Nothing unusual other than the change of executive officers.

We had fire and collision drill during the forenoon, and nothing further than this happened during the day.

The same old humdrum, nothing of note. I read as much as I can.

Only a lack of heavy rains has made a difference in these two days.

Remained aboard all day and read most of the time. Spent the day about as yesterday. Spent the day as I did the 18th. Spent the day aboard reading. [These are all excerpts from one week in February, 1912.]

Was not able to sleep at all during the early morning hours but lay in berth and rose about 7:00 A.M. or little after and had breakfast. The rolling of the ship increased during the forenoon and at 12:00 we had lunch under difficulties, it consisted of sardines on toast and a stew of beef carrotts [*sic*] and potatoes and finished with fruit, oranges and bananas.[70]

How similar these comments are to those of a World War II soldier, who wrote:

Every night we go to a movie or drop in at the U.S.O. dance but it doesn't help the boredom any. In the morning up at six, make the beds, sweep and then chow. Back from chow and mop the floor, then there is nothing to do for the rest of the day but dodge the sergeant when he is looking for men for fatigue details.[71]

One of the concomitants of such living is the inevitable camp rumors. These wild stories, completely untraceable in origin, circulate like fire in dry timber. In the Civil War they were called "grape cuttings," and they were passed along a "grape vine." In more recent days the Navy term "scuttlebutt" has been used to describe them. Both Federal and Confederate soldiers were avid rumormongers in 1863. One Northern soldier wrote that, because of the rumors that Grant had taken Vicksburg, "everybody is laughing and in good spirits about going home . . . the next day we hear that our men are getting whipped everywhere." Another Federal soldier, tired of such rumors, bluntly wrote: "I don't believe anything, only that Cairo (Illinois) is a damned mud hole."[72]

There were probably more rumors in 1898 than actual fighting. The long wait of the troops at Tampa before boarding ships for Cuba didn't help. First, according to the rumors, the Spanish fleet had bombarded New York, next it was off to Norfolk, and lastly it was waiting off Key West for the American transports.

Nor was it any different in World War II. An American soldier in Italy wrote in 1944: "You know we soldiers live on rumors and the rumor was that we were going to guard prisoners that were being taken back to the States. Everybody was happy but there was a non-com meeting called and when they came back the picture was changed completely." During the Normandy invasion a wild rumor passed through the ranks of American soldiers about a complete German surrender. Another concerned the capture of a German field marshal. The experienced combat man tried to live with these wild stories, and in the end, developed a very cynical attitude. "I don't bank on rumors anymore. . . ." one American fighting man in Hawaii finally concluded.[73]

The one indelible characteristic of the American fighting man is that he has generally borne all the hardships of military life with equanimity and patience. Furthermore, he has leavened his years in the service with romantic memories of civilian life; a condition he has reversed in later life by carrying the memories and characteristics of military life throughout his remaining years in mufti. The chinked huts of Fort Arbuckle, a solitary outpost in Indian Territory in 1851, were decorated with souvenirs and mementos of each soldier's family. During the Civil War both Billy Yank and Johnny Reb made their mud caves or log huts as homelike as possible. One of the problems of the old frontier army of post-Civil War days was that so many soldiers turned their attention to the raising of crops that military training was neglected. GI's in World War II decorated their Quonset huts with pictures of girls, and occasional civilian adornments. "Christmas trees are springing up all over Korea!" an American soldier wrote in 1951. "It has a regular holiday spirit. . . . You can't keep a GI from having a Christmas tree."[74]

On the reverse side of the coin, many a good military habit has been carried over into civilian life. Dirty soldiers and sailors in both world wars were taught to keep clean; indeed, they were often scrubbed down by their comrades with hard-bristled brushes. And the service has always taught a good deal of self-reliance and maturity. A World War II soldier, writing to his father who was about to be drafted, advised: "Mind your own business. . . . Never volunteer for anything. . . . Never under any circumstances raise your voice above the conversational tone. . . . Lend money to nobody. . . . Don't gamble; you can't win."[75]

The simple matter of learning how to live is only one by-product of military life. The U. S. Navy, in a 1931 study of men recently discharged from that service, discovered some interesting facts. Almost 90 percent of the men worked at trades learned while in service, and almost 100 percent thought their naval service to have been invaluable. The study further showed that in one of the nation's largest cities one out of every fifteen policemen was an ex-sailor. In New York, the country's largest city, one out of twelve policemen and one-half of all firemen were ex-sailors. Perhaps the former Secretary of National Defense, Robert McNamara, was right when he claimed that the military service can be an effective sociological instrument in raising the aspirations and level of training of many young men for later life. Those old Army and Navy recruiting posters which proclaimed "We Build Men" may have had some meaning after all.[76]

6

The Depths of Privation

ONLY FOR THE UNINITIATED AND THE OLD are there glories in war. For those whose duties carry them into the front lines of fighting, it becomes a wearisome, terrifying, and brutalizing business. For those in the rear war is filled with the endless boredom of routine.

No amount of training can really train one for the shock of war—the dead and bloated bodies of friends, or the paralyzing of the unknown. Since the transition from peace to war has come almost invariably without warning for the American people, the shock is even greater; mainly because the amount of training allowed for the men of the services has been too small. In any conflict, however, what really counts is what has been learned on the battlefield. These lessons have never been absorbed painlessly by American fighting men.

Washington's pathetic little army of 1776 was filled with novices at war; farm boys who were good with rifles, but who had little comprehension of what it was like to receive an enemy bayonet charge. The great general, himself, characterized his men as being "totally unacquainted with every kind of Military skill . . . timid and ready to fly from their own shadows," and as evidencing a "want of confidence." The War of 1812 involved too many Americans who saw war in terms of glory rather than sacrifice. The American soldiers of the Mexican War were tough adventurers who also were occasionally shocked by the exigencies of war.[1]

The Civil War was begun by two armies of amateurs, and sometimes the impact of battle upon the participants was amazing to behold. A young soldier at Shiloh found himself simply unable to pull the trigger of his gun, despite the fact that Confederate soldiers were almost upon him. A soldier of the Thirty-Third Illinois, a regiment composed partially of college students, was caught by Missouri bushwhackers as he was filling his canteen near a stream. His surprised reaction was: "Please gentlemen, don't shoot, I'm not well." Soldiers on both sides threw away equipment with utter abandon. The line of march for Grant's army from Fort Henry to Fort Donelson was littered with overcoats; accouterments the soldiers really needed a few nights later. In some Civil War battles, the fury of combat, along with the inexperience of the men, caused some soldiers to lose all sense of equilibrium. Rifles were found after the Battle of Gettysburg which had been muzzle-loaded five or six times by soldiers too overcome with the emotion of battle to know what they were doing.[2]

In the Spanish-American War—as brief as it was—there were instances when soldiers could not bring themselves to fire their weapons or to charge. The Seventy-First New York Regiment, one-third of whom had never fired their guns, could not be rallied from their prone positions before San Juan Hill. The spell was broken only by Army Regulars who charged over them and up the hill.[3]

The doughboys of World War I showed considerable inexperience in their earliest encounters in the trenches. A number of young Americans were captured by German soldiers while playing poker in dugouts on the front lines, while others failed to post sentries at the appropriate time and place. President Harry Truman, an artillery captain in the Meuse-Argonne offensive, remembers an incident illustrating the inexperience of his outfit:

We fired our first barrage on the night of September 6 (1918). We were occupying an old French position which probably was fairly well known to the Germans, and as soon as we had finished the barrage they returned the compliment. My battery became panic-stricken, and all except five or six scattered like partridges. Finally I got them back together without losing any men, although we had six horses killed.[4]

World War II was such a global conflict that it was virtually impossible to thoroughly train men for all types of combat. The worst experience for any young soldier of that war was to be placed far out in advance of front lines on picket duty. Next in terms of terror was a sudden enemy attack. In North Africa, when first experiencing German rifle fire, many young Americans rushed about their camps firing at anything, while their officers ran after them shouting: "For Christ's sake hold your fire, you God damned crazy bastards."[5]

The fears of the untrained fighting men in World War II were always worse than reality. General Marshall blamed it on the vivid imagination of the American fighting man, but it is doubtful the soldiers of any particular army in World War II were any different.[6] The fears of such inexperienced soldiers were, by all accounts, the most indefinable emotions of World War II. "Few men fear bullets," wrote one new soldier. "They are swift, silent, and certain. . . . Mortar shells are terrifying." There was what Ernie Pyle described as that "irresistible pull to get close to somebody when you are in danger. . . ." On Omaha Beach men refused to seek individual places of safety. They huddled together seeking the kind of mutual security Federal soldiers had sought at Shiloh in the Civil War. Even in the early stages of the war in the Pacific, Americans sometimes charged as if in close-order drill. *Yank,* trying to analyze the importance of experience in World War II, came to some interesting conclusions. It was almost impossible to predict which man in a platoon would be the bravest—"The loud, tough guys in the States turned out to be the weak sisters." The biggest mistake in combat was to bunch together. One should always know the sounds of his own guns. The best weapon was the BAR (Browning automatic rifle). One should dig his foxholes deep. And one should never sleep with his blanket over his head. Curiosity, also stated *Yank,* was the "American's worst fault. . . . He's just like a turkey. He wants to see what's on the other side of the log."[7]

The suddenness of the Korean War threw too many inexperienced American troops against fairly hardened North Korean units. Many Americans were unused to their weapons, and they had little experience in skirting mine fields. There was a good deal of aimless firing at anything that moved. On a few other occasions it was almost impossible to get the men to fire their weapons. The American dependence upon equipment was noted by more acute observers. "Americans are much too mechanized minded. . . ." wrote one veteran soldier, "so the job [of carrying equipment] falls to the Koreans." General Dean, who fought with his Twenty-Fourth Division until his capture, saw the same deficiencies, stating: "How am I going to teach these boys that they can't all jeep to battle?"[8]

Some of the same problems have presented themselves in Vietnam. Some Americans going out on patrol have failed to remember passwords. Patrols have been far too noisy, because they have attempted to carry loose metal equipment through the jungle. One group of men was annihilated because some of the young soldiers gave their positions away by lighting cigarettes. Many of the earliest arrivals fired at anything that moved—oxen, chickens, or innocent peasants.[9]

One of the gravest problems for American fighting men through the years has been sheer carelessness on the part of some individuals. Sickness was common in the Revolutionary Army because men failed to wash their utensils, and camped in poorly drained places. Sanitation among the volunteers in Mexico was almost nonexistent. Latrines were badly placed, and the troops drank contaminated water.

The same practices existed on both sides in the Civil War. Troops camped downstream from latrines. They were allowed to buy pies and foodstuffs from any peddler who came into camp. General officers failed to understand and control the dangers of contamination. An Illinois general who was charged with neglect along these lines gave a stinging but characteristic reply. "All I have to say in reply to this report," he wrote, "is that if he [an inspector] smelled any stink around my camp it was one of his own creating, and I am not disposed to be held responsible for every smell he might sniff up a mile around this camp."[10]

The earliest American arrivals in France in 1917 showed a characteristic inexperience in many ways. It was almost impossible to get some of the new troops to hold a grenade long enough before throwing it. "Captain," complained one private, "I just can't hold these grenades any longer because I can feel them swelling in my hand." The ordinary doughboy's notions about gas and its quick effects also needed redefining, for some of the earliest Americans at the front considered it most unmanly to wear a mask. As a consequence some regiments had to be taken out of the line because so many men were gassed. Some men suffered from a fear of being smothered while wearing a gas mask, and they ripped them off before the danger receded. Other men died because they underestimated the quickness of gas, and attempted to fit horses with masks before themselves.[11]

Once again, much disease resulted in World War I because of indifference. There was a good deal of dysentery in the trenches. Dampness and cold were the real offenders, though. Too many men failed to keep their feet dry, or to change their socks often enough. For these reasons and others, trenchfoot and respiratory illnesses were quite common among American soldiers in 1918. Pneumonia has consistently been the strong arm of the Grim Reaper, being the greatest killing disease in World Wars I and II. Over 23,000 Americans lost their lives with this illness in World War I, and in World War II it was the largest nonbattlefield cause of death. Between seven hundred and eight hundred GI's fell victim to this disease in the European theater.[12]

The inexperience of American troops brought about numerous casualties in World War II. Japanese pilots, having flown combat in China for years, had the edge on American carrier and land-based pilots. On some islands in the Pacific a standard Japanese trick was to place a wounded American along a trail and force him to scream for help. Rescue parties or medics would be shot. During the invasion of Normandy, scores of American troops were drowned by the incoming tide because they were pinned down on the beaches by German fire. The fact that so many were carrying banjos, tennis rackets, Bibles, and mirrors not only made it impossible for them to move quickly to the bluffs, but literally caused them to be drowned by the dead weight of their packs.[13]

Nor was the Navy immune to the problems of inexperience. The hurried stationing of ships in Britain in preparation for the invasion allowed for no training period whatever. It was reputed that one LCT skipper failed to turn to port at Land's End, on the southern coast of England, and sailed directly into a German-occupied harbor. Another landing craft, caught by a fog in the Irish Channel, sailed all night in the lee of a horseshoe-shaped island before being able to escape. These poor Naval officers were more to be pitied than condemned, however. Neither they nor their crews had any real experience in navigation. This, plus the fact that they were sailing the slowest and most unmaneuverable vessel afloat, provides sufficient excuse for error.

Much illness in World War II and Korea was a result of oversight. Men going overseas crammed themselves with candy bars, with much illness resulting. Many tough units like Merrill's Marauders were hard hit by the drinking of contaminated water. More than 80 percent of all sickness casualties in the Pacific in 1943 came from intestinal disorders. Dysentery in Korea was common, for many of the troops, inexperienced as they were, drank water from open holes used as latrines by Korean farmers. Trenchfoot, frostbite, and "the crud," a fungus problem caused by too little bathing, took many men out of the lines in both wars.[14]

The first months of Korea were part of one giant nightmare for the American fighting man. Too many men were psychologically unprepared for the struggle, and the impulse to panic was strong. Inexperience showed itself in many ways. "Once I was going to get out of the hole and throw my rifle away and go over the hill," stated one soldier. "You can't explain how it is. You just think you can't stand it any more." To veterans of the previous war, the weaknesses of the early American arrivals in Korea were glaring.[15] The young men were too prodigal with their equipment, they were too noisy, they lacked in motivation and desire, and they were deficient in little things. Two comments by a veteran of World War II tell part of the story:

The men are kept busy sweeping the snow from around their guns. Shoes wet, clothing damp, the men look something like an old hen that is standing in the barnyard after she has been caught in an unexpected rain. I feel so sorry for them, but they haven't learned to live outside in the winter. My year of the winter warfare in Germany in 1944–1945 taught me to work while the sun shines in preparation for the winter. Perhaps they will learn their lesson too.

Most of the men in Korea are "first-timers" at the art of war and have a lot to learn—maybe they have never been in a line company and shot at and hit to know how bad war can really be! Most complain without having anything to complain about.[16]

No fighting man is really experienced until he hears the sounds of enemy bullets. Fortunately, however, the disposition of the ordinary American is such that he adapts himself to war very quickly; probably because of the nature of the free society in which he is raised. The natural ingenuity of the Yankee soldier or sailor has always been given a freer rein in the American armed forces than in other armies and navies, and it has paid off rather handsomely.

In the American Revolution the adaptability of the American to war was quickly perceived by friend and foe alike. "There is such a mixture of the sublime and the beautiful together with the useful in military discipline," wrote John Adams, concerning the American armies, "that I wonder every officer we have is not charmed with it." In 1776 a group of American privates, officerless and surrounded by Hessians, improvised so well that they tactically outfought their opponents. On the high seas the privateers were so ingenious at trapping various British vessels they became the scourge of the seas.[17]

Civil War Americans quickly dropped the unessentials from their behavior, and in doing so, they created two of the most powerful armies in all history. Confederate soldiers learned to carry as little as possible while on a long march; a practice Union soldiers adopted with a horseshoe-shaped blanket roll hooked about the shoulders. Both sides had their natural fighters. John A. Logan, on the Federal side, was a politician who quickly learned military practices. Nathan Bedford Forrest was an illiterate but instinctive fighter for the Confederacy. Both generals readily took advice from their lessers. During the Battle of Raymond, when Federal troops had been stalemated by a stubborn enemy defense, Logan was approached by a private who said: "Gineral, I hev been over on the rise yonder, and it's my idee that if you'll put a regiment or two over thar, you'll git on their flank and lick 'em easy." Logan did, and a crucial Federal victory was won.[18]

On both the Federal and Confederate sides soldiers sometimes took matters into their own hands in order to achieve victory. At Lexington, in Missouri, a Confederate victory resulted when Southern soldiers rolled large bales of cotton ahead of them in their attack. Federal troops used the same technique at Vicksburg, when they placed the cotton bales on wheels. Other privates filled empty barrels with dirt—these were called "sap-rollers"—and used these as moving cover. Also on the Federal side, many victories resulted when ordinary soldiers threw away their official Harpers Ferry Muskets, and bought repeating rifles with money out of their own pockets. As far as illness was concerned, the ordinary Civil War soldier soon learned that self-administered medicines were often as good as those given by the company physician. Diarrhea, the common soldier knew, was best cured by drinking only boiled water and the use of blackberry wine.

Thus has a period of experience been the necessary phase in the creation of the veteran soldier. In World War I the early disregard for the effects of gas changed to a wholesome respect. The gas mask, with its handwritten phrases—"In Thee I Trust," or "I Need Thee Every Hour"—became an important part of the doughboy's equipment. Front line combat knowledge was quickly assimilated by American troops. Officers became merciless in their discipline. One major, finding his sentries resting rather casually, administered the new discipline as follows: "You are all wrapped up like an Egyptian mummy. Somebody could lean over the top and snake off your head with a trench knife before you could get your feet loose." Another warned his sentries in this manner: "What's your aim in life—hard labour in a German prison camp or a nice little wooden cross out here four thousand miles from Punkinville? Why wasn't there any sentry at the door?"[19]

The first Americans on the front lines in 1917 were a noisy bunch. As a lieutenant with an Austro-Hungarian division put it: "The constant hammering, moving of wagons, placing of lumber, plainly audible, mixed with some unknown shout like 'Hipp Ho' indicate preparations. It must be new American troops over there, who are making so much noise."[20] Within due time, however, such innocence faded, and the Americans became as swift and silent in their killing as were more experienced German troops. Indeed, to many of the French advisors in American regiments, the adaptability of the newcomers was "amazing."

The doughboy was ingenious in other ways too. His bill-of-fare in the trenches was unappetizing—usually consisting of canned beef, canned tomatoes, hardtack, and coffee. By trading with the French troops alongside there was a good deal of supplementation of the diet, however. Wine, cheese, and bread were taken from those allies in exchange for the hated canned salmon. In the mountains American troops ate heartily of fresh trout by the simple method of throwing hand grenades into streams or ponds.

Much of the early training in World War II was absolutely worthless and unrealistic. With the increase in the intensity and frequency of the fighting, however, methods of indoctrination were changed. Live ammunition practice was introduced into basic training, and many GI's learned the need for prayer while crawling under a hail of machine-gun bullets in simulated battle conditions. By 1942 it was possible for the Chief of Staff to announce that out of the 572 hours of basic training given each recruit, only 20 hours were given over to close-order drill.

In actual combat the earliest Americans overseas faced and overcame the inevitable difficulties of inexperience. A young officer, writing about his own personal struggle off the Normandy beachhead, declared: "It looked like another big tactical scheme off Slapton

Sands, and I couldn't get the feeling out of my head that it was going to be another miserable two-day job with a hot shower at the end." Once on Omaha beach, many young Americans were pinned down by enemy machine gun and mortar fire. By watching the patterns of German fire, the men soon learned "with surprise how much small-arms fire a man can run through without getting hit."[21]

In every World War II campaign American inexperience was soon modified by the sounds of gunfire. The fighting in Normandy was so bitter and close that Germans and Americans could converse over the hedgerows. One inexperienced American lieutenant was shocked by a German voice, which whispered through the bushes: "Evidently the Herr Lieutenant is a recent arrival." In other parts of Europe, American tank commanders soon discovered that Germans were tuning in on the American radio frequency and were ordering them to retreat to headquarters. The lowly landing craft crews quickly developed a self-imposed obligation to land infantry properly and to protect them whenever possible. Off Sicily one LCT moved in so close that it was able to silence several machine-gun nests with 20 mm. fire.[22]

As in the Civil War, the American fighting man of World War II was inventive and ingenious, even to the point of advising his officers as to the proper course of action. Noncoms and privates alike felt no compunction about following this course of action whenever necessary. A Marine colonel on Iwo Jima, after being advised by enlisted men for several days about what should be done, finally exploded. "All right, lad," he informed one private, "but just between you and me I'm getting damned tired of taking orders from privates." Earlier, in the fighting in the Admiralty Islands, G Troop of the Fifth Cavalry Regiment took it upon themselves to outflank a Japanese position by wading into a lagoon. This action, though not exactly according to orders, caused the enemy to flee in confusion.[23]

There are countless examples of American ingenuity and many of them involve men from the lower ranks. The Thirty-Sixth Division in Italy learned that the best way to unfreeze a gun after a cold night was to urinate on the trigger mechanism. An American noncom devised a contraption in Normandy which allowed tanks to better penetrate the hedgerows. Another soldier in France managed to rig up what he called a "Schnitzelwerfer"; eight bazookas which would fire in concert.

Marines in the Pacific quickly learned to leave their helmet straps loose so that shell concussions would not snap the neck. They also found that, by doing push-ups in fox-holes, they kept their bodies limber enough to take Japanese *banzai* assaults. The axiom soon evolved in the Pacific that the only good Jap was a freshly killed one; those killed several days before were likely to be mined. On Bougainville, American infantrymen devised a "Rube Goldberg" contraption which could fire gasoline cans from mortars—a sort of explosive flame thrower.[24]

The ingenuity required of American airmen in the Pacific in World War II is legendary. Old airplane engines were used to develop lumber mills. Damaged planes were pieced together in surprising fashion. A C.B.I. bomber which landed in the mountains was brought back to base by means of trailers. A B-24, disabled in an attack on Iwo Jima, limped back with two engines running wild. The top turret was blown off, and the navigator and observer were wounded. Only one wheel would come down. The remainder of the crew rigged two parachutes at the waist windows and tail, and tripped them at the moment of landing. The plane and crew were saved.[25]

The important characteristic of Americans in World War II was again their adaptability, and their willingness to defy military procedure when necessary. "Most of us would disobey an order if it interferes with the work of keeping up our plane. . . ." wrote one airplane mechanic. Infantry companies soon learned that although combat brought inevitable death, the most aggressive and tough units suffered the least. "Indifferent but watchful!" one Marine wrote of his reeducation on Guadalcanal. A *Yank* photographer, asking whether a certain forward area on Gloucester Bay was safe, was given the reply: "Go ahead. . . . If they get you, we'll get them." Inexperienced American soldiers, hesitating about carrying a corpse, heard this advice from their sergeant: "Go on, take hold of him, dammit. You might as well get used to it now, for you'll be carrying plenty of dead ones from now on. Hell, you may even be carrying me. . . ." As brutal as it seems, even today, this was a necessary order. When the young men finally reached the burial ground, they had overcome their squeamishness, one of them saying to the corpse: "Now don't run away while we're gone."[26]

As soon as any area in the Pacific was secured, it was the general practice of American military authorities to turn their talents toward providing entertainment for the troops. Theaters were carved out of hillsides or jungles, recreational buildings were constructed, and post exchanges were established. Individual Americans in specific situations, using army tools and metal, fashioned bracelets, necklaces, or rings to be sold by enterprising salesmen to newly landed units. Almost every military unit, if it was stationed on any island for a prolonged period, cultivated patches of corn, watermelons, or beans. One officers' club, located on Saipan, carried on a brisk restaurant business with such produce, using native Chamorro girls as waitresses.[27]

The early stages of the Korean War demanded much improvisation on the part of the American fighting man. The large North Korean T-34 tanks outgunned anything the United Nations forces had; that is until the United States brought in the General Patton tank. The Chinese assault down from the North posed new problems, because U. N. troops sometimes panicked upon hearing enemy bugle calls and whistles. Then there was the cold, which froze guns so hard they became unusable.

In every case, however, the American fighting men met their challenges with fortitude and ingenuity. Recoilless 75 mm. guns and mines slowed the large Russian-built tanks. The Army captured enough Chinese whistles and bugles that the GI's were able to give noisy replies to opposing troops. The situation was soon reversed, with Chinese troops tending to panic, and with American search-and-destroy operations causing huge enemy losses. As far as the cold was concerned, most infantrymen found that candy provided an excellent energy supply for the body, and that ordinary hair oil was a perfect lubricant for any gun. As one American private described the problem of survival in Korea: "We learned the tricks. We knew what to watch for and when to fire and how to take care of yourself. If you can live through the first couple of days, you got a chance."

Fortunately, the happy combination of characteristics in the American fighting man has affected the course of the Vietnam War. A young Army officer, surrounded by Viet Cong, called for an artillery barrage upon his own position and survived. An aging flier, seeing his comrade's plane unable to take off because of damage, landed his own machine amidst enemy fire and rescued his friend, and got a Congressional Medal of Honor for doing so. A squad of the Twenty-Fifth Division was decimated, its officers killed or wounded, with the command of the unit falling into the hands of a twenty-three-year-old private. For twenty-two hours the young soldier stayed at his radio, commanded his position, and held out until he was rescued. As General Westmoreland has said, in describing the character of the fighting man in Vietnam: "Our country, with its free-enterprise system, has taught Americans resourcefulness. Americans have an amazing lack of regimentation, and it pays off."[28]

No war in which Americans have been involved has been easy, including the Spanish-American War. In a way far more than other peoples or ideologies care to admit, Americans have shown a great capacity for suffering in time of stress. Even among the Royal Americans, a decade before the Revolution, life was so difficult on the frontier posts, and supplies so short, that certain companies within the regiment literally starved to death.

The first expeditionary force of the American nation was the Montgomery-Arnold march into Canada in the winter of 1775–1776. With just a few hundred men, and with Montgomery killed during the campaign, the Americans performed an almost superhuman feat. Through terrible snows, with no food except a little flour, an occasional baked dog, and shoe leather, these men managed to get to the outskirts of their objective. So weak were they from starvation and dysentery, however, that they were easily captured by British defending Quebec.

The remainder of the Revolutionary War was one great ordeal. The authorized ration of flour, meat, and whiskey was rarely met.

The troops wintered in huts made from fence rails, sod, and straw. In 1777 two-thirds of Washington's little army was barefoot; few had coats, stockings, or blankets; and in one case the Army was without bread for six days in one week. It was during this last occasion that an officer's dog was trapped and eaten by some of the men, entrails and all. Because of the lack of clothing and blankets among the troops, many of the men had to sleep in a standing position.

The amazing fact of history is that the Americans could fight at all during the Revolution. Prior to the Battle of Trenton, almost 3,500 of Washington's 10,000 troops were unfit to campaign. In several instances—during the winter of 1776 and in Greene's march to the Dan River—the men could be tracked by the bloody footprints left behind. On another occasion, one American unit had only six hours of sleep during a three to four day march against the British. Lafayette indeed spoke the truth when he felt that Revolutionary Americans could endure more than any other peoples on the face of the earth.[29]

Such hardships continued to exist for many fighting Americans after the Revolution. During the War of 1812 the troops in Fort Defiance on the Maumee River suffered from deplorable conditions, in respect to both food and clothing. The American in the Mexican War endured heavy mountain dews, hot and dry desert marches, wolves, lizards, sand flies, chiggers, sand, wind, sun, and heat. Some of the frontier garrisons, prior to the Civil War, were forced to eat prairie dogs stuffed with bacon.[30] The winter cold of the frontier was barely endurable, and many of the barracks were infested with fleas and mice, plus an occasional snake. Life in the Navy was no different. The sailors slept in closely packed quarters overrun with rats and fleas. Each ship had its quota of bedbugs and roaches. Water was often unfit for drinking, the pork was rancid, the hardtack was eaten through with weevils, and death by sickness or accident was always at hand.

The hardships of the Civil War soldier have been well described in hundreds of books. Every soldier who fought in Missouri, it was said, developed an Ozark cough; a racking and sleep-delaying bronchial infection. Troops were marched long distances, twenty-five or thirty miles a day, and they sometimes fell asleep standing. One Federal sentry at Shiloh, exhausted after a twenty-seven-mile march, fell across a campfire and was severely burned. All soldiers on both sides fought a continual war against lice and ticks; the occasional boiling of clothes offering only temporary relief. On both sides there were food shortages. Lee's army at Appomattox was reduced to roasted acorns and parched corn. During the siege of Chattanooga by Bragg, Federal soldiers ate acorns, kernels of corn, which had fallen from the feed bags of horses, or anything else they could obtain from the countryside. One Western soldier, after having eaten of ox meat, wrote: "The heart of an ox sometimes skinned and sometimes scalded and then boiled made a splendid feast for the lucky mess that could get hold of it. . . . I have been glad to get most of these dishes and the only one of them that I did not relish hugely was a liberal slice of ox-lung. . . ."[31]

In the Spanish-American War and World War I the American fighting man was forced to face similar conditions. The food given to the soldier of 1898 left much to be desired in quality and quantity. There were times when he wasn't fed at all. San Juan Hill was taken by troops who hadn't eaten for twenty-four hours, and who had had only four hours sleep the night before. The doughboy of World War I, as spirited as he was, was sometimes thrown into battle under the most terrible conditions; the worst of which was the Battle of the Argonne. Here the Americans took on solid fortifications and veteran troops in bad weather; an assignment the French would have ignored forever. Lice, or "cooties" as the Americans in 1918 called them, were ever present during the campaign. Rats lived in such close proximity to the trench fighter that they were sometimes adopted as pets.

After the Japanese attack on Pearl Harbor in 1941, the Americans fought an uphill war. American pilots had been equipped with *Buffaloes, Airacobras,* and *Tomahawks;* none of which could be rated on the same level as German fighter planes. The Japanese air forces—so underrated that one American magazine had claimed it consisted of only two hundred outmoded planes—came up with the

Zero, an exceptional fighter for the early stages of the war. Only the infinite courage of young American pilots kept the Pacific war effort intact. They flew the slow, cumbersome American fighters under the worst possible conditions, and held on until American industry produced the superior *Lightnings* and *Mustangs.*

In almost every theater of war after 1941 the American fighting man showed his staying power. Landing craft crews sailed their vessels under terrible conditions—no workable sanitation facilities, no stoves, and cranky engines. The Marines, yellowed with Atabrine or shivering with malaria, fought off the Japanese at Guadalcanal. In Italy, where the fighting was particularly grueling, the GI fought a cold, bewildering, and unappreciated war. At Bastogne, one-fourth of the Twenty-Eighth Division was reported killed, wounded, or missing during one week's action, and yet it managed to slow the German advance. In *Galahad,* Stilwell's campaign against Myitkyina, every single American was ill. Most had malaria or dysentery, virtually all of them had leech sores, and there was a good deal of dengue fever. Utterly exhausted, they occasionally fell into hysterics. Yet they fought off numerous Japanese attacks, and still managed to reach the outskirts of Myitkyina.[32]

The fighting in Korea had no breathing spells. At the time of the initial Communist invasion in 1950, the Twenty-Fourth U. S. Army Division was rushed north to meet the challenge. This garrison unit was under strength by one-third, it had only light tanks, no real antitank guns, and just a few light bazookas. Within weeks the Twenty-Fourth had lost 2,500 men, one-sixth of its original number, and had been driven back to the perimeter at Pusan. Told by their commanders that they had retreated their "last step," they and the Marines held on and reversed the course of the war.[33]

From then on the Korean conflict was a battle for the ridges. Men went twenty-four hours without food from time to time, frostbite was just something that most soldiers had, and each hill seemed more steep than the last. As S. L. A. Marshall stated, the men became "wise beyond their years," and developed a "toughened outlook toward the job far beyond anything dreamed of in recent times." There was no relief from battle; no warmth from the cold.

Pancakes froze before the men could eat them; coffee cooled before drinking. The only relief from the war lay in the daily mail deliveries and a comradeship-in-arms. When, at last, armistice negotiations were resumed in 1953, it was exceedingly hard to keep morale to a sensible level. A young officer described the situation:

I'm having a time keeping the morale of my men within reasonable limits. Most of them think the war is practically over. This morning they even asked me if we could still fire our mortars since the line had been settled. I try to convince them that it is O.K. to feel good about it, but that it isn't over yet. There doesn't seem to be much doubt in their minds but that it is all over except the shouting. I tell them that it is all over except the *shooting!*[34]

Part of the explanation for the excellent behavior of Americans under the hardship of battle rests in their very character. S. L. A. Marshall noted this when he contrasted the Chinese and American fighting men in Korea. The Chinese, he argued, might surrender one day and fight like "Mad Mullahs" the next. "In contrast," he concluded, "the great redeeming quality of the American GI is that he stays pretty much on an even keel, come hell or high water."[35]

There is an indescribable patience in the American fighting man, and it goes back to the very roots of his past. His resilience and fortitude, when wounded, has surprised his enemies. During the American Revolution hospitals were virtually nonexistent. The wounded walked, or were tended by comrades until they died or recovered. Pleurisy and pneumonia dragged many soldiers down to mere skeletons. Dysentery was so common it was considered one of the lighter ailments.

The Civil War brought forth the same American stoicism. Hundreds of Federal wounded at Pea Ridge remained undiscovered by advancing Confederate Indian units because they lay silently in the bushes until all danger had passed. A Federal private, wounded in the May 22 attack at Vicksburg, jokingly said, when he was informed that his leg was gone: "Now I can go home and make stump speeches." On the Confederate side the infinite patience of a wounded man facing death was legendary. Describing the enemy, one Federal officer stated: "Their great characteristic is their stoical manliness; they never beg or whimper, or complain; but look you straight in the face. . . ."[36]

The frontier Regular of post-Civil War days followed the same pattern. One wounded cavalry soldier, whom troopers had to leave behind for the Sioux, calmly told his friends: "I'm just all in, and I don't care a hang whether the Injuns get me or not." In a fight with Indians in 1865, a soldier was hit in the mouth with an arrow, which lodged in the root of his tongue. The point could not be removed surgically, so the soldier lay quietly while his comrades cut out his tongue. He lived and was eventually mustered out of the service.[37]

In World War I the doughboy could be as tough as they came. "The nerve that the boys display when they come in wounded is certainly remarkable," stated one observer. "They don't even whimper, and some of them even walk in when they are so shot up that they can hardly 'tottle' along." A Red Cross worker in France wrote that she had never seen such patient men before. One of her patients was a veritable basket case—one eye gone, unable to walk, move, or to talk—yet he never indicated any distress.[38]

After Ernie Pyle accompanied American troops in their invasion of North Africa in 1942, he was able to write that the GI's took their battle casualties "in a way to make you proud." Later in Normandy, where the fighting was so close and intense, the reaction of many wounded soldiers was similar to certain instances in the Civil War and World War I. A young GI was found sitting up in plain sight of the enemy. Told by his officer to lie down, he replied that he had a small wound on his heel, and he didn't want to "get blood poisoning. . . ." Two minutes later he was hit directly by a low trajectory shell.[39]

Stephen Crane's characterizations in *The Red Badge of Courage* are paralleled by many examples in World War II. Many men died in Normandy, swearing that they had never been hit by enemy fire. One GI, hit in the eye, argued that he had really lost his arm. Another, carrying the shard of an 88 mm. shell in his abdomen, discharged his duties another twenty-four hours before he realized his injury. And like Crane's dying soldier, many GI's crawled into bushes in order to die alone; none realizing that every man dies alone no matter where he is. Ernie Pyle, in his *Brave Men,* wrote of watching a wounded GI die in a field hospital. The chaplain uttered a few perfunctory words to the dying man, and then left. The "aloneness of that man as he went through the last minutes of his life was what tormented me," Pyle mourned. "I felt like going over and at least holding his hand while he died, but it would have been out of order and I didn't do it. I wish now I had."[40]

In most instances the courage of the GI was most clearly seen in his defiance or acceptance of death. He could and did suffer patiently and with fortitude. A Marauder, caught in ambush in Burma, was wounded in the neck and forced to wander through a swamp for three days. Covered by giant leeches, he passed so close to Japanese soldiers he could hear them snoring, and yet made it safely back to his own base camp. Other Marauders, sick, wounded, or dying, exhibited no "fear of death, no panic, no complaining." During the Cape Gloucester campaign a member of the Army General Staff noted: "The Marines are careful, brave fighters. . . . They were like hunters, boring in relentlessly and apparently without fear. I never heard a wounded Marine moan."[41]

The Navy comes in for its share of praise also. A medical officer, who floated to safety after the sinking of the U. S. S. *Vincennes* off Guadalcanal, later wrote:

Among them were several major casualties—men with wounds, which, if suffered in civilian life, would almost surely have been fatal. Here on the raft, still under fire, they were calm and astoundingly determined to stay alive. They would not give up. A few of them were, I was sure, clinging to the threads of life by sheer will-power. Perhaps any soldier of any country acts that way, but I suspected otherwise. There was something peculiarly American in that attitude of "of course, I'm not licked."

A young Naval officer, later killed at Midway, wrote after the sinking of the aircraft carrier, *Hornet,* in the South Pacific:

When you hear others saying harsh things about American youth, know how wrong they all are. So many times now that it has become commonplace, I've seen incidents that make me know that we were not soft or bitter. . . . Many of my friends are now dead. To a man, each died with a nonchalance that each would have denied was courage. They simply called it lack of fear, and forgot the triumph.

The battered American carrier, *Yorktown,* on the edge of a safe retreat from Midway, was finally sunk by a Japanese submarine. Most of the men got off, but five decks down, three veteran sailors were trapped by rising water. An officer telephoned to the men, "Do you know what kind of a fix you're in?" "Sure," was the reply. "We know you can't get us out but we've got a helluva good acey-deucey game down here right now."

These are examples of the ineffable kind of courage found in the majority of American fighting men in World War II. They fought and died in far-off places which they had never heard of before 1941. They suffered and bled in the fulfillment of plans too obscure for their understanding. An American Army nurse, killed an hour after writing these words, expressed it thusly: "We have learned a great deal about our American boy and the stuff he is made of. The wounded do not cry. Their buddies come first. The patience and determination they show, the courage and fortitude they have is sometimes awesome to behold."[42]

The same determination persisted for the most part of the Korean War. In 1951, when the Marines came out of the Chochin trap, they carried out their seriously wounded; the ambulatory patients walked.

Early in the Vietnam War, when most of the Americans were acting as advisors to ARVN troops, one Green Beret, who was wounded near the eyes, stayed with his men until he had completely lost his eyesight. He simply refused to be evacuated. In the Ia Drang Valley fight of 1966 all but two in an American platoon were wounded. Though surrounded, those still living made a no-surrender pact, and continued to fight until the Viet Cong overran the position and bayoneted all the Americans they could find. The two who escaped, a Guamanian and a Negro, both Regulars, pledged revenge, saying: "We're going back into the fight."[43]

The reaction of these young men to the sight of blood and death at Ia Drang is a standard one for the American fighting man. He may grouse and complain about the complexities of life which bring him to the edge of death, but he accepts them very much as a burden to be carried. This notable ability to accept life and death, with all the hardships they may bring, grows deeply in the subsoil of American history. A Connecticut doctor at Valley Forge wrote: "Why are we sent here to starve and Freeze—what sweet Felicities have I left at home; A charming Wife—pretty Children—Good Beds . . . ; a pox on my bad luck." A young soldier of the Mexican War, after viewing the dead at Cerro Gordo, was amused at his own "calmness and . . . indifference" during the experience.

The Civil War soldier, in most cases, was cut from the same mold. Early in 1861 a Federal soldier quipped upon hearing the ominous sounds of cannonfire: "Hark! from the tomb a doleful sound." Soldiers on both sides quite frequently referred to death as that "*grim* old Monster." A Federal soldier, just prior to one of Grant's ill-fated assaults on Vicksburg, wrote "there will be bloody work . . . we are ready for it." A Confederate sentry, when asked by a Union Soldier on the other bank of the Chattahoochee just how many Southern soldiers were available for the next battle, replied: "Oh, about enough for another killing."[44]

Preparations prior to any Civil War battle followed a routine familiar to any fighting man. There were always "tender thoughts" of home, hurriedly written "last letters," and occasional comradely promises. On the night before the Battle of Chickamauga two soldiers knelt and repeated together the prayer, "Now I lay me down to sleep," and swore that if either was killed, the other would take charge of the remains. The fear of occupying an unidentified grave haunted Federal and Confederate soldiers alike—perhaps more than death itself. Prior to one of Grant's assaults on Petersburg, soldiers of the Army of the Potomac calmly pinned to their clothes pieces of paper on which were written their names and addresses.[45]

The post-battle impact of Civil War fighting, so well described in letters and diaries of the time, evokes a sympathetic response from anyone who has heard the sounds of shot and shell. A young soldier, tired of fighting in Missouri, showed the effect of shock when he wrote that he "had rather be shot and done with it. . . ." A similar reaction was illustrated by the words of a Pea Ridge soldier when he stated: "I was so sure that I should lose my life, that I really felt no concern about it." During the Battle of Shiloh, Federal troops were driven to the banks of the Tennessee. Reinforcements arrived at just about sundown. Years afterward a young private remembered his emotions at that moment. "I gave one big, gasping swallow and stood still," he recalled, "but the blood thumped in the veins in my throat. . . ."[46]

America's participation in World War I, though short, was a ghastly and harrowing experience for the men who reached the front-line trenches. There death was so omnipresent that it was in sight and in the air. Many doughboys lived through such days and nights they would never forget. A young lieutenant, after the Battle of Saint-Mihiel, told his parents that of all the horrors of war—the overwhelming smell of death, and life in the trenches—the one sight he could hardly bear was of "brave fellows lying . . . to blacken in the sun and rot where they fell." Yet, he concluded, the "Hun, man for man, is no match for the American. . . ."[47]

Everywhere along the borders of "no man's land," men "slept with nerves taut with anticipation and in the consciousness of a night-mare. . . ." Some tried to evade the sounds of war by sleeping in deep dugouts; others, oppressed with a consciousness of space, slept in the open. Everywhere, and always, there was shock. A young Marine wrote his mother that the fighting in Belleau Wood was so horrible that it was sheer luck, and not prayer or supplication, which allowed for survival. A young officer described death as a horrible sight, "tho one becomes more or less accustomed to seeing the dead. . . ." In the Argonne, the fighting resembled all of the horrors of past Wildernesses and of future Ardennes. As one First Division soldier put it: "I have lost all track of time and hardly know when one day ends and another begins—and, as for the days of the week, I haven't known that for weeks."[48]

The numbness of this World War I doughboy to time and battle was a commonplace occurrence in World War II. Ernie Pyle could find no one word to describe it. "It's a look that is the display room for what lies behind it," he wrote, "exhaustion, lack of sleep, tension for too long, weariness that is too great, fear beyond fear, misery to the point of numbness, a look of unsurpassing indifference to anything anybody can do." It was present from the beginning of the war to the end. A Bataan soldier wrote: "I suppose this awful war has really just begun, but nine weeks has seemed an eternity. I'm so tired of killed men littering the jungle path, of the stench of dead bodies being always in the air." A Marine, back from Guadalcanal, wrote his parents of his nightmares: "So many of my platoon were wiped out, my old Parris Island buddies, that it's hard to sleep without seeing them die all over again."⁴⁹

For some men it was natural that World War II appeared as an unrewarding game of chance. Especially was this true in France and Italy. There was a sensation of "deadly unrelenting fatigue and danger"; a notion that each hedgerow gained was "like those already behind and those still to take." The fighting around the German forts at Brest was so intense that much of the previous American aggressiveness waned. As one junior officer put it: "These men do not want to go on because they have already taken great risks. . . . So, the farther you go, the greater the difficulty."⁵⁰

Yet, for many Yanks, it all depended on time, circumstance, and place. And it depended, to some extent, on the quality of the American unit involved. An Army Regular wrote just before the fall of Bataan: "In spite of all this, officers and men are cheerful and optimistic and crazy for a chance at the Japs. It is well known that this is just a temporary setback and that when help arrives we shall push the Japs clear off the Island." A Marine, writing to his parents before a 1943 island assault, claimed that the Corps was the best fighting force in the world, and that it could "lick the people that we are opposing." In December of the same year, a Marine corporal noted that his unit sang both ribald and religious songs before making an assault, and that there were eleven card games which were interrupted by embarkation. A Yank in Europe pronounced a bitter "hatred of the Jerries, a burning desire to avenge what they have done to us." And a young private, writing his mother about the raising of the siege of Bastogne, exclaimed: "If we hadn't been so nearly frozen and exhausted I think we would have raised up from our holes and cheered in spite of the snipers a stone's throw away from us."[51]

Crack American units in World War II could always summon at least one more effort in times of crises. The Marines at Tarawa and Iwo Jima proved that, as did the Army's Rangers in the European theater. The latter troops were tough, big, and willing. After the severe fighting in the Battle of the Bulge, where the Americans had thrown off the best the Germans had offered, the morale in such special American units soared. When one Ranger unit called for fifty special volunteers for some extremely hazardous duty, it was rewarded by over a thousand applications.[52]

The same could be written about the war in Korea. Crack units, with the special sense of duty imparted to them by able commanders, gave more than the last full measure of devotion. It was a gift which came in various shapes and forms. An Army officer, having returned from a terrible fight with Chinese troops, wrote: "I saw the dead carried from the hills they had died to secure in this war that is not a war. . . . I heard the terrified screams and the uncontrolled sobs of battle fatigued—the men who could not stand the war that is not a war." The late Marguerite Higgins wrote of seeing Marines playing gin rummy just before the landing at Inchon, and being "elaborately calm" about it all. And during the retreat from Chochin Reservoir, a Marine officer told his troops: "We're going to come out of this as Marines, not as stragglers. We're going to bring out our wounded and our equipment. We're coming out, I tell you, as Marines or not at all."[53]

This is not to say that few fighting Americans have experienced the anxiety of fear. No matter how elite an outfit is, or what its past record has been, the sounds of battle always create some fear of the unknown. During the *Bon Homme Richard's* fight against the *Serapis* during the Revolution, there were several instances in which frightened American sailors hoisted white flags, only to have them torn down upon the orders of John Paul Jones. There were other instances on land, when Washington's men simply quit on him; a development the great general attempted to curb by breaking certain officers from rank. Early in the war the militia gave way far too willingly in the open, having much more fear for injury to the lower parts of the body than the head. And, as shall be illustrated, the real emotion of fear was no different in the Revolution than it is in Vietnam today. As one American at King's Mountain expressed it, his feelings before battle "were not the most pleasant." He described his battle emotion thusly: "The first shock was quickly over, and for my own part, I was soon in profuse sweat."[54]

The young Revolutionary of King's Mountain is echoed down through every battle in American history. A soldier at Perryville in the Civil War wrote: "I was not shocked, surprised or startled, but I suppose I was too green to appreciate my danger." A year later, the same man, writing about Chickamauga, stated: "Well, war is a great thing, and I tell you that amid the terrible fighting of Saturday and Sunday, whenever I had time to think, I had some very serious thoughts about how I was going to get out of that tornado alive." A Federal soldier remembered his feelings before a Vicksburg charge as follows:

> We lay there about eight minutes and yet it seemed an age to me, for showers of bullets and grape were passing over me. . . . Oh how my heart palpitated! It seemed to thump the ground . . . as hard as the enemy's bullets. The sweat from off my face run in a stream from the tip ends of my whiskers. . . . Twice I exclaimed aloud . . . "My God, why don't they order us to charge?"[55]

Fear, and its natural consequence, "bugging out," went hand-in-hand during the Civil War. At Belmont and Donelson the slightest scratch from a thorn caused some men to report to physicians in the rear. At Shiloh a few Federal troops ran wildly to the rear, and "skulkers" lined the banks of the Tennessee at the end of the day. At Stone's River the right flank of the Union line collapsed, and hundreds of men vanished in retreat shouting "We are sold" (a phrase also used by skulkers in Arnold's 1775 attack on Quebec). On the Confederate side there were similar instances of cowardice. There was some "bugging out" by Rebels at First Manassas, and at

Shiloh on the second day. At Missionary Ridge the Confederate positions disintegrated once they had been pierced. At Nashville the Federal attack on Hood resulted in a Confederate rout.

There were skulkers in Cuba in 1898. The Seventy-First New York, a National Guard outfit, performed badly at San Juan Hill and literally could not be whipped into making a charge. Other soldiers, pulling an age-old trick, purposely lagged behind their own outfits and became "missing" so to speak; only to show up after the battle. One young private from the Midwest noted that one trail alongside San Juan Hill was crowded with "scrimshankers . . . unwounded men crawling for safety."

As minor as San Juan Hill seems alongside Gettysburg or Normandy, the fear and anxiety was there just as well. A sentry on night duty prior to the fight wrote that he was frightened during his entire watch—a mere land crab "sounded for all the world like battalions of Spaniards hell-bent upon surprise and massacre." A young American officer told a reporter before the famous charge: "I'm sweating blood with fear; but I will go ahead all right, and keep my men in line, too, never fear." And a private, recalling his emotions on San Juan Hill, wrote: "But through every minute my stomach was cold and clammy and rippled in little chills in time with my pulse. It was a comfort—almost—to bury one's nose in the rank vegetation of the jungle floor; anything to shrink in size."[56]

The great improvement in the art of military defense, along with heavy artillery, machine guns, and barbed wire, caused World War I to be little more than four years of slaughter. Any offensive was preceded by an artillery barrage, and was concluded with a direct infantry assault upon enemy trenches. Most drives failed, for it was almost impossible for the human element to overcome the natural advantages of the defender. The wonder of it all is that men could be made to assault impregnable positions time and time again.

The real break in the war came when the United States, with its vast infusions of manpower, threw the previously existing stalemate of defense versus infantry assault out of balance. The doughboys charged with such energy and in such numbers that German reserves were quickly exhausted, or were spread so thin that penetrations were made all up and down the Western front.

Still, with all of their numerical advantage, it was no easier for American fighting men to make that charge across "no man's land" than it had been for the British and the French. The fear syndrome was just as present at Château-Thierry and the Argonne, as it had been at Vicksburg a half-century before. Fresh American troops incurred heavy casualties when, under the strain of an attack, they tended to draw into groups. This wasn't the "gregarious instinct," as one writer described it; it was simply that natural reaction of men to anxiety.

All of the symptoms of fear were present during any attack. "There was nothing to do but sit there and wonder if your time had come. . . ." wrote one private. "Well, do you know I was just helpless; I couldn't even talk. In fact, my mouth became so dry I couldn't even spit." Another private, who while on patrol had run smack into an enemy party, wrote that his "heart almost stopped beating entirely." These are true reactions to fear—by men who confronted the German face to face. It was all very well, but not in the least correct, for a rear echelon staff officer to describe an attack in the following terms: "One ceased to listen to his heartbeats. The emotion became that of action. Suspense became objective, merged in responsibility for every man in watching where he stepped as he moved toward his goal. . . ."[57]

Fear symptoms were given close study by military authorities and sociopsychologists in World War II. Both groups produced percentages of fear cases, and clinical analyses of the effects of fear. One study found that the fear symptoms in a military unit corresponded with the number of deaths and atrocities witnessed by the unit. Another found that only 1 percent of those Americans fighting in the Mediterranean area admitted to having no fear. The most common physical symptoms of fear, according to such studies, included violent pounding of the heart, stomach distress, cold sweat, faintness, vomiting, and the loss of bowel and urinary control. The reaction of heart action to fear was just as common to officers as enlisted men, though the former admitted to fewer of the other symptoms than did enlisted men.[58]

There are many descriptive passages of the fear syndrome as written by men who had experienced it. A commonly described reaction was that of shock drowsiness; soldiers who had been through harrowing experiences simply passing into a deep sleep. A whole platoon of Americans in the Carentan Causeway fight in Normandy went to sleep after a terrible firefight. One American soldier, fighting in Germany, fell into such a sound sleep while under German sniper fire that his companions thought him dead. A young naval officer, having dislodged his landing craft after sustaining a number of direct hits at Omaha Beach, fell into a sound five-hour sleep.

As in the Civil War, fear sometimes brought on some immediate and violent reactions in the ranks of GI's. A sergeant in Normandy, running to the rear to get first aid, found himself being followed by his entire platoon; all of them shouting "Withdraw! Withdraw!" In another instance, an officer in Normandy simply couldn't get his men off the ground. They could neither go forward nor retreat. The officer finally broke the spell by firing wildly at a farmhouse while hollering: "God damn, I don't know what I'm shooting at, but I gotta keep on." During a heavy mortar attack in the Pacific, a number of Marines fell victim to the fear instinct by running in circles and crying "Stop the guns!"

The fighting American of World War II could be frankly descriptive of his experiences with fear. A Marine wrote of an artillery barrage: "After about ten minutes of this, Old Man Fear began to creep into me, and into everyone else lying in the same area. A cold hand seemed to reach in and clasp me by the brain. . . . I was just one big lump of quivering flesh trying to burrow my way into the earth." A tough Marauder wrote: "Fear has an identifiable taste. At least it has for me. It is a taste of brass. Every time a shell exploded it was as if my tongue had been touched by the two poles of a dry cell." An infantryman at the Battle of the Bulge confessed: "During this I was frozen with fear."[59]

Nothing can be more understandably descriptive than the words of fighting men. A paratrooper on his first training jump wrote:

"Well, looking at the sweating faces opposite me, all just as white as a ghost, just bloodless, made it 1,000 times worse. God knows what I looked like." A sailor after an action at Midway wrote that his "knees began to play drum-boogies," and that the "toughest guys were the same way." In another naval action, a lookout kept muttering: "Lord, I'm scared. Nobody has any idea how scared I am. . . . My God, I'm scared." Down below, in the same engagement, a sailor in the engine room read a magazine through the entire battle. Later, when he saw the damage topside, he had to be physically supported by members of the deck crew. An American infantryman, describing a fire fight in which he was wounded, wrote:

> Generally when I went into an attack I was nervous but was calm. The evening I got hit I was really nervous—my hands were shaking and I hated to leave the place we were in. All that day I just felt that I was going to get hit—I guess it is some sort of sixth sense. . . . I guess that I just worked myself up to such a point that I became careless or something.[60]

From all of the above one might suppose that such men would be worthless in action. In most instances, however, each man had his own devices for overcoming the effect of fear. A study of four hundred battle-tested Marines just returned from Saipan and Tinian pointed up some very interesting conclusions. First of all, almost 98 percent of these men indicated that prayer had fortified their courage. Others said that prayer had stopped them from running. One indicated that he had prayed while lying behind the dead body of a fellow Marine. Another stated that several Marines and himself had prayed together in concert.

More than 80 percent of the same Marines indicated that companionship was a factor in combatting fear. Other psychological supports against fear were the sense of duty (63 percent), anger (50 percent), and the do-or-die motivation, faith in firepower, and belief in luck.

All of these are substantiated by the comments of American fighting men in World War II. One Marine wrote: "I had lots of faith in the men who were at my side and they had faith in me. . . ." Another leatherneck commented: "I thought I would be nervous during the hours prior to the day of attack. But I wasn't. . . . That's what all these months in the tropics, under intensive training, have done for us." A Marine officer on Guadalcanal noted that he had not seen one instance of cowardice—only "cool bravery and courage." A 1943 Marine added: "I am not afraid. No man is ever afraid of something he knows he can lick."[61]

The sense of duty among American fighting men was a strong impulse in World War II. "I think that I overcame my fear because I knew that a fellow buddy of mine lay out there seriously wounded, and it was our responsibility to save his life if at all possible. . . ." A dive-bomber pilot in the South Pacific, looking upon the hazards he faced as part of his job, commented: "You get scared to death in the morning, come through it, and spend the afternoon reading or playing cards."

Anger and revenge are impulses much to be desired in any fighting man. An American infantryman in Italy explained his lack of fear by his "bitter hatred of the Jerries, a burning desire to avenge what they have done to us." A tough Marine on Saipan stated: "When I saw all my buddies getting hit, I just got mad and wasn't scared any more. . . . I was downright mad." These comments have a familiar ring to them. Stephen Crane wrote an entire novel about this particlar motivation in *The Red Badge of Courage*.

The other supports for courage—the do-or-die feeling, faith in fire power, and belief in luck—are easily understood. The first was an important part of the indoctrination of the doughboy in World War I. It pops up in World War II as a natural reaction. As expressed by a Marine of the Central Pacific, it was simply a case of survival. The last, a belief in simple luck, is part of any war. Civil War letters, World War I correspondence, and the comments of the GI, illustrate that a good many of these men merely felt that no enemy bullet had "his number" on it.[62]

All that was written about the World War II GI—the most analyzed soldier in history—can be repeated to a degree about the American of Korea or Vietnam. The soldiers of the American Twenty-Fourth

Division, which was rushed into Korea to halt the North Korean tide, faced some particularly difficult hardships. Their bazookas were so inadequate they bounced off the shells of enemy tanks. Their rifles, radios, and machine guns were leftovers from World War II. Thus it was quite natural that many of these young men made "strategic" retreats before being ordered to do so.

Yet all in all the American fighting man in Korea followed patterns of the past. Elite forces fought well, individuals died heroically in fulfillment of their duty, there was the do-or-die motivation throughout the war, and there was a good deal of elemental anger. There was also fear. Some men panicked early in the war; other units gave way to the same impulse after the entry of the Chinese. Men cried in shock, and suffered from psychoneurosis. On the Koto-ri plateau, during the horrible period of the surprise Chinese offensive, tough Marines fell victim to battle fatigue. They reported to sick bay in tears or with high levels of anxiety. The severe cold, it appears, added to the problem.[63]

One of the greatest defenders of the American soldier in Korea was S. L. A. Marshall, one of the best known American military historians. He admitted, after the Chinese onslaught, that some individuals had "bugged out" in search of "cooler ground"; but there was no wholesale panic. Combat fatigue, Marshall claimed, was a "forgotten term among the troops"; there was no time for it. "I will say, without a qualifying word," concluded Marshall, "that the men of the Eighth Army are the hardest-hitting, most workmanlike soldiers I have yet seen in our uniforms in the course of three wars."

Marshall has had good words about Americans in Vietnam as well. He reports that, at Ia Drang, some infantrymen bolted into the underbrush, that some men couldn't bring themselves to use their weapons, and that some men cried. Quoting an officer, however, Marshall concludes that if the men cried "it was because they were so damned mad," and that, on the whole, their performance was excellent. Thus, in Vietnam, the old story of war is repeated. Most Americans stand, fight, and die if necessary. Some run, for fear is as compulsive in the rice paddies as it was in the woods of the Ardennes. One young American, back from a fire fight in Vietnam, expressed it very well when he said that he was "a little nervous, but not actually scared. . . . Not chicken, but not another John Wayne either."[64]

The facts and figures of wars are so often misinterpreted or misused. All in all, in relation to simple battle fear, the American has a very good record. Far more Germans than doughboys surrendered in World War I; in fact, one of the demoralizing aspects of the war for the enemy was the realization that so many American soldiers were willing to fight to the death when surrounded. In World War II more Japanese soldiers than Americans were captured in battle. Those who didn't surrender, killed themselves. More Germans were captured in battle by Americans than conversely. In Korea there were many more Communist prisoners taken than GI's, and in Vietnam the enemy will to fight is rapidly declining according to recent American figures on defections.

As far as real psychoneurosis is concerned, the United States has had some troubles—but so has every nation involved in war. The Japanese argued that there were "nervous troops, but no neurotics" in the Imperial forces. How they were able to present this viewpoint is beyond comprehension. Japanese troops in World War II either fought to the death, committed suicide, or they surrendered.

By June, 1945, in World War II, approximately 300,000 psychoneurotics had been sent home by United States military authorities. Some of these resulted from real battle fatigue; others already had psychoneuroses, which were uncovered by the slightest military activity. Battle fatigue acting upon basic nervous deficiencies was the major problem in World War II, however. Some men fighting in Normandy under sustained conditions, and from hedgerow to hedgerow, became so drowsy that they were unfit for further duty. Some of Merrill's Marauders suffered from the same difficulty. Marines evacuated from Okinawa after weeks of bitter fighting showed no interest in anything; in fact, five such men in one unit received "Dear John" letters from their wives and showed not the slightest reaction. On Anzio the problem was severe. Most Amercan fighting men there suffered from some form of the "Anzio anxiety"; a trembling of the hands, and a scare reaction to the slightest sound.

There was little question in World War II that some men had neuroses which were quite near the surface. A Regular Army private went into hysterics during the Pearl Harbor attack, and had to be knocked out by his sergeant. Some men went into hysterics or began to act strangely during the Ardennes battle, and had to be sent to the rear. An LST officer, a gentle and unoffending soul, was chased around the deck three times by a razor-wielding sailor before the attacker was restrained. These cases could be duplicated by the score with other examples.[65]

Studies of psychoneuroses in World War II show some interesting findings. First they point up that most such soldiers were married in greater proportions than the average fighting man, and that they were older. They also showed that companies that had more aggressive and favorable precombat attitudes were inclined to have far fewer cases of psychoneurosis. This would tend to support the argument that elite regiments which have a high *esprit de corps,* are low on the psychoneurosis scale.[66]

Extreme anxiety cases were not new in World War II, nor have they ceased to exist since that time. Federal soldiers of the Thirty-Fourth and Eighty-Sixth Illinois Regiments went insane during the Battle of Kennesaw Mountain, and walked about the battlefield with pots and pans in their hands. To the eternal credit of the Confederates, who recognized the symptom, they were not shot. At Stone's River and at Shiloh there were cases of battle neurosis on both sides. A young private at San Juan Hill broke at the command to charge, and said to his commanding officer: "I can't, Captain—I can't. . . . I can't stand it . . . for God's sake send me back to the hospital corps—I can't go on. . . ."

Shell shock, an earlier name for battle fatigue, was common in World War I. These men were withdrawn from the front quickly if theirs was a sudden case. The more insidious type—the actual mental breakdown of an apparently normal human under the stress of war —was a more difficult situation. Many of these never did recover, and still live or relive their terrible visions of combat in Veterans Hospitals. The great army surgeon Harvey Cushing presented one such case history in his journal of the war. A soldier, somewhat of a hero at Belleau Wood and at Vaux, suddenly became a stutterer. As the fighting man himself expressed it:

The chief trouble now is the dreams—not exactly dreams, either, but right in the middle of an ordinary conversation the face of a Boche I have bayoneted, with its horrible gurgle and grimace, comes sharply into view, or I see the man whose head one of our boys took off by a blow on the back of his neck with a bolo knife and the blood spurted high in the air before the body fell.[67]

Such cases are to be found on all sides and in all wars. In Remarque's *All Quiet on the Western Front,* the hero is traumatized by the killing of a French soldier. In the Korean War Chinese soldiers wandered aimlessly about after heavy American shellings. An American machine gunner, in the same conflict, shocked by the results of an enemy attack, turned his gun on his comrades. In Vietnam dazed soldiers of the Viet Cong have emerged from heavily shelled areas crying, "Enough, enough."

In Vietnam the number of psychoneurotic American soldiers has dropped sharply; perhaps to one-twenty-fifth of those in World War II, using comparable scales. As Robert Sherrod, a recent visitor to Vietnam points out, the reasons for this lie in the fact that each soldier knows his length of duty in the war area is only twelve months, that most battles last only a short time, that there have been no long artillery shellings of American troops, and that the casualty rate in Vietnam for Americans is on a considerably smaller ratio than that of World War II.[68]

Sustaining the American fighting man in his times of troubles is his enormous and imaginative sense of humor, and his great resiliency. In the Civil War, and one suspects in every war, the American had much to say about his food. The Federal soldier, for instance, noting that his hardtack was stamped with the initials *BC,* concluded that these must have been an abbreviation for "Before Christ."

The same good-natured derision of army or navy food was true in the Spanish-American War and World War I. The soldier of 1898 simply could not eat the canned meat of that time, and concocted dozens of terms to describe it. A doughboy of World War I, typifying the general comment in the Army, wrote:

We had corn Willie for breakfast Corn Willie and Potatoes for dinner and Corn Willie for Supper. Quite a variety. You may not know what corn willie is but it is known in the states as corn beef, then the following day we had Gold Fish (Salmon) three times in three different styles—raw, stewed, and baked. Try them for two weeks straight, they are fine. . . .[69]

The World War II soldier had much to say about canned ham (Spam), K-Rations, C-Rations, and chipped creamed beef on toast. The last—an especial favorite of Navy cooks—bore an unrepeatable but familiar name on every ship in the service.

Despite the fact that service food is generally good, the American always dreams of home. The Civil War soldier conjured up memories of coffee; good coffee boiled on the kitchen range at home. A soldier in the Spanish-American War, a private, lay in his trench before San Juan Hill and dreamed of roast beef, mutton chops, roast goose, mince pie, and beer. The doughboy of 1918 envisioned ham and eggs, but always with a table cloth. Dependent on where he was at a particular time, the GI's dream of food was varied. A sailor in England wrote of his memory of a "little beer garden in the Bronx where for a nickel you can get a beer so big." A Mississippi soldier informed his parents that all he ever thought about was a plate of fried catfish. Soldiers in New Guinea dreamed about eating turkey while watching a winter snowfall through a dining room window. Everywhere and anywhere the GI thought about milk; fresh, cold milk. One private, just returned from the Pacific in 1943, drank so much milk at one sitting that he became ill.

There have been a great many times when life for the American serviceman was dire and difficult. Unlike the German or Japanese enemies of recent wars, who always sustained themselves with romantic legends of the national past, the American fighting man has shown an amazing adaptability and pragmatism. A Federal soldier, writing from a Missouri camp, asserted: "What do I lack to be happy? Shelter, boy, horse, groom, dog. . . . I am as happy as a young coon. . . ." A World War II soldier in Italy wrote about his living conditions: "It's quite comfortable even if made from scrap materials, nice place to spend the winter if necessary." Not only had he equipped his tent with a stove and a sink, but with a skylight as well. An American soldier in Korea told of the relative comfort of his hastily built dwelling, asserting: "My winter home, stove and lamp is a blessing today."[70]

The Civil War soldier wrote lengthily, and usually humorously, about his sleeping quarters and his frequent bouts with the "gray-backs" or lice. To one such soldier, his bed felt like the "soft side of a board"; to others the war against lice was as exciting as the war against the enemy.

The World War I soldier was no less adaptable to the same conditions. One doughboy admitted that wearing the British helmet was a real chore, and jokingly claimed that his collar size was rapidly expanding because of the weight of this protective device. As for the lice, or "cooties," the doughboys sang about them, and wrote long voluminous letters about their existence. One American claimed that he didn't mind the fact that they ate of his flesh, but he objected to their attempts to carry off the meal. Another, writing to his parents, stated that he had just had a long talk to a friend about them. Had his friend got them from a German trench, he asked? "Hell," ran the reply, "I just raised mine myself."

And always there have been the practical, and sometimes impractical, jokes. Soldiers in the Vicksburg campaign once set off a charge of powder underneath a Negro servant, and were delighted to see him go thirty feet into the air and come down unharmed. At an airport in France in World War I there was considerable argument over whether a chicken could fly. After bets had been laid, a flier took a poor fowl five hundred feet up and threw it out. It flew! In the Korean War it was considered quite funny to be photographed with corpses from uprooted Korean graves, or with the bodies of Chinese soldiers killed several months before.[71]

In World War I the almost insurmountable good humor of the American fighting men amazed the French. They shouted at the girls, they hooted at rear-line officers, and according to a French observer, they even "jested at the stalling of trucks." A GI in World War II once wrote that the ricocheting sound of German machine-gun bullets was quite similar to the song "Remember Pearl Harbor." An American in Vietnam, knocked cold by a spent Viet Cong bullet, later recalled it as one of the most humorous episodes in his life.

It is this kind of mental elasticity that has made enemy propaganda efforts of the past somewhat useless. Ernie Pyle remembered that an Italian propaganda leaflet in North Africa caused a soldier to remark: "Go to hell, you lousy spaghetti eaters. We'll tear your ears off before this is over." A GI writing in December, 1944, remarked that he had just seen a German propaganda leaflet, and it had made him laugh. "Never have I seen such poor propaganda!" he asserted. "The papers told us think about home and our folks, and the big turkeys and minced meat we would miss." German and Japanese radio propaganda in World War II was the source of much amusement to American fighting men. And in the Korean War Chinese propaganda leaflets were considered to be so humorous that special details were sent out to pick them up from where they fell.

There is a grim sort of humor in Vietnam. The enervating aspects of the monsoon seasons, and the very nature of the war, allow for a cynical twist to American good humor. Yet there are some special moments and incidents. One favorite device is to trick up battle helmets or combat jackets with mottos. A Marine helmet was spotted by one reporter, bearing the words "Boston 9669 miles to the rear." Another was marked "Charles [argot for Viet Cong] not here!" Some helmets bear titles indicating the place of origin of the owner, such as "Tennessee Rebel" or "St. Louey Baby."[72]

Even with the fighting American, however, there are times when the weight of a particular war becomes too heavy for the bearing. On such occasions his will to fight has been overbalanced with his anger and discontent at conditions. Mutiny is a harsh word. To use it in connection with American military history, with all its implications, is rather unfair. The United States has never experienced anything like the mutinies in the British fleet during the Napoleonic

Wars, or the mutinous condition of the French armies in 1917. There have been smaller and more isolated incidents, however, and these ought to be mentioned.

Conditions in the Revolutionary period were so hard that several instances of mutiny or near-mutiny existed. The New York militia gave much trouble in 1777, and there was a good deal of discontent at Fort Ticonderoga. Soldiers at Valley Forge came to the brink of mutiny in 1777 and 1778. At different times, Revolutionary soldiers at Charlottesville (Virginia), West Point, Fort Schuyler, Albany, and at Saratoga gave officers much difficulty. In 1780 the Connecticut line almost mutinied, and it took pleas from Washington and others to put conditions right.

The worst incident in the Revolution occurred in 1781, however. Troops of the Pennsylvania line mutinied, killed several officers, ignored the pleadings of General Wayne, and marched to Princeton, New Jersey. There the men formed a defensive perimeter, and threatened to kill any general who might appear. Only Washington's promise to discharge or furlough the men brought the condition to an end.

A later revolt by the New Jersey line was dealt with differently. Occurring in the same month as the mutiny of the Pennsylvania troops, the New Jersey uprising was met with vigorous action of the authorities, and the execution of the leaders of the mutiny.

Looking back on these incidents from the distance of almost two hundred years, it is amazing that Washington had so little trouble with his army. Conditions were extremely bad at times, and as Wayne pointed out, the Pennsylvania mutineers were "not devoid of reasoning." They had been faithful to the country for five years, unpaid for a good portion of that time, nearly naked, and poorly fed. What they seem to have wanted was justice. British promises of food and clothing, were they to switch allegiance, were not even considered. These men were simply patriotic Americans who had reached the limit of tolerance with regard to their living conditions.[73]

During the Civil War there were several instances in which troops failed to turn out for duty. Whole regiments, after the Emancipation

Proclamation, either failed to muster, or did so in sullen silence. A Western colonel was driven out of camp by his regiment because his men could not tolerate him. Almost all such incidents between 1861 and 1865 resulted from a complete lack of confidence by men in their officers, or by a serious disagreement of the troops with the principles of the war.

The American fighting man in World War II proved the extremity of his tolerance. An American in the Battle of the Bulge wrote that it was "impossible to realize the feeling of despair which grips a man when his comrades abandon him," but he continued to fight. Air Force units took heavy losses in Europe, and the appearance of vacant chairs at evening mess was so depressing that officers took special pains to match the number of chairs to the number of surviving men. Yet, in so far as all available research shows, there were no mutinies among fliers.[74]

The worst case of "near-mutiny" occurred among Merrill's Marauders. This unit was more properly known as the 5307th Composite Unit (Provisional), and was formed from nearly three thousand volunteers. Though it was in action only a few months—from February to May, 1944—it participated in five major and thirty minor engagements. The unit's commander was Brigadier General Frank D. Merrill; an amiable and confident man who had a history of heart trouble.

The story of the 5307th is one filled with hardships, unfortunate circumstances, and broken promises. The campaign towards Myitkyina was carried on through jungles and over mountain ridges. None of the soldiers had completely dry clothing during most of the march. Fire fights with the Japanese sometimes closed to within twenty-five yards. Merrill suffered from a new series of heart attacks, and virtually all of the Marauders became victims of one illness or another. Figures relating to the last difficulty are quite revealing. Slightly more than 1,900 men had become ill by the close of the Myitkyina effort. Of these there were 135 cases of total exhaustion and forty-two cases of psychoneurosis. The remainder suffered from malaria, "Naga," or leech sores, dengue fever, and dysentery. The battle casualties for the campaign amounted to 424 killed, wounded, or missing. Thus almost every man in the unit became a campaign statistic.[75]

The sorriest phase of the march to Myitkyina involves the relationship of the 5307th to General Joseph Stilwell, who not only commanded the Marauders but the Chinese troops in the area as well. Somewhere in the course of the war a promise had been made, either by Stilwell or by those subordinate to him, that the 5307th would be relieved once it had captured the Myitkyina airfield. This the troops did, but then sick and wornout, they were ordered to continue the siege of the town itself. Convalescent soldiers with fevers well over one hundred degrees were ordered out of their sick beds, and exhausted men were sent back into the line.

At this point the story becomes obscure. Discipline disintegrated within the unit, and it was soon announced that *Galahad,* the code name for the Myitkyina campaign, "was shot." Withdrawn to a rest camp, the men became even more sullen; there was violence within the camp, and the officers lost control of the men.[76]

The true story of the last hours of *Galahad* may not be known for decades. At this point in time one can only ask questions. Did Stilwell really expect too much of these men, or were the Marauders a unit from which little could be expected? Obviously the men had little respect for Stilwell, and he for them. When the unit reached the Ledo Road after a long grueling march, "Vinegar Joe," who was nearby, did not even go out to meet them. Stilwell apparently minimized the troubles of the 5307th and seemed to fail to recognize what they had done. The number of Japanese killed by the Marauders is impressive; yet Stilwell neglected to award any medals until after the damage to morale was done. Then, when it was too late, six Distinguished Service Crosses were given as well as forty Silver Stars. No Marauder won a Congressional Medal of Honor.

It is certain that recognition of the unit's efforts and some rest might have helped. An officer, viewing the unit as it was being pulled out of the line, remarked: "They look as if it were the end of the war for them, don't they. . . ? But you know, all they need is a pat on the back . . . maybe a parade—and they'd be back in here next season ready to do it all over again." Years later, and in retrospect, a close observer of the Marauders made this comment:

> The truth of the matter is that no one in the theater seemed to have the slightest concept as to how to handle combat troops; especially those sick, disgusted, disillusioned, aggressive, over-strained Galahad troops. No doubt about fifty, pretty little Indian, Chinese, Burmese prostitutes might have been the simplest solution to the whole problem.[77]

All in all, and in every war, it is apparent that all that any fighting American has ever wanted is a fighting chance. Given that, and with reasonably good leadership, the vicissitudes of misfortune have generally been met with good humor and reason. One can suspect that even Merrill's Marauders could have done without Chinese or Burmese women had the other conditions of their situation been normalized. The same was undoubtedly true of disgruntled American Civil War and Revolutionary soldiers, who, from time to time, were placed in the depths of privation.

7

Conquerors and Deliverers

WAR IS A CONTEST OF POWER from which neither side emerges completely unhurt. Property is destroyed, men are wounded and killed, and one side usually comes out as the victor. Fortunately, the United States has never lost a war. Excepting the War of 1812 and the Korean War, the country has won more glory in each struggle than it has lost. Thus has the American fighting man been a conqueror in most cases; a deliverer in others. In some instances—the two world wars, as examples—he has been both at the same time. How has he behaved in moments of triumph?

The circumstances of American history are such that the American armed forces have taken a great many prisoners. The first significant victories of this sort took place during the Revolution. Large numbers of German mercenaries and British-Canadian elements at Saratoga were surrounded and forced into surrender. Other major American land victories occurred at Stony Point, in the Illinois country, and at Yorktown. Hundreds of British seamen were captured as well by the Continental Navy and privateers.

Taking everything into account, it can be written that the American treatment of the captured in the American Revolution was far better than the treatment of American prisoners by the British. The large numbers of prisoners from Burgoyne's army were treated to no jeering or mishandling by Revolutionary troops after their surrender at Saratoga. Even the hated Hessians were dealt with fairly. Eventually this group of men—"convention" troops as they were called— were taken to the Boston area, where they were allowed great quantities of seafood and vegetables for their ration. If there was any difficulty at all, it lay in the bitter personal animosity that arose between some American and British officers. The latter refused to recognize the rank of the Americans, and in several instances, attempted to violate their privileges by sneaking out of camp. On the lower levels the relationships between the King's troops and the Revolutionaries in Boston were quite good.

At Stony Point the victorious Americans treated their British prisoners with exceptional kindness, and at Yorktown the surrendered forces were treated with such dignity that British officers were surprised. Only after the Battle of King's Mountain did American troops get out of hand. There the fight between American Tories and Revolutionaries had been so bitter that some of the Loyalists were shot after surrender. On the whole, however, one would have to agree with G. M. Trevelyan, the British historian that, when prisoner exchanges were made, the British prisoners were in a better condition than returned Americans.[1]

The customarily excellent treatment of captured enemy soldiers continued into the War of 1812 and the Mexican War. In 1815, following the Battle of New Orleans, a British officer wrote: "It is but justice to state that the Americans have behaved with some degree of kindness to our wounded prisoners. . . ."[2] Though it was not uncommon for Mexican soldiers to use the lance on wounded Americans in the war with Mexico, the Americans seldom retaliated in kind. After the major battles of this conflict—all American victories—United States soldiers were usually kept busy giving water to wounded Mexicans and helping to ease their condition.

In most cases the rules of war prevailed in the American Civil War. There were instances, however, when emotions or circumstances erased their effect. Negro Union soldiers were mishandled, and in some cases, massacred by victorious Confederates. Prison camps on both sides left much to be desired; particularly the Confederate prisons at Andersonville in Georgia, and Camp Ford in Texas, and the Union prisons in Illinois and New York. By far and away the worst of these was Andersonville (properly called Camp Sumpter), and the large numbers of prison deaths from starvation and disease in that camp is to this day inexcusable. Though the death rate in Federal prisons was sometimes high, this was usually the result of epidemics among Confederate prisoners already weakened by malnutrition at the time of their capture, rather than of poor food or facilities in the camp proper.

The treatment of Spanish prisoners in 1898 was exceptional. Spanish officers and men were treated with great courtesy, one of them writing that the Americans had vied "with each other in supplying our wants. . . ." Once on the American mainland, the prisoners were deluged with letters of sympathy, flowers, books, and by delegations of Protestant clergymen, who were anxious to make sure that the Spanish Catholics were treated well.[3]

Only one incident marred the record of Americans in this rather gentle war. Rookie American sentries, thinking that a commotion among the prisoners taken at Santiago indicated an attempted prison break, fired upon the Spanish and killed five of them. Even this was slightly excusable, however, for the near riot occurred near an American ammunition storage quarters, and it is understandable that the sentries had become concerned. Admiral Cervera's last word on the war was indicative of the treatment his men received. He wrote: "I wish to state that wherever we went there were demonstrations of the greatest sympathy with our misfortune. I have received many visits and many kind services from prominent people, some of very high rank, and at Annapolis the whole population was very kind to us."[4]

In 1917 the American fighting man went to war with sentiments well conditioned by American and British propaganda. He disliked the "Huns" or "Boche," as he was wont to call them, and sometimes let his zeal carry him too far on the field of battle. Once taken prisoners, however, Germans were well treated. Below are some comments by prisoners and German civilians on the conditions in American prison compounds.[5]

COMMENT OF CAPTURED HUNGARIAN LIEUTENANT—1918

All day long [we] were moved from one place to another until at 9:30 we arrived, soaked, in a large prison cage. . . . Later we received blankets from the Americans, which was very good of them. . . . Woke up in the morning at 5 o'clock. We received breakfast. Heavens, lovely white bread, a large piece which even in peace times is better than our cakes. Also meat and vegetables, conserve, and coffee that had some kick to it. Dinner, this priceless bread; a large piece, meat stew and coffee. . . . If this keeps up this way I shall even forget that I slept in such a condition. It is royal time the Americans give us.

EXCERPT BY POSTAL CENSORS—1919

Prisoners of war under American jurisdiction continue to send home glowing reports of good treatment. It is clearly deducible that they are more satisfied with their present condition, than they would be at home.

MEMORANDUM OF INFORMATION OBTAINED BY CENSOR —3RD ARMY, 1919

Returning prisoners of war are preaching American gospel in their homes. A Liburg student writes that he has talked with many of these and that they have nothing but praise for American treatment. The food, clothing and housing conditions while with the Americans were all of the best and as a consequence they were in excellent spirit and physical condition on their return. Those under French control tell another story. They say that those who are still in France will be kept quite a while because they are not in fit physical condition to be returned.

Despite the bitter emotions of Americans concerning Hitler, German prisoners in World War II were treated extremely well; in fact, much better than American prisoners in German prison camps. Though there were some bad incidents on the front line, there was nothing on the American side to compare with Malmédy. During the heat of battle most Americans allowed reason to rule emotion. In one instance a captured German sergeant in Italy who had refused to disclose information was vigorously defended by his captors. To the Americans the sergeant had shown himself to be a "real soldier," and was therefore excused from the usual ordeal with intelligence officers.[6]

Once brought to the rear, the German prisoners were most often transported to America. Here they were lodged in camps in various parts of the United States. The food they received was good—not equal to that of the American soldier—but on a par with the British ration. Though security in these prisons was barely adequate, only a very small number of Germans attempted to escape. So good were conditions in general that many of Hitler's "supermen" made plans to live in the United States as soon as the war was concluded.[7]

The Japanese, as well as the Italians and Germans, expected far worse treatment at the hands of the GI's than they received, which accounts for the numbers of Japanese suicides during the various battles for Pacific islands. Yet Japanese prisoners were taken, and these usually cooperated to the extreme with American intelligence authorities. On Bougainville Japanese prisoners not only "sang" loudly, but asked for the privilege to broadcast loudspeaker appeals to their comrades to surrender. Japanese prisoners taken during the hard fighting on Guadalcanal, one of the earlier battles of the war, were extremely well treated. An American soldier wrote concerning them:

They look well-fed, healthy, and well-behaved. There are a couple of aviators among them. A few look alert and quick, but the average looks like an ordinary boy who's spent too much time down on the farm. I'm not sure that Americans kept in captivity for as many weeks would look as good.[8]

Though resented by some GI's, the kind treatment of the Japanese and Germans brought some dividends. German rocket scientists, for example, chose the American Army to surrender to rather than the Russian. Many Italian units surrendered quickly in combat, and mocked American soldiers with statements that while the latter were going to Italy, they were going to New York. On Okinawa, late in the war with Japan, a number of Japanese began to give up rather than face more artillery barrages, and these included some officers.

The treatment of North Korean and Chinese prisoners during the Korean War varied according to circumstances. There were problems, however; not so much because of lack of food and clothing rations, but mainly because of hard-core Communists being allowed to dominate the prisoners for a rather long period. The situation was eventually cleared up, right at the close of the conflict, and many thousands of Chinese and North Korean prisoners decided to stay in South Korea rather than return home.

The control of Viet Cong prisoners in the present war has remained in the hands of the South Vietnamese. Unfortunately, and in all fairness, it must be said that the treatment of these people could be better. But then, the Vietnam War is a most peculiar one, demanding the utmost in patience and fortitude in American policy.

The various conditions described above relate to prisoners taken in battle. But there is another side to the whole question of the American fighting man as a conqueror—or even a deliverer—and that is his relationship with conquered or rescued civilian populations.

There is comparatively little to relate along this line during the first several decades of American independence. The Revolutionary War was fought principally in the thirteen states, and if one is to consider American Tories as conquered peoples, then it must be said that the attitude of the victors was harsh. Most of the families were stripped of their property, and were forced to flee to Canada. In the War of 1812 an American army struck again at the descendants of these same people by destroying part of the Canadian village of York; an act which was used as an excuse by the British to burn Washington.

Outside of the steady conquest of the Indians in the West, the first real American invasion of foreign territory took place in the Mexican War. In this conflict small American armies struck down from the north, and westward from Vera Cruz. The behavior of each—that is, the armies of Taylor and Scott—was both good and bad, depending on place and circumstance.

On the bad side it may be said that many of the volunteer soldiers behaved poorly. There were times when they plundered, drank too much, destroyed property, and shot civilians for amusement. They also bought women who accompanied their units as camp followers; an offense in the eyes of many Mexicans.

It may be added, on the other hand, that there were almost as many offenses committed by Mexicans against Americans. Shopkeepers charged extremely high prices for goods sold to Americans; American soldiers were waylaid on dark streets and jackrolled; and some Americans were provoked into quarrels.

In general, however, the behavior of Americans in Mexico was quite good. The Americans went out of their way to please the Catholic Church of Mexico by asking priests to accompany some of their units. Protestant officers made a point of attending local religious festivities whenever possible. At Saltillo and Tampico, which towns the Americans had shot up, the American soldiers were curfewed and forced to pay for stolen property. Puebla, after its occupation by American troops, had such unprecedented enforcement of the law that murder became almost unknown. Taxes fell everywhere; gouges by landowners were restricted; and the occupation government of the Americans was "clean."

When all was said and done, there were many Mexicans who regretted the American departure at the end of the war. Tears flowed in some communities, and General Winfield Scott was even tendered the offer of a monarchy. As is the nature of history in such developments, these aspects of the American venture in Mexico have been forgotten by the people of both countries. Even the Treaty of Guadalupe-Hidalgo, which was gentler to the defeated nation than most treaties of that day, is viewed today only in the rather simplified terms of Manifest Destiny or American imperialism.[9]

The intentions of both sides in the American Civil War were, in the beginning, quite honorable. Confederate troops, marching through parts of Maryland where Union sympathies prevailed, tried very hard not to offend these people. Federal troops in Missouri and Kentucky in 1861 were punished and fined when caught foraging off the general population.

But this excellent behavior was only temporary. Bushwackers in Missouri and Kentucky killed Federal troops out on patrol, and the attitudes of the Northern soldiers hardened. Stories of the castration of Federal cavalrymen, whether true or untrue, made the Federal Army susceptible to notions of revenge. On the other side, Lee's invasion of Pennsylvania in 1863 indicates that the Confederates were not above an overzealous penalization of civilian populations.

In the long run it was the Federal effort in the war which stood more often in the light of condemnation. Because of the bitterness of the conflict, and because the Northerners were the principal invaders, it was they who bore the onus of what many Confederates called wanton destruction. Sherman foraged his way through Georgia; that much is an established fact. He burned his way into South Carolina; that, too, is history. What is generally forgotten, however, are some other facets of the war. It is hard, for example, to find a single instance of rape committed by a member of Sherman's army (Southern writers claim that this was because of the large numbers of Negro campfollowers). Very little destruction if any was committed by Federal troops in North Carolina. Too, many of Sherman's men felt they had sufficient reasons to take revenge. The stories of Andersonville Prison and other supposed atrocities did not assuage any notions of Federal retaliation. Many Yankee cavalrymen, particularly Kilpatrick's men, were given no quarter after capture. Yet, in the end, Sherman's surrender agreement with Confederate General Joe Johnston was as generous as could be expected from any conqueror anywhere.[10]

In the immediate sense, the treatment of the Confederates in 1865 was exceedingly good; particularly when one considers what it might have been after four horrible years of conflict. Broadly speaking, it was the Southerners who brought upon themselves the punishment of Reconstruction. Unrepentant as losers, the institution of "Black Codes," the refusal of the South to accept racial equality, and the assassination of Lincoln; all of these factors allowed the Radical Republicans to successfully wave the "bloody shirt" for the next thirty years.

It was probably the realization of what such vengeance could do that formulated the outlines of American policy in 1898 and 1919. The Spanish in Cuba and Filipino nationalists were handled with comparatively good sense after the Spanish-American War. Within weeks of the American conquest of Puerto Rico the people there were quick to assert that they were "no español—pero Americano."[11]

At the end of World War I American military authorities instructed their occupation troops to behave with coolness and discipline toward German civilians. There were strongly phrased orders against fraternization of any sort. These policies were given muscle, and violators were punished in the beginning. Used to such frigid treatment from their own military units, the reaction of the German population was surprising. Submissive, fawning, or overweening, the Rhinelanders quickly broke down official American military policy. Former German generals pronounced Americans to be their "friends," and the "most honorable of all of our enemies." One American private wrote concerning the Germans: "They sure did give the Americans a royal Welcome for anything they had left . . . they wanted to give us boys while going through. . . ." Within weeks of the American occupation of Coblenz, the destruction of the American nonfraternization policy was complete, and occupation troops were freely distributing chocolate and other supplies to friendly children.[12]

At this point there began a rather strange honeymoon between the victorious American troops and the conquered Germans. To the doughboys the Germans seemed infinitely cleaner than the French had been. Their roads were good; their government bureaus were efficient. Their houses were sparkling clean and were open to all American troops. One American soldier, showing the effects of such a reception, wrote:

The ladies little girl and I are buried eyebrow in cake and chocolate trying to eat our way out. She thinks there is nobody like me. . . . When any one tells you that we were fighting the German people you tell them that I said they were mistaken as the Kaiser and his gang were the ones we were after.[13]

Once situated in the Rhineland, American Army authorities maintained a close but quiet watch on German attitudes toward the occupation troops. German mail was studied, and the press observed, in order to keep a barometric check on public opinion. The initial reactions of the civilians was invariably good. Below are a list of quotes from formal statements by German public officials or from censored mail treating with the American occupation.[14]

STATEMENT OF THE MAYOR OF KASCHENBACH

When your troops finally reached here, we watched their every movement with mingled feelings of fear and uncertainty. But today, after living 24 hours with them, we have no longer any apprehension. They are wonderfully mild mannered men and a great contrast to the domineering attitude of our own soldiers. Your troops, not even one, have spoken a single disagreeable word to anyone, and when we offered them wood for cooking and heating purposes they accepted with what seemed to be a certain shyness. They sit in our living rooms with us, and we smoke and try to make ourselves understood.

CLIPPING BY MAIL CENSORS, MAY 14, 1919

I have had soldiers in quarter all winter . . . ; it is certain that these people possess a secret method which raises the most common fellows into an individual who stands up boldly and moves about freely and unconcerned. I think we can learn some things there which later could be used to advantage here. I do not mean this personally, but as a better education nationally.

GERMAN WOMAN'S ACCOUNT OF AMERICAN ARRIVAL, NO DATE

While on duty the relations between men and officers are very strict, but on the other hand, when off duty, they are without restraint. The officers sit in the same rooms with their men. . . . There is no evidence of lack of discipline or of disobedience. Rumors to that effect are simply fairy tales spread by the Kultur of Kiel and Berlin. . . .

GERMAN WOMEN'S STATEMENT CONCERNING AMERICANS, NO DATE

Now let us come to the Americans. . . . They passed through the town . . . strong young people, of whom at least every tenth man could speak German. These people arrived in a friendly—almost modest manner, and therefore, are given a good and friendly reception. . . ."

STATEMENT BY RHINELAND CIVILIAN

The people of our village were worried at first about the occupation by American troops. Instructions were given as to how the inhabitants should conduct themselves in order to avoid any unpleasant incident. Children have constantly talked of the Americans' arrival, and pictured them as a band of wild Indians. However, when the troops arrived, we were astonished at their behavior and pleasant attitude toward our people. The men knocked at our doors, before entering our houses, and asked for what they wanted in a kindly manner. Not a single man acted disagreeably. Our people could not be more satisfied with the conduct of the American soldiers.

Many comparisons were made by German civilians about the behavior of American troops as compared with the French and British occupation troops, and with the comportment of German troops in the late stages of the war. Here are a few of those comments.

INTERROGATION OF GERMAN SHOPKEEPER OF DERNAU

As in statements made by others the warm reception given the American troops is not so much due to the fact that they like us as it is to the fact that they like the French and English less. Reports are circulating through this part of the country at the present time of the ill treatment received by the people around COLOGNE from the English troops. These reports have not been confirmed but they are generally known and talked about among the German people all of which causes bitterness of feeling against our Allies and increased liking for our own troops against whom no such rumors have been started.

CENSORSHIP CLIPPING OF MAIL FROM COBLENZ

I really dread to go to Wiesbaden and it is on account of the French occupation. Yes! If Americans were there it would be a pleasure. Coblenz may consider itself fortunate. They are likeable, neat and sensible people. I readily noticed the wide contrast in my journeys to and from Wiesbaden.

INTERROGATION OF GERMAN CITIZEN OF NEUNAHR, FEBRUARY, 1919

Hahn states that all the people in the town are admiring the clean-cut American soldiers. He states that the impression the American soldier is leaving, with the people of Germany, is the impression that Germany will have of America for years to come. He notices the contrast between the American and German armies in their forms of discipline, stating that if the German army had been as free with their men as the American Army is, they would not have had the success that was theirs at the beginning of the war.

INTERROGATION OF GERMAN SCHOOLTEACHER, DECEMBER, 1918

The American soldiers are well liked by the inhabitants as they are clean and generally treat the people with respect. He does not think our army well disciplined as compared to the German army but it is the universal feeling among the people that the spirit of the American army is much better than the German army ever has been.

CENSORSHIP NOTES FROM LETTER OF GERMAN CITIZEN, MAY, 1919

Johann Vogelsang of Westfalia [sic] who has visited the American Occupied Zone writes to Anna Wold of Niederahr that he would rather be among the gentlemen from America than the brutes who call themselves government soldiers.

The eventual growth of bitterness between American soldiers and German citizens was slow and gradual, and it was caused principally by mutual suspicions. The Americans claimed that the Germans were gouging them on prices, jackrolling them in alleys, discriminating against Negro soldiers, and were generally unrepentant. The Germans were sure that the American soldiers were responsible for the increase in crime, they disliked Negro soldiers, and they looked upon Americans as uncultured foreigners.

An American soldier who entered Germany in 1919 phrased the growing dislike of the Germans when he wrote: "If they [the American people] would see this Country over here they would say that Germany could have another larger army than she had, in fifteen years. There is the biggest gang of dirty snotty-nosed sore-eyed kids in this town that I ever saw." Another American soldier—a sergeant—sadly noted that many smaller German towns immediately stopped sales of liquor to the occupying army because of troubles which arose in bars. In early spring a German citizen, seeing the growing disillusionment on both sides, wrote: "By August, the Americans will have turned their backs to us. . . ." And in May, 1919, a woman of Wollstein, Rheinhessen, wrote:

> I want you to forbid Herman using such bold and insolent terms in speaking about the Americans. Let him be more decent and by all means do not accept any chocolate. . . . They can make things warm for you if they want to, and above all do not say that you are right. We do not touch their pockets or anything. . . . Here Katchen Schroder was thrown into jail from Monday to Tuesday because she told a soldier to ———. Another girl was unceremoniously spanked in broad daylight, and she is 23 years old too. . . . Stores were also closed because the owners were unfriendly and impudent. . . . Anna is painting beautiful roses upon white velvet which she intends to make into sofa pillows to send to you. You are to sell them to the Americans for a high price because they are good buyers and send many articles to their rich relatives in America.[15]

United States Army censorship reports in 1919 indicated a rapid turnabout in the relationship of the Germans with the American soldiers. Some occupied areas claimed that the Americans had requisitioned too much housing and equipment, leaving the civilians with very little. These Rhinelanders generally failed to note that American Army authorities usually paid handsomely for the items. Gone were the written and spoken statements that Americans were a chivalrous people who would not take revenge. Now the conquerors were "greedy" because they hampered black market operations, and they were "spiteful" because they punished German citizens for illegal possession of American goods or food. This was fault-finding of the lowest order, for without American food and financial support, much of occupied Germany might well have starved.

Evidence of the end of the honeymoon is plentiful. American authorities chlorinated the water supply in the town of Mayen, and became the victims of a malicious charge that the water had been poisoned. Newspapers in unoccupied Germany, particularly those in Berlin, added to the growing antipathy. A Berlin publication charged the Americans with overburdening the food supply of the Rhineland by buying at "fabulous prices," by ordering all peasants to keep their windows open at night so as to encourage the spread of influenza, and by censoring religious sermons. And in May, the same newspaper wrote:[16]

The American on the street is always chewing. If he does not chew tobacco, he chews gum and when he is not chewing he is spitting. I walked behind an American officer who spat five times every 100 meters. . . . Everybody knows that the American is practical. I noticed this particularly in their substitute for handkerchiefs. I saw even officers blow their noses by placing them between their thumb and index finger. . . . The childishness characteristic of primitive peoples crops out with all its frivolities and weaknesses in American character. They may be seen by dozens in shops, handling everything and buying useless articles at any price. . . . Liquor regulations were at first very strict, but liquor may now be sold until 10 p.m. and insults to women and indignities to men are often offered by drunken soldiers.

A second Berlin newspaper hit upon the same theme when it complained that the Americans on the Rhine had created a "strange, foreign world, which has no feeling for this old seat of culture. . . ." The Americans were out of place with the "fragrance, history, culture, and poetry" of the region. Searching for faults, the paper contended that "the populace is obliged to listen to Americans who speak German and have German names, when they tell how they won the war and are going to see that Old Germany does not get the severe peace terms."

It is an amazing fact that, with the admitted faults of Americans, the Germans could see none of their own. The high prices for farm produce were not being charged by the Americans but by German farmers. It was not the girl who was out after dark who was condemned, but the American who approached her. And those terrible Americans were the ones who enforced the laws. This peculiar Teutonic ability to put a reverse spin to logic is shown in the following clippings by American censorship authorities.[17]

FROM A RHINELANDER'S LETTER, FEBRUARY, 1919

Electricity plants are overburdened and the inhabitants get a feeble current so that the Herr American may burn 3 lamps in every latrine. This is the way things are here with the much praised American Occupation. If one smokes an American cigarette, one goes to the pen or pays a 3,000 M. fine. All in the name of Foch. Poor Germany how low you have sunk. The saddest is that all women folk run after them for the sake of candy.

FROM A LETTER WRITTEN AT NIEDERBREISING, N.D.

What are your Americans doing? Do you get as much chocolate as I do? I am tired of the stuff and also of the entire pack, although I have had many very very pleasant hours with them. The Americans cannot grasp that we have so much work to do. Those lazy people. Things are better for them in America than for us here. I may yet go with them. Then you would indeed make eyes. . . .

FROM A LETTER WRITTEN AT NEUWIED, N.D.

And these people want to bring Kulture to us barbarians? It makes me laugh. They are so many kilometers beneath us in reference to this kultur that it should be impossible for them even to try to compare themselves with us. . . . I haven't found any yet with any conception of the beauty of art and nature. One hears only music-hall tunes among them. Of course there are exceptions as in everything else, but some of these men are so far beneath that their origin from the ape can be plainly seen upon their faces. . . . They are the wildest when they are after the girls. But thank God that they cannot at once recognize the difference between a "decent" and a "common girl."

From a Berlin Newspaper, May, 1919

American women are more disagreeable to billet. They are supposed to be nurses and office helpers but the popular name for them is "Comforters." Worn out and painted, typical adventuresses, they walk arm in arm with officers, squeezed between their "protectors" in autos, or ride in the Coblentz woods.

As may be gathered from the above statements, much of the trouble between the Americans and Germans concerned women or stemmed from the quartering of occupation troops upon the general population. There was also some antagonism on the part of the Germans arising from the American readiness to thwart illegal operations, and the willingness of French occupational authorities to overlook such tedious details. One may see hints of all these difficulties in the following comments.[18]

From the Letter of Spinster Schoolteacher of Coblenz

All of the beautiful buildings and pretty restaurants they reserve to themselves. Our school is also occupied. Yesterday we had to clear out the last room in the building, which was used for our library. All books were placed in a furniture wagon and today we took them to another building. . . . And we were compelled to do it because the Americans wanted it done. Many German girls go around with Americans. I simply can't understand it. If any American talks to me I am prepared to give him an answer.

Third Army Censorship Report, May, 1919

The American troops are in general not as well spoken of as during the earlier part of the occupation. The French troops on the contrary are becoming more popular. The reason for these changes is probably that the Americans are continuing to enforce all their regulations very strictly while the French allow the inhabitants of their zones much more freedom than formerly.

One finds constant complaining from the Germans that American soldiers in 1919 were poorly behaved during the occupation of the Rhineland. Forgotten was the extremely poor discipline of the German army in the same area at the end of the war. Now every night stabbing was blamed on American soldiers, and every girl seen with an American soldier was suspect as a prostitute. A Grenzhausen citizen wrote:

> Am glad you are not at home, for we have serious conditions here. One of the boys was shot last night and two others were stabbed. It is unsafe to cross the street at night. Am not going to take any chances either. Many of our young girls have gone wrong since the A———are here; it is almost hard to believe of some of them. Martha Strodter is engaged to an A——— Isn't she crazy?[19]

The facts on crime during the American occupation of the Rhineland throw a different light on the subject than that seen by the Germans. Generally speaking, the behavior and discipline of the American soldier *was good,* and suffered only a slight deterioration when first line troops were sent home. During the first ten months of the occupation six Americans were convicted of larceny, twenty-three for assault with a deadly weapon, and 256 were accused by Germans of felony. Dixon Wecter, who compiled these figures, claims that, out of the quarter of a million Americans stationed in Germany in this period, the criminal cases amount to only two thousand per year.[20]

Such figures indicate that the American Occupation Army was fairly well behaved; especially in view of that fact that, for the same ten months of 1919, nearly ten thousand Germans were convicted for the same offenses against Americans. This last fact shows that, if it was unsafe for a German to "cross the street at night," it was five times as unsafe for an American to be out in the dark. With his comparatively high pay, the American soldier out on the town in the Rhineland in 1919 was the usual victim of gang attacks, sandbagging, jackrolling, and knifings.

History does have a habit of repeating itself, and in the case of the American occupation of part of Germany after World War II, it did. The brutalities of the Germans during the war years were well known by American GI's, and they entered Germany with every intention of being cool and distant victors. Instructions, pamphleteered to each GI who crossed the Rhine in 1945, read as follows:[21]

You are entering Germany, not as a liberator but as a victor. Do not keep smiling. Never offer a cigarette to a visitor whom you do not know well, nor offer him your hand. The Germans will respect you as long as they see in you a successor to Hitler, who never offered them his hand.

Forget the American habit of meeting everyone in an open way. Distrust everybody who has given you no proof of his honesty.

Always wear a uniform, never wear civilian clothes.

Never give way. Anything that is granted as a favor will be regarded by the German as his right, and he will subsequently demand twice as much. He thinks fair play is cowardice.

The only way to get along with the Germans is to make them respect you, to make them feel the hand of the master.

There was really very little need to inform American combat troops of the character of many Germans, for they had seen it in such places as Buchenwald and Dachau. A young private, writing in 1945 after seeing the charnel houses of these camps, told his mother that the Germans would have to pay and pay hard. An American captain, having also seen the slave laborers of Germany, expressed his own feelings:

The destruction is inconceivable. And, curiously enough, the roads and houses and fences are draped with flags. . . . As a matter of fact, they are all white. . . . I think we have learned our lesson. Unfortunately I can feel no compassion whatever for those folk.[22]

John Dos Passos ran across the same sentiment among American soldiers shortly after the German surrender. It was a sense of resentment; a notion that Americans were too soft with everyone. "We apologized to the French for saving their country and we apologize to the British and we apologize to the Russians. . . ." a soldier told Dos Passos. "First thing you know we'll be apologizing to the Germans for licking them. . . . And they all hate our guts and it damn well serves us right."[23]

The fear expressed by Dos Passos' GI is supported by fact. A study of the attitudes of American soldiers shows that in April, 1945, 71 percent of the GI's blamed "all of the ordinary Germans" for the war. By August the figure dropped to 61 percent. In April, 55 percent of the American soldiers felt that Germany could not be trusted again; in August, the figure was 40 percent.[24]

It was hard for the World War II American to maintain official policies of nonfraternization in Germany. As the first American troops entered Leipzig, flowers were thrown at them by some of the German civilians. The qualities of German character—the submissiveness, the discipline, the cleanliness, and the servility in defeat —once again broke down all barriers. In a sense the American GI liked Germany for many of the same reasons he did not like France. The *autobahns* were impressive, and the neatness of German towns clearly exceeded that of French villages. And there were the children and the girls. The little blond children quickly broke down GI resistance by unhesitatingly approaching the Americans. The girls, according to a New York *Sun* reporter, were immediately very friendly, and wore extremely short dresses in order to attract the attention of the occupation soldiers. Within a short time it was difficult for the ordinary American to remember that the men he met on the streets were the same ones who had shot American prisoners at Malmédy, or who had operated the ovens at Dachau. Thus did the policy of nonfraternization become a horrendous failure by the end of 1945.[25]

The German reaction to American occupation followed the World War I pattern. The one great difference was that Germany itself had suffered badly in this war. Berlin, Nuremberg, Cologne, Mannheim, Essen, Coblenz, and other German cities were heavily damaged. Everywhere there was ruin and devastation. Rumors passing about throughout the American zone of occupation indicated that if treated properly the Americans might invade Russia; that all German marriages (plus children) would be forbidden for ten years; and that all surplus butter was being used to polish boots of the American soldiers. Thus, with the appearance of the first American troops, there was the familiar tendency of Germans to attempt to curry favor with the conquerors.[26]

Once the initial fears were passed, however, the ordinary German civilian resumed his more aggressive nature. More and better food supplies were demanded from occupation authorities. Americans were criticized for poor discipline, and the informality and "sloppiness" of their soldiers. Negro Americans were particularly disliked. As far as the conduct of the war was concerned, most Germans returned to the notion that they had *not* been wrong in fighting the war—but just *unlucky* in not winning it. One study conducted in 1948 showed that the German population disliked the Russians, French, British, and Americans in that order. Most Germans felt that their cities should not have been bombed. "Why did English and American bombers destroy our cities and factories while we were fighting the Russians?" was a common complaint. Few Germans understood how their troops had behaved during the war, and claimed that American air attacks had been "unethical" and that the discipline of American soldiers was "disappointing."[27]

The truth and fiction in the post-World War II years in Germany are difficult to separate. The Germans complained of looting by GI's, fights by American troops in Berchtesgaden and Garmisch-Partenkirchen, attacks upon German women, and general misbehavior by GI's. The same twisting of logic, first seen in the Rhineland in 1919, appeared again. Signs appeared on fences calling for Americans to go home; yet there were public statements everywhere that the Americans now had a responsiblity to feed and protect the German people. Germans protested against American "brutality," and read books such as that by the German General Guderian. Guderian, a crack German tank commander in Russia, claimed that he could not have taken part in the plot to kill Hitler because he was a "Christian" and did not believe in murder. A German bartender, protesting against the loud behavior of Americans in his place of business, claimed that "this could not happen in the German army." How quickly had the early years of German successes in France and Russia been forgotten![28]

How valid were the German complaints about the lack of discipline among GI's? By May, 1945, there were already complaints that American soldiers had committed the sexual offense of rape against some German girls. Immediate investigation showed that many of the supposedly offended women were still virgins, and that others were known prostitutes. In July, 1956, the town of Bamberg, Bavaria, asked the U. S. Army to keep its soldiers out of town, mainly because of supposed rapes, attacks on German civilians, and brawls by soldiers with beer bottles. In the same year there was considerable unrest with American airborne troops in Munich over the alleged lack of restraint. Other German towns asked American authorities to keep their Negro soldiers in hand, because these were the subjects of much German resentment.

Investigations by American Army officers divulged the following facts. First, the behavior of the airborne troops near Munich was considered well above the average. Secondly, many cities such as Munich were partly to blame for various incidents because of local conditions, which German authorities allowed to continue. Munich had many bars—most of them filled with prostitutes. Five out of six of the rape cases involving Americans were established to be caused by an "underpaid or badly-used lady of the evening." Most of the beer-bottle brawls were between Americans and Germans with "zoot-suit persuasions." Thirdly, whenever the Army provided enough base facilities to keep American soldiers out of the German cities, the Germans protested. This was particularly true in the case of Heidelberg, where the German businessmen argued that Americans were being placed into "ghettos."

As far as American Negro soldiers were concerned, the problem presented two aspects. Despite the continued argument by Hitlerized Germans that Negroes were "inferior," there was no shortage of German girl friends for these soldiers. The complaints that the German population was being mongrelized by mulatto children is easily answerable that it took the compliance of German girls to accomplish this fact. In respect to the alleged Negro misbehavior in Germany, it might be added that many of the American colored soldiers, for the first time in their lives, had money in their pockets and could "operate" in a white world. This brought pleasures and hazards; both at the same time. Negro soldiers visiting bars with white prostitutes were often followed home by gangs of German youths. "Then a colored boy has to walk along quick," stated one American Negro soldier, "or its German rock and roll, but rough."[29]

Still, there was sufficient smoke in the German allegations of misbehavior for there to be some fire. With the motivations for hating Germans gone by 1946, there had occurred some decline in morale and conduct in the occupation armies; some of it on the upper levels. Older army officers had rented small apartments and installed mistresses. "Laundresses" were shared by enlisted men who couldn't quite carry the financial burden of the "single key." Venereal cases reportedly went up in 1946 from 52 cases per 1,000 soldiers to 427 cases for the same number of men. GI's had reputedly entered bakeries or restaurants and flung about dishes and bread. There were rumors of immorality among American Wacs; one was supposedly found dead and nude under an officer's window six days after her arrival from the United States.[30]

The black market, and the arrival of second-line American troops and replacements, intensified the problem. At the Alexanderplatz and the Tiergarten in Berlin, some rather substantial illegal operations were established. American soldiers wore twenty to thirty watches on either arm, and sold them to Russian soldiers. There was a reputedly large American black market operation involving American officers and soldiers who purchased watches and perfume in Switzerland and sold them in Germany.[31]

In 1956 the conduct of American troops in Germany fell under the glare of widespread publicity. A cartoon in the German newspaper, *Kasseler Zeitung,* showed an American soldier throwing a whiskey bottle through a window, with the caption reading: "Our army will protect us from our enemies but who will protect us from our friends." A twenty-year-old American private reputedly received thirty years in prison for raping a seventeen-year-old German girl and assaulting two others. Another soldier, eighteen years old, was placed in the Dachau stockade for throwing a hand grenade. An eighteen-year-old private reputedly killed a German ferryboat operator with a hunting knife. And a twenty-six-year-old veteran of Korea was convicted of an indecent assault on a German girl. According to one source the response of the American high command in Germany to these incidents was to ask the American government to stop sending soldiers with "low mentality" for occupation duty in Germany.[32]

The American magazine *Newsweek* sought for and found some answers to many of the German complaints. The GI side of the story, so said this publication, was that the total crime rate among GI's really was low; that Germans magnified everything out of proportion; and that the Germans themselves were responsible for many incidents. "The Germans are pretty cocky," claimed one American, "jeering us about having to get in by midnight, like school kids." From another GI came the complaint: "One of my buddies got in an argument with a couple of German sharpies in a restaurant. . . . They waited outside and worked him over good. You don't see stuff like that in the papers."

Concerning the charges of sexual misconduct, *Newsweek* pointed out that old German "semiprofessionals" preyed on young American boys. An Army official was reported as stating: 'You know how many rapes are reported—probably one a day somewhere in the command. I've investigated dozens. Usually they're just plain nonsense stories. The girl gets caught and hollers rape. Or maybe the boy won't pay, and she tells the police the same thing."

If figures mean anything, there are facts which support some of the claims of American military officialdom. Despite the widespread complaints of Germans in 1956, the records show that for the period from 1 December, 1953, to 30 November, 1956, there were 32,059 *alleged* offenses by American troops which fell under jurisdiction of foreign courts. Of this number slightly over 9,000 were actually tried, and only 305 American soldiers were condemned to serve jail sentences. Considering that these were total figures and that they included offenses in other countries besides Germany, and considering that America's manpower commitment to the globe was large in those years, the 305 convictions represent an insignificant figure. If these were all for sexual offenses alone—which they were not—one might conclude that Japan exceeded that number in the single incident at Nanking, and that the Russians went far beyond that number in the few days after their capture of Berlin.[33]

The American role in the conquest of Italy followed quite the same pattern as that of Germany in World War II. Internally, however, Italy presented some differences. While Germany's main cities were badly damaged by bombings, Italy's were not. While Germany committed itself entirely to the Axis war effort; Italy did not. And while there was an active Communist partisan effort in Italy, there was none in Germany.

As in World War I, when Italy entered the war only when it thought that political rewards were possible, this nation was never sure which way it should commit itself after 1940. There were times when its troops fought against British and American forces quite creditably in Africa; there were other times when they did not. Italian bombers were massed for use against the British Isles and other civilian areas (Malta) after 1940, but the Italian people bitterly resented token Allied bombing of themselves. Yet, when Naples and Rome were captured, both were bedecked with American and British flags, and the entering armies were given enthusiastic welcomes.[34]

The role of Italy in the remainder of the war was a peculiar one. An Italian Fascist army fought with the Germans; another Italian army sided with the Allies. Most of the Italian people, poverty stricken by 1943, passively hoped for an American and British victory.

The attitude of the fighting American in 1942 toward Italy and the Italians was also guided by split motivations. There were many boys of Italian descent in the American armies who could scarcely be expected to hate the land in which their fathers had been born. There were many American Catholics, who tied by their affection for the Holy City, could not look upon the Italians as enemies. But there were still other American boys, like one interviewed by Ernie Pyle, who could say: "I look at it this way—they've been poor for a long time and it wasn't us that made them poor. They started this fight and they've killed plenty of our soldiers, and now that they're whipped they expect us to take care of them. That kind of talk gives me a pain. I tell them to go to hell."[35]

Perhaps the Italians never understood it, but it was this dual emotion which colored the American war effort in Italy in World War II. By August, 1943, almost 90 percent of the food and other external supply items were coming from the United States. The Italian army was totally supplied by the United States. So much dried milk, vegetables, canned meat, soap, matches, cheese, and other food products were brought from the United States that an inevitable and vast black market came into existence. It is not fiction but a fact that Italy would have suffered terribly from famine had it not been for the American efforts at supplying the country.

Yet, while giving so much to the Italians, there were still many American soldiers who looked upon these conquered peoples as enemies whose streets and houses were dirty, whose women were immoral, and whose society was corrupt. Women could be bought for chocolate bars from little children who acted as pimps. Some GI's were accused of drunkenness, assault, looting, rowdyism, and rape. Liquor was "requisitioned" by ordinary soldiers who presented the producers with worthless slips of paper. One winemaker lost 22,000 liters of good Chianti in this manner; though investigation later proved that British soldiers in the neighborhood were greater offenders than GI's. American Rangers killed cows in some parts of

Italy in 1943 in order to obtain fresh meat; though it must be added that the American Government repaid the injured farmers.[36]

If there was one aspect of the American behavior in Italy about which one could moralize at length, it would be sex. Although more will be written below in respect to this, it might be said here that sexual standards virtually disappeared during the Allied invasion of Italy. But it must also be added that this lapse in morality occurred on both sides of the fence—with Italian women as well as with American and British soldiers. The Italians have forgotten this aspect of the problem since 1946—both in their movies and in their writings. To them it was always the uncultured American soldier who provoked the problem; not the complacent and willing teen-age Italian girl. Some evidence of this peculiar blindness is seen in the following excerpt from an Italian newspaper in the 1950's.

American soldiers were the most relaxed, carefree and sociable that Europeans had ever seen. They were even less formal than the Italians—that is, absolutely below the minimum level of discipline expected of a soldier. Before the Americans came you rarely if ever saw a drunken soldier in Europe. European armies simply do not permit troops to disgrace themselves and their services by intoxication in public. . . . The arrival of the Yanks will go down in history as the landing of the army that didn't care whether soldiers got drunk. In other matters of morals as well, the American troops turned out to be different from any seen in Europe up to the time of their arrival, with the possible exception of Hannibal's men during their stay in Capua.[37]

Such remarks can only provoke the following questions. Who has been drinking all that Italian wine produced in the last five centuries? Could the black market activities in Italy have survived without solid and important assistance from the Italians themselves? Were the excesses in drinking committed by a few American soldiers any more immoral than Italian anti-Jewish campaigns during Musolini's time? And where did all those girls, with whom the Americans were supposedly misbehaving, come from?

The surrender of Japan in 1945 brought another Axis nation under American occupation forces. As in the case of Germany, here was a nation which had fought to the bitter end. Two major cities had been virtually wiped out by atom bombs; other Japanese cities had been firebombed into destruction. One authority estimated that nearly two million Japanese lost their lives in the war; 668,000 of them from air raids alone. Over 2,250,000 Japanese buildings were destroyed by the bombings; 695,000 of them in Tokyo. At the end of the conflict, Japan had not only lost its industrial capacity, but its merchant fleet, its navy, and its transportation system as well.[38]

The first American soldier to enter Tokyo reputedly was Private Paul Davis, First Cavalry Division, from Fairfield, Oklahoma. Within weeks after his arrival the occupation of Japan was total and complete. The early American occupation units were met with a strange mixture of fear and obeisance. There is one story which, whether apocryphal or not, describes the emotions of the Japanese people soon after American troops began to arrive. Japanese electricians, put to work to repair facilities on one barracks, asked its lone occupant to what branch of the American services he belonged. His reply that he was a Marine caused a stampede to the door by the workmen.[39]

Much of this fear was rooted in Japanese war propaganda that the Americans were rapists and murderers. These notions were quickly dispelled, however, and a peculiar relationship between the Japanese and their conquerors came into being. It was, as described by Edwin O. Reischauer, the famed Asian scholar and former ambassador to Japan, "a strange fraternization between American battle veterans, who often had a bitter hatred of the Japanese they had just been fighting, and Japanese civilians who had lost loved ones and all their possessions in American air raids."[40]

The American occupation of Japan, during its first few months, presents a most interesting period in modern history. Most of the battle-seasoned Americans maintained a careful and cool approach to the beaten civilians. As one 1946 visitor put it: "One does not have to be here very long to discover that both the Americans and the Japanese know who won the war." On the other hand, the first

Americans to administer Japanese affairs were dedicated and sincere men. Reischauer writes: "It is hard to imagine a conquering army that could have undertaken the physical and spiritual rehabilitation of the erstwhile enemy with greater good will and deeper sincerity." General MacArthur led the way. "He showed all the virtues that the Japanese admire," wrote Reischauer. "His strength of will rivaled that of the strongest Japanese hero; his dignity and the firmness of his authority were all they could hope for in their leaders. . . ."[41]

Unfortunately, however, problems in the relationship between the Japanese and the Americans soon began to appear. The battle-tested veterans, whose "honesty, discipline, and fairness" had been admired by the Japanese, went home. In the case of the aforementioned First Cavalry Division, the turnover was rapid. By January, 1947, virtually all of this unit had been filled with American teen-agers who had never heard a shot fired in anger.[42]

In some ways, though, the trouble which was to come had deeper roots than the mere appearance of untried American soldiers. Japanese women, from the beginning, threw their love-starved attentions on the occupying soldiers. Within the hours after the landing of the Fifth Marine Division at Sasebo, Japanese girls attempted to force their way into the American compound. One blond Marine on sentry duty was so bothered by a Japanese girl who was stroking his hair that Japanese police had to be called to take away the offender.

There were other factors as well. The Japanese soon began to resent having to pay for the American occupation, and for certain supposed American privileges. The demobilization of Japanese soldiers—most of whom had never fought Americans in battle—brought back a built-in resentment. Returning from the islands and from Manchuria, they found their country under the American flag, members of their families in menial positions to American soldiers, and GI's now holding all the privileges that had once been theirs.[43]

The Korean War, placed on top of these irritations, caused more trouble. Japan was a "rest and recreation" area for Americans on leave from the fighting on the Korean peninsula. Many of these young fighting Americans took the phrase "R and R" to mean sex and liquor. Perhaps this was understandable, in view of the time and circumstances. General Mark Clark, the over-all commander of the American effort in Korea, saw it that way, writing: "These men, who knew that after five days they would go right back into grueling battle in Korea, played every minute they could stay awake while they were in Japan. Nobody has the right to ask a soldier just out of battle to do anything else."

What happened then in Tokyo and other Japanese cities from 1950 to 1953 merely added fuel to anti-American sentiments in the country. There were brawls between Japanese civilians and American soldiers; some caused by one group, some by the other. Prostitution flourished in Japanese cities. It was reported by one shocked American that there were over 8,400 prostitutes in the town of Chitose alone. The same reporter claimed that it was impossible to rent a hotel room in the town of Nara without a girl, and that he had seen Americans parading about Kyushu stark naked.[44]

It is doubtful that the situation was ever as bad as some shock articles in American newspapers and magazines claimed it to be, but it was not good. The result was a growth in leftist and anti-American activity in Japan. Japanese intellectuals spoke "caustically" of the behavior of the American soldiers, forgetting the earlier Japanese "rape of Nanking." Many Japanese leftists accepted Chinese propaganda about American atrocities in Korea—particularly those concerning the disfigurement of Korean women and alleged bacteriological warfare. In Japan, and even in Okinawa, students paraded and chanted on cue the slogan "Americans go home."[45]

What was never widely publicized in Japan and the United States were the real humanitarian activities of American fighting men. American officers stationed in Yokosuka gave monthly contributions to Japanese charitable organizations, even while anti-American pickets walked outside the gates of their camp. American Catholic soldiers and sailors supported parishes in Hokkaido, Muroran, Otaru, Hongkong, and in Korea. The American Twenty-Fifth Division "adopted" a Japanese orphanage in Osaka and kept it going even after the Division had gone into the fighting in Korea. In the 1953 typhoon disaster American servicemen and supplies helped the Japanese to recover. In 1959, when Nagoya was hit by a typhoon, which killed

4,200 and made over a million people homeless, the Americans quickly came forward with supplies and food. American helicopters moved Japanese civilians to safety, and thousands of lives were saved. Unfortunately, in all these incidents, the Japanese tended to feel that such help was to be expected of the Americans, and that it did not call for any public expression of appreciation.[46]

One of the greatest complaints of the Japanese concerning the Americans was that their presence caused an upsurge in crime on the streets of the nation. General Mark Clark's "official statistics" for the period from May to August, 1952, tend to contradict such claims. Clark argues that there were only 167 Americans who were charged with crimes against persons during the three month period, and these misdemeanors were mostly of the pushing and shoving variety. Crimes against property, the breaking of windows, etc., committed by American soldiers only totaled 129, according to Clark. If true, these would probably represent smaller totals than those committed by Japanese against Japanese, or by Japanese against Americans during the same period.

The strange ambivalence of emotions present in Germany with respect to Americans can also be seen in Japan. During the 1950's the Japanese people gave no great sentimental support to the fight against Communist incursions into South Korea; yet Japanese firms and businesses were willing to accept American Army contracts. In the 1960's there have been anti-American expressions in Japan over the Vietnam War, but the continuing Japanese prosperity resulting from that conflict has made the nation the strongest industrial power in Asia. The Japanese, like the Germans, have been happy to accept American protection and dollars but not the occasional excesses of some American soldiers.[47]

The relationship of the American fighting man to allied civilians and to liberated populations is a story unto itself, and can never be covered in full. Yet, because of its many-sided nature, it deserves to be briefly scanned.

The first large American expeditionary force stationed in an Allied country was the A.E.F. in World War I. Most of the American soldiers were taken directly to France, though some were passed through Britain while going to the front in 1917 or coming back from the fighting in 1919. Viewing this war in a broad sense, there were three distinct periods in which excellent relations between the Americans and their allies prevailed. The first was wrapped around the emotional arrival of American troops in 1917, when both the French and the British were on the verge of defeat. The second resulted from the American performance in the Second Battle of the Marne, when a pierced Allied line was patched with newly arrived American divisions. The third honeymoon was the shortest of all, and lasted through Armistice Day and a few days thereafter. Then both French civilians and American soldiers celebrated wildly together by dragging captured German guns about Paris while singing "Hail, Hail, the Gang's All Here. . . ."[48]

In between, however, there was some occasional bad feeling between American soldiers and the French and British. Many Americans regarded both French towns and French soldiers as being too dirty. American Army medical authorities carried on brisk campaigns to clean up many towns by scrubbing the streets, with a liberal use of disinfectants. In one French town, where zealous Americans washed the streets with a carbolic disinfectant, the citizens raised a great cry of protest, claiming the air was being poisoned. In another town that underwent the cleaning process, the mayor argued that the streets were being worn away by daily American washings.

As for the French soldiers, the attitude grew among American soldiers that the Gallic temperament allowed for too much personal dirtiness and too little appreciation of the United States. One American billet bore a sign which read "No French soldiers allowed here." And toward the end of the war most doughboys became tactlessly outspoken. "These French soldiers are a lot of ginks," asserted one American. "We can't have them around." Another commonly heard statement was "America *bon,* France *pas bon.*"[49]

Patience wore thin on all sides. The French claimed that the Americans drank too much; the Americans claimed that the French did likewise. American soldiers, while souvenir hunting, stole virtually the entire altar and clock at the Cathedral of Verdun, and the French (whose Louvre is filled with "liberated" art works) screamed foul. The French claimed that all the Americans were concerned about were French women; the Americans claimed that it was impossible to enjoy a leave without being approached by women or peddlers of pornographic literature. By the time of the American occupation of the Rhineland, the coolness between the French and the Americans had reached such a point that a German woman observed:

> The harmony between them [the Americans] and the French is very lukewarm. Everywhere one hears strong shrill discords. The French population sheared the Americans. While the French soldiers paid two francs a bottle of wine the Americans were made to pay 4, 6, and even 8 francs.[50]

The departure of American troops from France and Britain was surrounded with an emotion which was contrastingly cool to the warmness of their arrival. Most of the homeward-bound Americans in France were taken to large demobilization camps such as Camp Pontanezen in Brittany. These were, in the beginning, muddy and dirty places which offered little in the way of recreation and entertainment. Many doughboys became so dispirited with these conditions that their last memories of France were the most terrible. In England, where conditions were better, the memories of departure could be equally bad. An American sergeant was robbed of everything he had while staying at the Royal Buckingham Hotel. Later, while visiting a nightclub, he felt that the British regarded him with such "scorn and disgust" that he made it a point to show his own distaste. He wrote: "After sipping our drinks which were served to us in a hurry, because they were anxious to get us out, we leisurely lit a cigarette, talked and smoked a little and then slowly left the table giving the glad eye to all the belles who deemed it necessary to turn and look us over."[51]

The relationship between the doughboys of 1917–1919 and the French, and the relationship between the GI's and the same people in World War II bear some startling resemblances. From the beginning, while fighting with and against the French in North Africa, the

American was never considered by these people to be as disciplined as he ought to be. And in Normandy both the British and American troops were met with a surprising coolness, which reputedly had its roots in some alleged British misbehavior in the province in 1917 and 1940.

American reactions to France were usually adverse. Most American soldiers could not bring themselves to accept the bad roads, the squalid villages, the poor transportation, and French bureaucracy. Bill Mauldin, the great cartoonist of the war, hit this attitude squarely with one of his cartoons captioned "Did ya ever see so many furriners, Joe?"[52]

On the French side of the coin it may be stated that once again there was a problem with French women, whom the local inhabitants claimed were seduced by bars of chocolate. There were a few American deserters—some from the lowest class possible—who roamed about France allegedly committing depredations on poor French farmers. By 1946, with the conclusive defeat of the Germans, the French finally became outspoken in their feelings about American soldiers. The French weekly, *Samedi-Soir,* complained that GI's had taken over the Eiffel Tower, that they were constantly clambering to the top by means of ladders, they they were breaking an average of two hundred glasses a day by throwing them to the ground below, and that they were keeping Frenchmen out of the structure by force.

Nothing is ever all black or white in this sort of problem. At about the same time the French were complaining about the Eiffel Tower, American troops were being forced to pay nine dollars for a total of three drinks at most Parisian cafes. On the Montparnasse two drinks and two ham sandwiches cost Americans twenty dollars. GI's were badly overcharged for bottles of champagne, which went for twenty dollars.

The result of these practices was that American bases began to establish large post exchanges, much to the resentment of local businessmen. The Americans, as a result, fell into greater and greater isolation within France. By 1966, when the Americans were pushed out of France by President de Gaulle's policies, many of their wives complained that the French had nothing but contempt for them.

Some French comments at the American departure in 1966 were: "The only ones we will miss are the Negroes. . . . They are the big spenders. The other soldiers—cheap skates! Clods! Bores! Nothing!" A cafe owner offered this remark: "I will miss their patronage but not their brawls. Your soldiers do not hold their liquor well. I would say they started half the fights around here."[53]

That the above bartender failed to account for the blame in the other 50 percent of the fights, and that the French failed in general to understand that black marketeering and sexual promiscuity really involved the French as well as the Americans, are real clues to the problems of Americans abroad. It is interesting to note here by contrast that the more affluent French soldiers in the American Revolution faced somewhat similar problems. They, too, were accused of contributing to sexual promiscuity with American girls, and of general misbehavior.

Since the end of World War II the general disaffection with the GI throughout the world has followed a familiar pattern. American soldiers in the Philippines in 1946 were faced with so many aggressive Filipinas they had to place signs about their camps warning them away. The well-being of the American soldier, his apparent prosperity, and his carelessness with money provoked a good deal of envy wherever he went. The Viennese grew angry, not because the American came to that city and spent his money, but because the GI expected something in return. "The whole of Europe is envious of America. . . ." wrote an Italian, "envious of her power, her well-being. . . . And the Americans do nothing to help us overcome this ignoble but very human sentiment."[54]

The arrival of Americans in Britain in 1942 provided a cultural shock for that nation from which it has never recovered. Most GI's were taken to Britain on such passenger ships as the *Queen Mary,* the *Queen Elizabeth,* and the old *Aquitania.* The food served to the Americans was exceedingly poor—and usually consisted of boiled fish two times a day. It was a bad beginning. Ernie Pyle described what happened:

Second lieutenants, muscular and still growing, would order a complete second dinner after finishing the first. And between times they'd get up and serve themselves with bread, carry off their own plates, play loud tunes on their glasses with their forks, make rude jokes about the food and generally conduct themselves in a manner unbecoming to the dignity of a British cruiseship waiter. . . . I must say, in behalf of the British, that they finally broke down and entered into the spirit of the thing.[55]

What happened to the British Isles from 1942 to 1945 is a story that teeters midway between humor and tragedy. Millions of Americans were quartered throughout the United Kingdom. Their comparatively higher pay, their better equipment and clothing, and their lighthearted relationships with British women were irritations with which the Britons lived, but which they did not wholly accept. Staid hotels, where previous to 1942 the most exciting incident of the day was the nightly B.B.C. news broadcast, were now taken over by GI's on liberty. The Americans were everywhere; in London, Liverpool, the Midlands, Glasgow, Edinburgh, the Scottish Highlands, and in Northern Ireland. To the British—as the old quip went—there was nothing wrong with the Americans except that they were "over-paid, over-sexed, over-fed, and over here." The American reply, very aptly phrased, was that the British were merely vexed because they were "under-paid, under-sexed, under-fed, and under Eisenhower."

As will be discussed in greater detail below, there was an easy availability of British women. Many married girls, whose husbands had been fighting with the British Eighth Army in North Africa and Italy for years, became sexually aggressive toward the American soldier, and salved their loneliness with his presence. Not only was this true of white American fighting men, but of Negro-Americans as well. Racial discrimination, though not present in large parts of Britain in 1942, gradually grew throughout the war, mainly because of such liaisons between American Negroes and British women.

It is very likely true that Americans were the source of some trouble in Britain during the war. Rumors had it that white American Southerners resented the sight of Negroes with British women, and that there were brawls between colored and white soldiers in Birmingham and Chester. American fighting men were, on occasion, given to wild parties—particularly airmen—and these did not go down well with the British. Some American soldiers of low mentality, and from the lowest class, accosted women on the streets with direct propositions.

In actual fact, however, everything that could be said of the Americans could be repeated about the British themselves. American soldiers picking their way down Sauchiehall Street in Glasgow might be propositioned by a dozen women, all seemingly from a fairly good class. To stray off the beaten track in towns like Liverpool or Glasgow could be disastrous, for so-called "razor gangs" lay in wait for any lost GI. Pickpockets in Pickadilly Circus, working in conjunction with the famous "commandoes" of that part of London, took an estimated $2,000 a night from the pockets of American soldiers.

In 1951 there were still over twenty thousand American airmen living in Britain, along with five thousand of their dependents. Morale, discipline, and morals were relatively high, and the British were responding accordingly. There was still some irritation at the flaunting of wealth and possessions by the visitors, but Americans were still received in British drinking places "with a smile."[56]

The fact of the matter was that by the 1950's Americans and American business had become vital to the survival of the United Kingdom. In 1955 the returns from sales to GI's were three times as much as from sales of Scotch liquor in the United States. At the Brize Norton base in England, American servicemen spent over $2,000,000 a year for rent and other items, and $2,800,00 went to pay the salaries of Britishers employed on or about the base. American military purchases in that same year amounted to 300 tons of doughnut flour, 96,000 gallons of ice cream, $9,000 for soft drinks, $500,000 for assorted British foods, and $500,000 for British-made clothing.[57]

There have been times when the American military, attempting to protect its own rights in foreign lands, has been subject to controversy. Filipinos resented the fact that thieves were fired upon when they were stealing from American bases in their country. The South Korean press verbally manhandled GI's for shooting at looters in American camps. The general atmosphere in many countries has been one that called for American protection and dollars wherever necessary, but held that American troops should neither be seen nor heard.

In America's most recent conflict, the Vietnam War, the local press has also leaned heavily on United States fighting men for the usual reasons. The "Ugly Americans," one Vietnamese newspaper claimed, have changed the "color of love" to "the shade of green in the American dollar." The Vietnamese intellectual class reluctantly admits that, without the American presence, they would be living under communism; yet they freely criticize American boys for being "boorish, rough, and tactless."

These irritations are rooted in the feeling of many that the war is now an American one; that the Vietnamese Army has been slighted by being placed on pacification duty; and that the relationships between GI's and Vietnamese girls are undesirable. Marine Corps studies have substantiated the fact that the Vietnamese are extremely sensitive about the sexual liaisons between American men and Vietnamese girls, and that only 2 percent of the local population approves of such relationships.

The Marine Corps studies also pointed up other interesting conclusions. First, it was discovered that less than half of the Vietnamese interviewed felt that Americans liked them. Forty-two percent belived that the Americans thought themselves to be superior to the Vietnamese. Yet 78 percent stated that they liked Marines, while 62 percent of the Marines claimed to like the Vietnamese. The leathernecks, so said the Vietnamese, were brave, honest, kind to children, and expert soldiers. The Vietnamese, the Marines stated, were a tough and resilient people, who had survived great hardships.

Each serviceman entering Vietnam is handed a card which carries printed instructions on how to behave with the Vietnamese. Every American is told that he is a guest, that he must not be rude, that women must be treated kindly, and that local customs should be respected.[58]

The distribution of printed instructions is not new. It was done in World Wars I and II and the Korean War. The problem is, however, that between the printed word and actual happenings is a good deal of misunderstanding. The French, ever critical of American public behavior during and at the end of World War II, could never quite stabilize their reasons for disliking the GI's. In 1946 the most common complaints centered around the alleged drunkenness and sexual promiscuity of the Americans. In 1966, when the American forces withdrew from NATO bases in France, the visitors were contradictorally called a "Mongol horde" for dragging their families with them. "Their principal concern," the French said of the Americans, "is not to fraternize, but to create as quickly as possible a sort of sanctuary where they can withdraw and feel at home." The same French who criticized the Americans for spending too much money on their bases also complained that the GI's never learned French, that they didn't know how to behave, and that they never learned "how to drink wine, nor even to eat as we do."[59]

Though there are obviously basic cultural problems for Americans who come as liberators, protectors, or conquerors, the main difficulties have always seemed to center on sex. Young and vigorous men can scarcely be expected to ignore aggressive female sexual behavior, especially in time of conflict. Women who are lonely can hardly be expected to scorn the companionship of soldiers, particularly if the men have a definite material and financial edge on the local males. These conditions can quickly create an atmosphere in which trouble occurs.

This is what happened in Vietnam, for example. Prostitution, which was an encouraged industry under the French, has undergone boom times since 1963. Such places as the Josephine, Sporting, Capital, and Tu Do are famous as bordelloes which cater to Americans in Saigon. In Danang there is an equally famous whorehouse which bears the probably appropriate name *Forget-Me-Not*. Prostitutes have sometimes followed the troops into the rural areas. In the cemetery of a Catholic church there was a sin tent called "The Graveyard": a somewhat analogous historical coincidence with one called "The Holy Ground" during the American Revolution.

Recognizing the inevitability of the world's oldest business, especially in a country like Vietnam, has brought the Army to some interesting decisions. In several instances army authorities have brought prostitutes into proximity to American servicemen by placing them in supervised housing. This is particularly true in the case of "Sin City," the An Khe Plaza, where whoring is conducted under the close medical inspection of the First American Air Cavalry.[60]

During the American occupation of Japan and the war in Korea, prostitution underwent a tremendous growth in both affected countries. In Korea, Army authorities attempted to curb the more disastrous results of sexual intercourse—venereal disease—by encouraging medical inspection and control of prostitutes. In Japan, from 1946 through the Korean War, the problems caused by prostitution were manifold. Chitose, and its reputed 8,400 prostitutes in 1953, has already been mentioned. Actually, however, these Japanese houses which were never homes had rather colorful histories which went back to 1946, when American troops first arrived in great numbers in the island empire. In one case a large munitions plant, closed because of the result of the war, was soon reopened as a brothel for American and allied troops. Called "Willow Run" by the troops, it was partitioned into fifty cubicles, and it was operated for twenty-four hours each day. The 250 girls working there had all previously worked on the munitions assembly line. Now, in eight-hour shifts, they were expected to handle fifteen GI's each during their daily working time.

When public pressure built up to the maximum, General MacArthur closed the factory, much to the concern of the Japanese owners. These entrepreneurs were making more money than they ever had fitting out shell casings for the Japanese Army. The girls were even more upset. Having been democratized and unionized, they petitioned MacArthur that he should reopen "the Palace, and let us cheer up the homesick Americans."[61]

Many of the sexual contacts between American fighting men and girls of other countries during World War II were of a much less formal nature than those brought about by prostitution. Pickups came easy in Korea and on the Ginza in Japan, and required little more than the promise of an evening on the town. The same was true in Italy during the war. Sometimes, because it was difficult for the GI to sense the outward differences between a lonely woman and a woman whose moral standards were sullied, advances were often made to the wrong types in the British Isles and France.

In the years of war and of the occupation thereafter, however, there was never too much difficulty encountered by Americans in making feminine contacts. American military police allegedly acted as scouts for nearby houses of prostitution. John Dos Passos, touring Europe shortly after the end of the war, wrote that many American soldiers whom he encountered had become saturated with sex. After visiting the Berlin nightclub Femina, Dos Passos wrote of seeing well-dressed German women with American officers. "They consider four cigarettes good pay for all night. . . ." a soldier was quoted as saying. "A can of corned beef means true love."[62]

A postwar study of Americans and German women revealed some interestnig facets of the relationship between the two groups. It was claimed that Teutonic girls of the lower and middle class quite often preferred Americans because they were rougher and more disdainful of feminine feelings than German men. This was taken by such girls to be indicative of a greater "masculinity" on the part of the GI's. The same study indicated most American-German sexual contacts existed between soldiers and adolescent girls and widows, and that they were basically business arrangements.

From 1946 on through the 1950's there were many complaints from Europe that American soldiers were destroying French and German moral standards with their crude and blatant sexual liaisons. Out of West Germany, and from the upper class in that area in particular, came charges that occupation American troops were sexual "cavemen." Actually, however, the facts show that offended Europeans only saw what they wished to see. They ignored the simple truth that many of the American postwar camps of France—"Lucky Strike," "Pall Mall," "Old Gold," etc.—were deluged by young French prostitutes. Near Saint-Pierre, where "Twenty Grand" was located, scores of girls took apartments and set up businesses; the reaction of the local police being that such girls were "licensed," and fully within their rights as French citizens. As far as the West German accusations were concerned, it must be remembered that most of these charges came from the upper class; the same people who, as part of the German officer class, had forced adolescent Polish girls into brothels in order to serve Nazi troops.[63]

The difference between America's experience in Europe in World

War II and World War I is almost infinitesimal. Prostitution and its effects on American troops plagued Pershing and other military authorities from 1917 onward. One officer claimed in a 1922 study that 71 percent of American troops in France had engaged in sexual relations while in the country. During the war there were some Americans who saw the moral decline as part of the price of conflict. "A lot of nonsense has been talked about its refining influence," a *Saturday Evening Post* argued. "Most of this mash has been contributed by scholarly divines and such, who see the world through the mists of their own emotions." So, concluded the *Post* writer, because of the real horrors of the war, men could not be blamed for heading straight for French prostitutes on their return from the front. As for the occupation in the Rhineland in 1919, the story has a familiar ring. "Neuwied is occupied by the Americans," a German citizen complained. "The women sell themselves for a piece of chocolate."[64]

Sexual contacts, like some new drug, often have uncertain side effects. General Pershing had no sooner arrived in France in 1917 than he found the "venereal and liquor problems" to be the most difficult problems he had to face. Figures show that the general never really solved them. Over 6,700,000 man-hours were lost by the Americans in World War I; these resolving themselves down to approximately 18,000 men out of action with such ailments for each day of United States participation in the war. In World War II the latter figure dropped to 606 men out of action in the European theater for each day of the war, or 221,184 man-hours lost to venereal disease. A more refined study in World War II shows that in Italy there were four cases of venereal disease per thousand sexual contacts. The least likely candidates among American fighting men to have such troubles were the lighter drinkers and married soldiers.[65]

A happier result of the American involvement in World Wars I and II was the tendency of single American soldiers to take overseas wives; "war brides" being the more contemporary title. By January 1, 1920, it was reported that overseas Yanks had acquired 3,059 French wives, 1,448 British wives, eighty-eight Luxemburg spouses, seventy-five Belgian wives, forty-six German wives, and forty Italian wives. A number of Siberian women were also married to Americans, possibly twenty-six or more, during the American occupation of that part of Russia. A darker side of the picture was that the Americans left a large number of illegitimate children both in France and in the Rhineland in World War I.

In World War II overseas marriages were contracted quickly between GI's and resident girls. Many members of the Marine Second Division, while stationed in New Zealand, found girls from that country almost irresistible, and brought them to the altar by the score. So many soldiers of the First Cavalry married Australian girls and later settled on that continent that even today the Division Association has an Australian chapter.

British and German girls were also married in large numbers both during and after the war. Japanese and Korean wives were also acquired in significant numbers in the years following the end of World War II. In Vietnam there were one hundred marriages of GI's to local girls in 1964, two hundred such marriages in 1965, and well over one hundred in 1966.[66]

Most World War I and World War II overseas marriages have held together despite the natural strains built into the relationships. Some have not. Interracial marriages, while partly acceptable in Europe, were difficult to keep cemented in the United States. In rare cases some really terrible mistakes were made: Americans who married amateur prostitutes; or British and German girls who married far beneath themselves. The happier marriages, which far outnumbered the failures, were generally good matches, and there was a gradual but sometimes slow adjustment of foreign wives to American society.

If wives can be considered as such, they are only part of the souvenirs collected by Americans during military service in the last one hundred years. Americans have always married the girls of conquered or liberated territories. They did in the South in 1865; they do so today in Vietnam. And they have always "liberated," bought, or otherwise collected vast quantities of mementos, relics of battle, or little items calculated to remind them in future years of days left behind.

This basic characteristic of the American fighting man was just as true of Sherman's "blue cloud," which swept through Georgia, as it is of the American in Vietnam. "Billy Yank" didn't buy his souvenirs of course; he merely took them. He marched through the South collecting and discarding carriages and horses, and blankets and glassware. There is one story, probably based in fact, that several years ago an Illinois family finally returned a set of silverware "borrowed" from a distinguished Southern clan by one of Sherman's men during the Civil War.

Souvenir collecting in 1898 was carried on in a much more respectable manner. A veteran of that conflict noted that after each American victory the defeated Spanish immediately exchanged items with the victors. The Americans, it was noted, got rid of their hated sowbelly and hardtack for Spanish insignia and hats. After the naval battle of Santiago, where the fighting went totally in favor of the Americans, the Spanish complained that Yankee sailors not only took money from the pockets of the losers, but actually cut the sleeves off the coats of Spanish officers for souvenirs.[67]

Souveniring in the First World War almost became frenetic. Helmets, preferably spiked ones, Iron Crosses, pieces of German shrapnel, or German pistols were prized items. One fighting American, writing from the trenches, stated: "The fellows strut around with a dutch helmet on, throw up their hands and yell 'Kamerad-Kamerad.'" Other soldiers' letters in 1918 were almost tragicomic in their discussion of souvenir hunting. One doughboy, having been gassed and confined to a hospital, told his parents: "This time I was gased [*sic*] and shocked . . . but . . . I have a surprise for you, I have . . . two German watches and will give you one." Another wounded soldier wrote his mother:

> You asked me to send you a German helmet but I am afraid I cannot get to do that at present unless I get out of the hospital very shortly. . . . Altho an officers helmet is hard to get ahold of the others are not worth the sending. . . . I put the ribbon of an Iron Cross in one of my letters. . . . I had the Iron Cross also but lost it when I got wounded.[68]

The great souvenir thirst of the doughboy was never thoroughly sated, even during the Rhineland occupation. Here are three items from American intelligence reports which tell part of the story.[69]

INTERROGATION OF TRAVELING SALESMAN FROM COLOGNE, 1919

As to the soldier trade, he says that they have lots of money and buy foolishly. Articles that just before our occupation were sold to the people and the German soldiers for 25 to 30 marks are now bought by the Americans for from 80 to 100 marks. . . . He also stated that a great many articles are being made expressly for the American souvenir hunters and that in almost every case these are made of cheap imitation material. . . .

INTERROGATION OF NEUENAHR CITIZEN, 1919

She cannot understand the general desire of the American soldier for the "Gott mit uns" buckles and the German Iron Crosses, as these seem to be the only souvenirs they care to buy. She states that she alone has sold more Iron Crosses to American soldiers than the Kaiser ever awarded to his subjects. . . .

TRANSLATION OF LETTER OF COBLENZ DENTIST, 1919

An enormous business era is reigning here at present. A fabulous "Occupation Industry" has sprung up. It is laughable to see even the smallest of shops endeavouring to meet the demands of the Americans. . . . Naturally all things are outrageously expensive but they are bought up extravagantly. Since the American dollar is now worth from 10 to 12 marks, it does not seem so high in their estimation.

Returning American soldiers in 1919 presented amusing dockside scenes in New York. One doughboy was so loaded with souvenirs he had to be supported down the gangplank by his comrades. Less amusing were the problems of Hoboken, New Jersey, dock authorities who were faced with sorting out the returned effects of dead American soldiers. The piers of that town were piled high with letters, live grenades, Iron Crosses, German helmets, and French road signs. One American soldier had even sent his parents an entire German machine gun.[70]

The craze for souvenirs affected fighting Americans in World War II from the beginning into the period of occupation. An American soldier fighting on Bataan wrote in December, 1941, that he just found a "surrender card." "I'm keeping it for a souvenir," he concluded, "in the event I ever get back." He didn't get back; he died in a Formosan prison camp.[71]

As American troops lapped away at the Japanese and German defense lines in the Pacific and Europe, the business of souveniring became a brisk one. Lugers and German helmets were big items in North Africa. More valuable souvenirs were "liberated" during the advance into France and Germany. It was reputed that valuable stamp collections disappeared from the homes of philatelists in Germany, and that expensive cut glass pieces were sent home by GI's in Belgium.

In the Pacific theater souvenirs were more plebeian and hard won. On Bougainville, Japanese rifles sold for $30, and Japanese light machine guns went for $150. Shortly after landing on one contested beach, a Marine was seen running up and down the American line offering a captured rifle for $50. On Guadalcanal, a pilot wrote: "The Marines have all manner of loot, such as Jap cigarets, rifles, pistols, compasses, medals, parts of wrecked planes, underwear, drawers, trucks, rollers, etc." A Marine on the same island complained that he had nothing to trade with—just money, and nobody wanted that. On Okinawa the cave graves of the local people were looted. Skulls made into ashtrays and ornaments were sold to incoming troops.[72]

After the end of the war, and in the period of occupation, the collecting of souvenirs by American soldiers and sailors almost saved local economics. Iron Crosses were again big in Germany, and in Japan there were so many Japanese swords for sale there were dark rumors that Japanese plants were manufacturing them as souvenirs. Wooden trinkets, kimonos, cheap Japanese imitations, scrolls, and odds and ends were sold to Americans from flourishing street-side businesses in Tokyo. Nazi flags and party emblems, German pipes, and cuckoo clocks (always supposedly made in the Black Forest) were transported home from Germany in the duffle bags of American GI's.

The souvenir craze still continues. Local Vietnamese economies are partially supported by souvenir purchases of Americans on liberty. It is even suspected that some Vietnamese enterprises have been operated by Viet Cong in order to acquire American currency. When Richard Tregaskis visited Vietnam in the early 1960's, he noted that some American soldiers were carrying nonregulation weapons, partially because it was thought they were better than some American weapons; partly because of the souvenir impulse. Swedish submachine guns were highly prized, as were locally made hunting knives.[73]

Yet, with all of the present and past complaints about the behavior of American fighting men in overseas billets, it can be unequivocally stated that these representatives of the United States have acted with uncommon restraint in the roles of conquerors and liberators. That they brought about the so-called black market in Germany in 1946 is a claim based upon shallow facts. A diary written by a citizen of that country *during* the war claims that in February 1945 the Berlin petrol market was "doing a roaring trade." This was prior to the arrival of Americans in that city.

The argument that GI's have wrecked the moral codes at Europe also is not supported by fact. The same German diary indicates that in late 1944 German legations were publishing and distributing magazines containing nude photographs. In relation to the claims that GI's were and are too sexually motivated, the following quote might serve as an answer. Taken from a diary entry of February, 1943, and written by a German in Milan, it reads:

Milan's female beauties are considered more forthcoming than the girls of Sicily, who refused to associate themselves with Kuderna's men. An amicable agreement has been reached regarding the brothels. Our divisional Medical Officer has declared the supervision by the Italian authorities to be excellent, and praises the business-like organisation of these houses of professional leisure, which enables them to arrange a fortnightly alternative roster of girls.[74]

If there is any excessive fault of the ordinary American fighting man, it lies in his excessive naïveté. He assumes that the world can be made better, and he is totally unacquainted with the overwhelming sophistication of other societies. This does not mean that he does not have his own faults. But the proof is really in the pudding, to use an old cliché. Two of the five or six most prosperous nations on the face of the Earth today are West Germany and Japan. Obviously the American people have not been harsh conquerors. Insofar as souveniring is concerned, one may simply state that it is a fault related to innocence. And innocence, Jean Jacques Rousseau used to claim, was a virtue.

8

In the Hands of the Enemy

Discounting the peculiar aspects of the American Civil War, and excepting the instance of the War of 1812, it can be well established that American fighting men have taken more prisoners than have their enemies in each major conflict. Nevertheless, Americans have fallen into the hands of the enemy during the course of history. How were these men treated? And how have captured Americans behaved under this particular misfortune of war?

As general as the statement may sound, the record of the enemy in the handling of American prisoners has been bad. Many atrocities were committed against American fighting men during the Revolution; a fact seemingly overlooked or forgotten by many present-day historians. At Waxhaw Creek, near Charleston, General Tarleton established a widespread reputation for ferocity when he allowed his men to shoot, bayonet, or slash nearly three hundred surrendered American soldiers. "Tarleton's quarter," as it was known throughout the Continental Army, was actually not a new policy of the British Army, nor did it fail to survive the rest of the war. At Fort Washington a British officer was heard to shout to his troops: "What!

Taking prisoners! Kill every man of them." In another instance, probably more excusable in terms of the type of battle, a number of somewhat helpless Americans were massacred in a night attack upon a unit commanded by "Mad Anthony" Wayne.[1]

The major reason for the mistreatment of captured Americans in the Revolution was that the British simply refused to recognize that the Americans were fighting for a legitimate cause. Prisoners were looked upon as "transported convicts" or "jailbirds," deserving of nothing but the most contemptuous and inhumane imprisonment. The fact that most Americans wore such tattered and worn uniforms, when captured, caused the British to regard them as subjects for sport and amusement, and worthy of nothing but the worst type of prison conditions.

Therefore, the entire record of the British in the treatment of American prisoners in the Revolution was far from good. Out of the nearly 2,400 Americans captured by the British at Charleston, nearly one-third of the prisoners died within thirteen months, and another one-third became unfit for further service upon exchange. On the British prison ships, where most captured Americans were kept, the living conditions were terrible. The holds were overcrowded. The food was bad or in insufficient quantity. British soldiers were guilty of poking swords or pikes through the bars in order to deliberately wound the imprisoned men.[2]

The result of all this was that many men gave up and simply refused to eat; a common reaction of prisoners to severe mistreatment. Many broke, and lost their hearing, their voices, or their sensibility. Others died from starvation. As many as five or ten prisoners expired each day on certain prison ships. The bodies, taken ashore and buried in the sand, usually refloated at high tide and drifted out to sea.

The facts of the British mistreatment of Americans during the Revolution are not difficult to find. A young American, stuffed into one British prison ship like a sardine, wrote: "Paleness attends all faces. The melancholyst day I ever saw. . . . We are treated worse than cattle or hogs. . . . Three men of our battalion died last night. . . . Small pox increases fast."[3] And General Washington, noting that exchanged Americans were usually so emaciated and thin they were unfit to serve again, complained to the British: "How different was their appearance from that of your soldiers, who have lately returned to you, after a captivity of twelve months. . . . If you are determined to make captivity as distressing as possible, let me know it, that we may be upon equal terms, for your conduct must and shall mark mine."[4]

Despite Washington's protests the British failed to moderate their handling of American prisoners in the Revolution, and actually carried the same policy over to the War of 1812. In that conflict American officers were held in very close confinement, especially in the British prison near Quebec. At Dartmoor, in England, where about 6,000 Americans were kept by 1815, conditions were equally bad. Some of these prisoners were impressed Americans who had been held by the British for as long as eleven years. In April, 1815, when the British delayed in exchanging prisoners, there was a general riot of the Americans at Dartmoor. Demanding bread instead of hardtack, the prisoners became insubordinate and struck back at their captors with a passive resistance policy. Several days later the British guards opened fire on the prisoners, killing five and wounding thirty-five.[5]

Very little is understood about the Mexican treatment of captured Americans in the Mexican War. It is known that before and after the capture of the Alamo, which had occurred in the Texas Revolution, the Mexican General Santa Anna initiated a policy of no quarter. Much of the same approach was carried over into the war between the United States and Mexico ten years later. Wounded Americans were sometimes bayoneted or killed by the lance. Any American lucky enough to escape death after a battlefield capture was usually kept in a Mexican village jail; the conditions of which left a great deal to be desired.

The handling of prisoners by both sides in the Civil War was bad. The food and housing of Federal prisons was not nearly as poor as that which existed in Confederate prisons; yet the death rate among Confederate prisoners was quite high. Twelve of every one hundred men in Federal prisons died during the war; the major reason being that many captured Confederates were already suffering from malnutrition when taken. These men, when subjected to the cold of the North, fell prey to pneumonia and many smallpox epidemics. One might also add that the poorest Northern doctors were allowed to treat captured Confederates, and this did not help matters. The worst Federal prisons were located at Camp Douglas in Chicago and in Elmira, New York.

One almost has to view the Southern treatment of captured Yankees in a different light. Most Union soldiers came to Confederate prison camps as well-fed individuals. If they left alive, they did so as semi-starved and pitiful cases. A good many never left, of course; the death rate in Confederate prisons amounting to fifteen out of every hundred prisoners.[6]

The worst Confederate prison was that of Camp Sumpter (Andersonville, Georgia). Here, nearly 25,000 Federal soldiers were crowded into a very small plot of ground. No sanitation facilities existed. The only source of water was a thoroughly polluted stream. The prisoners lived (or died) on a diet of crushed corn and corncobs. Some individuals, as is always the case in these conditions, gave up and refused to eat. Those who survived did so in many instances because of personal loyalties within particular group situations.

It has often been argued by Southern historians that the Federal prisoners did not help themselves; that the failure of the men to live by certain standards of behavior caused the death rate at Andersonville to reach several hundred a day in specific months. In rebuttal, however, it must be stated that medical treatment at this most noted Civil War prison was virtually nonexistent; that some prisoners were shot by young and immature guards without reason; and that the very conditions of the camp were such that men were virtually forced to become animals. Fortunately, for the sake of historical truth, photographs of Andersonville as it really existed survived the war. These pictures tend to support the diaries and reminiscences of Federal survivors of Camp Sumpter, and serve to spite claims of many later historians that the majority of such descriptions were overblown.[7]

What is true about the Civil War is that no two camps were the same; that while one Northern or Southern camp might be bad, another would present comparatively good conditions. A similar situation existed in German prison camps in World War I. Some Yanks in 1917–1918 were housed in vermin-ridden prisons. Many Americans survived such imprisonment on thin soup, two hundred grams of black bread a day, and acorn coffee. Other captured doughboys lived in conditions in which no toilet facilities were provided, no fresh water was allowed, no heating or light was allowed, no mail was given out, and no soap was provided for the inmates. Conversely, other German camps provided a daily ration of fish, meat, bread, and margarine, and gave their American prisoners straw mattresses on which to sleep.

The first American prisoners taken in 1917 were sailors—thirty-nine men who were housed in a camp in Brandenburg. As the American participation in the war increased in scope, the number of prisoners taken by the Germans likewise rose. Red Cross and Y.M.C.A. officials attempted to regulate conditions within the German camps throughout 1918, meeting with only minor successes. Some American prisoners were known to have been threatened with sabers; others were forced to work under bad conditions. At one German prison, Camp Tuchel, the Americans were forced to chop wood from daylight to dusk. This may or may not have been an immoderate situation, depending upon the other conditions existing within the camp. Even so, it was very different from the treatment accorded to captured Germans by Americans. As one of the Kaiser's men wrote his parents, the conditions in his camp were "ritterlich" (princely), and that he would send food packages *to them* rather than the reverse.[8]

The treatment of captured Americans by World War II Germans was extremely bad. Over seventy American soldiers were shot near Malmédy after their capture in the Battle of the Bulge. In March, 1944, captured members of the 267th Special Reconnaissance Battalion were shot by the Germans in Italy. In September of the same year forty-seven American, British, and Dutch fliers were murdered in the Mauthausen Prison Camp in Germany, mostly by beatings. In other instances American and British fliers were severely manhandled by civilians after their bombers were downed in Germany.[9]

Though prisons were checked by the International Red Cross, the flouting of rules by the Germans regarding prisoners of war was common. Food was generally bad, and consisted mainly of potatoes, dehydrated greens, and turnips. The last named vegetable was ever present. Despite the good treatment of Germans in American prison camps, captured Yanks were sometimes singled out for especially bad treatment within German camps. A South African prisoner, describing the treatment of Americans in 1945, stated: "They quickly developed dysentery and were treated shockingly. They were put in double-decked barns with no sanitation facilities. There was no place for them to go and you can imagine the condition of their living quarters."[10]

The conditions in German prison camps deteriorated from bad to worse in the late months of the struggle in Europe. American airmen, captured in raids against German cities, were crowded into railroad cars in such density that some men lost their mental equilibrium and became hysterical. The latrine of each soldier was the portion of the car on which he stood. Other GI's were forced to march through Upper Silesia in deep snow, and those who lagged behind were beaten with rubber hoses. A number of Americans were placed in more infamous concentration camps usually reserved for Jews.

Virtually every American prisoner, when finally freed by the onrushing armies of the Allies, was found to be in bad physical condition. At Mooseberg, where Patton's army freed captured American airmen, the average loss of weight during the confinement of the prisoners was from thirty-five to forty-five pounds. A signal corpsman, who was released in Upper Silesia, found that his weight had dropped from 192 to 118 pounds during imprisonment. At Duderstadt, where Americans had been forced to live on turnip soup, there were seventy-five GI prisoners who were too weak to be moved.

The psychological impact of imprisonment in Germany was a profound one. Newly released prisoners, forty to sixty pounds down in weight, ate themselves into field hospitals within several days. Other released prisoners quickly developed anxiety neuroses which will plague them the rest of their days on earth. One GI, a man who had survived eighteen months of the worst kind of Nazi treatment, jumped to death from a New York City skyscraper two days after his return to the United States.[11]

Americans in the hands of the Japanese underwent even worse ordeals. Some pilots, members of the Doolittle raid and others, were beheaded. Americans who had fought to the final surrender in Bataan also received some special mistreatment. These men were assembled at Mariveles Airfield on Bataan on April 10, 1942, and were marched toward San Fernando in Pampanga Province. They were deprived of their canteens, bayoneted if they faltered, and flattened by trucks if they collapsed on the road. They were forced to drink from carabao wallows, and shot if they were too weak to keep up a pace set by the Japanese guards who rode bicycles.

Though there was enough food for the prisoners to be fed and fed well, the Japanese deprived the marchers of any opportunity to eat. An American colonel who asked for food for his men had his cheek slashed open by a Japanese guard. Some men, too weak to go further, were deliberately buried alive by their captors.

The prisoners finally arrived at Camp O'Donnell; a prison camp under construction. They had made the march of eighty-five miles in six days (twelve for later arrivals); the food ration for the entire experience consisted of one mess kit of rice, and whatever the men were given by a few friendly and courageous Filipino people.

There were almost no water facilities at Camp O'Donnell, and the prisoners were forced to stand in line for six hours in order to drink. Bathing, in the earliest period of the camp's history, was a dream. Many of the men who were released three years later were still wearing remnants of the same clothing they took into the camp.

There were other such incidents; all of which are excruciatingly difficult to relate. Americans captured on Wake Island were beaten almost daily during their imprisonment aboard the *Nitta Maru;* a ship which took them to Japan. Five of the American fighting men were picked from the Wake Island personnel and told: "You have killed many Japanese soldiers in battle. For what you have done you are now going to be killed." The execution of the Americans was by decapitation.

The stories of other repugnant incidents survived only by circumstance. When *Sculpin,* an American submarine, was scuttled by her crew after heavy damage, forty-two of the men were taken prisoner on board a Japanese destroyer. One of them was immediately thrown overboard because he was severely wounded. The remainder underwent very bad treatment. Later, some twenty-one of the men went down with a Japanese carrier which was torpedoed by the *Sailfish.* One of the twenty-one was picked up and survived the war.

In the midst of the war with Japan much enemy propaganda was devoted to the supposedly excellent care which was being given captured American prisoners. *Domei,* the Japanese news agency, declared: "All the prisoners have a very happy life. They are grateful to the Japanese Government for the just and good treatment accorded to them." A Japanese general also stated in the same year that "conditions in the war prisoners' camps leave nothing to be desired."

Facts do not substantiate these claims. The daily ration within Camp O'Donnell consisted of rice and camotes, a root vegetable. Meat, less than an inch square, was provided twice in the first two months. Occasional mango beans, a kind of cow pea, flour enough to make a paste gravy for the rice, and some coconut lard were sometimes given to the prisoners. Survival depended on black market arrangements with Japanese guards, or upon British and American Red Cross packages.

The death rate during the first week at Camp O'Donnell was twenty a day among Americans, one hundred fifty a day among the Filipino soldiers. Two weeks later the rate increased to fifty a day for the Americans, five hundred a day for the Filipinos. Hospital facilities for those who became ill were terrible. No water was available to the physicians, and men lay in their own excreta. Some patients dropped from two hundred pounds to ninety in a matter of weeks.

Several months after the opening of Camp O'Donnell, the American prisoners were moved to the Cabanatuan concentration camp in Luzon. Adequate drinking water was available here, and there was some water for bathing. The daily ration showed some improvement—an occasional chicken and some eggs—but it still consisted principally of rice.

The work details and the beatings continued. Shovels, golf clubs, or rifle butts were the principal weapons used by the guards to hit the weakened prisoners. Once, when three officers attempted to escape and were caught, they were beaten and hanged from overhead ropes for four days in the sun. After periodic beatings while in this position, two of the men were shot and the third beheaded.

The death rate at Cabanatuan for June through July of 1942 was thirty Americans a day. In September it decreased to fifteen a day. It went up to nineteen a day in October. By the end of October, approximately three thousand of the American prisoners had died, and there were 2,500 in the hospital. The causes of most deaths were starvation, dysentery, malaria, scurvy, diphtheria, and dengue fever.

Eventually some of the prisoners were taken to Japan, and others to Davao on Mindanao. In each case the voyage was made under such terrible conditions that men died in transit. At Davao the prisoners were so weak when they disembarked that the Japanese had to carry them in trucks to the stockade or penal colony. There was a slight improvement in the food rations; both at Davao and in Japan. Camotes, green papayas, and cassavas helped many of the prisoners to survive at Davao. The opportunities to increase the daily food intake were improved in Japan when many of the prisoners were put to work unloading vessels in various harbors. Again it must be repeated that what really allowed some Americans to live through these ghastly experiences was the occasional appearance of Red Cross packages.[12]

Also, as in the case of Andersonville, the survival of some men was really a matter of sheer luck. Having a partner when one was ill, being equipped with enough antibodies to withstand attacks of dysentery or influenza, and having an occasional chance to pick up a little vitamin C were major factors in making it to the end of the war. By 1945 most of the men were skeletal in appearance, and were existing on sheer nerve. John Dos Passos, who saw American prisoners in the Philippines shortly after their release, wrote: "They all looked strangely alike. Their heads looked very large for their bodies. Gray skin hung in folds from skinny necks. Their eyes were large and sunken, the whites clear, the pupils sharp and small, the iris bright."[13]

What Dos Passos saw was the same kind of animal Federal photographers had recorded at Andersonville, and what some newsmen had seen in the concentration camps in Germany. One may well imagine that Americans on board British prison ships during the Revolution had the same appearance. It may be recorded here again that in no case, even in the handling of the Japanese in California, did the American record of treatment reach such cruel levels. The Korean and Japanese prisoners held in concentration camps on Saipan during the war came out fatter and healthier than they were when captured.

American prisoners held by the Japanese in China experienced similar inhumane treatment. Very early in the war some twenty-five enlisted men and two officers, all American, were placed in a dark dungeon in Shanghai. They were allowed to use the toilet once a day; they were fed fish heads and rice, and given contaminated water to drink; ground glass was placed in their shoes so that they could not escape. In another prison in China, recalcitrant Americans were straitjacketed in leather jackets which were then watered down. These shrank when dry, almost crushing the prisoners.[14]

The treatment of Americans who managed to make it to Japan varied according to the particular prison camp involved. In some camps, the vitamin content of the daily ration was so deficient that some prisoners went temporarily blind. In other camps, American prisoners learned to roast grasshoppers, and to eat them like popcorn. In still other prison camps it was sadistic Japanese guards with whom the Americans had to contend. One captured Yank, describing one such experience with a Japanese doctor, wrote: he "stuck the big naked Samurai sword between my legs, and then, slowly, gently, he started to flick it with his wrist so that the sharp edge of the blade beat a steady, easy tattoo at my crotch. . . . Happily for me, Matsui tired of the fly-flicking sport. . . ."[15]

The complexities of the Oriental mind add some rather bizarre aspects to the treatment of captured Americans by the Japanese. Despite the savage bombing of Japan by American air power late in the war, downed American airmen were rarely mistreated by the Japanese civilian population; a distinct difference from the problems faced by American fliers in Germany. When American aircraft crashed in rural areas, it was not unusual for some Japanese farmer to bury dead Americans with respect and mark their graves with reverence.[16]

The contradictory treatment thus accorded Americans by some Japanese civilians saved many prisoners' lives. In fact, many of the Americans who were farmed out to work on docks alongside Japanese laborers struck up strange relationships with their supposed enemies. Perhaps this was because the Japanese civilian population realized the inevitability of defeat much sooner than the Japanese military. At any rate, both Japanese and American dock workers conspired to split sacks of rice taken from merchant vessels in various harbors. In other instances, when American prisoners were forced to work in mines or for Japanese families, Japanese civilians not only slipped them occasional food supplies, but treated them as humanely as was possible under the circumstances.[17]

American fighting men came up against the most brutal kind of Oriental savagery in the Korean War. Battlefield massacres of captured Americans were far more savage than those inflicted by the Japanese in World War II. In August, 1950, thirty-four members of an American cavalry regiment were killed with their hands tied behind their backs. In the infamous "Sunchon Tunnel Massacre," it was reputed that over 130 Americans were machine-gunned within a railroad tunnel. Approximately eighty other American soldiers were shot or killed by other methods during a "death march" from Seoul to Pyongyang. Some captured Americans were castrated and burned, and then shot. The fact that some 244 American prisoners were still unaccounted for as late as 1959 indicates the severity of the treatment meted out to prisoners who were force-marched by the Communists into North Korea.[18]

The full story of the treatment of the Americans in Korean prison camps may not be fully revealed for years. Diaries kept by prisoners on toilet paper, or on whatever materials writing could be kept, have never been fully released by the Department of the Army. This much is known, however. Beri-beri and pellagra were both common among the prisoners. Dysentery and pneumonia were big killers. Hepatitis was widespread. The reasons for the prevalence of these illnesses lie in the poor diet—cracked corn, millet, fishheads— and in the severe cold and the poor medical treatment afforded the sick. Some Americans were actually experimented upon by doctors who transplanted chicken livers under the skins of prisoners. Others were deliberately injected with infected hypodermic needles.

Besides the poor diet and medical treatment, some Americans and Allied prisoners were tortured to death or killed outright. Some prisoners were shot when refusing to confess to "germ warfare" charges; others were shot because they refused to divulge information. One American officer was kept in solitary confinement for three weeks. During this period he was beaten and tortured. Fortunately he survived and was returned to his comrades, though he was "morally and physically broken."[19]

Of the 7,190 Americans who were captured, approximately 2,730 died in prison. According to one writer over 90 percent of these deaths occurred in the first year of the Korean War. The death rate of Americans in Korean prison camps was the highest of all wars in which Americans have been involved. Nearly 38 percent, it beats the death rate of World War II American prisoners by 27 percent, and that of the American Revolution by 5 percent.[20]

Little is known about the treatment accorded American prisoners in North Vietnam. Treatment of American prisoners by the Viet Cong is not good, however. Kept in cages, given a substandard diet, and possibly subjected to air raids by their fellow countrymen, the prospects for survival for these men are not good. One may also hazard a guess that a good deal of indoctrination of American prisoners is being attempted. Radio broadcasts from Hanoi indicate that "confessions" have been extracted from some American airmen concerning supposed "atrocities." *Izvestia,* the Russian newspaper, has printed so-called interviews with some captured American pilots; each one indicating that the Pentagon had "lured" pilots into "criminal" activities with the promises of "more dollars."[21]

This smacks of what happened during the Korean War, when there were sensational press releases about the poor discipline of American soldiers in Korean prison camps. Such stories indicated that Americans collaborated with the Communists for favors; that they "snitched" on less cooperative comrades; that some Americans exhibited cruel and inhumane behavior towards ill GI's; and that many Americans simply gave in to the terrible conditions in the prison camps and died.

Because of the nature of the Korean POW story, it would be well to examine charges made concerning American soldiers, and the rebuttals that have developed relative to those charges. On one side of the case are the accusations that there was no natural leadership in the Korean POW camps; that many Americans had considerable evidence piled up against them for acting as collaborators; that American soldiers assaulted their officers on occasion; that officers readily confessed to charges of germ warfare; and that at least one American soldier threw helpless comrades out into the snow.[22]

There is no doubt that there is some truth in these charges, and this is probably the very reason many of the diaries kept by captive Americans may not be released for publication for decades. There *was* "ratting" by some GI's, there *was* some vicious bullying by certain Americans, and there *was* some collaboration. There were even twenty-one American soldiers who declined to come home during the 1953 prisoner exchanges; though it might be added that all have done so since.

How many American prisoners were involved in such unsoldierly incidents? Figures differ, according to the particular source used. One national magazine wrote that 192 men were suspected of "ratting" on comrades. Of these, the article claims, sixty-eight were separated from the services, three resigned, and six were convicted by courts-martial. The remainder either were absolved, or received relatively minor punishment. Another writer has stated that out of two hundred Americans suspected of collaboration, about forty-seven cases were approved for courts-martial. Of these only fourteen were actually brought to trial. Nine of the soldiers were enlisted men, eight of whom were convicted. Five were officers, three of whom were convicted. The same source indicates that pilots and Marines were most resistant to indoctrination, although in the case of the former many were severely mistreated.[23]

One of the charges made against American POW's during the early 1950's was that they were "soft," and that other United Nations units, particularly captured Turks, exhibited far greater discipline than the Americans. An objective look at the situation reveals some qualifying factors, however. First of all, the Americans were much more severely treated than all other U. N. soldiers. Chinese and Korean attempts to build a good public image in the Middle East and Africa may well have led them to treat Turkish prisoners much better than the captured GI's, for instance.

Furthermore, the United States and South Korean (ROK) troops were the most nonselective forces fighting in Korea. The Turks represented the elite of their army. The Commonwealth Brigade was composed of the best troops the British could send. The U. S. Marines, whose record in Korea was exemplary, was an elite unit. Yet there were instances in which even these men failed to withstand Communist pressures within the prison camps. About forty British soldiers returned home as indoctrinated Communists; and it was estimated that one-third of the captive junior NCO's in the Commonwealth Brigade were affected by indoctrination processes. David Rees, a respected British writer, has admitted that British POW's showed a considerable weakness to prison pressure. And despite the claims of U. S. Marine Corps historians, even a few leathernecks failed to meet the standards of the Corps.[24]

An important claim made, relative to the Korean War, is that, to a degree found in no other war, American POW's in Korea "snitched" on comrades or provided the enemy with intelligence in exchange for favors. This is a highly disputable argument. One authority has claimed that, if information were given to the enemy, it lacked any substantial value. The facts of history present another coloration to the claim as well. The passing of information to an enemy by a captive is common in any war. When John Paul Jones raided Whitehaven on the British coast in the American Revolution, a young American sailor was forgotten and left ashore. He sang to the British in beautiful fashion. At Andersonville Prison, during the Civil War, one of the great problems of patriotic Union soldiers was that most of their escape attempts were revealed by so-called comrades before they could be put into effect.

World War II presented numerous examples of "ratting," or the passing of information to the enemy. American prisoners in Normandy provided German intelligence with a great deal of information of the Allied build-up on the beaches, and the effects of the weather conditions on landing operations. An American airman, shot down and captured by the Japanese during the Battle of Midway, gave the enemy the following information—that there were about five thousand Marines on Midway, the exact number of planes available to the Midway Island defense command, and the exact location of Midway artillery emplacements.[25] And an American Marine, describing his experiences in a Japanese prison camp during World War II, remembered this incident:

> One of the prisoners knew a little bit about communications and signal codes and had a smattering of our decoding techniques. After a couple of years in the POW camp he flipped his lid and decided to spill . . . to the Japs. . . . No one wanted to kill him outright, so an elaborate plan was hatched that would enable them to do away with the guy without any one man's laying a glove on him.[26]

What was the enemy record of passing information in the Korean War and World War II? The simple answer is that it was far worse than that of the American fighting man. Chinese and Korean prisoners readily gave information after capture in the Korean War. German prisoners, especially in Russian prison camps in World War II, kept their captors well informed. Of all German prisoners, however, probaby none talked as readily as German generals, who were veritable fountains of intelligence. Even the Japanese in World War II, when captured, gave in easily. A Japanese corporal, captured in New Britain, was persuaded to give information which saved many American lives, and the feat was accomplished with a box of K Rations and a cigarette.[27]

The American Expeditionary Force of World War I, to which so many "old soldiers" point with pride, also had its informers. Some, like soldiers in any war, were frightened young men who would tell anything they knew. Others were far less innocent. American POW's at the Giessen Prison reported at the close of the conflict that a member of the Second Division was a known "Stool Pigeon," and "showed marked friendliness towards the camp authorities."[28]

All in all, the record of American POW's throughout history has been as good as or better than that of most other nations. In Korea it is doubtful that whatever information was given by Americans to the enemy proved to be of a useful variety, mainly because of the nature of that conflict. POW resistance in the Korean War, though perhaps unequal to certain periods of World Wars I and II, did have its moments of sublime courage. David Rees, the British writer, points out that there were many tough American prisoners who refused to give in to the Communists. Puerto Rican and Negro-Americans, on whom the Chinese concentrated, were never won over to the Communist ideology. General Mark Clark, who commanded U. N. forces in Korea during part of the war, has concluded: "There were heroes in those prison camps, great heroes. There were but few rats."[29]

As Albert D. Biderman, an American sociologist, points out: "Most of the American prisoners of war had an unquestioned belief in their own superiority of things American, and feelings of rightness and wrongness which the Chinese never were able to alter fundamentally. . . ." Biderman's refutation of the various charges concerning American POW's in the Korean War is most scholarly. This writer points out that nearly one hundred citations were awarded to returned Americans for resistance to indoctrination, and for acts of bravery and courage. One Medal of Honor was also won by a Navy helicopter pilot for his resistance activities while a POW.[30]

What about the twenty-one Americans who chose to stay behind during the Korean War prisoner exchange? One interesting study shows that twenty of them were Regulars, eighteen had grown up in poor circumstances, seventeen were school drop-outs, fifteen were twenty-one or under in age, two were married, and only one was a city boy. Considering the number of Americans who were POW's, the fact that there were only twenty-one real defectors indicates a strong personal patriotism on the part of the prisoners. Indeed, matching this number against the number of defectors of the enemy during the same conflict truly tells a story. Of the total 132,000 prisoners captured by U.N. forces, only 83,000 wished to return across the armistice line. Out of the 22,000 Chinese taken as prisoners, approximately 15,000 refused repatriation.[31]

If there is anything that stands out in the historical record of all American POW's, it is that the enemy has seldom understood the real nature of American character. Biderman, for example, points out that American prisoners in the Korean War exhibited a fine sense of humor. They signed written promises never to refer to enemy camp commanders in ignominious terms. They arranged "crazy weeks," in which all of the prisoners acted mentally ill. They organized latrine calls for all camp members at odd hours in the morning. These acts of resistance were beyond the understanding of Chinese camp authorities.[32]

The same individualistic and courageous behavior was seen during World War II. The crew of the *Grenadier,* a sub sunk by the Japanese, was subjected to abnormal and extreme punishment for the purposes of deriving intelligence. Not one American sailor talked, however, and all but four captives survived the war. Wake Island prisoners were treated very badly, but none of the Marines or captured civilian employees talked.[33]

The one advantage the World War II American had over Korean War soldiers, however, was the experience of surviving the great depression of the 1930's. The GI of 1941–1945 was more toughened to the ordeal of hardship. Captured Marines from Bataan soon accepted the fact that stewed fishheads, eyeballs and all, provided some rather elemental and needed nourishment. GI's learned that, while unloading ships in Japanese harbors, they could secrete food in socks pinned inside their clothing. The more elite the service from which the captive came, the stronger his will to survive. Captured American airmen in Germany became expert at ferreting out planted Nazi spies. Americans in Japan learned never to admit anything to the Japanese; "it was a good defense," as one old Marine put it. The same leatherneck explained the code of a Marine's behavior in rugged terms. It was the result of an *esprit de corps* which is "hammered into his thick skull and ass from his first soul-shattering meeting with a drill instructor until he picks up his retirement papers twenty years later."[34]

Neither the Allies nor the Germans really understood American national psychology in 1917 and 1918. German intelligence experts, attempting to work over captured doughboys, found in the end that they were quite unable to separate truth from fiction. Some young American soldiers were very naive, and told German officers a good deal about Allied troop movements. Others affirmed anything that the Germans wanted to establish, and denied everything the Germans wanted to negate. In the end German intelligence agents came to the conclusion that most captured Americans were totally "ignorant" of all Allied military activities.

The evidence that some doughboys played a deliberate cat-and-mouse game with their captors is rather strong. A German intelligence report on prisoners taken from the American First Division states: "The prisoners . . . give a poor impression and are totally ignorant of military affairs." Writing about some Americans captured at Cantigny, an enemy agent complained that they didn't seem to have good memories, and they didn't seem to be "able to state much about" the fight. The postwar conclusions of another German intelligence agent were these:

> He comments on the fact that the Americans were what might
> be called bad prisoners. A group of 14 were brought in one day

and when asked about their units refused to talk. They refused to work and talked back to the officers, much to the annoyance of the officers and the concealed delight of the men.[35]

The German argument that the 1918 doughboys were difficult to handle is echoed in other sources. A Y.M.C.A. official visited Camp Rastatt, an American prison in Baden, and found that the German guards were astounded at the discipline "manifested by our boys." The 2,600 men who were interned at Rastatt were not in good physical shape, they had little clothing, and some very strong attempts to indoctrinate them had been carried out by German prison officials. Yet their patriotism was still strong. The same Y.M.C.A. officer described his experience with them:

And how they did sing! . . . One night by a happy inspiration I pulled out my silk American flag which I always carried with me. . . . The effect on the men seeing Old Glory thus displayed in the camp can be imagined. There was a spontaneous outburst of wild cheers and ringing applause, and then all joined in with even greater intensity than ever in the singing of the last verse ("My Country Tis of Thee").[36]

The rugged individualism of the doughboy under pressure was what irritated the Germans most. What the American was proud to call freedom, the German regarded as a lack of discipline. Most Yanks, even while in 1918 German prisons, felt that they had certain inalienable rights, and were not above letting the Germans know about them. Note the peculiar contradictions within the following statement by a European observer of American prisoners of the Germans.

A few American prisoners were brought here in June 1918 and were not mistreated. The Americans were the chief complainers when the food was bad which was always. The Americans occasionally received packages containing hard tack and other luxuries but their packages were usually rifled.[37]

The general resistance of Americans to POW conditions goes far back beyond World War I, however. There were numerous attempts by Confederate prison officials to persuade Andersonville prisoners to switch loyalties, but the attempts were without much success. Federal prison officials found a similar resistance among their Confederate prisoners, despite the fact that by the end of the war there were six thousand "Galvanized" Yankees (ex-Confederates) serving in Federal frontier posts. Most of these men had been born in the border states, however, and their loyalties were not as deeply fixed to the Confederacy as those born further south. From thirteen hundred to two thousand Federal soldiers changed sides; these being mostly immigrant Americans. Considering the nature of the war, and the numbers of men involved, such defection on both sides may well be considered fractional.[38]

The stubbornness of American character was even noted in the British POW camps of the Revolutionary War. Though the death rate was high, it was never easy to bring captured Americans back into the service of the King. General Burgoyne found this out during his ill-fated strike into New York. Having taken some American prisoners, he ordered them to hear a proclamation concerning newly won British victories. When one or two of the captives cheerfully responded to the announcements, the others turned on the would-be defectors and savagely beat them.

The number of American escapes during the Revolutionary War was not as high as one might suppose, however. If they did occur, it was during the period when the prisoners were being marched overland to the various British-held harbors, where the men were to be put aboard prison ships. Once aboard the ships, escape for the prisoners was extremely difficult. Some British prison-ship captains allowed only one POW to be on deck at a time, and then only in chains. Yet, one may suppose that, at one time or another in the entire war, individual Americans attempted and completed prison breaks.[39]

The great difficulty faced by any historian in treating with American escapes during the Revolutionary War, the War of 1812, and the Mexican War, is that few records of these efforts were ever kept. Those who did succeed in escaping seldom wrote memoirs of those events. And when escaped troops returned to their commands, the entire episode was accepted as one of the many normal concomitants of war.

The situation was entirely different during the Civil War. Americans had, by then, become a highly literate people. Veterans' associations, formed at the end of the conflict, encouraged the printing of reminiscences; so much so that there are times when it is hard to distinguish truth from fiction in the claims of many of these old soldiers.

What is true is that there were numerous escapes from various prisons during the war, and some of them were quite spectacular. On the Confederate side it may be noted that even some generals got away from their Federal captors. General Bushrod R. Johnson, captured during the Confederate surrender of Fort Donelson, simply took a daylight stroll, found that he was not challenged by Federal sentries, and eventually walked back into the Confederate Army. A year and a half later Johnson was one of the leaders of the brilliant Confederate breakthrough of the Federal line at Chickamauga. Another Confederate general who escaped, and who was later to plague Federal posts in Tennessee, was John Hunt Morgan; the redoubtable leader of Morgan's Raiders.

Many Union soldiers made successful escapes from Confederate prisons in Georgia and elsewhere, and made their way to Sherman's advancing armies. Some men didn't succeed, of course; but it is a matter of fact that any time a Federal soldier could get out of a prison stockade, he had a chance to prolong his life by supplanting his camp diet of ground corn with blackberries and other fruit. There are hundreds of diaries which tell the same story. A Federal prisoner escapes, he hides in the woods several days and survives by eating fresh fruit, he is hunted down by hounds and captured, and he returns to prison vowing that he will try again.

As one reads such stories, it appears that the actual problem of escaping from a Confederate prison was not difficult. The hard part for the escapee was in making his way back to Federal lines. Even at Libby Prison in Richmond, a notorious Confederate prison for captured officers, several Western officers were able to gain a temporary freedom by merely walking through the gate.

One of the most amusing stories of the Civil War concerns a young Illinois soldier who was imprisoned at Belle Isle, near Richmond. This young man—Dalrymple by name—attempted to escape but was later apprehended. He was then placed in solitary confinement in a room next to the camp bakery. Cutting a hole through the wall, he managed to steal bread for two months before he was caught. Now the fattest and healthiest prisoner in any Confederate compound, he was moved to Andersonville; where escape was extremely difficult. Dalrymple made it, however, by stealing away from a wood-cutting party. Living for thirteen days on a rabbit killed with a thrown hatchet, he found his way to the Federal lines.[40]

Despite the fact that the number of American prisoners taken by the Germans in World War I was never large, there were numerous attempted and successful escapes by Yanks in that war. The first American to make it to freedom was an aviator, an Everett Buckley of Chicago, who had been captured by the Germans and imprisoned in a Black Forest camp. He escaped from there, but was recaptured and sent to a work farm near Varingenstadt. Again he escaped but was recaptured. There followed now a period of mistreatment, in which he was kicked and closely confined by his captors. In July, 1918, he escaped again. Walking at night, sleeping by day, and eating raw potatoes, he made it to the Swiss border.

Another American who escaped was Thomas Hitchcock, an aviator from New York attached to the French Flying Corps. He ran away from a German prison at Ulm and walked seventy miles to the Swiss border. Hitchcock and the previously mentioned Buckley were officers. A few enlisted men tried escape, and there were some who made it. One interesting case was that of Private Frank Sovicki of Shenandoah, Pennsylvania. Sovicki had been sent to Camp Rastatt after his capture at Château-Thierry. Placed into forced labor on a German farm, he also evaded his guards and walked the necessary distance to the Swiss border.

Sovicki's success was an unimportant exception to the rule. In both World Wars I and II the usual escapee was an officer or a high ranking noncom. The highest percentage of attempted and successful escapes involved such ranks in the Army Air Corps, the Navy, and the Marine Corps.[41]

American airmen who were captured by the Germans in World War II were most troublesome prisoners. Their *esprit de corps,* and their native intelligence and higher educational levels, were the major reasons for this. By all accounts the American fliers shared discomforts together and commonly kept the escape theme going. Somehow they gathered radio equipment together, only to have it taken from them by German "ferrets." With great daring, the Americans would then steal it back. Numerous escape tunnels were dug, and several airmen were killed attempting to escape. One American pilot managed to get out of the notorious *stalag* at Sagan, and traveled by freight car to the front lines. Only at the last moment was he apprehended by a German patrol.[42]

There are some rather spectacular stories concerning American airmen who were shot down in enemy-held territory, but who managed to escape capture until they crossed neutral borders. The entire crew of a B-17, downed in France, worked its way across the Spanish border. A single American airman, the survivor of a plane that crashed after the famous Schweinfurt raid, not only was able to travel through France and Spain, but was back with his flight wing in less than six weeks. An American glider pilot, captured during the Normandy invasion, was able to pull off a fascinating feat of derring-do. When Allied planes proceeded to bomb German headquarters during his interrogation, he managed to steal a grenade and explode it, after which he effected his escape. Showing light-fingered proclivities, he then filched a German motorcycle and rode it into American lines. A glider pilot, who was shot down in the same invasion, not only escaped but reputedly talked 156 enemy soldiers into coming with him.[43]

Some American airmen had similar successes in Italy. Running away from gangs of prisoners being moved to the rear, these men gained the help of sympathetic Italians until they reached the mountains, where they usually waited for the Allies to come up the boot of Italy. Some walked by night, until they reached Allied lines. A most spectacular escape in Italy was recorded not by airmen, however, but by a tough pair of infantrymen. These GI's had ensconced themselves in a deserted Italian farmhouse with some liberated Chianti, and were easily surprised there by a German private armed with a machine pistol. When the German attempted to remove a grenade from the jacket of one of the Americans, one GI knocked him through the door and then killed him with his own weapon.[44]

Escapes in the Pacific theater were a slightly different matter. The most successful ones were usually made in the Philippines. There were a number of Americans who managed to get away during the Bataan death march, or at the time of the surrender of American forces in the Philippines, and these men participated in guerrilla activity for the remainder of the war. Some of them fathered children with sympathetic Filipinos during the Japanese occupation of the islands.

As in the case of Europe, there were some spectacular escapes in the Pacific during World War II. A Japanese prison ship bound for the homeland with American prisoners was the scene of one of these. The vessel was torpedoed by an American submarine, whereupon the Japanese guards commenced to shoot the prisoners one by one. A mass break for the rail during the confusion allowed for the escape of eighty-three prisoners, all of whom made it to the nearby shore. Cared for by Filipino guerrillas, these men eventually were taken out of the islands by American submarines.

Here, also, is the report of Technical Sergeant Denver R. Rose, a prisoner on board a Japanese ship torpedoed September 7, 1943:

> Using his sword a Jap cut the rope to turn loose the first man in line. He was taken to the stern of the boat and shot in the back. He fell into the water. Then they cut loose the second man and took him back to be shot. I found the frayed end of steel cable on the rail behind me. I rubbed the ropes across the sharp edges until I got my hands free. . . .
>
> I ran to the front end of the ship and slipped down into the anchor hole. I hid there about twenty minutes. They were searching the ship for me. I heard more shots.

While the shooting was going on, I let myself down into the water. I treaded water very softly, so as not to stir up the phosphorescence. Gradually I moved away from the ship and finally lit out for shore.[45]

There was, as indicated previously, much criticism of the lack of spirit of American prisoners in enemy camps during the Korean War; one of the major complaints being that captive GI's made no attempts to escape. This was a generalization which had an element of untruth in it. When American pilots were shot down in an area in which escape was possible, they certainly attempted to reach American or U. N. lines. One American airman lived for a month off the enemy countryside, and finally reached the safety of a U. N. position. Other pilots also escaped, but the U. S. Army never divulged the details of these successful dashes to freedom. And while captive American troops were marched northward, there were several successful escapes from captivity.[46]

Such attempts were made in rather fluid situations however; usually when troops were in transit from one point to another. Once within various Communist stockades far to the north, escape was well nigh impossible; even though some Chinese camps were not surrounded by barbed wire or machine-gun emplacements. The questions each GI undoubtedly asked himself in such situations probably involved his chances of success. Not knowing the country well, and having no understanding of the language, where could he go? Moreover, a white or Negro American attempting to escape in North Korea was highly visible to the local population. The weather was unpredictable; the distance to friendly lines was almost imponderable. For these reasons there were no successful American escapes out of established prison camps in the North.

In attempting to understand whether all such excuses were valid, one would have to envision himself in a similar situation. Would he have the nerve to cross a terribly hostile countryside over such a great distance? He must also consider historical similarities. Of all the Germans imprisoned in the United States during World War II, not one POW managed to make his way back to Germany.[47] A similar situation has existed in the Vietnam War. A few escapes have been effected by ordinary GI's held by the Viet Cong. Another escape was achieved by Lieutenant Dieter Dengler, a German-born pilot in the U. S. Navy. Dengler, who got away after five months in the hands of the Communists, was finally rescued in a state of shock by American helicopters.

Though the end to Dengler's story was a happy one, it should be remembered that this pilot's partner in escape was beheaded, and that Dengler was a wreck of a man at the time of his rescue. Furthermore, Dengler's escape seems to have been made from a temporary base camp in North Vietnam, and not from a regular prison stockade. Because of the more rigid security in the latter type of prison, it appears probable that, as in the case of the Korean War, there will be few successful American prison breaks from North Vietnam.[48]

Whether the conditions of any particular prison camp are good or bad, life for the prisoners is usually reduced to a rather elemental existence. The prison ships in the American Revolution happened to be very bad, and the Americans who were shut up within them became naked and skeletal creatures. With nothing to look at but the bulkheads of the hold, they lost all sense of reality and time. When, on occasion, the British did provide better daily rations, it was not uncommon for some of the men to eat themselves into comas. Many literally became drunk from too much food; a condition often paralleled in other wars. A Federal prisoner at Andersonville wrote of becoming mesmerized by his ration of bacon, for instance. "It seemed as though the little morsel was magnetized," he concluded.[49]

The same condition was common in World War II. American soldiers, weak from the lack of a well-balanced diet, became "high" on cigarettes. One GI prisoner in Japan almost starved himself to death, because he traded his rice allotments to fellow prisoners for tobacco. Similar instances were seen in Korea. A tough World War II Marine, describing the exposure of such psychological weaknesses in prison, hit the nail on the head by stating: "Nothing in a person's make-up really changes much—a crybaby is always a crybaby, a weakling is a weakling, a man is still a man. . . ."[50]

One of the peculiar problems faced by American POW's in each period of war has been that of living through each day. Passing the time is not always easy. In the Civil War men kept busy making various little trinkets. A canteen, carefully separated, made two dishes—or even two scoops, if escape was contemplated. The Federal prisoners at Camp Ford in Texas made combs and chess pieces from the bones of cattle. Violins or musical instruments were also produced. In World War II any trinket that could be produced might prove to be good trade-bait, especially on the days when Red Cross packages arrived.

All in all, however, life in a prison camp can be a shattering experience and a source of trouble to a man for the rest of his life. A Federal officer, imprisoned at the infamous Libby Prison, wrote: "My daily life: I go to bed about ten, get up a little after daylight for roll-call, then breakfast. Read, write, walk and talk and grumble for a while. At two p.m., roll-call, then have dinner. Read, write, walk, talk and grumble till bedtime." "We are strange, restless, discontented creatures. . . ." the same officer wrote after his exchange.[51] Undoubtedly this man's mental anguish, during and after his prison experience, is akin to that suffered by every American POW in history.

The greatest moment in the life of any American POW prisoner is that which comes with his release from captivity. Former Andersonville prisoners who were passed through the lines to Sherman's advancing armies wept with joy at their good fortune. Their first request was for coffee, which when provided, caused some of the men to fall over as in a state of intoxication. A Federal officer, freed from Confederate captivity in 1865, wrote:

Very soon we came to a turn in the road, and could see on a hill our troops waiting for us, with the OLD STARRY FLAG in full view, and the band struck up "Red, White, and Blue." Then such a shout. We did not stop for mud or water, but ran to the river and went pell-mell over the pontoon bridge and into camp. . . . One went up to the flag, hugged and kissed the bearer, and wept.[52]

The return of Confederate prisoners was infinitely more subdued.

Those released on the battlefield simply made their way home by whatever means were available. Others, who were prisoners of long standing, were taken to discharge points, released, and allowed to drift back to the towns or villages from which they came. Emotionalism for these men was wrapped around the return to their families.

Sometimes the disorientation of returning prisoners is such that, for a few, the returning is an event they cannot really comprehend. An Army nurse, witnessing the liberation of American prisoners in Japan in 1945, wrote: "I think the biggest moment of my life was when the first trainload of fellows pulled in. They had spotted us long before we could see them. . . . At first they didn't know what to do or say. . . . They expect so little and are grateful for anything." The behavior of Americans who were exchanged at the end of the Korean War was slightly similar. Most seemed utterly submissive; some were even slightly frightened; and all had the appearance of men who were expecting something other than what was really happening.[53]

When victory is complete, as it was in World War II, there are always a few who manage to relieve some long pent-up emotions. Before the landing of occupation forces in Japan in 1945, the Americans in one camp had painted on the top of a nearby building a large sign, which read "Three Cheers for the U. S. Army and Navy." And the tough ones got their revenge. Marines who had been imprisoned since Bataan caught their most hated Japanese guard before he could escape. They then allowed retribution to be taken by an ex-Pennsylvania coal miner who had been beaten savagely by the guard only two weeks before. When the American was finished, the Japanese soldier was a toothless and quivering form on the floor.[54]

One fact comes through in the search for information on the records of Americans imprisoned by an enemy, and that is that most Americans have always retained a deep and abiding faith in their country. Enemy propaganda efforts have been fruitless. In the War of 1812, when techniques of propaganda were fairly undeveloped, American prisoners were given pamphlets urging a defection to the British cause. The pamphlets were a complete failure. In the Civil War, Federal prisoners returned north knowing that their cause had been just. Confederates went home and sang:

> Oh, I'm a good old rebel, that's what I am;
> And for this land of freedom I don't care a damn,
> I'm glad I fought agin' her, I only wish we'd won,
> And I don't axe any pardon for anything I've done.

German propaganda attempts in prison camps in World War I met with a resounding failure. Doughboys were told that they had fought for "Big Business," and that their cause was ridiculous. The Americans nodded their heads, a gesture of understanding the Germans took to be agreement, and then went back to their huts to snicker in glee.

In World War II the efforts of "Tokyo Rose" and "Axis Sally" were regarded by all American fighting men, free or in prison, as the most humorous radio programs on the airwaves. The reaction of most GI's was that if only these women were available to them for a few days, the troops might convince them of the strength of American character. And in Korea the serious classroom indoctrination presented by dedicated Chinese Communists was always tolerated but never really absorbed.

In a sense it is the happy mixture of discipline and freedom within the character of the American fighting man which has allowed him to survive the ordeal of prison life. An American released in Japan at the end of World War II expressed a part of this characteristic when he stated: "I think most of us who lived lived out of pure meanness. . . . The old army discipline helped." And an old Marine, writing of his own release from a Japanese prison camp, displayed the other side of the coin. Faced by a young lieutenant and told by him to line up and present their serial numbers, the prisoners reacted thusly: "That was about all he got to say before we barged past him, almost knocking him down, as we scrambled to get a seat on the homeward-bound train." The phrase *homeward-bound* is the key one. Home, to any imprisoned United States soldier, is a special place. It is America.[55]

9

The All-American Fighting Man

Hıstory shows that american fighting men have never been from one particular ethnic or religious background. America's armed forces have always been a composite of all the races and religions to which America has provided a haven. This is a national characteristic which other nations have always recognized in the United States. Hitler, for instance, looked upon the American Army as a "mongrelized" body of soldiers, and his own *Wehrmacht* as an "uncontaminated" force.

An opposing point of view is taken by a few Americans, and a few American ancestral organizations. These people have managed to conjure up a historical image of the American fighting man as a tall and lean soldier who carried his musket in one hand, and the King James version of the Bible in the other. And he is white.

The truth is that these people are no more correct about American history than Hitler was about the German past. Long before the American Revolution, the men who composed American militia units came from dozens of different national backgrounds. They followed one of several different religious beliefs, or in some cases, they were the products of an age of religious skepticism. Most of them were white. Most of them were Protestant. But some were Catholics and Jews; and some were Negro and Indian.

The first professional American fighting unit, the Royal American Regiment, was an amalgamation of soldiers from a dozen different places. Some were English, French, Swiss, Scottish, Irish, and German, and were recruited overseas. Others were men who had been persuaded to join the Regiment in the colonies. The Royal Americans, as described by one historian, was a "weird" collection of types. One-fourth of the men were "colonial" in origin, and the rest were continental Europeans or "refuse of the army of Ireland." By order of the King, all of the men were supposedly Protestant. Yet it is probably right to suppose that just a few of the Irish and German privates carried a Rosary out of habit or family tradition.[1]

The Revolutionary Army of 1775–1783 was mainly composed of white Protestants. Many of the enlistees were German or Scots-Irish by birth. The latter two types came out of Pennsylvania or the South, and though Washington distrusted them greatly, preferring native-born Americans, one cannot discount the numbers of foreign-born soldiers in the war for independence.

Each regular or militia regiment of the Revolution differed in terms of its composition. Most of the excellent Virginia units were recruited from native-born Americans. Pennsylvania, on the other hand, provided a wide variety of national backgrounds. Out of the twenty-five sergeants in one Pennsylvania line regiment, seven were Irish born (probably North-Irish), seven came from England, one came from Scotland, four were colonial born, and the remainder came from other European nations. Of the twenty-two corporals in the same regiment, two were Scots-Irish, three English, two Scottish, five American, and the rest had unspecified origins. Northern-Irish and Americans predominated among the private soldiers of this regiment, but there were other men who had come from England, Scotland, and Germany.[2]

The point having been made that most Revolutionary soldiers were white Protestants, it may be added that, all in all, an infinite variety of types fought for independence. The *Bon Homme Richard,* John Paul Jones's creaking warship, was manned by American,

English, French, Maltese, Portuguese, and Malay sailors, and was captained by a Scotsman. Numerous Indians fought for the Revolutionary cause. One of the heroes of the Saratoga fighting was a Narragansett Indian. There were Abenakis who were present during the terrible hardships at Valley Forge. Albigence Waldo, an Army physician who kept a diary during those hard days, wrote:

> I was called to relieve a soldier thought to be dying. He expired before I reached the hut. He was an Indian, an excellent soldier, and an obedient, good-natured fellow. He engaged for money, doubtless, as others do, but he has served his country faithfully. He has fought for those very people who disinherited his forefathers. . . .[3]

Negroes also played a significant role in the American Revolution. One Salem Poor, a New England Negro, fought heroically at Bunker Hill. Though many American officers disliked having Negroes in the service, they were eventually forced to accept them out of necessity. An August, 1778, return for regiments in Washington's command shows that seven brigades had fifty-four Negro soldiers each. Rhode Island encouraged Negro enlistment by guaranteeing freedom to each slave who joined the service of that state. Negroes fought heroically at Saratoga, and the Hessians were surprised by the number present in the conquering American Army. They were also in service at Lexington, Concord, Ticonderoga, Monmouth, and at Point Bridge, New York, where colored soldiers fought to the death. Privateering crews consisted to some extent of Negro sailors, and at times, they were used as spies in order to determine British operations in New Jersey, New York, and in the South.[4]

Nor was the makeup of the Revolutionary Army completely Christian. There were numerous and prominent Jewish officers under Washington's command. Of the reported 2,500 Jews in the American colonies in 1776, it was reputed that some six hundred served in the Revolutionary forces. Jews fought in the Carolinas, and in fact, there was a "Jews Company" from South Carolina. Jews fought at Crown Point and against the Indians who supported the British, and included such men as Solomon Bush, Nathaniel Levy, Moses

Cohen, Benjamin Sheftall, and Isaac Nuñuz Cardozo (the ancestor of the famous Supreme Court justice).

Jews continued to be active in the armed forces of the nation through the War of 1812. Some three thousand were reputed to have taken part in this conflict. Jews were listed among the defense units at Fort McHenry and among the American regiments which participated in the bloody encounter at Chrysler's Field. Uriah P. Levy was not only an active officer in the Navy during this period, but in years following, he rose to the rank of flag officer.[5]

Most of the men of the fighting forces of the United States from 1800 to 1840 were white Protestants, however; with Northern-Irish Presbyterians holding most noncommissioned positions in the ranks, and the people of British-Anglican extraction tending to fill the ranks of commissioned officers. Though stress may be laid upon white Protestant contributions to the action, it must also be remembered that American Negroes were again not exempt from participation in the fighting services during this period. Oliver H. Perry won a naval battle on Lake Erie during the War of 1812 with a crew consisting of white militiamen, Indians, and Negroes. Lawrence's hard fight on the *Chesapeake* was carried on with the aid of a Negro bugler. Jackson's clear triumph over Pakenham at New Orleans was accomplished with white militiamen and sailors, half-breed Indians, and Negroes.

The diversity of ethnic and national groups within the Regular Army and the Navy of the United States continued far after 1815. By 1820, for instance, there were so many foreigners in the American Navy that the Secretary of the Navy recommended that officers with bilingual qualities especially be given sea-duty. The increase in German immigration after 1830 was such that many of the frontier posts in Minnesota were manned almost entirely by German-speaking soldiers.

Irish immigration likewise had an effect upon the fighting forces. It has been estimated that 24 percent of Taylor's army during the Mexican War was Irish. Germans in the same army totaled 10 percent, the English 6 percent, and the Scots provided 3 percent of Taylor's men. The fact that 47 percent of the whole of this particular army consisted of immigrants indicates that other elements were also present. Numbers of Jews had volunteered from Maryland and Pennsylvania and were present in Taylor's units, and with Scott at such battles as Cerro Gordo, Contreras, and Churubusco.

The presence of so many immigrants in the American Army during the Mexican War created some problems. Some German and Irish Catholics were won over to the Mexican side, where they joined the excellent San Patricio Battalion. The language differences during this conflict posed handicaps for American officers. And the Irish were particularly hard to discipline, no matter from what part of the Union they had volunteered. Yet it must be stressed that, withal, most of these foreign-born soldiers were good fighters. One-third of Kearny's five hundred men who took Santa Fe were Catholic and Irish; yet desertions in that unit were at a minimum. Those who did desert from Scott's and Taylor's armies did so with great inducements from the enemy.

The peculiar aspect of this war, and others which followed for the United States in the 1800's, is that immigrant American soldiers were quick to grasp to their bosoms the patriotic folk myths of the time. A Jew, who witnessed the execution of captured members of the San Patricio Battalion near the end of the war, heartily approved of this treatment for defectors. When journals and newspapers pronounced early in the conflict that "Anglo-Saxon" steadfastness of the invaders would easily overcome the mixed-blood troops of Mexico, the Irish were among the first to regard themselves as qualified for this conclusion. This peculiar outlook by Celtic and Hebrew-Americans found an even greater expression in the Civil War.[6]

At the close of the Mexican War, when the Army was reduced to what was considered a normal peacetime size, the tendency of immigrant groups to look upon the service as a good introduction to American life grew in importance. Through the 1850's, therefore, it can be said that the frontier posts of the nation were truly manned by a mixed force consisting of Irish, Germans, Swedes, and Americans. Many of the latter had joined the service only because, as one observer expressed it, they had "been guilty of some misdemeanor."[7]

Thus by 1860 the U. S. Army was a strange admixture of excellently trained American-born (usually Anglican) officers, Irish Catholic noncoms, and privates from all countries and all walks of life. The privates of one dragoon company of the 1850's provide an excellent sampling of the composition of the whole army. One of these men was English, a teacher and a master of several languages; another, an Irish private, was a graduate of Dublin College; some were fairly well-read immigrants and Americans; and the remainder was made up of Irish and American "ruffians." Another unit, a company of the Second U. S. Infantry, which was stationed in the Dakota Territory, was made up of twenty German immigrants, ten Americans, and forty-two others from Ireland, Scotland, and England.

The outbreak of the Civil War had a profound effect upon the Regular military establishment of the United States. Many of the officers of the Army, Southern-born, went out of the Union with their states. The enlisted men however—particularly the Irish noncoms, the Germans and the English—remained loyal to the Union. The effects of disunion upon the Navy were equally disastrous. Many American-born officers resigned their commissions, but fortunately those who were foreign born stayed loyal. Since ninety-six of the 725 officers in the lower ranks were of non-American birth, this was extremely important. The importance of loyalty among the foreign-born enlisted naval complement cannot be underestimated. More than 200 of the 324 sailors on Farragut's flagship, the *Hartford,* were immigrants. Over one-third of the crew of the *Minnesota* consisted of twenty-six different nationalities. Twenty-nine nationalities were represented on the *Colorado,* and there were twenty-five different nationalities on the *Hartford.*[8]

The war in 1861 cut directly through all national entities, however. Though the Confederacy was inclined to think of itself as a cause supported and maintained by Anglo-Saxonism—Federal troops being regarded as "mudsills" or ethnic mixtures—this was not really true. Not only was Judah Benjamin, a Jew, one of the most trusted members of President Davis's cabinet, but thousands of Hebrews fought for the Rebel cause, and they fought well.

The peculiar aspect of Jewish participation on the side of the Confederacy is that these men were seldom reluctant to accept the aims of the Southern cause. A Jewish soldier, wounded during the Vicksburg fighting, wrote that he was dead set against "nigger" equality. Another, in a letter written just before Lee's surrender, stated: "Negroes are among masters and have the inclination to be tyrants. The extermination of this race is a necessary consequence of this state of affairs." A Jewish Confederate, expressing his faith in a famous Confederate general, wrote: "Can it be wondered at that this man has won our hearts and minds? Opposed as I am to hero worship, I shall never utter the name of Robert E. Lee unless with respect and veneration."

Nor were the Jewish Confederates ever easy to "reconstruct." A Jewish soldier wrote at the end of the war: "The four years that I have given to my country I do not regret. . . . My only regret is that we have lost that for which we fought." A Confederate officer, a Jew by the name of Raphael Jacob Moses, was still unrepentant forty years after the end of the war. As late as 1905 he carried a calling card which read: "Major Raphael J. Moses, C. S. A."

Bell Wiley, whose studies of soldiers in the Civil War are unequaled, found that not only were German, Irish, French, and English immigrants to be found in the Confederate Army, but Northerners as well. Some of these men were general officers; Cleburne, an Irishman, and Pemberton and Gracie, who were from the North, all three of whom present excellent examples. It is also possible, though not supported by sufficient proof, that "technical" Negroes may have fought for the "Bonnie Blue Flag." These would most likely be found as light-skinned volunteers from the Charleston, South Carolina, area, or from the Creole parishes of Louisiana.

Though it is true that there were many foreign-born soldiers in the Union Army, probably between 20 and 23 percent, the remaining 80 percent indicates that the Federals were mainly of

American birth. Wiley, who took 123 scattered regiments into consideration, found that New York was the greatest contributor to the Union cause. Pennsylvania, Ohio, Indiana, and Illinois were also high on the list. Some 814 of the men in Wiley's sampling came from slave-holding states; principally Virginia and Tennessee.

Among the foreign born who fought for the Union were the Germans, who counted up to nearly 200,000 enlistees; the Irish, who totaled almost 150,000; more than 53,000 Canadians; and some 54,000 English. Most of the German regiments came from New York, though there were scattered German units among the volunteers of Pennsylvania, Ohio, Indiana, Illinois, and Wisconsin. Two Illinois German regiments, the Eighty-Second and the Forty-Third, had notable war records; the first having the distinction of fighting in most of the eastern campaigns, including Gettysburg, and in several important battles in the West.[9]

The common denominator to all German regiments, North and South, was the plentiful supply of beer. A Western soldier, non-German, came to the conclusion early in the war that the German battle cry had to be "Zwei Lager und eine Union!" The tradition of keeping such regiments well supplied with alcoholic beverages both hurt and helped the German reputation in America. Native American regiments, or regiments filled partially with Irish volunteers, were wont to resent or envy this Germanic custom. In 1862 a classic fight took place at Camp Butler in Illinois between an American unit and the Eighty-Second, the aforementioned German regiment. There were other times when German-American soldiers, overstimulated by beer, plundered captured towns or villages.

On the other hand there were more sublime moments. When the fighting at Vicksburg ended, and the great Confederate fortress surrendered, the German soldiers of the Eighth Illinois invited German-born Confederates to share their supply of beer. It is needless to add that this was and still is a fairly successful method of making friends or influencing people amongst one's former enemies.[10]

The Irish were likewise splendid contributors to the Union cause, particularly among the various regiments from New York, Massachusetts, and Illinois. The blood of Erin flowed freely at Fredericksburg, and up and down the Shenandoah Valley. An Irish regiment, the Nineteenth Illinois, played an important role in the second day of the Battle of Stone's River.

Sturdy and brave as they were, many of the Irish troops did not measure up to some of the standards set by native Americans. They could not march at the forced pace to which Western troops of the Union cause were accustomed. They were often intemperate in tranquillity, and unwise in battle. Officers found them hard to discipline. Unlike German troops, who fell apart when pushed into improvisation, the Irish experimented too much and failed to follow orders well. When placed in close contact with native American regiments, the Irish tended to become overly belligerent, and fights resulted. In these extracurricular combats the Irish often came out much the worse, for they could not match the lean strength of their American adversaries.[11]

The variety of troops that made up the immigrant contribution to the Federal Army was almost infinite. Large numbers of Swedes served in certain Western regiments. One Nordic, a graduate from the University of Lund, served as a private in a Maine unit. Norwegians, Poles, and Hungarians were scattered freely amongst the regiments of the Northern cause. Illinois furnished two "Scots" regiments; the Twelfth and the Sixty-Fifth; better known as the "First and Second Scotch." A Russian officer, a former member of the Czarist forces in his native land, commanded the Nineteenth Illinois, a predominantly Irish unit.[12]

Though figures are highly conflicting, large numbers of Jews also wore the blue uniform. One estimate goes as high as fifteen thousand; another, probably more accurate, allows that there were six thousand Jewish enlistments in the Federal Army. Some Jews became officers of Northern units, and extremely good ones at that. Other Jews served in the Union Navy.[13]

As the war progressed into 1862, the American Negro also began to make a serious contribution to the Union cause. Many Negroes, used as servants in the first months of the conflict in 1861, had gotten in some earlier but unofficial licks at the Confederacy. A young Negro, a certain William Stains from Illinois, had spurred the

Union charge during the Battle of Belmont. In late 1862, Union Generals Hunter and Butler began the unauthorized recruitment of Negro battalions. Though these troops were used mainly in a support capacity, the building of bridges, and trench-digging work, their contributions to the Federal cause cannot be underestimated.

One by one the states of the North, running short in their quotas, began to organize combat Negro regiments. Such units fought well at Milliken's Bend, during the Vicksburg Campaign, and at Fort Wagner, in the middle of 1863. In the latter assault, the Fifty-Fourth Massachusetts Infantry, a Negro unit, lost two-thirds of its white officers and one-half of its men in the attack. Negro regiments in the IX Corps were also used in the unfortunate Petersburg Bomb Crater assault of 1864.

How good were these newly conscripted colored regiments? All in all, very good! They usually maintained a proud discipline, and their close-order drill was a sight to behold. They were hardy soldiers. One Negro regiment made thirty miles in one day in 1863 with not a single straggler. The defeat at the Petersburg Bomb Crater was less the fault of the Negro privates than it was that of the white officers and generals who commanded them. Their patriotism was surprisingly good, despite the fact that they received less pay than white troops, fewer supplies, and brutal treatment from the enemy if captured. Their enlistment rate, in spite of such dismal conditions, was extremely high, being one hundred a day in New York as late as 1865.

In the final days of the Confederacy, Negro troops were among those who breached the defenses at Petersburg and received Lee's last assault at Appomattox. And, when Federal troops finally got into Richmond, there were Negro cavalry units who rode into the town crying to Southern Negroes: "We have come to set you free!"[14]

It is truly difficult for the historian to arrive at the exact contribution of American Negroes to the Federal forces during the war. The reasons for this are numerous. First of all, there were many Negroes who were so light-skinned that they served in all-white regiments without question. One such Negro, H. Ford Douglass of Chicago, was a member of the violently antiabolitionist G Company, Ninety-

Fifth Illinois, for several years. None of his comrades knew that Douglass was of Negro ancestry.

Another factor in the difficulty of tabulating Negroes who served in the Union cause is that many freed slaves were used as "under-cooks" in many Western regiments. Listed on the muster rolls of the regiments as such, these men quite often picked up rifles and took part in fighting; all in an unofficial capacity of course.

Lastly, among the authorized Negro regiments, there was no real attempt by white officers to keep true muster rolls. If a Negro soldier was captured or killed, or if he went AWOL, another Negro, usually a freed slave, was picked up, given the same name as the departed soldier, and inserted into the regiment. For these reasons and others, the estimates of Negroes participating in the war vary. War Department records place the number at 178,895. Other sources state that many more than 200,000 Negroes fought for the Federal cause.

There are some hard facts, however. Negro soldiers did take part in 449 separate engagements. Their total casualties amounted to 68,178, of whom 2,751 were killed in action. Of the thirty-seven Medals of Honor awarded to men serving in the Chafin's Farm area near Petersburg in 1864 and 1865, fourteen of these were awarded to Negroes. These are figures on which to contemplate.[15]

It would be improper to leave the Civil War without discussing the contributions of the American Indian to both sides. Numerous Indians fought for the Confederacy, particularly in the Southwest. At Pea Ridge, where they were accused of scalping wounded Federal troops, Indians were partially responsible for the Confederate successes of the first day. In southeast Tennessee, where a number of Indians lived in 1861, there were many Redskin volunteers to the Confederate cause.

Five Indian regiments were authorized for the Federal Army, though only three were filled. These were the First Indian Regiment (Creeks, Seminoles); the Second Indian Regiment (Osage and various other tribes); and the Third Indian Regiment (Cherokees and half-breeds). All three regiments constituted the so-called Indian Brigade, which fought at Newtonia, Mississippi, Prairie Grove, Arkansas, and at Honey Springs and Perryville in the Indian Territory.

The muster rolls of the Indian regiments must have been something to read. They included such names as Stephen Killer, John Bearmeat, Alex Scarce Water, Mixt Water, Warkiller Hogshooter, and Swimmer Jack. Despite such fearsome names, however, the Indians were hard to keep disciplined and, though they were carelessly brave, they were not considered by many to be as good as the soldiers in the various Negro regiments. Furthermore, it was infinitely more difficult to obtain capable officers for these units; the better ones usually regarding service among the Indians as the lowest rung on the military ladder.

Though little used in the Civil War, the American Indian achieved a special role in the years following 1865. Every Regular Army unit stationed in the West carried Indian scouts on its payroll, and some of these were regarded as extremely able fighters. Pawnees were particularly prized for this purpose, but in the years from 1865 to 1880, scouts from the Arikara and the Crow tribes also served the country well.[16]

Only four Negro units were continued in service after the dissolution of the Federal Army after 1865. These were the Ninth and Tenth Negro Cavalry, and the Twenty-Fourth and Twenty-Fifth Negro Infantry. It was difficult to garrison these men anywhere in the country, principally because of local reactions to them. One United States senator, it was claimed, admitted to spending almost all his time during the Cleveland Administration forestalling the stationing of Negro units at Fort Ethan Allen in Vermont.[17]

This being the case, the only places in which Negro units could serve without objection were in the West. The Twenty-Fourth and Twenty-Fifth Infantry Regiments were committed mainly to garrison work on the frontier. On occasion, however, they were called into action. In 1889 Negro escort troops of one of these units performed so well in protecting an army paymaster during an assault by a marauding Indian band that every one of the soldiers was given a Medal of Honor or a certificate of merit.

The Ninth and Tenth Cavalry saw extremely hard duty in the West, following the Civil War. Called "Buffalo Soldiers" by the Indians, these men operated in almost constant peril. The Ninth

Cavalry alone fought in sixty separate Indian fights between 1868 and 1890, and the Tenth engaged in various skirmishes with Apache bands over the vast Territories of New Mexico and Arizona. In an 1881 fight in the Cushilo Negro Mountains of New Mexico, I Troop of the Ninth Cavalry, having lost its white officer to Indian snipers, fought on with such courage and bravery that its sergeant, Moses Williams, was given the Medal of Honor by "common consent."

This is not to say that the records of all four Regular Negro units were spotless. There were difficulties which developed between Negro garrison troops and several all-white communities in the West. The causes of these troubles have all but disappeared in the mists of time, but one can only surmise that they involved traditional resentments on both sides. The Twenty-Fifth Infantry shot up the town of Sturgis in the Dakotas in 1885, killing several civilians. In Winnemucca, Nevada, in 1899, soldiers of the Twenty-Fifth took over the town on one occasion and terrorized the inhabitants. In El Paso, Texas, in the same year, members of the Twenty-Fifth assaulted the local jail and killed several policemen; an incident that was repeated at Fort Niobrara in Nebraska a short time later. It might also be pointed out that, in 1867, E Troop, Ninth Cavalry, killed and wounded three white officers before the mutinous uprising was put down.

In every one of these incidents the troops may well have been provoked by the circumstances of segregation. One may also ask if the behavior of these men differed to any great extent from that of certain white units on the frontier. Shortly after the turn of the century there were some writers who claimed that Negro regiments had shown "greater sobriety and fewer desertions" than those composed of whites. It should also be added at this point that the Ninth Cavalry was able to report, at one period of the frontier wars, that not one single desertion had occurred during one twelve-month period of intensive campaigning.[18]

The white soldiers of America's frontier army during the Indian Wars were representative of a wide range of nationalities. A study of one particular post-Civil War frontier company showed ninety of the men to be former Federal soldiers, sixty-nine were ex-Confederates, nineteen were Irish, five were English, and the rest consisted of Canadians, Germans, Scots, Russians, Norwegians, Dutch, and Italians. The Americans in this instance came from every state in the Union, but mostly from Missouri, Tennessee, New York, Pennsylvania, and Indiana.

Many of the immigrants in the U. S. Army during this period were old soldiers who had served with the British in India, or in the Prussian army. The average age for all enlistments during the period was about twenty-three; thirty-two for reenlistments. The Irish still tended to dominate the noncom ranks, while Anglican Protestants held commissioned ranks far in excess of their percentage of the national population. A mere glance at the muster rolls of regiments serving in the battles around the Little Big Horn shows the range of national backgrounds. The names McIntosh, O'Neill, Berry, Criswell, Cunningham, and DeRudio are noted. Medal of Honor winners in Reno's fight near the Little Big Horn included a Bancroft, Brant, Callan, Goldin, Harris, Pym, Roy (first name Stanislaus), Scott, Stevens, Thompson, and Welch.[19]

The U. S. Navy after 1865 was given to the same ethnic variance. Anglican Protestants and Presbyterians held the officers' commissions, while enlistees consisted of native-born Americans and scores of other nationalities. There were so many immigrants in the U. S. Pacific squadrons in the 1880's that officers were forced to give commands in two or three different languages. On the U. S. S. *Ashuelot,* there were only nineteen native Americans; the rest of the crew coming from nineteen different nationalities. Though the majority of these immigrant sailors served well, it must be stated that the period from 1880 to 1890 was marked by an unusually large number of desertions; these mainly committed by foreign-born sailors.

So serious was the problem of immigrant sailors in the U. S. Navy by 1890 that Naval authorities made a concerted effort to "Americanize" the fleet. By 1898 the goal was almost completed, with the foreign-born complement of the Navy having been reduced to a low 10 percent.[20] Though most of the total fleet complement was white, no matter their national origin, it must be noted here that the Navy's attitude toward Negro enlistees was far more generous in

1898 than it was to be in years to come. Negro sailors, who could qualify as regular seamen, gunners, or gunners' mates, served without any exceptional discrimination at this time. They slept and lived together with whites in the crowded quarters of American warships of the predreadnought era. Within a few years, however, the Navy would virtually eliminate Negroes from the fleet, save for the menial classification of steward's mate.[21]

In 1898, when the war with Spain broke out, the American forces that were sent to Cuba, Puerto Rico, or the Philippines, once again covered the broad spectrum of race and creed. Some fifteen Jews went down with the ill-fated *Maine,* before the actual outbreak of hostilities. The first American killed in battle in Cuba was reputedly a Jew, and some four thousand to five thousand people of that faith volunteered for service in the Army. Spanish-Americans volunteered in large numbers from the Southwest, and some were actually listed on the rolls of Roosevelt's Rough Riders.[22]

American Negroes made a notable contribution in the Spanish-American War. The Twenty-Fifth Negro Infantry, along with the white Twelfth Infantry, captured El Caney. In the attack on San Juan Hill, the Twenty-Fourth Negro Infantry, with the Ninth and Thirteenth Infantry Regiments (white), got partial credit for the success of the assault. The color sergeant of the Tenth Negro Cavalry led a stirring charge of his regiment up San Juan Hill alongside the famed "Rough Riders," and there is probably some truth in the assertion that, when Roosevelt's men reached the crest, the Negro cavalrymen were already there. These colored Americans fought with exceptional gallantry; a fact which the Army recognized by awarding five Medals of Honor to Negroes who had taken part in the San Juan charge. One writer of the day stated that, in terms of service and sacrifice to the nation in 1898, no four white regiments could be compared to the four Negro units involved in the conflict.

The reward for some of these Negro regiments for such service was a slighting one indeed. General Shafter, commanding forces in Cuba, got the idea that Negroes would be far less susceptible to yellow fever than white soldiers, and proceeded to place the Twenty-Fourth Infantry on hospital duty at Siboney. The results were pitiful. Of the total regimental force committed to this onerous task, only twenty-four of the Negro troopers failed to get malaria or yellow fever.[23]

Though relationships between the white American troops in Cuba, who constituted a large majority of the invasion force, and the various Negro regiments were good in the beginning, there occurred a rather rapid deterioration after the defeat of the Spanish. The decline in the state of the Negro-American fighting man within the armed forces of the United States was indeed rapid after 1898. A number of incidents and developments account for this.

First of all a rather stupid Army directive had placed the Tenth Negro Cavalry on military police duty in Key West prior to departure for Cuba. Civilians in the community, as well as Southern white soldiers, objected strenuously to this, and racial incidents were frequent. Then, because several members of the Twenty-Fifth Negro Infantry had been arrested in Key West by civilian authorities, the members of that regiment went on a rampage, smashing the jail and freeing all prisoners. Following the end of the war some Negro units were sent into the Philippines. Here, along with white soldiers during the insurrection in the Islands, they found sexual contacts rather easy to make. Resentments and jealousies arose. Numerous Negro soldiers not only took Filipino wives, but deserted to the hills to fight with Aguinaldo, the local insurrectionist.

The fact of the matter was that by 1903 the U. S. Army still had its four traditionally Negro regiments with no place to put them. Congressmen in the United States used every political weapon available to keep them out of encampments in their own states. The Filipinos likewise protested the behavior of colored regiments in those islands. The Ninth Negro Cavalry, which had been stationed in the worst possible frontier posts, was never allowed to be encamped in any part of the Northeast due to local prejudice. Yet—in a strange contradiction—five Medal of Honor winners were still in service in these Negro regiments in 1903, while numerous other colored soldiers held certificates signifying meritorious conduct.[24]

Withdrawn from the Philippines, scorned by Northern states, some of the Negro regiments were sent to Brownsville, Texas; about as out-of-the-way a place as one could find in 1903. As one white officer expressed it three years later:

> The National prejudice has followed the flag across the Pacific Ocean. Five years ago, the colored regiments on duty in the Philippines were returned to the States at the demand of the Civil Governor of the Islands. No charge of misconduct was made against them; from the military point of view their service had been perfectly satisfactory.[25]

What happened thereafter only served to confirm rapidly emerging prejudices relative to the Negro soldier. Brownsville became a cauldron of rumors about the alleged misbehavior of soldiers in the Twenty-Fifth Infantry Regiment. There were stories about Negro attacks upon white women. Minor fights as well as a positive discrimination against the Negro troops followed. In August, 1906, the situation exploded. There was a shooting, reputedly involving three companies of the Twenty-Fifth, and resulting in the killing or wounding of three local inhabitants.

Because none of the soldiers would testify against those few Negroes who had fired into the town, a severe punishment was applied to virtually all of the members of the Twenty-Fifth. Three whole companies were discharged "without honor," including one Sergeant Mingo Sanders who had served for twenty-six years and was past retirement age. President Theodore Roosevelt, particularly, was most adamant in his determination to see the punishment through, in spite of the common knowledge the trials were "stacked" and that the innocent had been punished equally with the guilty.[26]

Despite the fact that Negro troopers of the Tenth Cavalry went into Mexico with Pershing in 1916, the relative gap between whites and Negroes in the services grew wider and wider. The Navy, following suit, partly because of the growing influence of Southern-born white officers in that branch of the service, began to limit the enlistments of Negroes. Treatment of Negro regiments in the Army declined from bad to worse. The 1917 Houston racial explosion, involving the Twenty-Fourth Infantry Regiment, seemed to clinch the fate of the colored American fighting man, at least for a while.

Here, in August, the troops fired into the town, reputedly killing seventeen white civilians and wounding many more. For this a dozen of the troops were hanged, and some forty-one were sentenced to life imprisonment.[27]

Nevertheless, the fighting American of 1917 still remains positively unidentifiable in terms of race and creed. He was white, Negro, or Oriental; he was Protestant, Catholic, or Jewish. His religions and national backgrounds were almost as varied as those of the entire globe; a condition that misled many German generals to the assumption that American loyalty to the Stars and Stripes simply *had* to be of an ephemeral nature.

This infinite variety was present in the very beginning. The U. S. Navy laid claim to getting the first enlisted men to the shores of France in 1917, simply because of the sinking of the merchantman *Aztec* off the French coast. The gun crew of that ship, Regular Navy men who managed to reach shore, consisted of several boys with Irish and Anglo-Saxon names, several with Polish and German names, and two Jewish sailors.

The varied backgrounds of the doughboy could be seen in the gathering of the American armies in 1917. Western regiments were generally taller and rangier than those from the East, while those from the East were inclined to have a larger percentage of immigrant Americans. Most of the men of the earliest divisions embarked were native Americans, but there was a sprinkling of German and Irish types as well. Later divisions, formed from the draft, sometimes had so many immigrants among them that there was a difficulty in communication between officers and men. One regiment which was formed in 1918 was composed of 80 percent immigrant boys. In almost every division there were American Indians. The 32nd Division was blessed with a five-foot-tall Chippewa, who was a terror on patrols. The Forty-Second, or Rainbow Division, had an Indian boy who killed seven Germans on one night patrol.[28]

Among the largest contributors to the American war effort in 1917–1918 were the German populations of Milwaukee, Chicago, New York, Cincinnati, and St. Louis. To the great disappointment of German commanders in the homeland, these people proved to be courageous fighters, and among the most patriotic of the drafted men. In the Belleville area of Illinois, where many Germans had settled, drafted German-American boys were honored before their departure by *Strassenfests*. Many young German boys looked upon the Marine Corps as a most appropriate means of serving their country, and lined up before the recruiting offices of that service.

The Irish still ruled the noncom ranks of the Army in 1917, and their influence was prodigious. One early unit in France was provided with British style uniforms, the unchanged buttons of which showed the British national symbol. Since the unit was mainly Irish-American, it was outraged and refused to move until an automobile was sent for a sufficient supply of U. S. Army buttons. In many regiments, such as the 165th Infantry (New York's old Sixty-Ninth Regiment), a traditional Irish unit, the organization was fleshed out with young boys of non-Irish backgrounds. This meant little to the Irish, however, for one Private Elanston Van Arsdale soon acquired the nickname *Clancy*. A Private Miguel DeGuerro of the same unit was given the more appropriate name *McNamara*.[29]

The Jewish contribution in World War I was substantial as well. The bare facts show that 20 percent of the Jews in the Army were volunteers, and that 48 percent of all Jewish-American soldiers were in the infantry. There were ten thousand Jews who were commissioned as officers in the war, and these included several prominent generals and admirals. Jews contributed almost 6 percent of the total deaths suffered by American armed forces in the war. More than 1,100 Jews were cited for valor, and of the seventy-eight Medals of Honor handed out, three were given to Jews. The youngest soldier in the war was Albert Cohen, a thirteen-year-old Jew killed in the Meuse-Argonne offensive. Altogether, there were approximately 250,000 Jews in uniform.

The Jewish desire for full acceptance as Americans has provided much literature on the subject of the Jewish-American fighting man. One finds the fascinating story of a Jewish mother who supplied seven sons to the American armed forces in 1918. One must also remember that the famous "Lost Battalion" of the Argonne Forest was saved by Private Abraham Krotoshinsky, a Jew who sneaked through the lines to bring relief.

Along with Sam Woodfill and Sergeant York must also be mentioned Sam Dreben, one of the great soldiers in American history. Dreben, a Russian Jew, served in the Philippines and Cuba as a United States soldier (he also fought in Nicaragua and Mexico between enlistments). In 1917 he got his big chance. Fighting with the Thirty-Sixth Division, he captured three machine guns and killed fifty Germans, and received as awards the D.S.C., the French *Médaille Militaire,* and the *Croix de Guerre.*[30]

The doughboy was really a composite personality. One draft division, the Seventy-Seventh out of New York City, was composed of men who spoke no less than forty-three languages or dialects. There were even Chinese-American soldiers of the Seventy-Seventh. One, a Sergeant Sing Kee, eventually won a decoration. In another unit, the 354th Infantry Regiment, obviously a late-drafted regiment of the Eighty-Ninth Division, the spread of nationalities was equally as great. A study of the medals awarded to B Company of the 354th shows that one was given to an Italian-American, two to German-Americans, two to Irish-Americans, two to Swedish-Americans, and one to a soldier with an English background.[31]

American Negroes in World War I were almost completely segregated from the remainder of the A. E. F. and within other U. S. fighting forces. The Navy, continuing its drive to become virtually an all-white service, allowed only ten thousand Negro enlistments; all in the messman category. The Army did create the Ninety-Second Division, which established one revolutionary concept in that it had Negro officers in the lower ranks. This unit fought with the French Fourth Army—a "trying assignment," according to one authority— and was the source of much trouble. The French felt, to a great degree in the beginning, that the Ninety-Second was poorly trained and represented more of a hazard to them than support.

There were also problems related to the officers of the division. These men, over 1,300 of them, had been trained in a "colored" officers' training school located in Des Moines, Iowa. With the arrival of the Ninety-Second in France, there developed cases of intimacy between French women and many of these officers; a situation which offended a good many local inhabitants, and most of the white Americans. There were further complaints that Negro enlisted men failed to respect the authority of their Negro officers.[32]

It would be hard to establish the real truth behind the developments that followed, but at any rate, the Army proceeded to replace many of the Negro officers with whites. In one week alone, over fifty replacements of this type occurred in the Ninety-Second Division. Many of the Negro officers were sent to the rear to command colored loading battalions at Saint-Nazaire.

There is no question that the fighting efficiency of the Ninety-Second Division did improve thereafter. It performed well enough for the Army to create a "provisional" Ninety-Third Division of colored troops. Consisting only of scattered regiments, which were assigned to the French, the "Black Watch," as the French called it, fought fairly well near the Argonne and around Saint-Mihiel. Later withdrawn, the various regiments were sent to the relatively quiet areas in the Vosges Mountains.

There were more than 400,000 Negroes in the U. S. Army at the time of the Armistice. Some 200,000 of these had been sent overseas, and about 40,000 were directly on the battle line. Total casualties amounted to more than 3,000 for the Ninety-Third Division, with 584 killed; and more than 2,100 for the Ninety-Second, with 176 killed in action. Several individual regiments of the two divisions provide some interesting historical data. The 367th Regiment, perhaps bearing some association with an earlier Negro unit, was known as "the buffaloes." The 368th, according to its white colonel, "behaved remarkably well" on the field of battle; the Third Battalion of this regiment winning eight D. S. C.'s for a September, 1918, attack in the Argonne sector.

The 369th Regiment (formerly the Fifteenth New York National Guard) was on the battle line more than 180 days. Fighting in the Champagne sector near the Aisne River, it suffered 851 casualties in five days of fighting in the late months of the war. The 369th claimed never to have lost a trench or to have had a prisoner taken. The unit, which was decorated regimentally with the *Croix de Guerre* and was known as "Hell's Fighters," had some special heroes. They were Needham Roberts and Henry Johnson; the latter having gained some fame from his assault upon twenty-two Germans with a bolo knife. The Regimental Band, a real "jazz band," was known throughout France for the special flavor of its music.

The regiments of the Ninety-Third Division were actually engaged in harder fighting than those of the Ninety-Second. The 370th Regiment, which was attached to the French Fifty-Ninth Division, suffered more than six hundred casualties and won seventy-five *Croix de Guerre* and sixteen D. S. C.'s. The 371st and 382nd also fought with the French, and suffered more than two thousand casualties in some very difficult combat.

A continuing lack of a high morale plagued both Negro divisions in World War I. The American Negro population had been carried along with the general national sentiment in the early months of the fighting. As one Negro enlisted man put it: "We really believed that it was going to be war to end oppression of all kinds and to make the world—of course the United States—safe for democracy." A rapid disillusionment set in once France was reached. Segregated in almost every possible way, far more even than Senegalese soldiers of the French army, many of the Negro soldiers lost their will to fight. There was an increasing lack of discipline, and a rise in the venereal rate among the Negro soldiers, especially among the loading battalions at Saint-Nazaire. The execution of eight Negro soldiers for murder or rape did not help the situation. And the men wanted to come home. A young Negro enlisted man put it this way. "I wanna git where I kin find some good United States dirt," he wrote, "and grab up a handful and kiss it."

There were profound echoes of these problems among the Negro population of the United States. Rumors were spread, particularly in New York City Negro areas, that colored American fighting men were being sacrificed by being placed in the most dangerous areas, and that the wounded were not receiving adequate medical treatment. The fact that these rumors were untrue and that the Negro divisions were given some of the quieter areas of the fighting line failed to end such tales. When General Pershing quietly pointed out the facts to Negro-American intellectuals, there were still further complaints that Negro soldiers were being discriminated against by the failure of authorities to give them more dangerous assignments.[33]

In the years to come, however, the Negro population of America had some solid basis for complaints. Numerous articles, written by white generals, denigrated the sacrifices of Negro soldiers in the war. In 1919 the burial and reburial of the bodies of American soldiers was assigned mainly to ten thousand American Negro troops, most of whom found a natural and understandable distaste for the task. In 1924, when a Federal office in Washington dedicated plaques on which were inscribed the names of killed servicemen, it was found that the names of Negro dead appeared on a separate tablet from those of the whites. And in the 1920's, when "Gold Star" mothers began their pilgrimages to the cemeteries of Belgium and France, those women who were Negro were placed on separate steamers from those of other races. All of this made it rather hard for the American Negro to accept the argument that the 1,300 Negroes who were buried in Flanders Field had died to make the world safe for democracy.[34]

How good were the Negro troops of the A. E. F.? An experienced French officer who served with them wrote: "I did not think so highly of the coloured troops from America whom I found in my sector." He did add qualifications, however, by stating that such soldiers needed respect from their fellow white soldiers before they could be expected to fight well. Pershing, who had not only served with Negroes before the war but did his best to defend them in 1918, undoubtedly felt that they should have been better. But Pershing was a professional soldier and not a sociologist; he could hardly have been expected to understand the real nature of the problem of the Negro fighting man. After all, it was he who had allowed many American Negroes to go into action wearing the French uniform.[35]

The enlargement of the role of the Negro fighting man since 1940 has been spectacular in scope. Before 1930 the U. S. Navy had virtually stopped the enlistment of Negroes, excepting a scant few for duties in the messman branch. In 1939 the number of Negroes in the Army had declined to less than four thousand; far fewer than the total of American Negroes in uniform in 1900. With the approach of war and the commencement of the draft, however, the numbers of Negroes, particularly in the Army, grew rapidly. Nearly 100,000 were in the service just prior to Pearl Harbor day. By 1942 there were 467,000 in the Army.

In terms of percentages, the number of Negroes in the U. S. Army never did exceed 8.62 of the total force during the war years, and in fact, never equaled the percentage of Negroes in the general American population. More than 70 percent of all Negro soldiers in World War II were in the quartermaster, engineering, or transport activities of the Army. Yet by V-E Day nearly three quarters of all Negro soldiers were overseas. As the war progressed to its final conclusion, the percentage of Negroes who were assigned to duty in the infantry actually declined from 18 percent in 1942 to 8 percent in 1945. The important fact to remember about these latter figures is that they represent percentages of all Negroes in uniform, and not percentages of all Americans in uniform. In other words there was an increasing tendency during the war to place Negro soldiers into duties other than those connected with the infantry.[36]

By V-J Day there were some 140,000 Negroes in the Air Force, mostly in supply, ordnance, and airdrome defense battalions. Three all-Negro flying units were created; the 332nd Fighter Group, the 447th Bombardment Group, and the Ninety-Ninth Fighter Squadron. A fourth—the 477th—was in training when the war ended. The Ninety-Ninth and the 332nd saw some hard combat by 1945, particularly the former. Its record was fairly impressive in that it flew 1,578 combat missions and 15,553 sorties. The Ninety-Ninth claimed 111 enemy aircraft destroyed in the air, 150 blown up or damaged on the ground, and considerable damage inflicted on enemy ground installations and transport.

Many Negro-Americans saw combat in World War II in widely separated areas and units. Negro tankers fought with Patton in France, and did well. Negro artillerymen, particularly those of the 333rd Field Artillery, gave excellent support to ground operations around Saint-Malo and Brest with 155 mm. cannon. Their chants while loading and firing—"Ramcke, count your men" or "Rommel, how many men you got now?"—became widely repeated throughout France.[37]

The Ninety-Second Negro Division, recreated and sent into the fighting in Italy, had a most luckless history. Mark Clark would claim later in a probable overstatement of the case that "It was the worst division I had." Still the record of the Ninety-Second did leave something to be desired. In December, 1944, when German units assaulted the Serchio River line, the division crumbled and gave way. Later, in February of the following year, Germans infiltrated the lines of the Ninety-Second quite easily and caused heavy casualties, creating much anxiety along the whole Allied line.

The major complaint about the Ninety-Second, and one voiced by Truman K. Gibson, a Negro and a civilian aide to the Secretary of War, was that the unit was trigger-happy and unstable, and that it had panicked before various German assaults. Yet it should be indicated that there were many individual feats of heroism, as indicated by the awards given to the unit. These included two D. S. C.'s, twelve Legions of Merit, eighty-two Silver Stars, and 542 Bronze Stars.[38]

As previously indicated, Negroes were strictly confined to the messman's branch of the U. S. Navy in 1939. A few of these men were almost accidentally given an opportunity to serve their country well. Dorie Miller, a messman aboard the U. S. S. *Arizona,* was awarded the Navy Cross for gallantry on December 7, 1941, and a number of other messmen won similar awards for courage under fire. By 1945, however, there were some evidences of a changing Naval policy toward Negro enlistees. Though 95 percent of them were still messmen, the rest had managed to move into general ratings. Two Negroes were listed in Naval officer's training schools in 1942, but by 1945 there were as many as fifty-eight commissioned Negro officers.

The major concern of virtually all Negro personnel in World War II was that of racial discrimination. The Negro fighting man, as one would expect, felt far less strongly about the aims of the war—

freedom of speech, etc.—than did white soldiers. What the Negro soldier and sailor faced almost every day of his life in uniform was the simple fact of segregation. Colored officers were forced to sit in the back of street cars and buses in the South. Negro soldiers were killed or attacked by civilians or military policemen in various parts of the South when they violated the "black codes" of a community. In one incident nine Negro soldiers were forced to eat outside a lunchroom while German prisoners were brought inside. "Why are we pushed around like cattle?" asked one young Negro. "If we are fighting for the same thing, if we are to die for our country, then why does the Government allow such things to go on?" Another Negro soldier, contemplating on his sorry existence in the service, expressed his hope for better treatment in years to come. "Such things are all I have to think about. . . ." was his pessimistic conclusion.[39]

Racial antagonisms were brought into existence by varying causes after 1941. White officers of Negro troops, especially in the South, tended to ride herd on their troops; possibly hoping to avoid friction with local civilians. Overseas there were incidents based on a multitude of causes. The early readiness of British women to accept Negro escorts caused bitter clashes to occur between whites and Negroes. The Army tried to solve the problem in several instances by having "white liberty nights" and "colored liberty nights." In the Philippines the competition between white and Negro-American soldiers for women brought about many ugly repercussions.

The Negro "complex," now more understood than it was in 1945, caused much difficulty in World War II. One white officer wrote in 1945 that the Negro fighting man presented a "marked problem when it comes to dealing with individuals." He saw his Negro enlisted men as expecting "more than those boys who do actual fighting," and "childish" in their petulance. Other white officers became quite upset over the disdain of the Negro for much-needed supply equipment. Trucks were driven without sufficient oil, or in low gear, until they simply burned out their motors. The greatest complaint of white officers was that the Negro soldier was insufficiently educated, and was sometimes prone to groundless fears and suspicions. Though this was not the fault of the ordinary Negro fighting man, there was some truth in this. Of Northern Negro soldiers 39 percent had received only a grade school education; 67 percent of Southern Negro soldiers had less than a high school education.

There are some studies which tend to support the claim that Negroes were far less motivated toward the winning of the war than whites. One survey, completed in 1945, indicated that Negroes had far less animosity than whites toward the Japanese. Another study in the same year showed that most Negroes felt that they had already done their share in the winning of the war, and that they should not be called upon to do more.[40]

Yet, out of these seemingly dismal facts, the performance of the Ninety-Second Division in Italy, and the racial animosities generated by the war, comes one interesting development: that of the experiments with racially integrated fighting units. Suggested as early as October, 1943, by *The New Republic,* the idea of forming integrated companies progressed slowly but surely toward actuality. Some rather startling discoveries emerged from these innovations. First of all it was found that the Negro fighting man was far more motivated to combat than ever before. Second, it was revealed that combat by integrated units tended to erase racial antagonism. Desegregated regiments, or regiments having Negro platoons, were found to be far less ressistant to integration than expected—on both sides of the color line.

In other words, the signs for the future were good. Negro platoons fighting in otherwise white regiments were highly praised. "After that first day when we saw how they fought, I changed my mind," a white South Carolinian stated. "They're just like any of the other boys to us." And when nine Negro soldiers were turned away from a Southern restaurant in favor of German prisoners, the reaction of many white soldiers was one of shame and disgust. *Yank,* the Army magazine, received 287 protest letters from all parts of the armed forces. One soldier, a white serving in Burma, wrote: "We are proud of the colored men here. . . . We are ashamed that the German soldier . . . is treated better than the soldier of our country, because of race."[41]

Another racial group which was forced to go through a twilight of anguish and discrimination was the Japanese-Americans. Pearl Harbor had made suspects of them all. Herded into relocation camps in California, or placed under close scrutiny in Hawaii, these people carried a special burden. Finally allowed to participate in the war, the *Sansei* (wrongly referred to as *Nisei*), proved their loyalty with a vengeance. Between 1941 and 1945 nearly eighteen thousand Japanese-Americans volunteered for service. Their motivation was well expressed by one such soldier: "America has given me all that I have. I want action. I know that I'm fighting so that my wife and four-year-old daughter in Hawaii can live in honor as loyal Americans."[42]

From the beginning the *Sansei* were excellent soldiers. Formed into two main combat units—the 442nd Combat Team and the 100th Infantry Battalion—they fought through some of the most harrowing campaigns of the war. The 442nd, whose men came from Japanese relocation centers in California, took as its slogan the phrase "Go For Broke"; a *sansei* phrase which is now an accepted part of the English language. It fought north of Cassino, Anzio, and elsewhere. More than 90 percent of the unit were awarded Combat Infantry Badges. Not once did the 442nd retreat. Its heroes—Private Masao Awakuni, Sergeant Kuzuo Masuda, and Captain Young Oak Kim—performed such feats as anchoring mortars on their legs, knocking out Mark IV tanks within twenty-five feet, and clearing mine fields of trip wires with their bare hands.

The 100th Infantry Battalion was made up mostly of Hawaiian-born Japanese. The unit fought at Salerno, on the Volturno and Rapido, Cassino, and elsewhere. There was not one single desertion or AWOL longer than an hour during the three years of the battalion's existence. That is, unless one should count the two wounded Japanese-Americans who left hospital beds in order to join their unit during one very severe battle. Only two members of the battalion were ever taken prisoner, and these were helplessly wounded. By 1945 the most heavily decorated unit in the history of the Army, it had won one thousand Purple Hearts, forty-one Silver Stars, thirty-one Bronze Stars, nine D. S. C.'s, three Legion of Merit Medals, and two Presidential Unit Citations. There were only 1,300 soldiers in the entire battalion.[43]

Though mainly in the European theater, the *sansei* were actually everywhere. One Japanese-American, a Private Kenny Yasui, captured sixteen Japanese prisoners during the Burma fighting. Others acted as interpreters for other branches of the service. No matter where they were, however, these fighting Americans were good soldiers. They were, as one American paratrooper phrased it, "Goddam good fighters." To a Texas unit, cut off in the Vosges Mountains in France, they were saviors. A *sansei* unit suffered 60 percent casualties in order to rescue that "lost battalion."[44]

A third "minority" which proved its right to a place in the American way of life was that of the American Indian. From Pearl Harbor day onward, Indians seldom waited to be drafted; they volunteered. By November, 1942, there were more than ten thousand in uniform, many of them in the Marine Corps, which encouraged their enlistment. A year later there were fourteen thousand Indians in the service. Of all able-bodied eligibles of the Crow Nation, 40 percent were in the fighting, while in other tribes not a single individual ever asked for deferment. By early 1945 there were more than 21,000 in the Army, nearly 2,000 Indians in the Navy, 121 in the Coast Guard, and 723 in the Marine Corps. Indians fought on Bataan, Corregidor, Iwo Jima, Okinawa, Anzio, and Normandy. A Ute Indian was the first American to meet the Russians on the Elbe.

The famous Indian of the war was Private Ira Hayes, one of six men to raise the flag on Mt. Suribachi. Yet in that same battle there were twenty-two other Indians who became casualties. Elsewhere there were Indian heroes of equal stature. Private Charley Ball and Joe Longknife, both Assiniboins, were two of the three hundred Indians who fought on Bataan. One unnamed Indian private killed four Germans in ten minutes at Bizerte. A Paiute Indian, his arm shot off in the tail turret of a bomber over New Guinea, fired his pistol until he died. A Pottawatomi, having bailed out over Yugoslavia, walked for six weeks through the mountains and managed to get back into action. Another, a Creek, was wounded on eight different occasions while in battle. One Indian who fought in both the European and Pacific theaters, killed six Germans with as many shots in Europe, and close to forty Japanese in the invasion of Attu.

One could go on and on indefinitely. Colonel Edward I. McClish, a Choctaw, fought as a guerrilla in the Philippines for three years. He was estimated to have participated in the killing of over three thousand Japanese soldiers. American Indians fought in the Royal Air Force as members of the famous Eagle Squadron. One Indian, General Clarence L. Tinker of Army Air Corps, was killed near Midway.

The Indian was a silent fighter; ideal for the Rangers or Special Force units. His ability to undergo ordeals and his ability to improvise harked back to frontier wars. An Indian, fighting with Merrill's Marauders, timed his mortar fire with exploding enemy shells in order not to disclose his own position. With unchanging expression, he proceeded to eliminate scores of enemy soldiers. Other Indians, talented at night fighting, ranged far into the Italian hills in order to garrote German sentries.

Thus did the American Indian establish a magnificent World War II record. By the Spring of 1945 they had won seventy-one Air Medals, fifty-one Silver Stars, forty-seven Bronze Stars, thirty-four Distinguished Flying Crosses, and two Congressional Medals of Honor. An enviable record indeed![45]

The American Jew of 1941 had a special stake in the war. Not only was he fighting for his homeland, but for the very existence of his faith. Perhaps it is for these reasons that a look at Jewish-American participation in World War II provides some interesting surprises. Approximately 550,000 Jews were in service between 1941 and 1945; almost 5 percent of the total American manpower committed to the war. More than 80 percent of these draftees and volunteers were in the Army; the remainder were in the Navy, Coast Guard, and Marines. A large number of those in the Army were attached to the Air Corps, and formed more than 6 percent of the U. S. A. F. flying personnel.

The affinity of the Jew to flying cannot be explained. A study of

Jewish-American fighting men from Pittsburgh indicated that one out of every four was serving in the air forces. In the Pacific theater it was estimated that approximately nine hundred fliers in that area were of the Jewish faith. Jewish fighting men were present, either directly or in support missions, for both the Hiroshima and Nagasaki atom bomb raids. On the other side of the globe, rarely did an American sortie or raid take place from any British base without the participation of American Jews.

There were plenty of Jews elsewhere, however. Sergeant Irving Strobing was an early war hero with his last wireless messages from Corregidor. Barney Ross, the prizefighter, was a genuine hero on Guadalcanal. Lieutenant Raymond Zussman won a Congressional Medal of Honor by killing seventeen Germans, and capturing thirty-two others. Sergeant Abraham Todres of Brooklyn not only served four years of war, but won thirty decorations, including the D. S. C., two Oak Leaf Clusters, the Silver Star, a Purple Heart, a *Croix de Guerre,* an Air Medal, a Bronze Star, and a Presidential Citation. Altogether, Jews won more than 61,000 awards of various types during the conflict. Besides these honors there were seven Jewish-American major generals, thirteen brigadier generals, one Jewish-American admiral, and two Jewish rear-admirals.[46]

The variety of ethnic groups that served the nation in World War II is impressive. There was an Eskimo unit—The Alaska Combat Intelligence Detachment—which was designed to scout the Aleutian chain for Japanese activity. A number of Chinese-Americans served with distinction; one of them with Merrill's Marauders. One out of every four men on Bataan was reputedly of Spanish-American origin, and in all, there were estimated to be 250,000 Spanish-speaking individuals in the American Army. A number of these fought with the crack First Cavalry Division. Among the Latin-American heroes of that unit was Corporal Armando Valencia who fired a machine gun by hand during one South Pacific battle until his hands were blistered. Two others were Private Damacio Romero and Sergeant Hilario Gutierrez, whose heroic but fatal action inspired the First Cavalry to greater heights in the Leyte-Samar campaign. Other Spanish-speaking soldiers included some five thousand Filipinos who made up the First Filipino Infantry, and the 35,000 Philippine Scouts who were technically a part of the American Army.[47]

The magnificent characteristic of American society, however, is that almost anyone might consider himself part of a minority group. The great bulk of the fighting forces from 1941 to 1945 was made up of white Protestants and Catholics and one must not overlook that fact. These, in turn, consisted of individuals with a broad spectrum of backgrounds. Robert Sherrod, who viewed the Second Marines as they prepared for Tarawa, noted that most of the unit were Midwesterners, Texans, and Californians. A leading *Thunderbolt* squadron in Britain carried such names on its rolls as Zemke, Schilling, Johnson, Carter, Gabreski, Goodfleisch, and Goldstein. The first five were possibly of German, Polish, and British backgrounds, while the last two were probably Jewish. There were even immigrants who were able to serve their adopted country with distinction. A German-born soldier was one of the real heroes of the fighting in New Guinea. One of the Americans who landed in North Africa was of Yemenese origin, and his parents still lived in Arabia. Thus it was that the GI of World War II came from many races, nationalities, and creeds.[48]

The breakdown of the service bar against integrated forces moved at an increasing pace in the years following World War II; that is, everywhere except in the Navy. The number of Negro officers in that branch of the service declined from fifty-eight in 1945 to four in 1949. Though Negroes had been allowed to move into ratings other than messman during the war, the Navy continued to enforce a 10 percent limit of Negro sailors for each ship.

In July, 1948, President Truman's Executive Order 9981 really broke down most barriers to the progress of the uniformed Negro. As was that President's manner, he bluntly ordered "that there shall be equally of treatment and opportunity for all persons in the armed forces without regard to race, color, religion or national origin." In some ways the Air Force had beaten Truman to the punch. That service had broken up the all-Negro fighter and bomber groups, and was well on its way toward the integration of Negroes into all phases of air force activity. By 1950 there were 25,702 Negroes in the Air Force, and 351 of them were officers. The Army followed suit in the same year and finally ended its 10 percent limit on total Negro enlistments in its fighting forces.[49]

Unfortunately the Army failed to move fast enough, and the outbreak of the Korean War found some virtually all-Negro units still in the field. These included the famous old Twenty-Fourth Infantry Regiment. Some of these Negro units did not do well in the early stages of the fighting, but for that matter, neither did most American units. The Army continued to work diligently on integration as the war progressed, and soon even the Twenty-Fourth was broken up; its soldiers being parceled out to other units, particularly within the Twenty-Fourth Division.[50]

As indicated, Negroes did no better or worse than other American soldiers during the ordeal of Korea.* There were some Negro heroes, of course; and these included the first Medal of Honor winners from that race since 1898. Private William Thompson and Sergeant Cornelius H. Charlton paid the price of their lives for the nation's highest military award. At the Hungnam Perimeter, when the Marines were trying to evacuate their personnel from a trap created by the Chinese assault, a Negro platoon threw off North Korean bayonet attacks through eleven hours of continuous fighting. As prisoners of the Chinese, the American Negroes behaved quite well, and refused to swallow the daily indoctrination of Communist propaganda.[51]

The effects of integration in Korea were quite significant. On-the-field reports indicated that the Negro not only developed more pride in his unit, but learned the necessity for the interdependence of one soldier upon another. One field officer declared his Negro soldiers to be his "best" men. A survey of 185 Army officers made just after the end of the Korean War showed that the great majority of them felt that Negro soldiers were every bit as good as whites, and that their over-all fighting ability was quite good. The same

---

* According to one writer, the "theme song" of the Twenty-Fourth Regiment, Twenty-Fifth Division, was "Bug Out Blues." In August, 1950, the Twenty-Fourth panicked and stampeded during a Communist assault, even though it was in reserve at the time. See n. 51.

study also indicated that most of the officers questioned felt the Negroes were more careless with equipment, sometimes inclined to panic, and less inclined to attack.

The total impact of integration in Korea was not to be dismissed, however. One United States senator argued that the Negro soldier was "fighting nobly for America that owes them much." More importantly, the attitude of those white officers and men who worked with the Negro changed perceptibly. "I got more men in my platoon. . . ." wrote one white officer. "That now gives me 10 colored soldiers and 38 white ones. . . . We have absolutely no trouble in the platoons, but the Negro soldiers tend to congregate to themselves. . . ." The same officer had written earlier:

I have 8 Negro soldiers in my platoon now and they are all as good soldiers as you could want. The best is . . . and I want to promote him to Corporal and then Sergeant before he goes home. I was a little worried about them at first, but there was no use worrying. They have been as good as any of the white soldiers, and in some cases much better.[52]

In a way that had never been seen before, the American Army in Korea proved the necessity and value of racial integration. Japanese, Puerto Ricans, Negroes, Hawaiians, Mexicans, Indians, and American whites fought side by side. General Mark Clark, while commanding the American Army in that theater of war, was so struck by the character of his men that he ordered that a study be made to determine the makeup of an average nine-man infantry squad in Korea. The results showed that four were white Americans, one was a Negro, two-and-a-half were ROK soldiers, and the remainder consisted of Puerto Ricans, Mexican-Americans, Indians, or Hawaiians. By the last, Clark may have been referring to Japanese-Americans, who performed exceedingly well in Korea, winning a number of honors. One, a Corporal Hideo Hashimoto, won a citation for attacking an enemy tank with rocks. Another, Sergeant Hiroshi Miyamura, won a Congressional Medal by killing sixty Chinese before his capture.[53]

As the smoke of the Korean War finally began to disperse, there were many critiques written during the 1950's on the behavior of the armed forces in the recent fighting, and in various encampments overseas. A great deal of attention was focused on the Negro soldier. Hanson Baldwin, *The New York Times* military expert, accused the Negro of presenting a "most difficult military problem" in terms of venereal disease, discipline, and courts-martial. There were complaints from West Germany about the behavior of Negro troops in that country. Much of the latter seemed to have been based upon the intermarriage of Negroes with German girls. Thirty-one Negroes of the Second Armored Division, and fifteen Negroes of the First Division, brought home German wives. Other Negroes left illegitimate children in Germany.[54]

The result of the general criticism against the Army in the 1950's was the upgrading of the selectivity of local draft boards. More sober minds saw the difficulties of the Army overseas not in terms of race, but in terms of quality of men available for the draft. The result was, by 1960, the creation of a highly professional and well-behaved fighting force; one trained to the ultimate for any eventuality.

What is the composition of the nation's fighting forces today? The leadership positions in the Army are still principally held by white Anglo-Saxon Protestants; most of them from the North Central sections of the country. The Navy's leadership positions are dominated to a large extent by white Anglo-Saxon Protestants. This is not to be unexpected, of course, since the majority of the national population is of that strain and creed. What has become very right about it all is that there do not seem to be any barriers in any of these areas to minority elements. One of the major United States commanders in the Far East, for example, is a Negro. It might be mentioned, parenthetically, that Roman Catholic participation in the leadership areas of the Armed Forces has increased substantially over the past twenty years; all of which indicates the fluidity of movement on these levels.[55]

The fighting forces still remain as an example of what integration of races and nationalities might accomplish. One of the first

Marines ashore during the 1958 "police action" in Lebanon was an officer whose parents had come from Syria and Lebanon. A Marine who was fighting in Vietnam in 1963 was the son of a German soldier who had been killed twenty years before in Stalingrad. A company of the Second Battalion, First Brigade, Twenty-Fifth Infantry, fighting in Vietnam in 1966, had a staff sergeant of Papago Indian parentage, a Specialist fourth class from the Virgin Islands, another sergeant from Comanche backgrounds, one private from Samoa, and a corporal with Japanese ancestry.

One would also have to agree with General Westmoreland's statement of 1966 that the Negro soldier had "come into his own." "He has the self-respect he didn't have before," claimed this white Episcopalian Southerner. "You can't tell the difference between Negro and white soldiers." The facts sustain Westmoreland's argument. Up to August, 1966, the number of Negroes killed in Vietnam amounted to more than 14 percent of the total American dead. The total number of Negroes in South Vietnam in that month came to 21,519; 16,531 of whom were in the Army, 3,580 of whom were in the Marines. There are still relatively few Negro officers, however; less than 1 percent in the Navy and Marine Corps, for example.[56]

Combat in Vietnam has served to eliminate many of the old attitudes between white and Negro fighting men. A Negro Marine has stated: "We're treated equal in the Corps—white, black, German, or Jewish." Another Marine argued: "Over here, it's different. A war's on. There's no room for prejudice. If you're prejudiced, you won't get along and it's probable that you'll get killed." A Negro of the 173rd Airborne Brigade was quoted as saying: "When you drink out of the same canteen and eat off the same spoon, you get real tight together. . . . When you sleep in the same foxhole, you're just like brothers." These claims are given strange support by the reputed complaint of one Negro civil rights leader who argued in July, 1966, that many officers didn't even know how many Negros were in their companies. This is a peculiar comment indeed from a man who wishes the Negro to lose his "visibility," and then complains when the Army accomplishes that goal.[57]

Nevertheless it is true, as many civil rights leaders have argued, that the Negro is somewhat out of proportion among the combat units in Vietnam. In December, 1966, some 23 percent of all combat troops were colored, despite the fact that only 11 percent of the national population is Negro. The reasons for this discrepancy are not hard to fathom, however. Negroes reenlist at a rate twice as high as that of whites. Then, too, there are opportunities for many Negroes in uniform which they cannot find on the outside. In a sense the armed forces have become the Harvard and Yale for many an underprivileged Negro boy from the slums. Former Secretary of Defense McNamara has stated that the service has given Negroes the right to learn "skills and aptitudes which for them and their families will reverse the downward spiral of human decay."[58]

The millennium in racial relationships has not been totally reached within the armed forces, of course. There are occasional setbacks. Negro boys seldom "liberty" with whites in Vietnam; in some ways preferring a separation at this point in their relationship. There have been some racially inspired fights among some of the units stationed in Vietnam; a memorable one taking place on an airfield landing strip. There have been rumors of race fights in Germany, particularly at Harvey Barracks, Kitzingen, Germany. Yet, after all, there were fights between Irish, German, and American regiments during the Civil War. And in 1846 there was a real wing-ding of a battle between an Irish regiment from Georgia and a Western regiment from Illinois. Soldiers of any age, it seems, can rarely confine all their aggressiveness to the enemy.[59]

White, Negro, Oriental, or Indian, the common experience of any American fighting man in real combat has been a rediscovery of his religious faith. Best expressed by a Catholic priest, Father William Thomas Cummings, who stated during World War II that there were "no atheists in the fox holes," the place of religion in war has been continuously reaffirmed throughout history.

Perhaps it was Ethan Allen who peremptorily established a firm relationship between God and the Revolutionary soldier when he is supposed to have proclaimed the taking of Fort Ticonderoga "in the name of the great Jehovah and the Continental Congress." At any rate, the poor ragged soldiers of Washington's Army found great consolation in their faith. God, according to the diaries and letters of these men, was most certainly on the side of the Americans. The more extreme the distress of the American fighting man of the Revolution, the closer he was to his God. A corporal inscribed in his diary: "About ten went to the Chapel and herd the Reverend Doctor Langdon from the Hebrews, 2, 10. . . . I find God has a Remnant in this Depraved, and Degenerated, and gloomy time."

With the upsurge of religious activity generally in the United States after 1800, it became customary for officers of both the Army and the Navy to enforce church attendance among their men. Each ship commander was obliged to hold regular services in which appropriate readings were given from the Bible. One such captain was known to have missed his regular service only twice in four years; both times because of savage storms.[60]

In the Mexican War it was customary for the American armies to carry chaplains from both the Protestant and Catholic faiths. When it became difficult to acquire enough of the latter, Mexican Catholic priests were brought in to conduct regular services.

Both the Federal and Confederate armies of 1861 to 1865 were mainly Protestant; but, as indicated previously, there were many Catholics and Jews. Chaplains were provided for most regiments, and though these men were sometimes held in low regard by the troops, there were many who established themselves as heroes. Two chaplains, one Catholic and one Presbyterian, won Congressional Medals for bravery. The latter, a Chaplain Milton Haney of Illinois, not only contradicted some of the tenets of his faith by supplying whiskey to his troops in time of battle, but at Atlanta he took up a rifle and led a vital charge.

Normally, both the ordinary soldiers of the Civil War and their generals were basically religious men. "Stonewall" Jackson approached the level of religious mysticism. One Confederate general, Leonidas Polk, was an Episcopalian bishop before the war. Oliver O. Howard, on the Union side, was a hard-fighting, Bible-reading general who scorned profanity and drinking. On the lower levels it was not uncommon for colonels or other officers to be former ministers. Some were so strict about church attendance that their subordinates had one of two choices on Sunday—attendance at a religious service, or a stretch in the guardhouse.

Amost every Civil War soldier carried a Bible or a prayer book; the latter sometimes called "the soldier's friend." Each regiment, Federal or Confederate, was given to the singing of religious songs; the "old familiar hymns" as they were described by one general. These were elements of faith which most soldiers took into battle with them, and with which some died. After the first bloody day at Shiloh, when night rescued the beleaguered Union troops, wounded soldiers could be heard moaning prayers from the woods behind the Confederate pickets. One such soldier began to sing "Jesus, Lover of My Soul," and the song was taken up by wounded men all over the battlefield. In the days following this and other battles, it was not uncommon to find soldiers who had expired with Bibles in their hands. Nor was it uncommon to note the sudden rush of soldiers to be baptized in the days after such bloody encounters.[61]

The Spanish-American War was fought during a period of frantic religious and missionary activity on the part of Protestant and Catholic churches. Every volunteer was given a prayer book or a rosary by his own church. The power of God was evoked and thanked during and after every battle. "I know I had my life in my hands but my mind and conscience did not trouble me much for I trusted to a *higher power*" was a statement typical of the soldier of the day. In the midst of war, however, some concessions to faith had to be made. Protestants, stranded in Cuba or Puerto Rico without a church of their own, attended Catholic churches. It really didn't matter; just so long as the organist played the *Star-Spangled Banner*. But pity the poor Jewish soldier of the time. The only meat that did not spoil in the humid Caribbean weather was salt pork, and this he either ate or went without any food.[62]

The intensity of fighting on the Western front in 1917 and 1918 had a profound effect on the fighting American's religious convictions. Father Cumming's World War II remark about atheists in foxholes had many earlier versions. "This war makes Christians out of lots of fellows," a young American corporal wrote. "The first shell that I saw hit near me was the greatest sermon I ever heard," stated one doughboy. One Yank wrote that, when he went over the top, he always breathed the phrase "God is with me and will guide me through danger." In order to make positive his survival, he followed this up by going through the words of the hymn, "I Need Thee Every Hour."

One thing was likely in 1918, and that was that God had probably never before heard as many prayers for succor. Almost every letter sent home by the doughboys of World War I indicated that the "Good Lord" was being banked upon for a lot of help. A Jewish doughboy of 1918 summoned up a remembrance of things past and wrote: "When I was at the front, I promised God to cut out everything if he would save me from the shells. . . " Those few who scoffed at faith found that their disdain was sometimes jammed back down their throats. A soldier wrote:

I was greatly amused to hear one of our most proficient "crap-shooters" and a self-professed gambler, circus follower and hobo become quite wrathy tonight when several of the other men began to knock "Billy" Sunday. "Billy" had a defender who I am sure never "hit the sawdust trail."[63]

There were a few other amusing incidents of this general nature. A pious Southern Baptist boy reportedly strolled into an Episcopal service, thinking it would satisfy his Protestant leanings, and became profoundly disturbed to find it too ritualistic for his taste. Most interesting of all, however, was the true account of a Catholic doughboy who made the similar mistake of wandering into an Episcopal Church in France. Thinking that the mild variances in service were due to the peculiarities of French life, he got as far as the communion before he realized his error. One may well wonder about the amused reaction of the priest to that boy's later confession.[64]

The number of chaplains assigned to the various branches of the armed forces reached a new level in World War II. At one time in the European theater, there were as many as 2,800 chaplains; the Roman Catholics having the largest single quota, to be followed by the Baptists, Methodists, Lutherans, and Presbyterians in that order. There were eight thousand chaplains assigned to the U. S. Army during the entire conflict. Seventy-seven of them were killed in action, 243 were wounded in action, and two were declared missing in action. There were seventy-four nonbattle deaths among these men; five of them dying in prison. Scattered among the 8,000 chaplains were 1,777 decorations, including eighteen D. S. C.'s, 148 Silver Stars, 320 Purple Hearts, and 1,022 Bronze Stars.[65]

Religion was a serious part of each fighting American's life after 1941. A soldier on Bataan wrote that he was sustained by a phrase from Psalms 91:7. It reads: "A thousand shall fall at thy side, and ten thousand at thy right hand, but it shall not come nigh thee." A Marine in the South Pacific pleaded in a letter home: "Dear God, spare our lives, for we are young and love life so much. . . ." An American officer in Italy asserted: "I haven't found a man yet who hasn't fervently prayed during a shelling and there are no fox-holes until you dig them." Every bombing mission from Britain was preceded by short services for those who wished to attend. And among the troops serving in New Guinea, a sociologist discovered that 76 percent of the men felt that prayer was a help in combatting fear. The other 24 percent were probably rear-echelon soldiers.[66]

As in almost every American war, there was a good deal of ecumenism in World War II. The facts of life made it so. A soldier in Hawaii wrote that, shortly after the Pearl Harbor attack, all his companions were in a deep state of shock. "We started to sing (a hymn). . . ." he wrote, "we started very softly and gradually everyone was singing at the top of their lungs." The same soldier, some months later, found a little country chapel on one of the islands. "Here you are as liable to sit next to a Japanese, Chinese, Filipino, or a Negro as you are to sit next to a service man. . . ." he told his parents. "The free people of the world sort of value their hold on the freedom of worship, don't they?"

There were times when the exigencies of conflict caused some interesting experiences. A Texan jumped into a trench filled with Negro soldiers during a Japanese attack in the Marshalls. One of the Negroes became frightened and hysterical, but was calmed by another who said: "If you had been living with your God like I've been living with mine, you wouldn't be so scared." "You know," wrote the Texan afterwards, "it made me think a little about myself." In North Africa an aviation ground crew, consisting of five Jews and two Catholics, occupied the same tent. Christmas was celebrated by all seven "in keeping with the principles of Americanism. . . ." A Jewish prayer was read, a Wisconsin Catholic sang the Lord's Prayer, and all sang carols. During the campaign into France in 1944 a tough sergeant decided to hold a roadside service. "Rustle up a blankety padre for a Mass," he ordered. The priest, finding that his congregation was mostly Jewish, proceeded to thank the men for their attendance. "Ah, forget it, Pop," was one reply.[67]

The circumstances of America's most recent wars—those of Korea and Vietnam—have provided experiences of a different nature. Yet the hold of faith is still there, and in times of stress the ordinary fighting man has been inclined to turn to his religion for psychological support. One priest has explained the consistently high church attendance as due to the need for a "sense of security"; the need for solace, understanding, and strength.

What is the religious makeup of the armed forces of the nation today? There are few hard facts available, except the claim by the Bureau of Naval Personnel that the religious affiliation of all servicemen tends to correspond with the various religious affiliations of the general population of the United States. If true, this would mean that little more one-half of the total manpower of the armed services have a definite religious allegiance of one kind or another. About six-tenths of these would be Protestant, and three-tenths would be Catholic. One-twentieth of America's fighting men today would be Jewish; slightly more than one-fiftieth would be Eastern Orthodox; and the remainder of affiliated fighting men would consist of Old Catholics, Buddhists, or Polish National Catholics.

It is truly evident that the American fighting man is *anyman;*

he is not specifically a Protestant, Catholic, Jew, Negro, white, or Oriental. It is doubtful that he has ever been. To claim anything else would be a great disservice to Reuben James, a Negro who died in the Tripolitan Wars; to Sergeant York, a Protestant, who fought in France in 1918; to Barney Ross, a Jew who fought on Guadalcanal; to Colin Kelly, a boy of Irish descent who tried to bomb a Japanese battleship off the Philippines; to Joe Longknife, an Indian who fought on Bataan; to Masao Awakuni, a Japanese boy who anchored his mortar to his legs in Italy; to John Basilone, of Italian extraction and the great Marine of World War II; and to all the rest of America's fighting men, who have made the great sacrifice, regardless of color or creed.[68]

10

A Summing Up

THERE IS NO QUESTION that the American fighting man is and always has been, on the surface, a fault-finder of unequalled intensity. One concludes that he complains because he feels it is almost a duty to do so; it is the one right left to him within his disciplined and regulated world. A Marine general in Korea in 1953, after studying 187 different units in that theater of war, found that almost every soldier had a gripe about some aspect of the service. Many were really centered on homesickness; some were based simply on hearsay. And a good many concerned the rations served to the men in combat.[1]

The last reproach has always been a standard one for the American in uniform. Revolutionary soldiers at Valley Forge, probably with much justification, lamented about the "good food" which they might be having at home, and the "smoke and cold" of army camps. The Civil War soldier was most outspoken about his rations. To one soldier, his pancakes seemed to be "cut out of a rubber blanket, and tasted accordingly." Hardtack, and it was truly hard, was sometimes called "animated cookies," simply because of the maggots customarily found within it. A standard refrain in the

Seventh Illinois Cavalry, a tough Western outfit, was that they had nothing but "Beans for breakfast, Beans for dinner, Beans for supper."

Men in blue and gray made their discontent known by letters to their parents and occasionally to public officials at home. Governor Richard Yates of Illinois was told by a private of the Thirty-Sixth Illinois Volunteers that "the victuals we get are not fit for a starving man to eat. . . ." And another bluecoat, living the hard life in the region of Jackson, Tennessee, in 1862 wrote concerning his meat ration:

> But it's awful poor beef, lean, slimy, skinny and stringy. The boys say that one can throw a piece up against a tree, and it will just stick there and quiver and twitch for all the world like one of those blue-bellied lizards at home will do when you knock him off a fence rail with a stick.[2]

The World War I doughboy complained mostly about the lack of variety in his rations. Tinned salmon, invariably called "goldfish" by the men, bacon, canned tomatoes, coffee, and hardtack were ordinary fare in the front lines. But the American of 1918 was a resourceful individual. The French liked salmon, and so there was a good deal of trading with nearby Gallic regiments for wine and good hard French bread.

The GI of World War II was ordinarily well fed. There was usually a plentiful supply of meat, citrus fruit, dairy food, potatoes, and various other items. There were still occasional indictments, however. American units bitterly censured the food that was usually given out on British transports; mainly because it was insufficient in quantity, poorly cooked, and unvaried. The standard menu of such British ships always seemed to contain tasteless and unappetizing boiled fish and the inevitable parsnip.

Even when the food was fairly good, however, American servicemen always felt it necessary to keep up a drumfire of recrimination. A sailor stationed aboard an LST in the Pacific theater wailed to the Secretary of the Navy by letter that the food on his vessel was simply horrible. Investigation proved that the weekly menus contained eggs, bacon, pancakes, ham, steak, potatoes, beans, and fried chicken. It also proved that the discontented sailor had gained twenty pounds since his induction into uniform. In Hawaii, where food was fairly good throughout the war, a soldier wrote his mother that her recently shipped oatmeal cookies would be a Godsend. "They'd taste good," he asserted, "and its been years since I've had any." In virtually every instance where complaints were followed up, it was found that the fighting man involved as the plaintiff was eating a better balanced diet than ever before in his life. General E. M. Almond's investigation of charges by troops in Korea found similar contradictions. One of his interviews with a complaining soldier went as follows: "How is your mess?" "Aw, it isn't any good." "What's the matter with it?" "We don't get any meat." "What did you have yesterday for dinner?" "Didn't have any meat." "Didn't you have chicken?" "Oh, sure, but that's not meat." "What is meat?" "Steak!"[3]

Another usual source of grumbling has concerned the medical facilities and treatment. Civil War soldiers argued that the usual prescription for any sick soldier was "two pills and a powder," to be continued "every ten minutes until death ensues." A soldier of the 116th Illinois complained that the "Damned Surgeons are not worth a Curse." Other soldiers of that war wrote (and probably with some justification) that their surgeons were too often drunk. Hospital care, said the soldiers of both sides, was often "barbaric." The usual treatment, argued one trooper, consisted of thin soup with "frequent and copious" doses of quinine. Another soldier of the same war, using a phraseology that could be well understood by the GI of 1943, stated that his main hospital ration was a "shingle" with pieces of boiled beef on it. Too frequently, said the men of 1861, the surgeons showed no sympathy and understanding for the mortally wounded man. It was not uncommon for a dying soldier to be measured for his coffin while he was still conscious.[4]

The foregoing Civil War complaints concerning medical treatment strike a familiar chord to the veteran of World War II. The standard pill, according to most men in the latter war, was the famous APC. It was handed out for colds, stomach trouble, sunburn, and a variety of other ailments. That single capsule, along with the ever-present sulfa pill, seemed to be considered the cure for almost everything. At least that was how the common soldier viewed the results of sick call.

Another familiar gripe of the American fighting man has always been the "man at home." Revolutionary and Civil War soldiers wrote countless letters about those too cowardly to volunteer. World War I provides similar examples. A soldier of the A. E. F., writing to a Midwestern newspaper, bitterly advertised for other boys to come across and "do your bit." Many men who joined the Navy were stuck for four years according to the terms of their enlistment. They just didn't think it fair that others who had been drafted into service should be discharged at the end of the war after a few months duty. And a front-line doughboy expressed himself about the people at home as follows:

I am overjoyed that Jim and Butch are at last making themselves useful and I heartily endorse what our Old Uncle Sammy is doing in that respect. If anybody at home doesn't approve of that, they just ought to get in the service once and see some of the things we're training to go up against, and they never would warble again.[5]

The GI of World War II and Korea made similar bitter imputations. "It is as hard as hell to be here and read in every paper that comes from home where Pvt. Joe Dokes is home again on furlough after tough duty as a guard in Radio City," one private complained in the midst of the war against Japan. Another soldier, upset at strikes on the home front, noted: "I don't suppose they know that there are guys who are getting blown to bits, trying to protect those very fellows that are howling for more cash in their pockets." An American in Korea writing in 1952 paralleled these sentiments with the following comments:

Many times I have heard it said, with the bitterness that only loneliness can bring, that the men in Korea were the forgotten men; that the U. S. was aware of the conflict in Korea only in the sense that taxes were higher. The soldiers in Korea envied those at home living in a nation mentally at peace while physically at war.[6]

A considerable number of the ordinary American soldier's concerns about his own situation have been wrapped around American officialdom, which they feel has either hindered or prevented victory. The fact is that most fighting men disdain the true politician. Civil War governors, many of them attempting to insure their political futures, made numerous and extensive visits to regiments from their own states. Genially received in the beginning of the conflict, these ambitious politicians soon found that too many excursions among veteran troops created nothing but cynicism and contempt for their high office. Pompous words and florid speeches were increasingly unpopular among seasoned troops on both sides after Shiloh and Antietam.

The Spanish-American War and World War I brought numerous visits by Washington bureaucrats, congressmen and senators, and various other officials to the camps or fighting fronts. When Governor Tanner of Illinois visited troops from his state who were training in Tennessee in 1898, he received a chilly reception. Congressmen who came over to "the front" in 1918 not only were generally resented by the doughboys, but were the recipients of denunciatory letters from the soldiers themselves. The reason for such written gripes was, in most cases, the necessity for each unit to provide a formal review for the visitors.

The GI of World War II and of Korea was probably the most outspoken of all American soldiers concerning American politicians and officials. A corporal in Hawaii wrote in 1944 that President Franklin Roosevelt—the "top soldier"—had made soldiers wait in the sun for hours and then had reviewed the troops in a "swish. . . ." There were hundreds of charges from American fighting men that the nation's policy of kindly treatment of captured Germans was really politically inspired. And a Marine corporal, noting the death of a prominent politician in 1943, wrote:

All over the world guys are digging through snow and ice and mud and volcanic soil with their little entrenching shovels and burying their buddies in shallow, hasty little graves, with just a helmet or canteen with his name scratched on it to mark the spot, and back home a politician dies from overeating and gets a $50,000 funeral. It's rather difficult to swallow.[7]

When President Roosevelt died in 1945, an enlisted man in France wrote his own personal analysis of the old and the new political leaders.

Although there have been a lot of times I disagreed with him [Roosevelt] I believe that he was doing a good job in world politics. I just can't figure the Big Three being Churchill, Stalin and Truman. I hope Truman will take the advice of men like ex-Sec. of State Hull, Sec. of State Stettinius, and John F. Dulles. I imagine Harry Hopkins will be rather powerful in an unofficial capacity—I don't believe that will be as bad as it sounds. . . .[8]

The GI's of World War II were, in most cases, a solid and realistic lot. The public reaction to Roosevelt's death was somewhat appalling to many of these men, for they had seen death in a multitude of forms in God-forsaken places they had never heard of before the war. Besides, the war still had to be fought and won. To deprive the troops of their dance music on Armed Forces Radio after a difficult reconnaissance seemed sacrifice enough, but to cancel their movies because of the mourning period neighbored on sacrilege. "I think they are carrying this further than Roosevelt would have wished," one American wrote after having been denied the privilege of seeing the nightly movie at a front-line headquarter's tent.

The Korean War GI was driven to the limit of his patience by what he thought were poorly reasoned policies established by his government. "The people in Washington are certainly following a wishy-washy policy," a soldier wrote. "It is as if they are afraid to call reserves, draft people, put on rationing and fight this war." The troops in Korea, so said one soldier, "don't like anything in Washington except the Finance Office."

In 1951 a tribe of Washington politicians descended on Korea. The reaction of one American to such a visit was as follows:

> The air is full of airplanes today and the roads are full of half-tracks with machine guns. What? No Communist breakthrough, no Communist offensive—but Vice-President A. Barkley is paying our Division a visit! We had heard nothing of it in advance, but he landed at our little airfield today. I presume he will give the voters the information that he has "been to the front and seen our boys in conflict with the enemy. . . ." I'd like nothing better than to roast the *Ass* of the peace loving United Nations supporters' Democratic Party. What a nimble-witted bunch of S.O.B.'s we have running the U. S. . . . I don't mean to be disrespectful, but our nation is full of half-assed politicians that don't deserve to hold the offices they've been elected to.[9]

These are harsh words, even from the pen of an American in Korea. Yet, one must view the sentiments of the ordinary soldier toward his political leaders in terms of what his political leaders have sometimes thought of him. Too often in American history the men who have worn the uniform have been considered mere pawns of official government policy. They have been regarded less as individuals than mere units in a military machine. Their sacrifices, as politicians through the ages have so often indicated, have been "glorious," but only to be expected. In this connection one might ponder the modicum of humanity to be found in a statement purportedly made by a United States senator in 1966. It reads: "It costs us nearly $50,000 to train a good non-com and deliver him to Vietnam. Then if he steps on a booby trap he is out of action, maybe for good. Costs are fantastically high for the U. S. in this kind of guerrilla war compared with costs of the enemy."[10]

The variety of gripes by the American fighting man throughout his long history has been infinite. A young Union soldier, grumbling that he had joined the Army to die of bullets and not measles, wrote: "We are so much fooled around that not only myself but all our boys get disgusted with the war." Another private in the same conflict wrote that his camp was a "lovely place—a gorgeous hole." A Federal soldier complained in 1861 that he had been transported from one dirty camp to another in "coal carrs [*sic*]."[11]

The doughboy of World War I gave vent to similar lamentations. The Y.M.C.A., some said, was "nothing but graft. . . ." The American Red Cross, others argued, never provided anything free to the soldiers. The French people and their army came in for some special grousing. At the end of the conflict in 1918 an official French communiqué was issued which read: "The French Army, with the aid of the Allies, has achieved the defeat of the enemy." Such Gallic pomposity was too much for most members of the A. E. F.[12]

In World War II and in succeeding wars there were numerous dissatisfactions about countries and places in which GI's were stationed. India, so said one American GI in 1943, was "a place where the American soldier is taken for a sucker." "It is hell living here in the Pacific," commented another soldier. "God damn it, get me out of these jungles. Have you forgotten the poor souls that have been overseas?" The disquietude of GI's in Korea centered to a great extent on the "gooks"—the Koreans who stole from Army supply depots, or who ran black market enterprises in Seoul and Pusan.[13]

Surprisingly, the American fighting man has complained relatively little about his duties in actual combat. He may have questioned the merits of certain commanders—Buell or McClellan in the Civil War, or Stilwell in World War II—but he has had comparatively little to chafe about in relation to battle conditions. Perhaps the reason for this is that, once a soldier completes his mission, he is so overcome with a sense of gratitude for having survived that he does not have it in his heart to complain. But there are exceptions. A doughboy, back from a mission in "no man's land" in 1918, wrote:

It was darker than 31st and State Streets, Chicago, and raining. The top sergeant informed me that I was to go along with the party and I thanked him for the favor he showed me in letting me in on a hero's grave. Even "Jerry" had more sense than to send someone out on a night like that.[14]

Griping as a characteristic is a common denominator to all American fighting units, no matter what branch of service or what unit is observed or studied. The manner of this seemingly overt discontent, which German commanders in World Wars I and II misread as a lack of morale, differs from battalion to battalion, or from regiment to regiment. And it differs in style and content from one branch of the service to another. Ernie Pyle observed, during the Sicily invasion of 1943, that the American sailor was "fundamentally friendly," but that there was a "subtle difference" between these men and the American soldiers in transport. The soldiers, said Pyle, seemed harder and tougher; more used to dirt and less needful of niceties, and more inclined to gross inquietude.[15]

Pyle's comparison was made on the basis of one crew and one Army unit. The Navy, along with every other American branch of service, has had its excellent ships and its "losers"; it has had its elite units and its ordinary ones. The fleet, fitting its complement to its various needs, would have no trouble digging up some hard-bitten sailors, gifted in scurrilous language.

Taking each service in order—the Navy, the air forces, the Army, the Marines, and the special forces—one finds that elite units are those which have that aggressive quality needed for victory. In the Navy aggressiveness has always assumed the form of an essential pride of the men in their particular ships. There is probably little question that the men of John Paul Jones had it for the *Bon Homme Richard.* How else could that commander have taken the *Serapis* after such a hard fight? By 1812 the pride of the infant American Navy was so great that bravery was "passed almost without notice," according to a contemporary, and was "therefore no object for praise." So high was American naval morale and aggressiveness in 1812 that man for man, ship for ship, the U. S. Navy was probably the best naval force on the globe.

In the middle years of the nineteenth century there was a steady but gradual decline in the spirit of the Naval complement, probably because the best men and officers were more inclined to ship out on clippers or merchantmen. Despite some hard duty during the Civil War, Admiral David D. Porter complained about the American fleet in the 1880's that "There is not a Navy that does not have the advantage of us in ships and guns."[16]

What brought the Navy back into public favor as a military service was a Treasury surplus, which could best be spent on ships, and a great deal of good luck in 1898. The fleet, rebuilt with ponderously armored vessels, won some surprising victories against the Spanish; all of which were celebrated in poetry and patriotic verse. Once again the Navy was in style. President Theodore Roosevelt, partial to a good big Navy, not only managed to get a canal through Panama as a favor to the Navy, but scrapped the old heavily plated battleships for the faster and more maneuverable ships of the dreadnought class. By 1917 the American Navy was not only easily identifiable by its peculiar cagelike masts, but it had a plentiful supply of good battleships and cruisers and fast destroyers. And there were even a few submarines.[17]

Still abuilding in the early 1920's, the Navy was cut back slightly by the Washington Naval Conference. Pride kept morale high, however, and the U. S. Navy began its pioneering in aircraft carriers and long-range subs. By 1941 the fleet was in generally good condition, poorly trained for night fighting, but on the whole a striking force to be feared. The manner in which it rebounded after Pearl Harbor is still a romantic and almost unbelievable story. By 1945 there was scarcely an American jacktar who was unaware of the fact that he was part of the largest and best navy in the world.[18]

The sense of being part of an elite force pervaded the entire fleet, even to those sailors who manned the tankers and the landing craft. To a real sailor a ship is his mistress, endowed with special qualities. "The old hooker is still kicking," a World War II sailor wrote. "She's a mighty good girl, Pop, I've had a lot of fun with her." Again he wrote: "She's too smart for the enemy—always one jump ahead of them. . . . She's a sweetheart!" A young officer, having lost his ship off Newfoundland, eulogized: "She was a whacky job, but she was a good old hooker and we were pretty fond of her. You get to know all her screwy actions, what she'll do in all kinds of weather, how she turns and handles, and get to feel she has a personality distinctly her own. She was a good ship."[19]

There have been many special ships in American naval history—the *Constitution,* the *Monitor,* the *Olympia,* the *North Carolina,* and others—but one branch of naval service that has served the country well in recent years is the "silent service"; the American submarine fleet. In World War II the performance of the men of these ships was superb. Only by facts and figures does this picture fully emerge. The German Navy in World War II lost between seven hundred and eight hundred submarines; the Japanese sub fleet of 128 was almost completely out of action at the end of the war. The U. S. Navy lost fifty-two subs, with a total of almost 3,500 officers and men. Not only did these American submarines paralyze Japanese shipping and sink numerous enemy fighting ships, but the individual acts of heroism performed by the sailors of these vessels were in the highest tradition of self-sacrifice.[20]

During the general chorus of discontent over the behavior of American forces in Korea in the early 1950's, Hanson Baldwin was one of those military experts who claimed that the fighting forces of the nation had lost their old fighting spirit. "We must bring back the bands. . . ." he argued. "The services must, at all cost, foster and build up unit *esprit*—regimental *esprit* in the Army, squadron *esprit* in the Air Force, ship *esprit* in the Navy." Baldwin's complaints were particularly directed at the Army, whose replacement system, the writer claimed, had wrecked the regimental sense of homogeneity and belonging. Baldwin was harking back to the older days when the Navy looked down on the "gyrenes," the Marines looked down on every other service, and when the infantry sang:

> The infantry, the infantry, with dirt behind their ears,
> The infantry, the infantry, that laps up all the beers,
> The cavalry, artillery, the bloomin' engineers
> They couldn't lick the infantry in a hundred million years.[21]

Baldwin had a point, for though the Navy and Marines were still prideful, the Army had destroyed, at least for the time being, that basic sense of *élan* and *esprit* necessary to each good unit. The

Continentals had it during the Revolution, and generally scorned the militia. Within the Continental Army some units had a margin of pride exceeding that of others. The Second Carolina had thought itself to be unbeatable. Virginia, Maryland, and Delaware troops were widely admired, while the Massachusetts soldiers from Cape Cod and Marblehead had created excellent reputations.

In the period of frontier development, from 1800 to 1850, the excessive regimental pride of certain units became most troublesome. The battalions of some regiments occupied widely distant posts, and yet maintained such unit arrogance that brawls with soldiers from other regiments were the bane of post commanders. *Esprit* in the Mexican War developed around state regiments. The Mississippians thought themselves best, and parenthetically speaking, they *were* pretty good. Georgian regiments fought the Mexicans and everybody else. An Illinois soldier, showing pride in a recent victory over the Mexicans, wrote: "I feel proud that I am a 'sucker' and that Illinois troops have conducted themselves in such a manner. . . ."[22]

Esprit in the Civil War armies underwent interesting changes. Initial loyalties were to one's company, but these were soon submerged into regimental pride. In the Confederate Army, regiments were usually referred to by the name of their commanders; this, despite the fact that there were certain numerical designations. Forrest's cavalry was known as just that, and it must certainly be considered an elite unit of its time. Longstreet's divisions were the pride of Lee's army, and Lee's army was the pride of the Confederacy. These were, in a sense, the elite forces of the Confederacy.

Working downward on the Federal side, one could say that the proudest force on the Northern side was the Army of the Tennessee. Its troops looked down on the Army of the Cumberland, and to a larger extent, on the Army of the Potomac. Yet, within each of these three Federal Armies, there were regiments which never seemed to give ground easily. The Iron Brigade (Westerners) in the Army of the Potomac fought that heroic delaying action in the first hours of Gettysburg. The Fifty-Fifth Illinois, a bitter and cynical regiment of brawlers, saved Grant's Army of the Tennessee at Shiloh. Opdycke's Brigade (Illinois and Ohio troops) saved the Army of the Cumberland at Franklin.[23]

The *esprit* some Civil War units had developed was carried into Indian Wars after 1865 and became deeply rooted in some regiments; particularly in the cavalry, since it seemed to be involved in most of the hard fighting in those days. The Fifth Cavalry, as late as 1941, could say that it had fought forty engagements against Indians prior to the Civil War; from Gaines Mill through the Wilderness to Appomattox in the Civil War; in numerous engagements against Indians until the 1890's; and then against the Spanish in Puerto Rico. The Seventh Cavalry had won forty-three Medals of Honor by 1941; its most famous battle, strangely enough, being the defeat at Little Big Horn. The Eighth Cavalry by 1941 had won ninety-two Medals of Honor. The Tenth Cavalry, a Negro regiment organized by Colonel Benjamin H. Grierson in the post-Civil War periods, scouted over 6,700 miles in 1878, and later helped to take San Juan Hill in 1898."[24]

The first divisions to achieve the elite classification in World War I were the First, Second, Twenty-Sixth, and Forty-Second. Other divisions soon to gain excellent reputations were the Twenty-Seventh, Twenty-Eighth, Twenty-Ninth, Thirty-Third, Seventy-Seventh, and Ninety-First.

Some infantry regiments (excluding Marines) whose records were good in World War I were the Sixteenth, Eighteenth, Twenty-Sixth, and Twenty-Eighth, all Regulars. The 132nd, a regiment attached to the Thirty-Third Division, established an enviable record as a National Guard unit. It won five Medals of Honor, the second highest total of any regiment in the U. S. Army in the war. Four of these awards were given for direct bayonet assaults upon enemy machine-gun positions.[25]

As in the case of the Civil War, pride or *esprit* in World War II was developed first with the regiments, only to be submerged later into a division or an *esprit de corps*. A GI stationed in the Pacific wrote early in the war that his own particular regiment was extra tough, and was noted for "its drinking and drunks." Some Texas and Oklahoma regiments particularly distinguished themselves in fighting in Italy.[26]

By 1943 divisional pride had become all important, particularly if the unit had distinguished itself in hard fighting. Mark Clark remembered years later, and somewhat nostalgically, that some veteran divisions of World War II "would clear the sidewalks of soldiers wearing the shoulder patch of newly arrived, untried outfits." Airborne divisions were composed of specially trained and exceedingly tough troops. The Eighty-Second Airborne, for instance, established a formidable reputation in Sicily, Normandy, at Nijmigen, and on the Rhine. In the Pacific area the First Cavalry Division fought from the Admiralties to the Philippines, and their battle record entitled them to be called elite troops. The First Infantry Division, which fought well in Normandy, and the Third Infantry Division, which probably engaged in tougher fighting than any other U. S. troops in the entire war, were also exceptional units.

On the corps level, the VIII American Corps fought exceedingly well in the Battle of the Bulge, and turned defeat into victory. Among the various American armies, the Eighth American Army was described by a British general as having done a "grand job of work" in Sicily. Outstanding among these military combinations, however, was General Patton's Third Army. It captured 81,522 square miles of enemy-held territory, took 12,000 towns, villages, and cities, killed 47,500 German troops, wounded 115,700 of the enemy troops, and brought in 1,280,688 prisoners. It is little wonder that General Patton was the one American officer viewed with considerable awe by Russian generals at the close of the war. Both he and his Third Army were elite in the broadest meaning of the word.[27]

Regimental and divisional pride were almost absent at the beginning of the Korean War, but gradually they emerged. The "Wolfhound" Regiment, the Twenty-Seventh, commanded by Lieutenant Colonel John Michaelis, fought extremely well in the early days and won the admiration of all. On a divisional level, the First Cavalry once again established itself as an elite unit. On one occasion 219 men of the division found themselves cut off, miles behind enemy lines. They marched for three days and thirty miles, avoided enemy patrols, ate only two meals, and still managed to bring out 211 men.[28]

By the end of the Korean War the *esprit* of American Army units had increased enormously. A young lieutenant could write of his troops that he had a "wonderful platoon—they know their job, they do it without being told, and they do it fast." S. L. A. Marshall, whose literary defense of the behavior of Americans in Korea was needed, further described the growing pride of Army units. He wrote:

> And I have watched them pass the bird, the boo, and the studied affront to some rival regiment as they passed. "Send up a battalion, bums, and we'll let it relieve one of our platoons." Shades of the past! Who ever expected that this could happen to the American Army again! It sounds like 1918.[29]

If there is one factor in the American military tradition that acts as a constant irritant to the pride of the Army, it is the exalted reputation of the Marine Corps. A bitter GI of World War II wrote: "I can assure you that the Marines are not glorified in the least. We found out from the Navy that the Marines were held in reserve at Makin. . . . But who got the credit—not the Army. . . . No, where the Marines are concerned we over here sort of laugh it off."[30]

The fact of the matter, however, is that the Marine Corps does have *esprit;* an indefinable something which makes each individual leatherneck feel just a little bit superior to the ordinary GI. The evidence is plentiful, and much of it comes from Army sources. Mark Clark has written: "The American Marines have it [pride] and benefit from it. They are tough, cocky, sure of themselves and their buddies. They can fight and they know it." Hanson Baldwin has written that the Marines "live tradition; the United States marine bears upon his shoulders the nation's past and the nation's hopes for the future." An American general, an Army officer, wrote of the World War II Marines: "The Marines are careful, brave fighters. . . . These men are in splendid physical condition and were spoiling for a fight. They were the hunters, boring in relentlessly and apparently without fear. I never heard a wounded Marine groan." Another World War II Army general wrote after Tarawa: "I can never again see a United States Marine without experiencing a feeling of reverence."[31]

There are some fairly objective as well as partisan statements concerning Marine *esprit de corps*. An Australian colonel, when awarded the American Legion of Merit in World War II, would not accept it until it was pinned to his chest by a Marine, so high was his regard for the leathernecks. In World War I German intelligence reported that the Marines were the "elite corps" of the American fighting force, and that each leatherneck felt his membership in the Corps to be a source of honor and pride. A more recent American military scholar, as late as the 1960's, concluded that the Marines are still the toughest of American fighting men. On the other side of the world, Russian newspapers have contended that the Marine Corps is recruited from the most "reliable" people —"men of Anglo-Saxon origin. . . ."[32]

The Russians are wrong, of course, for the Marine Corps is derived from all nationalities and races (6 percent Negro at present). What the Slavic mind doesn't comprehend is that the Marines are simply men of a special breed, from officers down through the lower ranks. General Lewis B. (Chesty) Puller wrote in 1956 that the Marine Corps to him was "more than self-preservation, religion, or patriotism." It was a basic loyalty which traveled both ways—"up and down." The tradition which is implied in all of this is not new. Marines in Belleau Wood refused to leave the field even when wounded; a courage which inspired an Army general of the day to write that he couldn't think of Marines without getting tears in his eyes. Robert Sherrod, who accompanied the Marines to Tarawa, wrote: "The Marines simply assumed that they were the world's best fighting men." When Sherrod asked one leatherneck if he was afraid, the answer was: "Hell no, mister . . . I'm a Marine." A Navy corpsman wrote from Tarawa that he had finally concluded that the Marines "must be the best fighting men in the world." And a 1944 Marine wrote his parents:

We're out to get you Tojo, each of us with our secret weapon. Sure we'll tell you what it is; it's very common, a little thing called pride. . . . Enough pride to keep after you until you're downed, once and for all. Enough pride that no matter how difficult the problem is, we'll never turn back, because we are the United States Marines.[33]

Iwo Jima and Tarawa were great tests of Marine courage, but the supreme ordeal came in the Korean War. Thrown into the war quickly and hurriedly, with some very weak support from nearby Army divisions, the Marines helped to save the United Nations cause at the Naktong Bulge. British observers, at this point of the war, saw them as swaggering reminders of the Coldstream Guards and Jackson's Confederate legions. The Marines merely saw themselves as men who were doing their duty. "These guys fight well because they don't want to let the rest of the guys down," one Marine was quoted as saying. "And the rest of the guys have pretty high standards."

The Corps, according to one writer, made the landing at Inchon in an elaborate "calm." Later, when the Corps was trapped near the Chochin Reservoir, its attitude was simply: "We're going to come out of this as Marines, not as stragglers. We're going to bring out our wounded and our equipment. We're coming out . . . as Marines or not at all."[34]

They did come out—by plastering "Tootsie Rolls" on leaking radiators to keep their machines going—and by discovering "reserves of strength they never knew they possessed." In fighting their way to safety, they inflicted 35,000 casualties on the Chinese, and as one writer put it, they "marched in, erect, in column, picking up a cadence without order." And concerning the Marines in Korea, there is one last significant fact: Out of the approximately 7,200 Americans captured by the enemy, only 227 were Marines. That figure in itself implies something about the Marine spirit.[35]

Simply because of the very nature of the duty involved, the men who fly the planes of the various air forces must be considered of an elite character. In World War I American pilots flew with much bravado and skill, despite the fact that they were really novices in the established patterns of the air war of the time. The American pilots in World War II were likewise more inexperienced than their adversaries after 1941. Japanese pilots had built up many hours of combat in China. German pilots were truly veterans at this stage of the war by comparison to the Americans. Furthermore, it must be admitted in all honesty that American fighter planes did not measure up to Japanese, German, or British fighter aircraft.

But the skill and bravery of the American pilots won time for the Allied cause. An entire squadron of cumbersome torpedo bombers was lost during the Battle of Midway in a suicidal attack. But while these men were going down in flames and causing a good deal of distraction to the Japanese, an American dive bombing unit was able to come down directly out of the sun and inflict a crippling blow to the Japanese carrier fleet. In Europe, American bomber crews, flying without fighter protection, lost heavily in early sacrificial raids on Schweinfurt and Ploesti.

But the Americans learned the techniques of air war quickly. By the end of the conflict they ruled the skies of Germany and Japan. Through all of the sacrifice of the war the *esprit* of these men remained abnormally high. It was still high in Korea five years later. There were times when they were shooting down Communist planes at a ratio of fifty to one. Their support to ground troops was fantastic. They paralyzed Communist transport in such a way that, by late 1952, front-line Chinese troops were suffering heavily from starvation and illness.[36]

Much of the same praise can be given to the American airman in Vietnam. Their courage under adversity has been so great that overstatement is virtually impossible. Their *esprit* is something special. One is reminded here of the story of a captured American pilot who was forced to make a public confession over Hanoi radio. He went through his performance all right, but also added the extra statement that there was much discontent among American carrier pilots. Two such airmen had recently been dishonorably discharged for refusing to take part in raids upon the North. Who were they? One was an officer named Clark Kent; another a pilot named Ben Casey.

Something ought to be written here about special force units in American military history. These are not new, and probably go back to the very beginning of the nation's military tradition. The Royal Americans, prior to the Revolution, were a special force; so were Rogers' Rangers. In the Civil War there were "Berdan's Sharpshooters," and Wilder's "Lightning Brigade" of the Federal Army. Morgan and Forrest had their raiders, special forces indeed, on the Confederate side.

Special forces truly came into their own in World War II. Merrill's Marauders, much discussed previously, the First Special Service Force (The Devil's Brigade), the Army Rangers, Carlson's Marine Raiders, and even the "Seabees" were special units. In every instance there was a deep instillation of pride into these various outfits, and a feeling that, for their particular kind of training, they were unequaled by any other unit on the face of the earth.[37]

Esprit de corps is conceived in comradeship and nurtured by sacrifice. Comradeship in the earlier days of the American military tradition existed largely because whole companies, or even regiments, came from the same small town or city. Glover's Marblehead troops in the American Revolution had grown up with each other; they could not be expected to leave their wounded on the battlefield without reluctance. Even in the War of 1812, a luckless conflict for American men of arms, the same spirit manifested itself. An American soldier in the Battle of New Orleans refused to retreat, saying "You can hang or shoot me, and it would be all right, but my best friend needed my assistance, and nothing on earth could have enduced me to neglect him."[38]

The volunteer aspect of the Civil War brought the same characteristic into a clear delineation. Many regiments which were recruited from the larger cities in the East performed less well than Western Federal troops because of the lack of ethnic or cultural cohesiveness. Confederate regiments, or Western units in the Federal Army, fought hard because each soldier knew most of the men in his own company, and each soldier felt a strong loyalty to his state. The sight of wounded friends dying, or of comrades, long known, frozen in death on the battlefield, were stimulus for revenge.

"*Oh God,*" a young Federal officer wrote after the first day at Stone's River, "my company and my regiment. We went into the fight with over seven hundred men and now have about 300. . . ." The "noble Rosecrans," and the Yankee desire for revenge, would win the second stage of battle, he concluded. This is but one example in this war between brothers, and not the best one at that. The entire conflict was filled with such incidents. One needs only to read one of the great war novels of all time, *The Red Badge of Courage,* in order to properly understand this peculiar quality of the Civil War.[39]

Comradeship was a vital factor in the Indian Wars as well. Many of the men in America's frontier army had been comrades-in-arms for decades. The sense of belonging pervaded every company, every regiment. The old and hackneyed story of regimental loyalty—particularly that concerning the U. S. Cavalry—is based on real fact. Men who rode thousands of miles each year together were not about to leave helpless comrades to the Indian knife unless there was no other solution. Even on the Little Big Horn, when Major Reno's unit of the Seventh Cavalry was fighting for its very existence, men risked their lives to help wounded friends over the shallow ford, through the reeds, and up the hill to safety.

One of the great problems in 1898, particularly during the charge up San Juan Hill, was that of keeping the men moving. There was too much disposition to fall back to aid wounded buddies; all of which slowed the American assault. One reporter, surveying the battlefield after the victory had been won, found a wounded American infantryman sitting by the body of a friend. The corpse was already in a state of decomposition, but the live soldier kept at the task of fanning away the flies, and shooting at the circling vultures. "I won't leave him alone, I won't," the boy exclaimed. "He dressed this here leg for me only five minutes before he was shot. . . ."[40]

The sense of comradeship comes through loud and clear in the letters of World War I doughboys. Draftees, volunteers, regulars, and guardmen were bound together by the very nature of the young and vigorous country that had produced them. They were further welded by patriotic fervor and song. "We sang together," a member of the Second Division wrote later, "when we marched, when we were out on the battlefield and even when things were hot." "Buddy" was such a popular word of the war that it was soon written into that poignant ballad of the 1920's, "My Buddy."[41]

The death of comrades in 1918 was never taken lightly. A young doughboy wrote that he could not stand to see the bodies of his friends rotting where they had fallen out of reach of stretcher parties. A Marine, fresh from Belleau Wood, wrote: "It sure is an awful feeling to see your comrades and friends killed all around. . . ." A tough young officer of the First Division had seen his best "buddy" killed by Germans. Henceforth, he added, he would "take no quarter from now on."[42]

A historical study of World War II, written and published in 1946, took note of the following characteristic of GI's:

Unit commanders were aware of, and disturbed by, the tendency of men to halt an advance to see that the wounded were safely taken back. Measures to prevent this were difficult to enforce. Two features of Pacific fighting differentiated it from that in Europe: the Japanese fought on in suicidal fashion if bypassed, even very small groups or individuals; and they killed wounded men without mercy. U. S. soldiers were aware of this and felt strongly about leaving wounded comrades in the wake of an advance, to fall victims to any bypassed enemy sniper.[43]

From what wellspring did this emotion derive? The answer would be hard to come by, but one guess is that common experiences and close relationships helped. A sailor, writing from boot camp, partially explained it when he stated:

So you march and wheel and 10,000 men are as one man, intent upon their marching, stiffly turning in tight trousers jammed down into leggings, hats pressed firmly upon the eyebrows, and all individuality gone, and it is good to lose yourself in the warm sea of young fighters, and you can die for them and they will die for you.[44]

A young American girl in England even noted the comradeship of the GI in the dancehalls and pubs of that country. "Soldiers took care of each other," she wrote, "and in general, though always noisy, and sometimes boisterous and profane, they were very agreeable and considerate."[45]

The American sense of belonging and his faith in his comrades was most evident on the battlefield, however. The last message from Corregidor in 1942, as the Japanese were overrunning the American positions, was: "Tell Joe wherever he is to give 'em hell for us. . . ." "Leave me here," pleaded a wounded American infantryman to his comrades in Normandy. "The rest of you had better drop back to the next hedgerow." None of the GI's retreated, even though the fight became a grenade-throwing contest at twenty-five yards.

The meaning of death was no different to the World War II soldier than it had been to the doughboys twenty-three years before. A Marine of the South Pacific asserted that the thought of comrades rotting in shallow island graves drove him to even greater desperation. A bomber maintenance mechanic admitted that he silently said a prayer for the crew and pilot of his ship before each mission. "God help them on this take-off," was his daily plea. A soldier on Bataan, admitting that artillery fire called down on his position had killed numerous Japanese, sadly added that it didn't bring a comrade killed in the barrage "back to me."[46]

How sad it is that the word "buddy" seems to be rooted only in war! A New Guinea soldier wrote that his worst experience in war was to see his "buddies" falling down dead and wounded. The hasty burials were worse still. A simple cross or Hebrew star, hung with a helmet or identification tag, just didn't seem to be enough. John Dos Passos, who visited the Guam cemetery in 1946, found little handcarved messages on the wooden markers—"In memory of a grand guy," "A Good Scout," and "He Served Us Well." A Marine grave on Guadalcanal carried the inscription:

> And when he gets to Heaven,
> To Saint Peter he will tell:
> One more marine reporting, sir—
> I've served my time in Hell.[47]

Marguerite Higgins saw the same sense of comradeship in Korea. "You know," she quoted a Marine as saying, "you hear stories about comrades of battle getting to be closer than brothers. I guess it's true." The same reporter saw many instances of loyal comradeship; she wrote that she had seen "young boys perform incredibly brave deeds to save a position, to help a buddy. . . ." During the retreat from Chochin Reservoir, as Miss Higgins noted, a number of wounded Marines had been stranded and left behind on the ice and snow. Marine units crawled back, on their stomachs and on the ice, to bring them back. Another Marine unit, some of its men too wounded to be moved, refused to retreat. Their company commander stuck a rifle in the ground and shouted: "This is Easy Company. Easy Company holds here."[48]

But there were some occasions when nothing could be done. The North Koreans or Chinese came in such waves—"hordes," the American newspapers called them—that American infantrymen could do nothing but retreat. These were the sweating-out periods; when each man felt that somehow he hadn't contributed enough. Even the artillerymen, sometimes far to the rear, felt the pangs of conscience. "We have fired a few rounds in support of an attack, but actually haven't been doing as much as I feel we should," a mortarman complained. "I know from my experience in W. W. II what it is to be a rifleman and how you like to have everything thrown at the enemy that you can."[49]

The American "fetish" for bringing out the wounded, or for driving through to rescue trapped companies, has been a great puzzle to soldiers of the South Vietnamese Army. In the fighting near Tin Binh in February, 1966, some men of the First Infantry Division were surrounded by strong Viet Cong forces. A twenty-four year old lieutenant took six men and a tank in to rescue them, only to find himself part of the surrounded detachment. He then called artillery fire down on his position and managed to extricate all the men. In another instance, near the Cambodian border, a First Infantry private was wounded five times in attempting to get assistance to a fallen comrade. A Chicago Negro boy was awarded a Medal of Honor, posthumously, because he fell on a live grenade to save his comrades.

Airmen also have fallen victim to the comradeship complex of the American fighting men. Helicopters have been shot down in making rescues, and their pilots killed. Others, more fortunate, have made night landings—a most hazardous action—in order to bring out wounded men. One fighter pilot, flying an old propellor-driven plane, landed and took off under direct enemy fire while rescuing a friend.[50]

These are all acts of bravery, but whether inspired by comradely devotion or not, bravery is so commonplace in the American military tradition that it would take volumes to recount every heroic deed. Yet there are some which do stand out among the others. There was an American artilleryman at Bemis Heights in the Revolution who fought by his cannon until he fainted from the loss of blood from a mouth wound. Another Revolutionary soldier fought a British raiding party at Yorktown with a spade, until he was finally shot. In the Battle of Lake Erie, during the War of 1812, the wounded men, lying in the welter of their own blood, continued to pull the lines until the battle was concluded.[51]

There were scores of such incidents in the Mexican and Civil Wars. An American artillery unit, during one battle in Mexico, took it upon itself to pursue a retreating enemy cavalry troop; a truly unusual sight. At Fort Donelson in 1862 a color sergeant of a Western Federal regiment reformed the Union line by carrying his banner far in advance of his fellows and shouting "See! See! See!" At Kennesaw Mountain, where Sherman rashly attacked solid Confederate defenses, the fighting became so close that spades, rocks, and lighted "turpentine balls" were the principal weapons.[52]

Perhaps the great fascination the Civil War holds for so many people lies in the question of motivation. How could men be so incredibly brave in a war between brothers? Why did Sam Davis, the young Confederate spy, allow himself to be hanged in Tennessee rather than reveal the spy network with which he was associated? What drove Day Elmore, the famous drummer boy from Illinois, into active participation in the battles of Pea Ridge, Perryville, Stone's River, and Chickamauga? Why, after he was seriously wounded in the last named fight, did he reenlist; only to die in the Battle of Franklin?

These are all part of the mystique of the Civil War. What made

J.E.B. Stuart's troopers so daring? What drove Nathan B. Forrest— that untutored genius of war—to perform such feats of heroism? What inspired Lee's men to the last bitter end at Appomattox? Why did Grant's troops charge to certain death at Petersburg?

If one could answer these questions, he could understand the character of every fighting American. He would understand why a fifteen-man American patrol, surrounded by an overwhelming German force in 1918, fought to the death. He would understand why a young American officer at Chipilly Ridge in 1918 bayoneted one enemy officer, shot two other soldiers, and captured seventeen Germans— all after part of one leg was blown away. He would also understand why a sergeant of C Company, 354th Infantry, Eighty-Ninth Division, took a shot through the heart in order to protect his officer. He would likewise understand why a French intelligence report of 1918 stated that "groups of American soldiers were killed to the last man, rather than surrender."[53]

All in all there were ninety-five Congressional Medals of Honor awarded to the Army in World War I; the Navy won twenty-eight, most of which went to the Marines. Each award is a story unto itself. If there is one incident in that war that pulls upon the imagination, it is the story of the "Lost Battalion." These were 679 men, surrounded by a strong force of Germans in a dense thicket of the Argonne Forest, and yet refusing to surrender. They held on for days, until one Private Abraham Krotoshinsky finally threaded his way through the German lines and brought help. Only 252 doughboys came out; a real tribute to the character of the American fighting man of 1918.[54]

To the men of the "Lost Battalion" and to every serviceman in American history, death was well understood as the irrevocable and final end to life. Yet the deeds continue. Marine pilots on Midway flew their lumbering "Buffaloes" to certain death in order to strike at Yamamoto's fleet. Winston Churchill reputedly wept when he heard of the annihilation of Torpedo Squadron I, the fifteen planes whose sacrifice made it possible for American dive bombers to hit the Japanese carrier fleet a smashing blow. In the European theater it was not uncommon for enlisted men to attempt to bring in Flying

Fortresses whose pilots had been killed. In one instance a co-pilot could not loosen the dead hand of his pilot from the control column of his Fortress. He flew his mission for two more hours, holding the dead pilot with one arm and steering with the other. A belly gunner of another Fortress came out of his bubble to find the plane afire. He jettisoned all inflammable material, manned waist guns for a brief interval, and put out a fire in the radio with his bare hands. He was eventually awarded the Medal of Honor, and incidentally, taken off kitchen police duty for having committed a previous misdemeanor.[55]

The bravery of airmen in World War II was matched by the men of the "silent service." The commander of the *Growler* (SS215) and two other men were wounded by machine-gun fire after close contact with a Japanese patrol ship. Unable to move from the bridge, the commander of the sub ordered his ship to submerge; thereby ordering himself to certain death. The *Sculpin* (SS191) was damaged in 1943 by an enemy depth-charge attack. Captain John P. Cromwell ordered all hands to abandon ship, with the exception of ten enlisted men, one other officer, and himself. A Navy report on the loss of the *Sculpin* reads:

About 12 men rode the ship down, including Captain Cromwell (John P.) and one other officer, both of whom refused to leave it. Captain Cromwell, being familiar with plans for our operations in the Gilberts and other areas stayed with the ship to insure that the enemy could not gain any of the information he possessed.[56]

The sacrifices of the airmen and the sub crews were heroic ones, of course; but the dirtiest and yet most commonplace duties fell to the infantrymen. These were the rifle carriers whose lives were in danger every time they took a step toward an enemy-held sector. If the threat wasn't a land mine which killed or castrated, it was an enemy sniper hidden behind some hedgerow or bush, or tied in a tree. One postwar writer has claimed that the infantry suffered 75 percent of the casualties in the European theater of war, while the air forces suffered slightly over 9 percent losses. But who received the decorations? The Army Air Corps in Europe reputedly received more than 82 percent of these awards, while the infantry was given slightly over 9 percent.

The heroism of the foot soldier apparently seems so commonplace as to be considered unworthy of special attention. An American soldier, fighting in Normandy, directed tank traffic for four hours while standing with one broken leg. Another GI in the same fighting continued to direct artillery fire despite the fact that he knew he had been spotted. His last words were "The next one [enemy mortar shell] will fall here." The crossing of the Remagen Bridge was accomplished by young American boys who inched their way across a heavily mined structure, which might have blown sky-high at any moment. On the Scheldt estuary American infantrymen fought to the death to hold hard-won machine-gun nests. The fighting in the Ardennes Forest was bitter, hard, cold, and frustrating. Here the specter of death hovered everywhere.[57]

The foot soldier in the Pacific fought a different kind of war; a fever-ridden, frightening, dirty kind of conflict. The story of the First Cavalry Division gives a true picture of the struggle. In the Admiralties, Sergeant Troy A. McGill won a Medal of Honor by holding a defensive position thirty-five yards in advance of the main line of resistance. Attacked by two hundred Japanese, he fired his automatic weapon until he ran out of ammunition, and then he swung his rifle as a club against the attackers. When dawn came, McGill was dead, but 105 Japanese bodies were found in front of his foxhole.

In the fight for Antipolo during the Luzon campaign, the First Cavalry won ninety-two Silver Stars and one D. S. C. Of these Silver Stars, 40 percent were awarded to men who rescued wounded comrades, 22 percent went to men who held positions in the face of overwhelming assaults, 20 percent were given to men who led attacks on enemy positions, 17 percent were won on reconnaissance patrols, and the remainder went for assorted deeds. One-fourth of the Silver Stars were given posthumously, and the names of all of the men of the First Cavalry who won the decorations ran the whole gamut of ethnic and national backgrounds.

Some specific examples of heroism in the Luzon campaign included that of a sergeant who ran twice through enemy fire to bring up ammunition, a Mississippi private who fired a machine gun until he was overrun, a truck driver who drove a burning ammunition truck to a safe position, and an officer who led a squad to an untenable position in order to rescue sixteen wounded men. All of these were exceptional actions, of course; though not quite equal to the heroism of Sergeant Louis Herbert, D Troop, Twelfth Cavalry Regiment, who fired a machine gun in the Leyte campaign in a standing position until he had sent seventy Japanese to their heavenly reward.[58]

The Marine Corps in World War II won fifty Medals of Honor. Thirty-two of these went to men who died in action; fourteen of them were given to sergeants, eight to corporals, and twenty-eight to privates. Twenty-six of the Marines won the Medal by attempting to smother live hand grenades; only three of these men survived. Five of these particular awards went to Marines, who within sight of the end of the war, died while smothering grenades on Okinawa. Another went to a 1943 Marine hero, who in an island assault, threw a grenade which hit a tree and bounded back. Without hesitation, he dived squarely on the grenade and was blown to bits.

The history of the Marines in World War II is filled with deeds far beyond the call of duty. A Marine officer on Tarawa cleaned out six machine-gun nests, and when he was wounded, he refused evacuation. In a last assault he was killed. Earlier, in the battle for Guadalcanal, a wounded Marine officer rolled off his stretcher, cleaned out an enemy sniper nest, then allowed himself to be carried to the infirmary.

The Marine Corps went through a special ordeal on Iwo Jima. On D-Day plus thirty-five, the casualties of the Fifth Marines came to almost nine thousand men. The Second Platoon, B Company, Twenty-Eighth Marine Regiment, went through twelve platoon commanders in three weeks of fighting; three of them were privates. Yet, after those thirty-five days of unadulterated horror, the unaccounted for were only two officers and seventeen enlisted men. It is slightly reminiscent of the Ninth Illinois, a crack Federal regiment, which listed less than ten men missing out of their nearly three hundred casualties at Shiloh during the Civil War.[59]

The special horror of the fighting in the Pacific was the closeness of it all. Bayoneting or hand-to-hand fighting involves exceptional courage. Private Donald J. Ruhl, a Marine in the Iwo Jima attack, made a personal assault on eight Japanese soldiers. He bayoneted one, killed another, ran through the nest of Japanese soldiers to rescue a wounded Marine forty yards away from him. All night long he held his place, only to be killed the next day, when he attempted to smother the blast of a poorly thrown grenade.

Another Marine at Iwo Jima was attacked by a sword-swinging Japanese soldier. He knocked his opponent down, and cut off his opponent's head with the Nipponese broadsword. Another Marine attacked a Japanese blockhouse on the slopes of Mount Suribachi and killed ten of the enemy before he was shot. And long before Joe Rosenthal of the Associated Press had arrived to take the famous Mount Suribachi flag-raising picture, the Fifth Marines had placed a flag stolen from the Navy on the top of the ashy peak.[60]

All of this was achieved with raw courage, and a strange aspect about courage is that it sometimes comes from the strangest sources. Ex-football athletes often became quivering shell-shock cases in the midst of battle, while thin, scrawny, pimply faced kids performed incredible feats of courage. A young Marine officer on Okinawa was one of the latter type. He wore thick glasses, and led his men in what they sometimes regretfully described as a "Gung Ho" fashion. "He would stand up during intense fire," wrote one observer, "and shout orders with complete abandon for his own safety." The only time he appeared to have been frightened was an occasion when he lost his glasses during the height of an attack. "Please help me find my glasses," he pleaded with his men, "please, I can't see without them."[61]

Of the 131 Medals of Honor awarded in the Korean conflict, most were designated as posthumous decorations. One can only conjecture about all the heroes of this and other wars, men whose deeds were unseen or untold simply because no one survived to write commendations concerning them. One may also wonder about the deeds of courage, which while noted, did not merit the nation's highest award. One example—somewhat of a strange contradiction—concerns the actions of Navy Lieutenant Eugene F. Clark, who before the Inchon landing was put ashore to scout enemy positions and batteries. Clark was ashore for fourteen days, he reconnoitered beaches, checked tides, had occasional fights with Communist troops, and managed to get an important landmark illuminated. For this he received only the Silver Star.[62]

Consider also the instance of a trapped company of soldiers in Vietnam. The GI's fought waves of Viet Cong assaults, and an enemy machine-gun nest was taken. "Some kid whose name I don't even know stood up and shot both the machine gunners in the face," an officer recalled later. This young boy—like Stephen Crane's "young soldier"—is another of those nameless heroes of the American military tradition.[63]

War is, as some have written, 99 percent boredom and 1 percent sheer fright. It is that 99 percent that gives the individual fighting man the time to assess himself and others. American soldiers in the Mexican War, those who could write, were inclined to argue that action was better than inaction. There was, they contended, too much marching, not enough fighting. But then, as in every war, there soon appeared the horrible sights of a battlefield once won; the corpses lying with arms akimbo and with bloated bellies.

Once having looked death in the face, each soldier may spend a good deal of his inactive time in some down-to-earth philosophizing. A Texas Ranger, fighting for the Confederacy in 1861, wondered: "Why do I subject myself to this life . . . ? Well I don't know unless it is the Quixotic desin [design] to work for nothing." A Federal soldier, far from home in Missouri, pondered: "Here I am in a strange land. Shall I ever see you again or shall I fall victim to the enemy? Shall I deliver my life to the God who gave it without being able to see you again?" A World War I doughboy wrote his family that the war intruded on his thoughts constantly. "Sherman didn't know what war was in his time," he concluded. And a World War II private, writing of a newly killed officer, stated: "Some of us find it hard to believe that he could be dead. But I guess in war there is no favoritism."

It is the very cheapness of life that impresses itself most upon the front-line soldier. A Marine on Guadalcanal told his parents that "we take it [life] for granted and so quickly and brutally it's taken away. Let me tell you that sudden death is horrible and absolutely inglorious." Another World War II soldier viewed it in a slightly different way. "Death is easy," he stated. "It happens often. The toughest part is going on, existing as an animal."[64]

But then, for some, the sheer danger of military life serves as an opiate for its more painful moments. Sometimes it has even served to dull the emotion of fear. The co-pilot of a downed Flying Fortress went to sleep in his cockpit, while Zeroes continued to make strafing passes at the plane. A Marine on Guadalcanal sat in a bomb crater during an attack and conjured up memories of "old movies about World War I," and in particular, of the film *What Price Glory*. A Korean War American GI, complaining mildly about the hills to be climbed, stated: "Maybe I look at life philosophically but I can always see that things can always be worse." And a Civil War soldier once inscribed: "I like the *business* very well. . . . You could not get one of our boys to go back home to stay."

Waiting a war out has always proved a problem, however; that is, with most soldiers. "According to the headlines in tonight's paper, the war with Japan will last until 1949," one GI wrote in 1943. "Ouch! Let's see, I'll be 30 years by that time." "I am in good health and spend my time pleasantly," a Federal soldier wrote in 1861. "I read the news till I become tired or disgusted, and then I go out on the hills and breathe the fresh air."[65]

It is the springtime that proves the hardest time of year for the American fighting man. A Civil War general, two weeks from his death at Shiloh, wrote his wife, about the beauty of the Tennessee spring and added: "Dear wife, when will our Good God in his providence permit a return to those happy times." Another Civil War soldier, charmed by the same spring, wrote home that he had just been for a walk in order to pick wild flowers. "Now Hattie," he concluded, "you may think that I am getting almost childish in my ideas . . . but no for it is all these small things which compose the whole of life's happenings." A World War II GI, writing from a trailside camp in the scenic greenery of Hawaii, commented: "It's been very quiet here, so quiet that this seems more or less like a glorified camping trip than a war." And from England an American soldier wrote in 1944: "Spring has begun to spring here in the Kingdom and rural England is beautiful. I have had the opportunity in the very recent past of seeing a lot of it. At times it is hard to believe a fight is going on for its very survival. . . ."[66]

Inevitably, by one process or another, wars all come to an end. It is not surprising to note that American fighting men, and probably those of all nations involved in war, have had similar reactions to peace. There is a great deal of disorientation. Nothing seems quite the same. "I sure am homesick since they quit fighting," a doughboy of 1918 wrote. "While they were fighting, it never entered my mind." One young private of World War I made one last trip out to a cemetery to visit the grave of a lost "buddy." "I am so blue," he lamented. Yet some doughboys at the front were quickly over the trenches to visit their former opponents. Sailors on naval vessels fired flares and rockets in 1918, just as they did in 1945 at Saipan, Guam, Okinawa, and elsewhere. Some just got drunk at the end of both World Wars, while others merely contemplated. "It's a wonderful feeling to be in a world where men aren't dying by other men's hands," a GI wrote from France in 1945. "I'm thankful that God saw fit to let me live, to let my friends live, to let our country live."[67]

Sometimes the homecoming has turned out to be the hardest part of all. A Civil War soldier wrote in 1865 that he couldn't stand the thought of living out his life in a small town in Illinois. World War I soldiers often underwent a strange and almost traumatic sensation of loneliness. *The Literary Digest* of 1919 noted that returning veterans seemed to want solitude more than anything else, and bitterly resented any questioning about the war. Many young men simply could not stay at home in 1919, and some even longed for a return to the uniform. One such veteran wrote that "I must admit to myself at least that I am lost and somehow strangely lonesome."

It was no different in 1945 and 1946. A World War II GI admitted that he was "as restless as a gony [*sic*] bird." Another wrote: "As funny as it may seem, I find myself beginning to wonder if I'm going to like it out of the Army—nearly three years in the Army gives you some sort of feeling that civilian life doesn't offer."[68]

In the long run, however—despite the long look back at some anchored ship or green-shingled army barracks—the slow adjustment to civilian life is eventually made. Nowhere has it been better described than in the reminiscence of an old Civil War veteran. Finally discharged, he packed his souvenirs in a great sack, caught a train to the town nearest his home, and began a long walk through the countryside. The road was dusty; it was a hot Midwestern summer. He passed a small country store, and a man sitting on the inside counter leaned forward, peered for a moment, and then returned to his business. A dog came to some fence palings and barked. There was nothing more. Soon he was back at his work, cutting and shucking corn; almost as if he had been "away only a day or two."[69]

As post-Civil War writers were inclined to describe it, for those who couldn't return, there was always the silent bivouac of the dead. For those who have been lucky enough to return from America's great wars, there are the long memories—ever changing—and never forgotten. Such is the strange and contradictory mystique of war. The American fighting man, no matter his decade or century, is no more immune to it than was the Roman centurion, or Napoleon's great soldiers of the nineteenth century. Like them, he never wishes to return to those sacred days of his past; yet in most instances he treasures each individual remembrance like the beads of a Rosary. And in all truth, he realizes that no person who has never known what he has seen could ever really understand.

Notes

CHAPTER 1

1. Quincy Wright, *A Study of War* (Chicago: The University of Chicago Press, 1964), pp. 5–6, p. 17.
2. *Ibid.*, p. 9.
3. Harry A. Ellsworth, *180 Landings of U. S. Marines, 1800–1934* (Washington, D.C.: U. S. Marine Corps, 1934). Russian propaganda says over 240 up to 1966.
4. R. Ernest Dupuy and Trevor N. Dupuy, *Military Heritage of America* (New York: McGraw-Hill Book Company, Inc., 1956), pp. 710–717.
5. *Correspondence Relating to the War with Spain, Including the Insurrection in the Philippine Islands, and the China Relief Expedition* (Washington: 1902), pp. 1327–1328.
6. St. Louis *Post-Dispatch,* July 17, 1966.
7. John M. Palmer, *America in Arms: The Experience of the United States With Military Organization* (New Haven, Conn.: Yale University Press, 1941), p. 20.
8. Dupuy, *op. cit.,* p. 77.
9. Celer Et Audax. *A Brief History of the King's Royal Rifle Corps: 1755–1948* (Aldershot, U.K.: Gale and Polden Ltd., 1948), pp. 3–10. The regiment is now known as the 2nd Battalion, Royal Green Jackets. It is presently stationed in Borneo.
10. T. Harry Williams, *Americans at War: The Development of the*

American Military System (Baton Rouge, La.: Louisiana State University Press, 1960), p. 10.

11. Gen. George A. Forsyth, *The Story of the Soldier* (New York: D. Appleton & Company, Inc., 1909), p. viii. U. S. Bureau of the Census, *Historical Statistics of the United States, Colonial Times to 1957* (Washington, D.C.: U. S. Government Printing Office, 1960), p. 737.

12. Gen. Emory Upton, *The Military Policy of the United States* (Washington, D.C.: Government Printing Office, 1912), p. 128. Benson J. Lossing, *The Pictorial Field Book of the War of 1812* (New York: Harper & Brothers, 1869), pp. 1005–1008.

13. Williams, *op. cit.,* pp. 36–37.

14. Percival Lowe, *Five Years a Dragoon ('49 to '54): And Other Adventures on the Great Plains* (Norman, Okla: Univ. of Oklahoma Press, 1965), pp. xii–xvi.

15. Ella Lonn, *Foreigners in the Union Army and Navy* (Baton Rouge, La.: Louisiana State University Press, 1951), pp. 80–81, pp. 618–619.

16. *Historical Statistics of the United States,* p. 735.

17. *Ibid.*

18. *Ibid.* John Dickinson, *The Building of An Army* (New York: The Century Co., 1922), p. 27.

19. *U. S. News and World Report,* Aug. 8, 1966.

20. Laurence Stallings, *The Doughboys: The Story of the A.E.F., 1917–1918* (New York: Harper & Row, Publishers, 1963), p. 25.

21. *Ibid.,* p. 380. *Historical Statistics of the United States,* p. 735.

22. Harvey Cushing, *From a Surgeon's Journal, 1915–1918* (Boston: Little, Brown & Company, 1936), p. 507.

23. Fred A. Sassé, *Rookie Days of A Soldier* (St. Paul, Minn.: W. G. Green, 1924), pp. 230–231.

24. *Historical Statistics of the United States,* p. 736.

25. *The War Reports of General of the Army George C. Marshall, General of the Army H. H. Arnold, Fleet Admiral Ernest J. King* (New York: J. B. Lippincott Company, 1947), pp. 274–276.

26. Austin Wheatley, "The Asian Retreat We've All But Forgotten," The Detroit *News,* Aug. 14, 1966.

27. David Rees, *Korea: The Limited War* (New York: St. Martin's Press, Inc., 1964), p. 185, p. 461.

28. *U. S. News and World Report,* Aug. 8, 1966. U. S. Bureau of the Census, *Statistical Abstract of the United States: 1965* (86th Edition) Washington, D.C., 1965, p. 270.

29. Samuel E. Morison, *The Oxford History of the American People*

(New York: Oxford University Press, 1965), pp. 212–213. Sir George O. Trevelyan, *The American Revolution* (New York: Longmans, Green & Co., Inc., 1905), vol. 1, p. 283.

30. Aaron Wright, "Journal of a Pennsylvania Rifleman At the Siege of Boston," *Boston Transcript,* April 11, 1862. Wayne is quoted in Carl Van Doren, *Mutiny in January* (New York: The Viking Press, Inc., 1943), p. 18.

31. Quoted in Charles K. Bolton, *The Private Soldier Under Washington* (Port Washington, N. Y.: Kennikat Press, Inc., 1964), p. 29.

32. Trevelyan, *op. cit.,* III, 80. Bolton, *op. cit.,* p. 248.

33. Edward J. Nichols, *Zach Taylor's Little Army* (Garden City, N. Y.: Doubleday & Company, Inc., 1963), pp. 101–102.

34. Private John A. Modglin to his sister, Sept. 28, 1918, World War I Collections of Illinois Historical Library. Poem is unsigned from same source.

35. Dixon Wecter, *When Johnny Comes Marching Home* (Cambridge, Mass.: Houghton Mifflin Company, 1944), p. 483.

36. Harry E. Maule, ed., *A Book of War Letters* (New York: Random House, Inc., 1943), p. 35, p. 268.

37. *Ibid.,* p. 278. Donald Marshall to his parents, Jan. 20, 1952, by his permission.

38. Charles W. Whitehair, *Out There* (New York: D. Appleton & Company, Inc., 1918), pp. 58–60. General Richard Thoumin, *The First World War,* ed. by Martin Kieffer (New York: G. P. Putnam's Sons, 1964), p. 358. Priv. Pearl Harlow to parents, June 16, 1918, Illinois Historical Library.

39. Howard H. Peckham and Shirley A. Snyder, ed., *Letters from Fighting Hoosiers* (Bloomington, Ind.: Indiana War History Commission, 1948), p. 241. Wecter, *op. cit.,* p. 554.

40. Donald Marshall to parents, Dec. 18, 1944, by permission.

41. Maule, *op. cit.,* p. 5, p. 267.

42. Wecter, *op. cit.,* p. 538.

43. J. George Fredman and Louis A. Falk, *Jews in American Wars* (Washington, D.C.: The Jewish War Veterans of the United States of America, 1954), pp. 216–217.

44. Richard Tregaskis, *Vietnam Diary* (New York: Holt, Rinehart and Winston, Inc., 1963), p. 351. The Chicago *Tribune,* Oct. 27, 1966.

45. Frederick Palmer, *Our Greatest Battle* (New York: Dodd, Mead & Company, Inc., 1924), p. 484. See also: Justin H. Smith, *The War with Mexico* (Gloucester, Mass.: Peter Smith, 1963), Vol. I, *passim.*

46. Wecter, *op. cit.,* p. 485. *Yank,* June 9, 1944. *Letters from Fighting Hoosiers,* p. 332.

47. Maule, *op. cit.*, p. 326. *Letters from Fighting Hoosiers,* pp. 21–22.
48. *Time,* Jan. 1, 1951. Tregaskis, *op. cit.*, p. 75.
49. Leander Stillwell, *The Story of a Common Soldier of Army Life in the Civil War* (Kansas City, Mo.: Franklin Hudson Publishing Co., 1961), p. 13. Philip Welshimer to his wife, June 6, 1861, Welshimer MSS, Illinois Historical Library.
50. Joseph H. Odell, *The New Spirit of the Old Army* (Westwood, N. J.: Fleming H. Revell Company, 1918), pp. 18–19. Wecter, *op. cit.*, p. 484. Ernie Pyle, *Brave Men* (New York: Henry Holt and Company, Inc., 1944), p. 401.
51. Wecter, *op. cit.*, pp. 556–557, pp. 486–487. H. Landes to parents, Landes MSS, Illinois Historical Library & Robert Sherrod, *Tarawa: The Story of a Battle* (New York: Duell, Sloan & Pearce, 1954), p. 116.
52. Marguerite Higgins, *War in Korea: The Report of a Woman Combat Correspondent* (Garden City, N. Y.: Doubleday & Company, Inc., 1951), p. 83, p. 84. John G. Westover, *Combat Support in Korea* Washington, D.C.: Combat Forces Press, 1955), pp. 52–53. Donald Marshall to parents, Jan. 1952, by permission.
53. Higgins, *op. cit.*, p. 219. Sevareid is quoted in Albert D. Biderman, *March to Calumny: The Story of American POW's in the Korean War* (New York: The Macmillan Company, 1963), pp. 195–196.
54. Tregaskis, *Vietnam Diary,* p. 83, p. 279, p. 330. Bart McLendon, "Teen G.I.'s Know Why They Fight," Detroit *Free-Press,* Aug. 18, 1966.
55. The Chicago *Tribune,* July 11, July 20, 1966.
56. Examples of the mutilation rumors are to be found in the David Givler and Ira Blanchard MSS, Illinois Historical Library. Quote is from Col. John Wilcox to his wife, July 11, 1862, Wilcox MSS, Illinois Historical Library.
57. Mark Sullivan, *Over Here, 1914–1918,* Vol. V of *Our Times: The United States, 1900–1925* (New York: Charles Scribner's Sons, 1933), p. 359. Odell, *The New Spirit in the Old Army,* p. 41, p. 67.
58. Musician Matthew I. Daniels to his brother, Sept. 15, 1918; Priv. Pierre Turch to Joseph Biller, n.d.: World War I Collection, Illinois Historical Library.
59. H. Landes to parents, May 8, 1945, Landes MSS. Sherrod, *Tarawa,* p. 58, p. 96. Wecter, *op. cit.*, p. 468.
60. *Ibid.*, p. 486. Pyle, *Brave Men,* p. 374, p. 446. William L. Shirer, *The Rise and Fall of the Third Reich: A History of Nazi Germany* (New York: Simon and Schuster, Inc., 1960), pp. 955–956.

61. *Small Unit Action No. 6, American Forces in Action Series* (Washington, D.C.: Historical Division, War Department, 1946), pp. 1–29. *Letters from Fighting Hoosiers,* p. 142, p. 175.
62. Wecter, *op. cit.,* p. 487. *Letters from Fighting Hoosiers,* p. 142, p. 165, p. 183, p. 187.
63. T. R. Fehrenbach, *This Kind of War: A Study in Unpreparedness* (New York: The Macmillan Company, 1963), p. 162, p. 199, p. 232.
64. Smith, *The War with Mexico,* Vol. I, pp. 193–194. Bell Irvin Wiley, *The Common Soldier in the Civil War* (New York: Grosset & Dunlap, n.d.), Book I, pp. 39–43.
65. E. S. Betts to sisters, Aug., 1917, Illinois Historical Library. Palmer, *Our Greatest Battle,* p. 319.
66. Oscar Lampley to Mrs. Geo. Winn, June 26, 1918; Seaman E. C. O'Brien to *Western Illinois Courier;* Priv. Cecil R. Lee to his parents, Nov. 6, 1918: Illinois Historical Library. Maule, *War Letters,* pp. 191–192.
67. *The Best from Yank, The Army Weekly* (Cleveland, O.: The World Publishing Company, 1945), p. 122. Maule, *op. cit.,* p. 186. The Chicago *Tribune,* Oct. 27, 1966.
68. A. L. Davis Scrapbook Relating to the Puerto Rican Campaign; Priv. John Schell to Mrs. Lindsay Lloyd, Jan. 13, 1919; Lt. J. F. Smith to parents, Sept. 14, 1918: Illinois Historical Library. Pyle, *Brave Men,* pp. 399–400. Donald Marshall to his parents, Oct. 22, 1951, by permission.
69. Samuel A. Stouffer and others, *The American Soldier: Combat and Its Aftermath,* volume II of *Studies in Social Psychology in World War II* (Princeton, N. J.: Princeton University Press, 1949), p. 109.
70. Odell, *op. cit.,* p. 42. *The Best of Yank,* p. 109.
71. Dupuy, *Military Heritage of America,* p. 679. S. L. A. Marshall, "Our Army in Korea—The Best Yet," *Harper's* magazine, August, 1951.
72. Forsyth, *The Story of a Soldier,* Vol. I, p. 91.
73. Eugene Bandel, *Frontier Life in the Army, 1854–1861,* ed. by Ralph P. Bieber (Glendale, Cal.: Arthur H. Clark Company, 1932), pp. 20–21.
74. E. A. Brininstool, *Troopers With Custer: Historic Incidents of the Battle of The Little Big Horn* (Harrisburg, Pa.: The Stackpole Company, 1952), p. 36. "Leatherneck Salesmen," *Marine Corps Gazette,* Aug. 1955.
75. Sigurd J. Simonsen, *Soldier Bill* (New York: Fortuny's Publishers,

1940), p. 9. C. C. Lyon, *Experience of a Recruit in the United States Army* (Washington, D.C.: War Department, 1916), p. 3.

76. *Illinois in the World War* (Chicago: States Publication Society, 1920), Vol. I, p. 57. Samuel Stouffer and others, *The American Soldier: Adjustment During Army Life*, Vol. I of *Studies in Social Psychology in World War II* (Princeton, N. J.: Princeton University Press, 1949), p. 439. *Letters from Fighting Hoosiers*, pp. 152–153.

77. *The Best from Yank*, p. 91.

CHAPTER 2

1. Bolton, *The Private Soldier Under Washington*, p. 103.

2. Marquis de Lafayette, *Memoirs: Correspondence and Manuscripts of General Lafayette* (New York: Saunders and Otley, 1837), pp. 378–379. Quoted in Bowman, *op. cit.*, p. 61. *The Fremantle Diary: Being the Journal of Lieutenant-Colonel Arthur James Lyon Fremantle*, edited by Walter Lord (New York: Capricorn Books, 1954), p. 97.

3. The Letter Book of Armand Tuffin, Armand MSS, letters 10 and 30, pp. 2–3, Special Collections, Columbia University.

4. Lynn Montross, *Rag, Tag and Bobtail* (New York: Harper & Brothers, 1952), p. 270. John A. Palmer, *Life of Steuben* (New Haven, Conn.: Yale University Press, 1937), p. 157. *U. S. News and World Report*, Nov. 28, 1966.

5. Smith, *The War with Mexico*, I, pp. 105–108, pp. 236–237, p. 440; II, p. 164, pp. 300–301, p. 306–308.

6. Jay Luvaas, *The Military Legacy of the Civil War: The European Inheritance* (Chicago: The University of Chicago Press, 1959), p. 22. *A Collection of Civil War Writings*, ed. by Jay Luvaas (Chicago: The University of Chicago Press, 1958), pp. 154–155.

7. Quoted in *Harper's Weekly*, January 7, 1865.

8. Luvaas, *The Military Legacy of the Civil War*, pp. 16–18, pp. 48–51, pp. 53–54, p. 58, p. 141.

9. *Ibid.*, p. 97. Major-General J. F. C. Fuller, *Grant and Lee: A Study in Personality and Generalship* (Bloomington, Ind.: Indiana University Press, 1957), p. 52.

10. Arthur J. Marder, *The Anatomy of British Sea Power: A History of British Naval Policy in the Pre-Dreadnought Era, 1880–1905* (Hamden, Conn.: Archon Books, 1964), p. 255, p. 445, p. 448. Frederick T. Jane, "The Maine Disaster and After," *Fortnightly Review*, April, 1898.

11. Captain Henry Taylor, "The Indiana at Santiago," *Century Magazine,* May, 1899. Marder, *op. cit.,* p. 448.
12. *Sketches from the Spanish-American War, War Notes No. III* (Washington, D.C.: Office of Naval Intelligence, 1899), p. 9–14.
13. Walter Millis, *The Martial Spirit* (Cambridge, Mass.: The Riverside Press, 1931), pp. 291–292. *The Manchester Guardian* is quoted in *Welding of the Nation,* 1845–1900, Vol. IV of *American History Told By Contemporaries,* ed. by Albert B. Hart (New York: The Macmillan Company, 1910), p. 587.
14. *War Notes No. III,* pp. 14–20.
15. William H. Carter, *The American Army* (Indianapolis: The Bobbs-Merrill Company, Inc., 1915), p. 84.
16. *As They Saw Us: Foch, Ludendorff and Other Leaders Write Our War History,* ed. by George Sylvester Viereck (Garden City, N. Y.: Doubleday, Doran & Company, Inc., 1929), pp. 8–9.
17. Quoted in Thoumin, *The First World War,* p. 355, p. 357.
18. Gen. John J. Pershing, *My Experiences in the World War* (New York: Frederick A. Stokes Company, 1931), Vol. I, p. 91.
19. Floyd Gibbons, *And They Thought We Wouldn't Fight* (New York: George H. Doran Company, 1918), pp. 81–83. James G. Harbord, *Leaves From a War Diary* (New York: Dodd, Mead & Co., 1925), 207–208.
20. George A. B. Dewar and Lieut. Col. J. A. Boraston, *Sir Douglas Haig's Command, Dec. 19, 1915 to Nov. 11, 1918* (Boston: Houghton-Mifflin Company, 1923), pp. 279–280. *The Private Papers of Douglas Haig, 1914–1919,* ed. by Robert Blake (London: Eyre & Spottiswoode, Ltd., 1952), p. 272.
21. Cushing, *From a Surgeon's Journal,* p. 404. Frank Hitt to his family, Jan. 13, 1919, Illinois Historical Library.
22. Pershing, *op. cit.,* I, pp. 187–191.
23. R. S. Tompkins, *The Story of the Rainbow Division* (New York: Boni & Liveright, 1919), pp. 30–31. Viereck, *op. cit.,* pp. 69–71. Colonel De Chambrun and Captain De Marenches, *The American Army in the European Conflict* (New York: The Macmillan Co., 1919), p. 123.
24. Pershing, *op. cit.,* II, p. 88.
25. Chambrun, *op. cit.,* pp. 144–145, p. 153. Blake, *op. cit.,* p. 315. Viereck, *op. cit.,* p. 75, p. 133.
26. Lt. E. H. Betts to his sister, Aug. 3, 1918, Illinois Historical Library. Betts was killed a short time later. Pershing, *op. cit.,* II, pp. 66–67.
27. Quoted in Pershing, II, p. 139.
28. Chambrun, *op. cit.,* p. 164, p. 166.

29. Viereck, *op. cit.*, p. 152, p. 155. Fuller, *Grant and Lee*, p. 53.

30. Viereck, pp. 162–163. Sir George Aston, *The Biography of the Late Marshal Foch* (New York: The Macmillan Company, 1929), p. 374. Pershing, *op. cit.*, II, p. 268.

31. Cpl. Ted Fatanyaro to his family, Oct. 6, 1918, Illinois Historical Library.

32. Aston, *op. cit.*, p. 382. Blake, *op. cit.*, p. 325.

33. *The Times History of the War* (London: The *Times*, 1919), XX, pp. 57–58. Lieutenant-Colonel C. à Court Repington, *The First World War* (London: Constable & Co., Ltd., 1921), II, pp. 393–394.

34. Maurice and Lilli Swetland, *These Men: For Conspicuous Bravery Above and Beyond the Call of Duty* (Harrisburg, Pa.: The Military Service Publishing Co., 1940), p. 151. The corroboration is found in Ed Radley to Bloomington (Ill.) *Bulletin*, May 28, 1919, Illinois Historical Library. Dewar, *op. cit.*, p. 326.

35. Repington, *op. cit.*, II, p. 399, p. 397.

36. *Illinois in the World War* (Chicago: States Publication Society, 1920), I, p. 222. Cpl. Frank Mansfield to brother, July 9, 1918, Illinois Historical Library.

37. Blake, *op. cit.*, p. 329. Viereck. *op. cit.*, p. 298. Repington, *op. cit.*, III, p. 404.

38. Mangin's comment on the American troops at Château-Thierry was: "You rushed into the fight as to a fête." Quoted in Pershing, *op. cit.*, II, p. 161.

39. Viereck, *op. cit.*, p. 10, p. 133. Thoumin, *The First World War*, p. 487. *Times History of the War*, XXI, pp. 64–65. While American writers may not have stressed the American Negro's contributions to the war, none wrote in such a vein as the *Times* historian. Thoumin described the Allied assault as a powerful blow delivered by French Generals Mangin and Degoutte.

40. Winston S. Churchill, *The Second World War: The Hinge of Fate* (Boston: Houghton Mifflin Company, 1950), pp. 386–387. Omar N. Bradley, *A Soldier's Story* (New York: Henry Holt and Company, Inc., 1951), p. 58.

41. Pyle, *Brave Men*, p. 298. Dos Passos, *Tour of Duty* (Boston: Houghton Mifflin Company, 1940), pp. 316–317. The long quote is from Martin Boyle, *Yanks Don't Cry* (New York: Bernard Geis Associates, 1963), p. 124.

42. Ernie Pyle, *Here is Your War* (Cleveland: The World Publishing Company, 1945), p. 3. Harry Coles and Albert K. Weinberg, *Civil Affairs: Soldiers Become Governors*, a volume of *Special Studies:*

U.S. Army in World War II (Washington, D.C.: Department of the Army, 1964), p. 272.

43. Hanson Baldwin, "What's Wrong with the Regulars," *The Saturday Evening Post*, Oct. 31, 1953.

44. Bradley, *op. cit.*, p. 90. Churchill, *The Hinge of Fate*, p. 734. Pyle, *Here is Your War*, p. 145, p. 196.

45. Winston Churchill, *The Second World War: Closing the Ring* (Boston: Houghton Mifflin Company, 1951), p. 39.

46. Montgomery, *Normandy to the Baltic*, p. 178. In this book Montgomery modified his wartime claims about the Battle of the Bulge, saying that British troops had merely relieved the American VII Corps so that it could go forward. See Bradley, *op. cit.*, p. 488, for Churchill's statement to the Commons.

47. Maule, *War Letters*, pp. 64–65. Ladislas Farago, *Patton: Ordeal and Triumph* (New York: Ivan Obolensky, Inc., 1964), p. 763. John Masters, *The Road Past Mandalay* (New York: Harper & Brothers, 1961), p. 283.

48. Churchill, *Closing the Ring*, p. 570, p. 652. Also see Churchill's *The Hinge of Fate*, p. 254

49. British criticism of the American air effort is to be found in *The New York Times* as early as July 5, 1942. Marder, *op. cit.*, p. 540, points out that the dreadnought, for example, was just as much an American idea as a British one. For information on the logistical abilities of Americans, see Bradley, *op. cit.*, p. 39; and Churchill's *Closing the Ring*, p. 149.

50. Montgomery, *op. cit.*, p. 102, 194.

51. Dos Passos, *op. cit.*, p. 160. Masters, *op. cit.*, p. 282. *Newsweek*, April 30, 1945. Montgomery, *op. cit.*, p. vi. Cyril Falls, *The Second World War* (London: Methuen & Co., Ltd., 1948), p. 174.

52. Otto D. Tolischus, *Tokyo Record* (New York: Reynal & Hitchcock, Inc., 1943), p. 107. Dos Passos, *op. cit.*, p. 312.

53. Pyle, *Here is Your War*, p. 45.

54. Julian Bach, Jr., *America's Germany: An Account of the Occupation* (New York: Random House, Inc., 1946), p. 270. *Letters from Fighting Hoosiers*, p. 327.

55. *Time*, Jan. 1, 1951.

56. London *Daily Telegraph*, Sept. 1, 1950. The long quote comes from Andrew Geer, *The New Breed: The Story of the U. S. Marines in Korea* (New York: Harper & Brothers, 1952), p. 56.

57. *The U. S. News and World Report*, August 25, 1950.

58. *Atlas*, April, 1966, quoting *Les Temps Modernes*.

CHAPTER 3

1. Trevelyan, *The American Revolution*, I, p. 281.
2. Eric Robson, ed., *Letters From America, 1773 to 1780: Being the Letters of a Scots Officer, Sir James Murray, to his Home During the War of American Independence* (Manchester, England: Manchester University Press, 1951), p. 18. Admiral Graves, quoted in Trevelyan, *op. cit.*, I, p. 280.
3. Quoted in Bolton's, *The Private Soldier Under Washington*, p. 9, p. 14.
4. Bolton, *op. cit.*, p. 52. G. D. Scull, ed., *Memoirs and Letters of Captain W. Glanville Evelyn, of the 4th Regiment from North America, 1774–1776* (Oxford, England: James Parker and Co., 1879), p. 55.
5. Bolton, *op. cit.*, p. 92. Trevelyan, *op. cit.*, I, p. 316.
6. Peter Force, ed., *American Archives: Fourth Series* (Washington, D. C.: M. St. Clair and Peter Force, 1837–1846), V, p. 425.
7. Robson, *op. cit.*, p. 29. Force, *op. cit.*, VI, pp. 1209n–1210n.
8. Ray W. Pettengill, ed. and trans., *Letters from America, 1776–1779* (Port Washington, N. Y.: Kennikat Press, Inc., 1964), p. 89. John Burgoyne, *State of the Expedition from Canada* (London: Almon Press, 1780), p. 163.
9. Pettengill, *op. cit.*, p. 112.
10. Trevelyan, *op. cit.*, I, p. 280. Edmund Kirke, *Rear-Guard of the Revolution* (New York: Appleton & Company, Inc., 1888), p. 265. Force, *op. cit.*, I, pp. 1682–1683.
11. Trevelyan, *op. cit.*, I, p. 280.
12. Force, *op. cit.*, II, p. 1021.
13. Edgar Stanton Maclay, *Reminiscences of the Old Navy: from the Journals and Private Papers of Captain Edward Trenchard, and Rear-Admiral Stephen Decatur Trenchard* (New York: G. P. Putnam's Sons, 1898), p. 9.
14. Lossing, *Pictorial Field Book of the War of 1812*, pp. 447–448, p. 464.
15. Entry of 11 Jan., 1815, Sir John M. Tylden Journal, New York Public Library.
16. Smith, *The War with Mexico*, I, p. 105, p. 106, p. 159, pp. 160–161.
17. *Ibid.*, II, p. 54, p. 65.
18. *The Fremantle Diary*, p. 133.

19. *The Spanish–American War: War Notes No. VI* (Washington, D. C.: Office of Naval Intelligence, 1899), p. 29, p. 56.

20. *Ibid.,* p. 37. Frank Freidel, *The Splendid Little War* (New York: Bramhall House, 1958), p. 15. Millis, *The Martial Spirit,* p. 185.

21. Herbert W. Wilson, *The Downfall of Spain: Naval History of the Spanish-American War* (London: Low, Marston and Company, 1902), p. 75. *The Spanish-American War: War Notes No. I,* p. 86.

22. *Ibid.* Stephen Bonsal, *The Fight for Santiago: The Story of the Soldier in the Cuban Campaign from Tampa to the Surrender* (New York: Doubleday & McClure Co., 1899), p. 98.

23. *History of the First Division During the World War, 1917–1919,* as compiled by The Society of the First Division (Philadelphia: The John C. Winston Company, 1922), p. 211.

24. The first intelligence quote comes from Viereck, *As They Saw Us,* p. 36. The German report on the Marines is quoted in Robert Debs Heinl, Jr., *Soldiers of the Sea: The United States Marine Corps, 1775–1962* (Annapolis, Md.: The United States Naval Institute, 1962), p. 207.

25. John McGrath, *War Diary of the 354th Infantry, 89th Division* (Trier, Germany: J. Lintz, n.d.), p. 13.

26. Stallings, *The Doughboys,* p. 112, p. 163. Viereck, *op. cit.,* p. 148.

27. Benedict Crowell and Robert F. Wilson, *Demobilization: Our Industrial Demobilization After the Armistice, 1918–1920* (New Haven, Conn.: Yale University Press, 1921), p. 89.

28. Chambrun, *The American Army in the European Conflict,* pp. 275–276. Viereck, *op. cit.,* pp. 39–40. *Current History,* June 20, 1918.

29. Ralph H. Lutz, ed., *Fall of the German Empire, 1914–1918: Documents of the German Revolution* (Palo Alto, Calif.: Stanford University Press, 1932), II, p. 478. Viereck, *op. cit.,* p. 231, p. 286.

30. All quotes from *Candid Comment on the American Soldier, 1917–1918 . . . by the Germans* (AEF, 1919), Records of the War Department, General Staff Record Group 165 (The National Archives, National Archives and Record Service, General Services Administration, Washington, D. C., 1967).

31. Viereck, *op. cit.,* p. 30, p. 41.

32. Crown Prince William of Germany, *My War Experiences* (London: Hurst and Blackett, 1922), pp. 317–323. Viereck, *op. cit.,* p. 124.

33. Japan *Advertiser,* January 17, 1934. Robert J. C. Butow, *Tojo and the Coming of the War* (Princeton, N. J.: Princeton University Press, 1961), p. 18.

34. Mark Gayn, *Japan Diary* (New York: William Sloane Associates,

1948), p. 35. Shirer, *The Rise and Fall of the Third Reich* (New York: Simon and Schuster, Inc., 1960), p. 875n. Hans Louis Trefousse, ed., *What Happened at Pearl Harbor? Documents Pertaining to the Japanese Attack of December 7, 1941, and Its Background* (New York: Twayne Publishers, Inc., 1958), p. 247, pp. 250–251.

35. John Deane Potter, *Yamamoto* (New York: The Viking Press, Inc., 1965), p. 35, p. 41, p. 43. Masatake Okumiya and Jiro Horikoshi, with Martin Caidin, *Zero* (New York: E. P. Dutton & Co., Inc., 1956), p. 61. The two sources are used here to further confirm Yamamoto's doubt about the war.

36. "The True Story of Pearl Harbor," *U. S. News and World Report,* December 11, 1961. Potter, *op. cit.,* p. 44.

37. *U. S. News and World Report,* December 11, 1961. Trefousse, *op. cit.,* p. 259. Tolischus, *Through Japanese Eyes,* pp. 7–8. Potter, *op. cit.,* p. 129.

38. Victor Hicken, "America Drifted," The Chicago *Tribune,* December 4, 1966.

39. See Shirer, *op. cit.,* p. 873, for "monumental miscalculations" of Nazis. Robert Sherwood, *Roosevelt and Hopkins: An Intimate History* (New York: Harper & Brothers, 1948), p. 357, p. 441. Trefousse, *op. cit.,* p. 267.

40. Otto Dietrich, *Hitler,* trans. by Richard and Clara Winston (Chicago: Henry Regnery Company, 1955), p. 167. B. H. Liddell Hart, *The Rommel Papers,* trans. by Paul Findlay (New York: Harcourt, Brace and Company, Inc., 1953), p. 295. Rommel's papers, which will be quoted extensively herein, were edited by Liddell Hart in an interesting and somewhat biased manner.

41. Dietrich, *op. cit.,* p. 167.

42. Potter, *op. cit.,* p. 82. Tolischus, *op. cit.,* p. 151, p. 111. Butow, *op. cit.,* p. 412. Gayn, *op cit.,* pp. 100–101.

43. These quotes come from Tolischus, *op. cit.,* p. 112, p. 164, p. 166. The last, concerning the "untrained and undisciplined" Americans, comes from the Japan *Times and Advertiser,* January 9, 1942.

44. *Ibid.,* December 23, 1941.

45. Butow, *op. cit.,* pp. 19–20. Potter, *op. cit.,* p. 154. *United States Submarine Losses* (Washington, D. C.: Naval History Division, Office of Chief of Naval Operations, 1963), p. 3.

46. *The Best of Yank,* p. 56. Sherrod, *Tarawa,* p. 136. Potter, *op. cit.,* p. 298. Toshikazu Kase, *Journey to the Missouri,* ed. by David Nelson Rowe (New Haven, Conn.: Yale University Press, 1950), p. 75, p. 78. Butow, *op. cit.,* pp. 425–426.

47. *St. Lo (7 July–19 July, 1944): American Forces in Action Series* (Washington, D. C.: Historical Division, War Department, 1946), p. 8, p. 50, p. 100. Pyle, *Brave Men*, pp. 379–380.
48. Dietrich, *op. cit.*, p. 99. *Decisive Battles of World War II: The German View*, trans. by Edward Fitzgerald, and ed. by H. A. Jacobson and J. Rohwer (New York: G. P. Putnam's Sons, 1965), p. 402.
49. Ernst Kris and Hans Speier, *German Radio Propaganda: Report on Home Broadcasts During the War* (New York: Oxford University Press, 1944), pp. 227–228, pp. 239–240, p. 252. *The Goebbels Diaries*, ed. by Louis P. Lochner (New York: The Fireside Press Inc., 1948), p. 244.
50. Kris and Speier, *op. cit.*, p. 229, pp. 239–240.
51. "Military Operations Against American Troops in Africa," trans. from Russian and German, by courtesy of General Services Administration and The National Archives, Washington, D. C. *The Rommel Papers*, p. 366, p. 407, p. 404, p. 408, p. 521. On p. 523 Rommel states that "The Americans . . . profited far more than the British from their experience in Africa. . . ."
52. Adolf Galland, *The First and the Last* (New York: Ballantine Books, Inc., 1957), p. 195. *Decisive Battles of World War II*, pp. 411–412, pp. 418–419. *Small Unit Actions*, p. 189.
53. Kase, *op. cit.*, p. 7.
54. Okumiya and Horikoshi, *op. cit.*, p. 234. Mitsuo Fuchida and Masatake Okumiya, *Midway: The Battle That Doomed Japan* (New York: Ballantine Press, Inc., orig. copyright, U. S. Naval Institute, 1955), p. 212.
55. Taken from Writings of German Officers by Department of Defense, used here through courtesy of General Services Administration and The National Archives.
56. *Ibid.*
57. Falls, *The Second World War*, p. 296.
58. *The Rommel Papers*, p. 295.
59. Higgins, *War in Korea*, p. 219.
60. Geer, *The New Breed*, p. 40, pp. 225–226. *U. S. News and World Report*, March 13, 1953. Higgins, *op. cit.*, p. 181.
61. The Chicago *Tribune*, November 12, 1966.
62. Trang Cong Tuong, "The Aggressors Will Not Escape Retribution," *International Affairs*, Moscow Edition, July, 1966. Tregaskis, *Vietnam Diary*, p. 327. The Giap statement comes from a translation in *Atlas*, April, 1966.
63. *International Affairs*, Moscow Edition, October, 1965. *Current Digest of Soviet Press*, XVII, No. 15, p. 25 (taken from *Izvestia*, 14

April, 1965). The comment on the Marines comes from *International Relations*, October, 1965.

64. *Current Digest of Soviet Press*, XVI, No. 25, p. 19 (taken from *Pravda*).

65. *Ibid.* See also: *Current Digest of Soviet Press*, XVI, No. 25, p. 19; and same for 4 and 24 Nov., 1965.

66. Material on U. S. Navy comes from *Ibid.*, XVIII, No. 2, pp. 28–29.

67. Georges Blond, *The Death of Hitler's Germany*, trans. by Frances Frenaye (New York: Pyramid Books, 1958), p. 93.

CHAPTER 4

1. Stanley M. Pargellis, *Lord Loudoun in North America* (New Haven: Yale University Press, 1933), p. 114.

2. Dickinson, *The Building of An Army*, p. 27. Harbord, *Leaves From a Diary*, p. 87. Sherrod, *Tarawa*, p. 32. Patton is quoted by William B. Huie, *The Execution of Private Slovak: The Hitherto Secret Story of the Only American Soldier Since 1864 to Be Shot for Desertion* (New York: Duell, Sloan & Pearce, 1954), p. 15.

3. Harriet J. Walker, *Revolutionary Soldiers Buried in Illinois* (Los Angeles: Standard Printing Co., 1917), p. 91.

4. Lowe, *Five Years a Dragoon*, pp. 4–5. Stillwell, *The Story of a Soldier*, pp. 14–15. Gerhard P. Clausius, "The Little Soldier of the 95th: Albert D. J. Cashier," *Journal of the Illinois Historical Society*, LI, No. 4, pp. 380–387.

5. Benjamin J. Gould, *Investigations in the Military and Anthropological Statistics of American Soldiers* (New York: U. S. Sanitary Commission, 1869), p. 34, pp. 86–88. Wiley, *The Common Soldier in the Civil War*, p. 303.

6. Bonsal, *The Fight For Santiago*, p. 391. Odell, *The New Spirit*, pp. 30–31.

7. *Physical Examination of the First Million Draft Recruits: Methods and Results* (Washington, D. C.: U. S. Medical Department, 1919), p. 15, p. 331. Cushing, *From a Surgeon's Journal*, pp. 375–377.

8. Frederick L. Allen, *The Big Change* (New York: Harper & Brothers, 1952), pp. 203–204. *The Commonwealth*, XIX, No. 21, p. 279. Kendall Banning, *Our Army Today* (New York: Funk & Wagnalls Company, 1943), pp. 4–7. R. R. Palmer, B. I. Wiley, and W. R. Keast, *The Procurement and Training of Ground Combat Troops, United States Army in World War II* (Washington, D. C.: Department of the Army, 1948), p. 3.

9. *What the Soldier Thinks* (Washington, D. C.: War Department, 1945), n. p. Allen, *op. cit.,* pp. 203–204. Bernard D. Karpinos, "Curent Height and Weight of Youths of Military Age," reprint from *Human Biology,* December, 1961, pp. 335–353.
10. Pyle, *Brave Men,* p. 49.
11. The material on the landing craft crews comes from author's own experiences. Also see *Statistical Abstract,* p. 269, and Karpinos, *loc. cit.*
12. Marshall, *War Reports,* p. 273.
13. E. E. Hale, "Naval History of the Revolution," *Proceedings of the American Antiquarian Society* (Worcester, Mass.: By the Society, 1889), p. 389, pp. 393–394. One might also note the aggressiveness of John Paul Jones in raiding Whitehaven on the British coast.
14. Lossing, *Pictorial Field Book of the War of 1812,* pp. 1005–1008.
15. Smith, *The War with Mexico,* I, p. 123, pp. 193–194.
16. Victor Hicken, *Illinois in the Civil War* (Urbana, Ill.: University of Illinois Press, 1966), pp. 74–75. Ira Blanchard, "Recollections of Civil War Service with the 20th Illinois," Typed manuscript, Illinois Historical Library, p. 30.
17. John Wilcox to his wife, Jan. 27, May 22, 1862, Wilcox Collection, Illinois Historical Library. Robert H. Strong, *A Yankee Private's Civil War* (Chicago: Henry Regnery Company, 1961), p. 20. E. H. Ingraham to niece, May 12, 1864, E. H. Ingraham Papers, Illinois Historical Library. *Three Years in the Army of the Cumberland: The Letters and Diary of Major James A. Connolly,* ed. by Paul M. Angle (Bloomington, Ind.: Indiana University Press, 1959), p. 240.
18. Charles J. Post, *The Little War of Private Post* (Boston: Little, Brown & Company, 1960), p. 184. Scrapbook of A. L. Davis relating to 3rd Ill. Vols., Illinois Historical Library.
19. Viereck, *As Others Saw Us,* pp. 296–297. Tompkins, *The Story of the Rainbow Division,* p. 89, p. 248. The Rainbow Division, in all of its fighting, took only 1,317 German prisoners.
20. Pershing, *op. cit.,* II, pp. 181–187. Palmer, *Our Greatest Battle,* p. 29. Harbord, *op. cit.,* pp. 303–304, pp. 329–330.
21. Cushing, *op. cit.,* p. 392. Gibbons, *And They Thought We Wouldn't Fight,* p. 263.
22. E. S. Betts to his sisters, April 4, 1918, Betts Collection; W. L. Buckner to friend, July 8, 1918, World War I Collection: Illinois Historical Library.
23. Ralph Capes to family, Sept. 24, 1918; Herbert Hessel to family,

Nov. 11, 1918: World War I Collection, Illinois Historical Library.

24. Maule, *War Letters*, p. 269. *War Reports*, pp. 690–691.

25. *Letters from Fighting Hoosiers*, p. 4. Maule, *op. cit.*, p. 194, p. 196. *The Best of Yank*, p. 117.

26. Maule, *op. cit.*, p. 115. *War Reports*, p. 363. Pyle, *Brave Men*, p. 330.

27. *Letters from Fighting Hoosiers*, p. 3. Charlton Ogburn, Jr., *The Marauders* (New York: Harper & Brothers, 1956), p. 90.

28. Sgt. Landes to his parents, June 21, 1944, Landes Collection, Illinois Historical Library. Maule, *War Letters*, p. 193. *Letters from Fighting Hoosiers*, p. 364.

29. *The Best from Yank*, p. 6, p. 17, p. 146. Ogburn, *op. cit.*, pp. 171–172, p. 111. *Newsweek*, Mar. 5, 1945, reported that Marines had been killed in crouching position.

30. Ogburn, *op. cit.*, p. 130. The story of the Jewish boy was commonly told in the Pacific theater.

31. Major B. C. Wright, *The 1st Cavalry Division in World War II* (Tokyo: Toppan Printing Co., 1947), p. 92, p. 155. *War Reports*, pp. 276–277.

32. *Small Unit Study No. 7*, p. 33, pp. 91–92.

33. *Small Unit Study No. 5*, p. 29.

34. *Small Unit Study No. 7*, pp. 44–45.

35. Farago, *Patton*, p. 414. *Small Unit Study No. 7*, p. 77, p. 90. *Small Unit Study No. 5*, pp. 4–8, p. 21.

36. *Small Unit Study No. 3*, p. 12. *Letters from Fighting Hoosiers*, p. 196.

37. Morris Janowitz, *The Professional Soldier: A Social and Political Portrait* (Glencoe, Ill.: The Free Press, 1960), p. 41. *The Best from Yank*, p. 55, p. 56.

38. Don Marshall to his parents, Feb. 20, 1945, by permission. *The Best From Yank*, pp. 91–93.

39. Stouffer, *The American Soldier*, I, p. 170, p. 331. Janowitz, *op. cit.*, p. 41.

40. *The Best from Yank*, p. 217. Maule, *op. cit.*, p. 113.

41. S. L. A. Marshall, "Our Army in Korea—The Best Yet," *Harper's* magazine, Aug., 1951, pp. 21–27. *Look* magazine, May 28, 1957, p. 39, pp. 35–43.

42. Geer, *The New Breed*, p. 179. *U. S. News and World Report*, Oct. 5, 1951.

43. Don Marshall to his parents, Nov. 27, 1950, by permission.

44. *Time*, Jan. 1, 1951. Don Marshall to parents, Sept. 6, 1951, Jan. 10, 1952, by permission.

45. Mark W. Clark, *From the Danube to the Yalu* (New York: Harper & Brothers, 1954), p. 29. Clark says 142 sons of American generals were in Korea; 35 of them were casualties. Heinl, *Soldiers of the Sea*, p. 587.

46. William S. White, "The End of the Old Army," *Harper's* magazine, June, 1959.

47. *U. S. News and World Report*, Nov. 28, 1966.

48. Pargellis, *op. cit.*, pp. 299–300. Trevelyan, *The American Revolution*, I, p. 307. Burgoyne, *State of the Expedition*, p. 163.

49. Fred J. Cook, *What Manner of Men: Forgotten Heroes of the American Revolution* (New York: William Morrow & Company, Inc., 1959), p. 94, p. 101.

50. J. Fair Smith to parents, Sept. 20, 1918, World War I Collection, Illinois Historical Library.

51. *The Best from Yank*, p. 53, pp. 124–125. *Letters from Fighting Hoosiers*, p. 196. Ogburn, *op. cit.*, p. 171.

52. *Time*, Sept. 16, 1966. *Associated Press*, Dec. 3, 1966.

53. Friedel, *The Splendid Little War*, p. 230. W. O. Stevens and A. Westcott, *A History of Sea Power* (New York: Doubleday, Doran & Company, Inc., 1920), p. 286.

54. Chambrun, *The American Army in the European Conflict*, p. 164. Viereck, *op. cit.*, pp. 37–38. *Candid Comment on the American Soldier*, p. 11, p. 15.

55. Charles S. Nichols, Jr. and Henry I. Shaw, *Okinawa: Victory in the Pacific* (Washington, D. C.: Historical Branch, U. S. Marine Corps, 1955), p. 103, p. 124.

56. *The Best From Yank*, p. 52. Wright, *op. cit.*, p. 99.

57. Pyle, *Brave Men*, p. 97. *Letters from Fighting Hoosiers*, p. 56.

58. Pyle, *Here Is Your War*, p. 115. *Rommel Papers*, p. 491.

59. *Letters from Fighting Hoosiers*, p. 168. *War Reports*, p. 261.

60. Fehrenbach, *This Kind of War*, p. 487.

61. Earl C. Ewert, *The United States Army*, with foreword by Hanson W. Baldwin (Boston: Little, Brown & Company, 1941), p. 32.

62. Quoted in *Newsweek*, April 30, 1945.

63. *War Reports*, p. 369.

64. Robert S. Johnson with Martin Caidin, *Thunderbolt!* (New York: Ballantine Books, Inc., 1963), p. 221.

65. Clark, *op. cit.*, p. 208.

66. Smith, *op. cit.*, I, pp. 275–276. Churchill, *Closing the Ring*, p. 149. Col. Randolph Leigh, *48 Million Tons to Eisenhower: The Role of the SOS in the Defeat of Germany* (Washington, D. C.: The Infantry Journal, 1945), p. 37, p. 66.

67. Sherrod, *op. cit.*, p. ix. Masters, *The Road Past Mandalay*, p. 282. Masters, an Englishman, says that the Americans achieved "real miracles" in Burma. *Newsweek*, Feb. 19, 1945.

CHAPTER 5

1. Lonn, *Foreigners in the Union Army and Navy*, p. 88.
2. R. Glisan, *Journal of Army Life* (San Francisco: A. L. Bancroft and Co., 1874), p. 120.
3. Lonn, *op. cit.*, pp. 83–85. Don Rickey, Jr., *Forty Miles a Day on Beans and Hay: The Enlisted Soldier Fighting the Indian Wars* (Norman, Okla.: Univ. of Oklahoma Press, 1963), p. 51.
4. Louis Pelzer, *Marches of the Dragoons in the Mississippi Valley* (Iowa City, Iowa: State Historical Society of Iowa, 1917), p. 47.
5. Lowe, *Five Years a Dragoon*, p. 60, p. 75.
6. Bandel, *Frontier Life in the Army*, p. 266.
7. Forsyth, *The Story of the Soldier*, p. 231, pp. 331–33. Soldiers on the frontier rarely knew they had been awarded the Medal of Honor until they found it on their bunks.
8. James R. Jacobs, *The Beginning of the U. S. Army: 1783–1812* (Princeton, N. J.: Princeton University Press, 1947), p. 125. Lowe, *op. cit.*, p. 38. C. C. Lyon, *Experience of a Recruit in the United States Army* (Washington: War Department, 1916), p. 13.
9. Jacobs, *op. cit.*, pp. 257–260. Williams, *Americans at War*, p. 18.
10. Sherwood, *Roosevelt and Hopkins*, pp. 381–382.
11. *Associated Press* Dispatch, Oct. 13, 1966.
12. The Chicago *Tribune*, June 9, 1917.
13. York killed 25 Germans, captured 135, and cleaned out 35 machine-gun nests. Sergeant Charles Kelly (World War II) killed 40 Germans at Salerno. Hayes died a tragic death. Even Audie Murphy, the most decorated American in World War II, has given away most of his medals.
14. Janowitz, *The Professional Soldier*, p. 227. The attitude of Americans toward their professional soldiers in uniform, and their professional soldiers in politics is almost impossible to analyze.
15. Palmer, *America in Arms*, p. 87. Hull's surrender of Detroit was blamed on the fact that he only had 300 Regulars—the rest being volunteers and militia. Actually, the British who opposed him had only 320 Regulars—the remainder of their soldiers being volunteers and Indians.
16. Gibbons, *And They Thought We Wouldn't Fight*, p. 245. Joseph L.

Schott, *Above and Beyond: The Story of the Congressional Medal of Honor* (New York: G. P. Putnam's Sons, 1963), pp. 99–100. Woodfill, whom Pershing called the "greatest soldier in the A.E.F." cleaned out five machine-gun nests in France. He died just a few years ago; little attention being given to his demise by the press.

17. Bonsal, *The Fight for Santiago*, p. 43. Priv. A. H. Mauley to his uncle, April 4, 1919, Illinois Historical Library's World War I Collection.

18. Palmer, *Our Greatest Battle*, p. 430. It has been estimated that, in March of 1918, there were 700,000 Americans of draft age who could not write in English.

19. Schott, *op. cit.,* pp. 195–200. *Letters from Fighting Hoosiers*, p. 33. Stouffer, *The American Soldier*, I, pp. 212–213.

20. *The Saturday Review*, Nov. 10, 1945. The feeling between volunteer and Annapolis officers in the Navy was deeply antagonistic, partially because of the notion on the part of the former that the service academy men were draft-dodgers.

21. Stouffer, *op. cit.,* pp. 76–77, p. 63, p. 61, p. 65.

22. Don Marshall to his parents, Nov. 13, 1950, Aug. 24, 1951, by permission.

23. Fehrenbach, *This Kind of War*, p. 607.

24. Stanley Pargellis, ed., *Military Affairs in North America* (New York: D. Appleton-Century Company, Inc., 1936), p. 241. Pargellis, *Lord Loudoun in North America*, p. 334, p. 128.

25. Lt. Col. Samuel Smith to General Washington, Sept. 27, 1777, Smith Collection, Columbia University Library. *Writings of Washington*, VII, p. 219; XIII, p. 96.

26. Bowman, *Morale in the Revolutionary Army*, pp. 73–74, p. 90. Smith, *The War With Mexico*, II, p. 190.

27. Pelzer, *op. cit.,* pp. 1–2. Glisan, *op. cit.,* pp. 105–106.

28. Wiley, *The Life of Billy Yank*, pp. 205–206.

29. Donald W. Mitchell, *History of the Modern American Navy: from 1883 Through Pearl Harbor* (New York: Alfred A. Knopf, 1946), pp. 31–32.

30. Bonsal, *op. cit.,* p. 391.

31. Wecter, *When Johnny Comes Marching Home*, p. 293. See *The New York Times*, March 9, 1927, for information on behavior of the 24th Infantry Regiment. Priv. George Nevill to Sam Nevill, Sept. 2, 1918, Illinois Historical Library, tells of self-inflicted wounds among Marines.

32. Bradley, *A Soldier's Story*, pp. 44–45. Ralph Lewis, "Officer-En-

listed Men's Relationships," *The American Journal of Sociology,* Jan., 1947.

33. Huie, *The Execution of Private Slovik,* pp. 11–12.

34. *Newsweek,* April 23, 1945.

35. Fehrenbach, *op. cit.,* p. 120, goes into detail on discipline in Korea. Also see p. 342, same source, for quotations.

36. *U. S. News and World Report,* Jan. 23, 1953.

37. The McKeon case is discussed in *Time,* July 30, 1956. Hanson Baldwin, "Our Fighting Men Have Gone Soft," *Saturday Evening Post,* Aug. 8, 1959. Bladwin states that military authorities were having much difficulty with venereal disease in the Army, and with black marketeering.

38. *U.S. News and World Report,* Nov. 28, 1966.

39. Lowe, *op. cit.,* pp. 151–152. Bandel, *op. cit.,* p. 114. Maclay, *Reminiscences of the Old Navy,* p. 89.

40. *The Civil War Letters of Henry C. Bear: A Soldier in the 116th Illinois Volunteer Infantry,* ed. by Wayne C. Temple (Harrogate, Tenn.: Lincoln Memorial University Press, 1961), p. 7. John Neff to Gov. Yates of Illinois, Oct. 30, 1863, Yates Collection, Illinois Historical Library.

41. Priv. Reuben Prentice to Lovina Eyster, Oct. 6, 1861, Prentice Collection, Illinois Historical Library. Diary of James Howlett, n.p., Illinois Historical Library.

42. Gibbons, *op. cit.,* p. 244. Priv. Leo A. Schopp to sister, Jan. 24, 1919, World War I Collection, Illinois Historical Library. Priv. Clyde Sisson to Centralia (Illinois) *Evening Sentinel,* April, 1919, Illinois Historical Library.

43. Sullivan, *Our Times,* V, p. 655.

44. *The New York Times,* July 1, 1942.

45. Johnson, *Thunderbolt!,* p. 96, p. 98. Ogburn, *The Marauders,* p. 63. Wright, *The 1st Cav. in World War II,* p. 99.

46. Tregaskis, *Vietnam Diary,* p. 195.

47 David McFarland to his wife, Feb. 2, 1862, McFarland Collection, Illinois Historical Library. Cushing, *From a Surgeon's Journal,* p. 508.

48. Jacobs, *op. cit.,* p. 129.

49. Wiley, *The Life of Johnny Reb,* pp. 55–56.

50. Luther H. Gulick, *From Morals and Morale* (New York: Association Press, 1919), pp. 103–105.

51. Civil War Diaries of Charles W. Wills, Illinois Historical Library. Peter Weyhrick to D. C. Smith, Jan. 30, 1863, D. C. Smith Collection, Illinois Historical Library.

52. Sherrod, *Tarawa*, p. 39.
53. *The Civil War Letters of Sergeant Onley Andrus*, ed. by Fred Shannon (Urbana: University of Illinois Press, 1947), p. 23, p. 69.
54. *Ibid.*, p. 96. Wecter, *op. cit.*, p. 338, p. 483, pp. 497–498.
55. Maule, *War Letters*, p. 55. *Letters from Fighting Hoosiers*, p. 327. George S. Patton, Jr., *War As I Knew It* (Boston: Houghton Mifflin Company, 1947), p. 337.
56. *What the Soldier Thinks*, pp. 5–6.
57. Ogburn, *op. cit.*, p. 233. Maule, *op. cit.*, p. 320. Vera Lynn, who sang much in the style of Julie Andrews, was very popular with American soldiers. Wiley, *The Life of Billy Yank*, p. 273; *The Life of Johnny Reb*, pp. 161–163.
58. The Greenwell diaries, The New York Public Library, by permission.
59. Maule, *op. cit.*, p. 114. Cpl. M. L. Miles to his aunt, Nov. 14, 1944, Miles Collection, Illinois Historical Library.
60. Don Marshall to family, Sept. 7, 1951, by permission.
61. Bandel, *op. cit.*, p. 105.
62. Cpl. M. L. Miles to aunt, n.d., Miles Collection, Illinois Historical Library. The soccer-football game, witnessed by this writer, lasted about a week, and was played over possibly mined ground.
63. C. J. Post, *The Little War of Private Post*, p. 98.
64. Clarence Hart to Mrs. John Hart, July 29, 1918; Lt. R. E. Farmer to parents, Feb. 19, 1919: World War I Collection, Illinois Historical Library.
65. There were dozens of other songs of course, among them verses too bawdy to repeat.
66. Marshall, "Our Army in Korea," *Harper's,* Aug., 1951. Tregaskis, *Vietnam Diary*, p. 85.
67. Ira Payne to parents, Sept. 21, 1862, Payne Collection, Illinois Historical Library. Seaman Verne Miller to father, Feb. 7, 1918, Illinois Historical Library.
68. Sigurd J. Simonsen, *Soldier Bill* (New York: Fortuny's Publishers, 1938), p. 47. H. Landes to parents, July 22, 1944, Landes Collection, Illinois Historical Library. O. P. Miles to his aunt, Aug. 19, 1918, Miles Collection, Illinois Historical Library.
69. Bandel, *op. cit.*, p. 289, p. 234. Sam Gordon to wife, Sept. 26, 1862, Gordon Collection, Illinois Historical Library.
70. All quotes come from the Greenwell diary, New York Public Library, by permission.
71. M. L. Miles to aunt, n.d., Miles Collection, Illinois Historical Library.

72. Payson Shumway to his wife, Jan. 4, 1863, Shumway Letters, Illinois Historical Library. Wells' diaries, Illinois Historical Library.
73. *Letters from Fighting Hoosiers,* p. 61. *Small Unit Action No. 7,* p. 75. Priv. H. Landes to parents, Oct. 8, 1941, Landes Collection, Illinois Historical Library.
74. Glisan, *op. cit.,* p. 81. Don Marshall to parents, Dec. 23, 1951, by permission.
75. Maule, *op. cit.,* pp. 252–253.
76. *The United States Navy in Peace Time: The Navy in Its Relation to the Industrial, Scientific, Economic, and Political Development of the Nation* (Washington: Navy Department, 1931), p. 143. The 1931 findings are probably still true today, with many of the nation's policemen coming from the services. McNamara's comments are detailed in *U. S. News and World Report,* Sept. 5, 1966.

CHAPTER 6

1. *The Writings of George Washington from the Original Manuscript Sources, 1745–1799,* ed. by John C. Fitzpatrick, VI, pp. 106–115.
2. Virgil G. Way, *History of the Thirty-Third Regiment Illinois Veteran Volunteer Infantry on the Civil War* (Gibson City, Ill.: Regimental Association, 1902), p. 24.
3. Millis, *The Martial Spirit,* pp. 285–286.
4. Quoted in Frank Friedel's *Our Country's Presidents* (Washington, D.C.: National Geographic Society, 1966), p. 206.
5. Maule, *War Letters,* p. 110.
6. Marshall's statement is in *War Reports,* p. 261. It reads: "The American soldier has a very active imagination and usually, at least for the time being, covets anything new and is inclined to endow the death-dealing weapons of the enemy with extraordinary qualities since any weapon seems much more formidable to the man receiving than to the man delivering."
7. Maule, *op. cit.,* p. 186. Pyle, *Brave Men,* p. 401. *The Best From Yank,* pp. 149–150.
8. Don Marshall to parents, n.d., by permission. Higgins, *War in Korea,* p. 204.
9. The Chicago *Tribune,* Sept. 1, 1966.
10. Oglesby to Ord, July 10, 1862, Richard Oglesby Collection, Illinois Historical Library.
11. Pershing, *My Experiences in the World War,* I, p. 137.
12. Leigh, *48 Million Tons for Eisenhower,* p. 106.

13. *The Best from Yank,* p. 10. Pyle, *op. cit.,* p. 367, reaffirms my own knowledge of the Omaha Beach landing.
14. *Fuehrer Confederences: On Matters Dealing with the German Navy* (Washington, D. C.: Office of Naval Intelligence, 1947), p. 155.
15. *Time,* Jan. 1, 1951. *U. S. News and World Report,* June 1, 1951, reported that only one out of every five soldiers would fire during fight.
16. Don Marshall to his parents, Nov. 25, Dec. 22, 1951, by permission.
17. John Adams to Abigail Adams, Aug. 24, 1777, *Familiar Letters of John Adams to His Wife, Abigail Adams,* ed. by Chas. F. Adams (New York: n.p., 1876), p. 298. Bolton, *The Private Soldier Under Washington,* p. 226.
18. Way, *op. cit.,* p. 39.
19. Gibbons, *And They Thought We Wouldn't Fight,* pp. 81–83, p. 155.
20. *Candid Comment on the American Soldier,* 1917–1918, p. 17.
21. *Omaha Beachhead (6 June–13 June): American Forces in Action Series* (Washington, D. C.: Historical Division, War Department, 1945), p. 39, p. 58.
22. *St-Lo, American Forces in Action Series,* p. 125, p. 76.
23. Wright, *The 1st Cav. Division in World War II,* p. 33. Howard Donner, *The Spearhead: The World War II History of the 5th Marine Division* (Washington, D. C.: Infantry Journal, 1950), p. 95.
24. *Small Unit Action No. 3,* p. 4. *The Best from Yank,* p. 76, p. 53.
25. *War Reports,* p. 322, p. 387.
26. Wecter, *When Johnny Comes Marching Home,* p. 491. Maule, *op. cit.,* p. 186. *The Best from Yank,* ix. Pyle, *op. cit.,* p. 372.
27. Any newcomers landing on Saipan or Tinian after the islands were secured were deluged by GI's who were selling trinkets.
28. Marshall, "Our Army in Korea," *Harper's,* Aug., 1951. Geer, *The New Breed,* p. 258. *Time,* Jan. 1, 1951. St. Louis *Post-Dispatch,* Nov. 8, 1966. Westmoreland is quoted in *Look,* Oct. 18, 1966.
29. Lt. Col. Samuel Smith to Gen'l Washington, 26 Sept., 1777, Smith Collection, Columbia University. Bolton, *op. cit.,* p. 84, p. 54.
30. Lowe, *Five Years a Dragoon,* pp. 107–108.
31. William Strawn to Newton Bateman, Nov. 12, 1863, Bateman Collection, Illinois Historical Library.
32. Bradley, *A Soldier's Story,* p. 475. Col. Charles N. Hunter, *Galahad* (San Antonio: Naylor Co., 1963), pp. 69–70, p. 131. The capture of Myitkyina was considered important during Stilwell's Burma campaign.

33. The Detroit *News*, Aug. 14, 1966.
34. Marshall, "Our Army in Korea," *Harper's*, Aug., 1951. Don Marshall to his parents, Nov. 2, 1951, by permission.
35. Marshall, "Our Army in Korea," *Harper's*, Aug., 1951.
36. Way, *op. cit.*, p. 45. Fuller, *Grant and Lee*, p. 53.
37. Brininstool, *Troopers with Custer*, pp. 217–218. D. Alexander Brown, *The Galvanized Yankees* (Urbana: Univ. of Illinois Press, 1963), p. 188.
38. Elmer F. Straub, *A Sergeant's Diary in the World War* (Indianapolis: Indiana Historical Commission, 1923), p. 210. Sarah Harley to Miss Brock, Oct. 20, 1918, World War I Collection, Illinois Historical Library.
39. Pyle, *Here Is Your War*, p. 108. *Small Unit Study No. 7.*
40. Pyle, *Brave Men*, pp. 50–51.
41. Hunter, *op. cit.*, p. 156, p. 160. Heinl, *Soldiers of the Sea*, p. 394.
42. Two long quotes are from: *Fighting for America*, ed. by Nathan C. Balth (New York: National Jewish Welfare Board, 1944), p. 71; and *Letters from Fighting Hoosiers*, p. 270. The material on the *Yorktown* is taken from Potter's *Yamamoto*, p. 236. The nurse's comment comes from Jacob Rader Marcus, *Memoirs of American Jews, 1775–1865* (Philadelphia: The Jewish Publication Society of America, 1955), I, p. 196.
43. St. Louis *Post-Dispatch*, Aug. 7, 1966.
44. Albigence Waldo, "Journal," *Pennsylvania Magazine of History*, XXI, pp. 308–309. John Seaton, "The Battle of Belmont," *War Talks in Kansas: A Series of Papers Read Before the Kansas Commandery* (Kansas City, Mo.: Hudson Publishing Co., 1906), p. 4. *The Civil War Letters of Sergeant Onley Andrus*, ed. by Fred Shannon (Urbana: University of Illinois Press, 1947), p. 118. E. H. Ingraham to aunt, May 21, 1863, Ingraham Collection, Illinois Historical Library. Strong, *A Yankee Private's Civil War*, p. 119.
45. Mary Livermore, *My Story of the War: A Woman's Narrative of Four Years Personal Experience* (Hartford, Conn.: A. D. Worthington, 1889), p. 674.
46. Lyman Needham to brother, Oct. 20, 1861, Needham Collection, Illinois Historical Library. *Warfare Along the Mississippi: The Letters of Lieutenant Colonel George E. Currie*, ed. by Norman E. Clarke (Mt. Pleasant, Mich.: Central Michigan University Press, 1961), pp. 24–28. Leander Stillwell, "In the Ranks at Shiloh," *Journal of the Illinois Historical Society*, XV, Nos. 1–2, pp. 474–475.

47. Lt. J. Fair Smith to parents, Sept. 26, 1918, World War I Collection, Illinois Historical Library.
48. Palmer, *Our Greatest Battle*, p. 80. Priv. Herb Hessel to father, Sept. 18, 1918; Lt. J. Fair Smith to parents, Sept. 14, 1918, Nov. 9, 1918: Illinois Historical Library.
49. Pyle, *Here Is Your War*, p. 145. Pyle, *Brave Men*, p. 270. *Letters from Fighting Hoosiers*, p. 15. Maule, *War Letters*, p. 182.
50. *St-Lo*, p. 125. *Small Unit Action No. 3*, p. 24.
51. Maule, *op. cit.*, p. 260. Maule, *op. cit.*, p. 28. *Letters from Fighting Hoosiers*, p. 245, p. 71, p. 168.
52. Bradley, *op. cit.*, p. 491.
53. Don Marshall to family, Jan., 1952, by permission. Higgins, *War In Korea*, p. 142, 182.
54. Bowman, *The Morale of the American Revolutionary Army*, p. 39. James Collins, *Autobiography of a Revolutionary Soldier*, ed. by John M. Roberts (Clinton, La.: Feliciana (La.) Democrat, 1859), pp. 259–261.
55. *Three Years in the Army of the Cumberland: The Letters and Diary of Major James A. Connally*, p. 22, p. 124. "With Grant at Vicksburg: From the Civil War Diary of Captain Charles E. Wilcox," ed. by Edgar Erickson, *Journal of the Illinois State Historical Society*, XXX, No. 4 (Jan., 1938), pp. 479–480.
56. Post, *The Little War of Private Post*, pp. 176–177, p. 150. Bonsal, *The Fight for Santiago*, p. 166.
57. Palmer, *op. cit.*, pp. 82–85. Priv. Harry Turner to Sycamore (Ill.) *Tribune*, Jan. 6, 1919, World War I Collection, Illinois Historical Library.
58. Samuel A. Stouffer, "A Study of Attitudes," *Scientific American*, May, 1949.
59. *Small Unit Study No. 7*, pp. 38–39, pp. 71–72. *Letters from Fighting Hoosiers*, p. 248, p. 163. Ogburn, *Marauders*, p. 181.
60. Maule, *op. cit.*, p. 17, p. 245, p. 266. *The Best from Yank*, pp. 45–47. Don Marshall to parents, April 15, 1945, by permission.
61. David Dempsey, "Fear in Battle," *The American Mercury*, June, 1945. Maule, *op. cit.*, p. 28, p. 184.
62. Dempsey, *op. cit.*, Wecter, *op. cit.*, pp. 492–493. *Letters from Fighting Hoosiers*, p. 71.
63. Lynn Montross and Nicholas A. Canzona, *U. S. Marine Operations in Korea, 1950–1953* (Washington, D. C.: Historical Branch, U. S. Marine Corps, 1955), p. 121.
64. Marshall, "Our Army in Korea," *Harper's*, Aug., 1951. S. L. A. Marshall," "Men Facing Death: The Destruction of an American

Platoon," *Harper's*, Sept., 1966. The Chicago *Tribune*, Oct. 25, 1966.

65. Col. Frank O. Hough and Major John A. Crown, *The Campaign in New Britain* (Washington, D. C.: Historical Branch, Marine Corps, 1952), p. 45. Dempsey, *op. cit.*, Pyle, *Brave Men*, p. 285. *Letters from Fighting Hoosiers*, p. 6.

66. Stouffer, *The American Soldier*, II, pp. 85–88, p. 115, p. 121.

67. Post, *op. cit.*, p. 197. Cushing, *From a Surgeon's Journal*, p. 489.

68. Robert Sherrod, "Notes on a Monstrous War," *Life*, Jan. 27, 1967. Sherrod's reasons for the low psychoneurosis percentage in Vietnam are echoed in many other sources. Higgins, *War in Korea*, p. 126.

69. Lt. R. E. Farmer to parents, Feb. 19, 1919, World War I Collection, Illinois Historical Library.

70. Post, *op. cit.*, p. 240. Maule, *op. cit.*, p. 273. Wecter, *op. cit.*, p. 497, p. 517. Major J. C. Black to parents, Black Collection; Cpl. M. L. Miles to Aunt Mary, Oct. 14, 1944, Miles Collection: Illinois Historical Library. Don Marshall to parents, Nov. 25, 1951, by permission.

71. Sgt. M. S. Jones to Alonzo Jones, Sept. 16, 1918, World War I Collection, Illinois Historical Library. Simonson, *Soldier Bill*, p. 72. Interview with Prof. Donald Marshall, Western Illinois University, Macomb, Illinois.

72. Viereck, *As Others Saw Us*, p. 152. Maule, *op. cit.*, p. 139. Pyle, *Here Is Your War*, p. 125. Don Marshall to parents, Dec. 18, 1944, by permission.

73. Bowman, *op. cit.*, pp. 35–36, pp. 36–39. William Reed, *Life and Correspondence of Joseph Reed* (Philadelphia: Lindsay and Blakiston, 1847), II, pp. 315–317.

74. Hicken, *Illinois in the Civil War*, pp. 124–130. *Letters from Fighting Hoosiers*, p. 163. *War Reports*, p. 269.

75. *Merrill's Marauders: American Forces in Action Series* (Washington, D. C.: Military Intelligence Service, 1945), p. 1. This source gives figure of 2,997 officers and men in 5307th Composite Unit. Other sources, probably because of replacements sent in, give differing figures. See also: Hunter, *Galahad*, p. 4, p. 200.

76. Some good sources on the Marauders are: Hunter's *Galahad;* Master's, *The Road Past Mandalay;* and Ogburn, *The Marauders*. These are all critical of General Stilwell. *The Stilwell Papers*, ed. by T. H. White (New York: William Sloane Associates, 1948) are critical of everybody.

77. Hunter, *op. cit.*, p. 178, p. 204. Masters, *op. cit.*, p. 147, p. 244.

Merrill's Marauders, p. 45, pp. 115–116. Ogburn, *op. cit.*, pp. 271–272.

CHAPTER 7

1. Trevelyan, *The American Revolution*, I, p. 294.
2. Journal of Sir J. M. Tylden, Jan., 1815, New York Public Library.
3. Severo Gómez Nuñez, *The Spanish-American War: Blockades and Coast Defense: War Notes No. VI* (Washington, D. C.: Office of Naval Intelligence, 1899), p. 126.
4. *Ibid.*, p. 106, p. 140.
5. All taken from *Candid Comment on the American Soldier, 1917–1918*.
6. *The Best from Yank*, p. 49.
7. *U. S. News and World Report*, Mar. 13, 1953. Pyle, *Brave Men*, p. 123.
8. Maule, *War Letters*, p. 194.
9. Smith, *The War With Mexico*, II, pp. 216–217, pp. 212–214, pp. 225–227.
10. Stories of mutilations of soldiers in Grant's invading army were quite common in 1862.
11. The Davis Scrapbook, Illinois Historical Library.
12. Chambrun, *The American Army*, pp. 316–317. Priv. Fred Knipping to his mother, Nov. 9, 1918, Illinois Historical Library.
13. Priv. Fred Long to his wife, Dec. 29, 1918, Illinois Historical Library.
14. All quotes taken from *Candid Comment on the American Soldier, 1917–1918*.
15. *Ibid.*
16. *Ibid.*
17. *Ibid.*
18. *Ibid.*
19. *Ibid.*
20. Wecter, *When Johnny Comes Marching Home*, pp. 286–287.
21. Roland N. Stromberg, *Readings and Study Guide in American History* (New York: McGraw-Hill Book Company, 1960), pp. 202–203.
22. Capt. M. L. Miles to his family, Mar., 1945, Illinois Historical Library.
23. Dos Passos, *Tour of Duty*, pp. 325–326.
24. *Scientific American*, May, 1949.

25. *Newsweek*, May 28, 1945.
26. Bach, *America's Germany*, p. 247.
27. *Ibid.*, pp. 251–252. David Rodnick, *Postwar Germans: An Anthropologist's Account* (New Haven: Yale University Press, 1948), pp. 98–99.
28. William L. White, *Report on the Germans* (New York: Harcourt, Brace and Company, Inc., 1947), pp. 115–116.
29. *Newsweek*, May 28, 1945; Aug. 6, 1956.
30. Oswald G. Villard, "Our Military Disgrace Abroad," *The Christian Century*, June 26, 1946.
31. Bach, *op. cit.*, p. 60.
32. *Time*, July 16, 1956.
33. *Newsweek*, July 30, Aug. 6, 1956. *The New Republic*, June 3, 1957.
34. This is not to say that Italian cities were spared from bombing. Actually, however, none were subjected to saturation bombing as in the case of German cities. Italian *Macchi* planes were stationed in France during the Battle of Britain.
35. Pyle, *Brave Men*, p. 118.
36. Coles, *Civil Affairs*, pp. 273–274, pp. 377–378.
37. *What Europe Thinks of America*, ed. by James Burnham (New York: The John Day Company, Inc., 1953), pp. 54–55. For perfect refutation to this, see: *While Berlin Burns: The Diary of Jans-Georg von Studnitz* (Englewood Cliffs, N. J.: Prentice-Hall, Inc., 1963), p. 35. This last reference indicates brothels were in full swing in Italy during German "occupation" of that country.
38. Reischauer, *The United States and Japan*, pp. 207–208.
39. Wright, *The 1st Cavalry Division*, p. 204. Donner, *The Spearhead*, p. 165.
40. Reischauer, *op. cit.*, p. 221.
41. Gayn, *Japan Diary*, p. 50. Reischauer, *op. cit.*, p. 224, p. 229.
42. Wright, *op. cit.*, p. 206.
43. Donner, *op. cit.*, pp. 138–139. Reischauer, *op. cit.*, pp. 206–207.
44. Clark, *From the Danube to the Yalu*, p. 123. Richard Deverall, "Wild GI's; Our Black Eye in Japan," *America*, Mar. 6, 1954.
45. Gayn, *op. cit.*, p. 135. John C. Clews, *Communist Propaganda Techniques* (New York: Frederick A. Praeger, Inc., 1965), pp. 184–185.
46. *America*, April 17, 1954, Clark, *op. cit.*, pp. 123–125. In 1967, five Americans stopped a rape attempt by a Japanese citizen in the Azabu district of Tokyo.
47. Clerk, *op. cit.*, p. 138, p. 141. Reischauer, *op. cit.*, p. 205, says:

"The history of the American occupation of Japan will some day form one of the most fascinating and important chapters in the history of the world in modern times. . . ."

48. Harbord, *Leaves from a War Diary*, p. 396.
49. Gulick, *Morals and Morale*, p. 150.
50. *Candid Comment on the American Soldier, 1917–1918*.
51. Straub, *A Sergeant's Diary in the World War*, pp. 279–280.
52. Pyle, *Here Is Your War*, p. 45. Bach, *America's Germany*, pp. 265–267.
53. *Ibid.*, p. 270. *Newsweek*, June 25, 1945. Lloyd Shearer, "Why the French Are Throwing Us Out," *Parade*, Oct. 2, 1966.
54. *Newsweek*, June 10, 1957.
55. Pyle, *Here Is Your War*, p. 7.
56. *Newsweek*, June 11, 1945. *U. S. News and World Report*, Aug. 31, 1951.
57. *Ibid.*, Aug. 19, 1955.
58. The Chicago *Tribune*, Feb. 19, 1967.
59. *Atlas*, Sept., 1966.
60. Tregaskis, *Viet Nam Diary*, p. 248, p. 195, p. 308.
61. *America*, Mar. 6, 1954. Gayn, *op. cit.*, pp. 212–216.
62. Dos Passos, *op. cit.*, p. 331, p. 323.
63. Rodnick, *op. cit.*, pp. 106–107. *Newsweek*, June 4, 1945.
64. *Saturday Evening Post*, Nov. 10, 1917. *Candid Comment . . . 1917–1918*. Wecter, *op. cit.*, p. 332.
65. Leigh, *48 Million Tons to Eisenhower*, p. 107. Stouffer, *The American Soldier*, I, p. 178.
66. Wecter, *op. cit.*, p. 333, p. 286. Sherrod, *Tarawa*, pp. 28–29. Wright, *op. cit.*, p. 242. *U. S. News and World Report*, Aug. 22, 1966.
67. Davis Scrapbook, Illinois Historical Library. Post, *The Little War of Private Post*, p. 269. Nuñez, *op. cit.*, p. 103.
68. Priv. Frank Gipperick to Mrs. Morrison, Sept. 20, 1918; Sgt. Wm. Jones to his father, Nov. 24, 1918; Sgt. Jones to his mother, Nov. 31, 1918: World War I Collection, Illinois Historical Library.
69. All quotes from *Candid Comment . . . 1917–1918*.
70. Crowell, *Demobilization*, p. 83.
71. *Letters from Fighting Hoosiers*, p. 13.
72. Dos Passos, op. cit., p. 56. Maule, *War Letters*, p. 190. *The Best from Yank*, p. 52. The author witnessed the looting of Okinawan cave graves.
73. Tregaskis, *op. cit.*, p. 75.
74. Von Studnitz, *op. cit.*, p. 35, p. 218, p. 249. This diary indicates

that all that Americans were accused of bringing to Europe was already flourishing by the time the Yanks arrived.

CHAPTER 8

1. Trevelyan, *The American Revolution,* III, p. 10.
2. Montross, *Rag, Tag and Bobtail,* pp. 409–410.
3. Danske Dandridge, *American Prisoners of the Revolution* (Charlottesville, Va.: The Michie Company, 1911), pp. 494–499.
4. *The Writings of George Washington,* coll. and ed. by Worthington C. Ford (New York: G. P. Putnam's Sons, 1890), V, p. 169.
5. Lossing, *The Pictorial Field Book of the War of 1812,* pp. 1067–1069.
6. *This Was Andersonville Military Prison as Told in the Personal Recollections of John McElroy,* ed. by Roy Meredith (New York: McDowell, Obolensky, 1957), pp. xix–xx.
7. Hicken, *Illinois in the Civil War,* pp. 343–364.
8. Conrad Hoffman, *In the Prison Camps of Germany* (New York: Association Press, 1920), pp. 150–157. See also: *Candid Comment on the American Soldier, 1917–1918,* for information on how German prisoners of Americans were treated.
9. Shirer, *The Rise and Fall of the Third Reich,* pp. 955–956.
10. *Newsweek,* April 23, 1945. The author has checked out the "turnip" story with several personal friends who were prisoners. It was true.
11. *Newsweek,* May 7, June 11, 1945.
12. Tolischus, *Through Japanese Eyes,* pp. 199–214. *U. S. Submarine Losses: World War II,* p. 71. W. Scott Cunningham with Lydel Sims, *Wake Island Command* (New York: Popular Library, 1962), p. 123.
13. Dos Passos, *Tour of Duty,* p. 135.
14. Gwen Dew, *Prisoner of the Japs* (New York: Alfred A. Knopf, Inc., 1943), pp. 306–307. The author records escape of two of imprisoned Americans from Shanghai to Australia. Cunningham, *op. cit.,* p. 178.
15. Boyle, *Yanks Don't Cry,* pp. 142–143, pp. 178–188.
16. This peculiar aspect of the Oriental mind appears frequently. Several Westerners who were in Japan during the war recorded that they had never seen Americans mistreated outside the camps.
17. Boyl, *op. cit.,* p. 111, p. 114, give good treatment of this.
18. Clark, *From the Danube to the Yalu,* p. 302. Fehrenbach, *This*

Kind of War, p. 199. Kinkead, *In Every War But One*, p. 84. Biderman, *March to Calumny*, pp. 118–119.

19. *Ibid.*, pp. 118–119. Kinkead, *op. cit.*, pp. 143–144. Kinkead's book is a savage attack on the behavior of Americans prisoners of the Communists. Biderman's book is a scholarly rebuttal to those charges. As to this writer's opinion, it would seem that, though Kinkead has some facts on his side, he tends to overlook the reality of history and human behavior.

20. Kinkead, *op. cit.*, pp. 16–17. Biderman, *op. cit.*, pp. 101–102. It must be pointed out that the death rate in particular instances in World War II, and in the American Revolution, was higher.

21. *Current Digest of Soviet Press*, July 21, June 29, 1965, quotes *Izvestia* stories on supposed "confessions" of an American airman.

22. Kinkead, *op. cit.*, pp. 64–68.

23. *U. S. News and World Report*, Aug. 26, 1955. Gladwin Hill, "Brain-Washing: Time For a Policy," *Atlantic Monthly*, April, 1955. Hill claims 225 GI's were originally accused of misconduct.

24. Kinkead, *op. cit.*, pp. 162–163, claims only one Marine out of every 570 engaged in combat was taken prisoner, and that only one Marine was dismissed for collaboration in Korean prison camps. Biderman takes other view: that there is some evidence that Turks collaborated. Biderman, *op. cit.*, pp. 161–163. See also: Rees, *Korea: The Limited War*, pp. 344–346; and *U. S. News and World Report*, Aug. 19, 1955.

25. *The Japanese Story of the Battle of Midway* (Washington, D.C.: Office of Naval Intelligence, 1947), p. 40. The flier even disclosed the types of planes the U. S. had on Midway.

26. Boyle, *op. cit.*, p. 153.

27. Lt. Col. Frank O. Hough and Major John A. Crown, *The Campaign in New Britain* (Washington, D.C.: Historical Branch, U. S. Marine Corps, 1952), p. 74.

28. Robert Cutler, *No Time for Rest* (Boston: Little, Brown & Company, 1965), p. 95. *Records of the 2nd Division in World War I* (Washington, D.C.: Second Division Historical Section, 1928), n.p.

29. Rees, *op. cit.*, p. 342. Clark, *op. cit.*, p. 313. *U.S. News and World Report*, Aug. 19, 1955.

30. Biderman, *op. cit.*, p. 257, p. 56, pp. 49–50, pp. 25–26, pp. 298–300.

31. Kinkead, *op. cit.*, discusses these on pp. 16–17. *U. S. News and World Report* analyzes their backgrounds, July 15, 1955. See also: Fehrenbach, *op. cit.*, p. 595.

32. Biderman, *op. cit.*, pp. 58–60.
33. *U. S. Submarine Losses*, p. 46. Cunningham, *op. cit.*, p. 118.
34. Boyle, *op. cit.*, p. 93, pp. 67–68, p. 152.
35. Viereck, *As Others Saw Us*, p. 235. *World War Records: First Division, A.E.F.* (Washington, D.C.: The Army War College, 1928), n.p. *Candid Comment on the American Soldier, 1917–1918*.
36. Hoffman, *op. cit.*, p. 177, p. 169. American prisoners of the British during the Revolution often sang patriotic songs.
37. *Candid Comment on the American Soldier, 1917–1918.*
38. Brown, *The Galvanized Yankees*, p. 1, pp. 211–213. Confederate soldiers from Tennessee, Kentucky, and Missouri were, on occasion, not as fervent in their patriotism as those from the "deep South."
39. Bolton, *The Private Soldier Under Washington*, pp. 166–167, pp. 187–191.
40. According to Lossing, *op. cit.*, pp. 788–789, American prisoners escaped from Beauport, near Quebec, in 1813.
41. Carl P. Dennett, *Prisoners of the Great War* (Boston: Houghton Mifflin Company, 1919), pp. 101–107, pp. 133–137.
42. Kenneth W. Simmons, *Kriegie* (Camden, N. J.: Thomas Nelson & Sons, 1960), p. 121, p. 161.
43. Johnson, *Thunderbolt!*, p. 130. *War Reports*, p. 365.
44. *The Best from Yank*, p. 49.
45. Tolischus, *op. cit.*, pp. 201–202.
46. Clark, *op. cit.*, p. 211. Biderman, *op. cit.*, pp. 86–89.
47. Biderman, *op. cit.*, p. 90. Germans escaped from prison camps, but never got back to Germany.
48. St. Louis *Post-Dispatch*, July 28, 1966. The fact that Dengler and others were kept in countryside prison camp indicates that it was not a major North Vietnam prison.
49. Henry H. Eby, *Observations of an Illinois Boy in Battle, Camp and Prisons, 1861–1865* (Mendota, Ill.: by the author, 1910), pp. 135–136.
50. Boyle, *op. cit.*, p. 152, pp. 203–215.
51. *Letters from Libby Prison: Being the Authentic Letters Written While in Confederate Captivity in the Notorious Libby Prison at Richmond*, ed. by Margaret W. Peelle (New York: Greenwich Book Publishers, 1956), p. 15, p. 57, p. 80. One must also add that rumors are part-and-parcel of prison life. There is a plenitude of evidence of this.
52. Edmund Newsome, *Experience in the War of the Great Rebellion by a Soldier of the 81st Regiment Illinois Volunteer Infantry* (Carbondale, Ill.: by the author, 1880), pp. 225–226.
53. *Letters from Fighting Hoosiers*, p. 382.

54. *Ibid.*, p. 378. Boyle, *op. cit.*, pp. 244–245.
55. Dos Passos, *op. cit.*, p. 136. Boyle, *op. cit.*, p. 245.

CHAPTER 9

1. Pargellis, *Lord Loudoun in North America*, pp. 111–112.
2. Van Doren, *Mutiny in January*, p. 43.
3. Peter Du Ponceau, "Autobiography," *Pennsylvania Magazine of History, LXIII* (April, 1939), pp. 189–227, p. 457. Albigence Waldo, "Valley Forge, 1777–1778. Diary," *Pennsylvania Magazine of History*, XXI (1897), pp. 299–323.
4. Bolton, *The Private Soldier*, pp. 20–24. Pettengill, *Letters From America*, p. 119.
5. Fredman and Falk, *Jews in American Wars*, pp. 8–11.
6. Nichols, *Taylor's Little Army*, p. 173, p. 33. Marcus, *Memoirs*, II, pp. 91–95.
7. Glisan, *Journal of Army Life*, p. 120.
8. Lowe, *Five Years A Dragoon*, p. 21. Lonn, *Foreigners in the Union Army and Navy*, p. 87.
9. See Wiley's *The Common Soldier in the Civil War* (a combined edition of *The Life of Billy Yank* and *The Life of Johnny Reb*), pp. 322–323, p. 307. Lonn, *op. cit.*, pp. 82–84, pp. 577–584. Marcus, *op. cit.*, I, p. 147; II, p. 43; III, p. 225, p. 304, p. 318.
10. Matthew U. Jamison, *Recollections of Pioneer and Army Life* (Kansas City, Kan.: Hudson Press, 1911), p. 152. Lonn, *op. cit.*, p. 644. William Schlay to D. C. Smith, July 10, 1863, D. C. Smith Collection, Illinois Historical Library.
11. One such fight occurred between the 3rd Rhode Island and the 33rd Illinois.
12. Lonn, *op. cit.*, p. 160, p. 171. The Russian officer was John Basil Turchin.
13. *To Bigotry No Sanction* (Philadelphia: Anti-Defamation Council and the American Jewish Committee, 1941), p. 27. It is difficult to count the Jews in the Civil War. So many German names sounded Jewish; so many Jews had changed or "anglicized" their true names.
14. *The New York Times*, Oct. 10, 1863, April 24, 1865. *Atlantic Monthly*, June, 1903. One clipping in Gumby Scrapbook Collection, Columbia University, indicates that two of Butler's regiments were officered by "intelligent mulattoes" who spoke French.
15. Hicken, *Illinois in the Civil War*, pp. 334–344. Victor Hicken, "The

Record of Illinois' Negro Soldiers in the Civil War," *Journal of the Illinois State Historical Society,* Autumn, 1963, pp. 529–551.

16. Wiley, *op. cit.,* pp. 316–318.
17. Stephen Bonsal, "The Negro Soldier in War and Peace," *The North American Review,* Vol. 185 (1907), pp. 321–327.
18. Oswald G. Villard, "The Negro in the Regular Army," *Atlantic Monthly,* June, 1903. Gumby Scrapbook, Columbia University. Bonsal, *op. cit.,* pp. 326–327.
19. Brown, *Galvanized Yankees,* p. 122. Rickey, *Forty Miles a Day on Beans and Hay,* p. 17. Forsyth, *The Story of a Soldier,* I, p. 91.
20. Robert Johnson, *Thence Round Cape Horn: The Story of the United States Naval Forces on Pacific Station, 1818–1923* (Annapolis, Md.: L. S. Naval Institute, 1963). No specific page given here because entire book indicates foreign influence in the Navy. Mitchell, *History of the Modern American Navy,* p. 5, p. 55.
21. New York *World,* June 10, 1917, states "Negro seamen, gunners, and gunners mates gave a good account of themselves at Manila Bay." Villard, *op. cit.*
22. *To Bigotry No Sanction,* p. 30.
23. Millis, *The Martial Spirit,* pp. 290–291. Bonsal, *The Fight for Santiago,* p. 300. *The Negro Reference Book,* ed. by John P. Davis (Englewood Cliffs, N. J.: Prentice-Hall, Inc., 1966), p. 615.
24. Bonsal, "The Negro Soldier in War and Peace," *The North American Review,* Vol. 185 (1907), pp. 323–327. See also: Gumby Scrapbook, Columbia University. This last collection of clippings indicates the plight of the Negro soldier in this period.
25. Matthew F. Steele, "The 'Color Line' in the Army," *The North American Review,* Vol. 183 (1906).
26. Joseph B. Foraker, "A Review of the Testimony in the Brownsville Investigation," *The North American Review,* Vol. 187 (1906). See Gumby Scrapbook Columbia University for further information.
27. *Ibid. The Negro Reference Book,* p. 615. *The New York Times,* Mar. 9, 1927.
28. Stallings, *The Doughboys,* p. 167.
29. Interview with surviving member of that unit. See also: Pershing, *My Experiences in the World War,* I, p. 316.
30. *The Hebrew Impact on Western Civilization,* ed. by Dagobert D. Runes (New York: Philosophical Library, Inc., 1951), pp. 271–273. Fredman and Falk, *op. cit.,* pp. 75–76. *To Bigotry No Sanction,* pp. 31–33. Lee M. Friedman, *Jewish Pioneers and Patriots* (Philadelphia: The Jewish Publication Society of America, 1942), pp. 272–273.

31. Robert Alexander, *Memories of the World War, 1917–1918* (New York: The Macmillan Company, 1931), pp. 107–108.
32. *The Negro Reference Book,* p. 624, p. 620. Stallings, *op. cit.,* pp. 360–361, p. 321. Gumby Scrapbook, Columbia University.
33. *The New York Times,* Feb. 23, 1919. Wecter, *When Johnny Comes Marching Home,* p. 299, p. 303, p. 293. *The Negro Reference Book,* pp. 622–623, p. 616. Pershing, *op. cit.,* II, pp. 116–117.
34. *The New York Times,* April 15, 1919. Gumby Scrapbook, Columbia University. *Amsterdam News,* Feb. 19, 1930.
35. Pershing, *op. cit.,* II, pp. 116–117. Viereck, *As Others Saw Us,* pp. 303–304. Stallings, *op. cit.,* p. 318, points out that many Negro soldiers wore the French uniform.
36. *The Negro Reference Book,* p. 625. Stouffer, *The American Soldier,* I, p. 494.
37. *The Negro Reference Book,* pp. 643–645. *Small Unit Action No. 3,* p. 5. *The Best from Yank,* pp. 134–135.
38. *The Negro Reference Book,* pp. 639–641. *Newsweek,* Feb. 26, 1945.
39. Gumby Scrapbook, Columbia University. *Report of President's Committee on Equal to Serve,* pp. 17–25. Stouffer, *op. cit.,* I, pp. 506–508. Wecter, *op. cit.,* p. 538.
40. *American Journal of Sociology,* Jan., 1947. Stouffer, *op. cit.,* I, pp. 486–495, pp. 521–524. Capt. M. Miles to his aunt, Aug. 2, 1945, Miles Collection, Illinois Historical Library.
41. *The New Republic,* Oct. 18, 1943. Stouffer, *op. cit.,* I, pp. 586–587, p. 592. *The Best from Yank,* pp. 212–213.
42. The Baltimore *Sun,* Jan. 10, 1943. *Nisei* means "those of the first generation"; *sansei* refers to those of the second generation. It is probable that most of the Japanese-American soldiers were second generation Americans.
43. *American Mercury,* June, 1945.
44. The Texans were members of the 36th Division. *The Best from Yank,* p. 223.
45. "The Indian Goes to War," *The New Republic,* Nov. 31, 1942. Donald C. Peattie, "Braves On the Warpath," *The American Legion Magazine,* July, 1943. Ogburn, *The Marauders,* p. 179. *Indians in the War* (Chicago: Department of Interior [Indian Affairs], 1945), p. 1, pp. 5–8, pp. 14–15, p. 28, pp. 50–51.
46. Fredman and Falk, *op. cit.,* p. 201, p. 216, p. 221. Runes, *op. cit.,* pp. 278–279. *Fighting for America,* ed. by N. C. Balth, p. 5.
47. The Chicago *Tribune,* Sept. 12, 1966. Wright, *The 1st Cavalry Division in World War II,* p. 31, pp. 82–83. *Philippines* (Published by Philippine Resident Commissioner to the U. S., Nov., 1942),

Vol. II, n.p. Franc Shor, "See You in Manila," *The American Legion Magazine*, Mar., 1943. Filipinos, like Negroes, were often subject to discrimination in the U. S. Japanese-Americans, who trained in Wisconsin, were not.

48. Sherrod, *Tarawa*, p. 31. Johnson, *Thunderbolt!*, p. 147. Maule, *War Letters*, p. 219. It may be added that WASP's have rarely been the subject of specific books concerning military contributions. Other white hyphenated Americans have been so celebrated however. See: Michael Musmanno, *The Story of the Italians in America* (Garden City, N. Y.: Doubleday & Company, Inc., 1965), p. 206, which claims that 10 percent of American soldiers in World War II were of Italian descent.

49. *President's Report on Equal Opportunity*, pp. 17–19, pp. 21–25, p. 43.

50. Tracking down information on the old 24th was difficult. It was apparently in the 25th Division at the beginning of the Korean War. Don Marshall to mother, Oct. 16, 1951, Marshall Letters, indicates that platoons were receiving transfers from "all-Negro" 24th in Sept.-Oct., 1951. See also: Robert Leckie, *Conflict, The History of the Korean War, 1950–1953* (New York: G. P. Putnam's Sons, 1962), p. 96, p. 107.

51. Negroes received only two Medals of Honor out of 131 conferred in the Korean conflict. Both American Indians and Spanish-Americans far exceeded this figure. The majority of winners were whites of European ancestry.

52. Gumby Scrapbook, Columbia University. *The New York Times*, Sept. 7, 1950. *U. S. News and World Report*, May 11, 1956. Don Marshall to parents, Oct. 16, Sept. 23, 1951, by permission.

53. Clark, *From the Danube to the Yalu*, pp. 197–198. *Time*, Jan. 1, 1951. Schott, *Above and Beyond*, p. 233.

54. Baldwin, "Our Fighting Men Have Gone Soft," *Saturday Evening Post*, Aug. 8, 1959. *U. S. News and World Report*, Oct. 11, 1957.

55. Janowitz, *The Professional Soldier*, pp. 87–88.

56. *The New York Times*, Aug. 28, 1958. Tregaskis, *Vietnam Diary*, p. 28. The Chicago *Tribune*, July 25, 1966. *Look*, Oct. 18, 1966. *U. S. News and World Report*, Aug. 15, 1966.

57. *Ibid.* Soviet newspapers make much of the Negro contribution to the Vietnam War, claiming that American whites are forcing colored peoples into combat against each other. Whitney Young's complaint, quoted in The Chicago *Tribune*, July 24, 1966, is a strange one. Other Negro leaders' complaints about Negro soldiers doing too much is in direct contradiction to what some Negro leaders were saying in 1944.

58. *Time,* Sept. 16, Dec. 23, 1966. McNamara's comment is in *Time,* Sept. 16, 1966.

59. Stories about racial problems in Germany have never been officially confirmed by the Army.

60. Amos Farnsworth, "Journal," *Massachusetts History Society Proceedings,* XII, pp. 74–107. Maclay, *Reminiscences of the Old Navy,* p. 26.

61. Hicken, *Illinois in the Civil War,* pp. 50–70

62. Davis Scrapbook, Illinois Historical Library. *The Little War of Private Post,* pp. 156–157.

63. Cpl. Ted Fatanyaro to father, Oct. 16, 1918; Conrad Zoeckler to Henry Hirsch, Oct. 3, 1918; Kent Diary: Illinois Historical Library. Wecter, *op. cit.,* p. 407.

64. Odell, *The New Spirit,* p. 25.

65. Leigh, *48 Million Tons to Eisenhower,* p. 124. Renwick Kennedy, "How Good Were the Army Chaplains," *The Christian Century,* June 5, 1946. There were many Protestant and Jewish complaints that Army chaplains were under the control of Roman Catholics.

66. Maule, *op. cit.,* pp. 258–259. Wecter, *op. cit.,* p. 482. *Letters from Fighting Hoosiers,* p. 70. "What the Soldier Thinks," Periodical Publication of the War Department, Dec. 1942–Sept., 1945.

67. Cpl. H. Landes to LaGrange (Ill.) Presbyterian Church, Nov. 18, 1943, Illinois Historical Library. *Letters from Fighting Hoosiers,* p. 276. Maule, *op. cit.,* pp. 141–143. William S. White, "The End of the Old Army," *Harper's,* June, 1959.

68. Peoria (Ill.) *Journal-Star,* Sept. 26, 1966. E. M. Eller, Rear Adm. (Ret.) to author, Sept. 20, 1966, writes: "Since these figures are fully as valid as personnel sampling, we refer you to *Yearbook* for such percentages over the past thirty-four years of its publication." The *Yearbook of American Churches,* as quoted in *Historical Statistics of the United States,* listed 104,190,000 Americans as having religious affiliations in 1957. This is over half of the total U. S. population. The percentages on religious affiliations of American fighting men is thus calculated from same source.

CHAPTER 10

1. Waldo, "Valley Forge," *Pennsylvania Magazine of History,* XXI, pp. 308–309. Lt. Gen. E. M. Almond, "What Happened in Korea When the Chinese Marched In," *U. S. News and World Report,* Feb. 13, 1953.

2. James Hatch to Governor Yates, Oct. 29, 1863, Yates Collection, Illinois Historical Library. Stillwell, *The Story of a Common Soldier,* p. 124.

3. The story of discontented sailor who gained weight comes from author's own experiences. Maule, *War Letters,* p. 253, contains statement from one soldier which reads: "They will tell you how much they think of the Army [World War II]. . . . Probably 70 to 90% of them never had it as good before in their lives." See also: Almond, *op. cit.;* H. Landes to mother, Oct. 13, 1941, Landes Coll., Illinois Historical Library.

4. Oliver Nixon, "Reminiscences of the First Year of the War in Missouri," *Military Essays and Recollections: Papers Read Before the Commandery of the State of Illinois, Military Order of the Loyal Legion of the United States* (Chicago: The Dial Press, Inc., 1899), III, p. 427. *The Civil War Letters of Henry C. Bear: A Soldier in the 116th Illinois Volunteer Infantry,* ed. by Wayne C. Temple (Harrogate, Tenn.: Lincoln Memorial University Press, 1961), p. 17.

5. Private John Crow to The Pontiac (Illinois) *Leader,* April 21, 1919; Seaman William Warren to his mother, Feb. 9, 1919; Priv. W. L. Buckner to a friend, July 8, 1919: World War I Collection, Illinois Historical Library.

6. Stouffer, *The American Soldier,* I, pp. 187–188. Maule, *op. cit.,* pp. 148–149. Don Marshall to family, Jan., 1952, by permission.

7. H. Landes to parents, Aug. 5, 1944, Landes Collection. Maule, *op. cit.,* p. 142. *Letters from Fighting Hoosiers,* pp. 246–247.

8. Don Marshall to parents, April 13, 1945, by permission.

9. Don Marshall to parents, April 15, 1945, Nov. 27, 1950, Nov. 24, 1951, by permission. Marshall, "Our Army in Korea," *Harper's,* Aug., 1951.

10. *U. S. News and World Report,* June 27, 1966.

11. Macomb (Illinois) *Journal,* Jan. 31, 1862. John Batchelor Diary, Illinois Historical Library.

12. Priv. Clyde Sisson to Centralia (Illinois) *Evening Sentinel,* Illinois Historical Library. Virtually every American soldier in France in 1918 had something to say about the French communiqué, dated Nov. 11.

13. Sgt. Geo. Williams to Mr. Herb Landes, June 1, 1943, Landes Collection, Illinois Historical Library. Stouffer, *The American Soldier,* I, pp. 187–188.

14. The author has found few comments on battle conditions excepting

those on fear or shock. The quote from Chicago comes from the Sycamore (Illinois) *Tribune,* Jan. 6, 1919.

15. Pyle, *Brave Men,* p. 3.
16. Abel Bowen, *The Naval Monument* (Boston, The Author, 1816), p. vi. Williams, *Americans at War,* p. 22. Michell, *History of the Modern American Navy,* p. 10.
17. A remnant of the fleet of the 1890 period was the old "Prairie State," the former U. S. S. *Illinois,* on which many naval officers in World War II were trained.
18. The standard British joke in 1945 concerned a supposed exchange of messages between a British and an American ship. "How do you like being the second largest navy?" the American message read. "How do you like being second best?" was the reply.
19. Maule, *op. cit.,* p. 276, p. 279.
20. *U. S. Submarine Losses* (Washington: Naval History Division, Office of Chief of Naval Operations, 1963), p. 3.
21. Hanson W. Baldwin, "What's Wrong with the Regulars," *Saturday Evening Post,* Oct. 31, 1953. Frazier Hunt, *Blown in by the Draft* (Garden City, N. Y.: Doubleday, Page & Co., 1918), pp. 19–20.
22. Lewis W. Ross to family, April 8, 1847, Illinois Historical Library.
23. To my knowledge, the only large scale action between part of Lee's army and a Western army was at Chickamauga. There Longstreet's men cracked the Union right wide open on the second day of the battle, only to be stopped dead by Thomas's stand on Horseshoe Ridge. Even from this it would be difficult to rate the two different armies, mainly because of the factor of luck in the early Confederate success.
24. C. B. Wright, *The 1st Cavalry Division,* pp. 2–3.
25. Stallings, *Doughboys,* p. 46, p. 143. The 42nd, or "Rainbow Division," was one of the most feared. See also: *Illinois in the World War,* I, p. 338.
26. H. Landes to parents, Nov. 15, 1941, Landes Collection. Ernie Pyle, in his *Brave Men,* seemed partial to the Texas and Oklahoma regiments.
27. Clark, *From the Danube to the Yalu,* p. 195. Bradley, *A Soldier's Story,* p. 475. Churchill, *Closing the Ring,* p. 39. The figures on Patton's superb Third Army come from Farago, *Paton: Ordeal and Triumph,* p. 790.
28. Higgins, *War in Korea,* p. 117. Fredman and Falk, *Jews in American Wars,* pp. 258–259.
29. Don Marshall to parents, Jan. 10, 1952, by permission. Marshall, "Our Army in Korea," *Harper's,* Aug., 1951.

30. H. Landes to parents, Jan. 15, 1944, Landes Collection. In World War I the feeling between Army and Marine troops was intensified, because it was supposed that the Marine Corps alone had won at Château-Thierry.

31. Clark, *op. cit.*, p. 195. Baldwin, *op. cit.*, Heinl, *Soldiers of the Sea*, p. 394, p. 484.

32. *Ibid.*, p. 207 Janowitz, *The Professional Soldier*, p. 42. *International Relations*, October, 1965.

33. *Newsweek*, Aug. 13, 1956. Harbord, *Leaves from a War Diary*, pp. 295–296. Heinl, *op. cit.*, p. 394, quotes an Army officer of World War II as stating that he "never heard a wounded Marine moan." Sherrod, *Tarawa*, p. 35, p. 117. *Letters from Fighting Hoosiers*, p. 37.

34. London *Daily Telegraph*, Sept. 1, 1950. Heinl, *op. cit.*, p. 542. Higgins, *op. cit.*, p. 83, p. 143, p. 182.

35. Montross and Canzona, *U. S. Marine Corps Operations in Korea*, III, p. 194, p. 243, p. 351. Fehrenbach, *This Kind of War*, p. 369. Heinl, *op. cit.*, p. 589.

36. Clark, *op. cit.*, p. 208.

37. Robert H. Adleman and George Walton, *The Devil's Brigade* (Philadelphia: Chilton Company, 1966), p. 181. It is claimed in this recent book that only thirty men of the "Devil's Brigade" were ever captured, that none surrendered, and that the unit took no prisoners during certain phases of mountain fighting in Italy. This unit was part American, part Canadian. The Rangers were called "the black death" by the Germans; the "Green Berets" have been called "picked cutthroats" by the Russians.

38. Fredman and Falk, *op. cit.*, p. 28.

39. Philip Welshimer to wife, Jan. 14, 1863, Welshimer Collection, Illinois Historical Library.

40. Bonsal, *The Fight for Santiago*, p. 158.

41. The Chicago *Tribune*, April 15, 1967.

42. Priv. Elsworth Wade, U. S. M. C. to friend, Oct. 12, 1918; Lt. E. S. Betts to sisters, Aug. 3, 1918, Illinois Historical Library.

43. *Small Unit Actions* (Washington, D. C.: Historical Division, War Dept., 1946), p. 110.

44. Maule, *op. cit.*, p. 287.

45. *Letters from Fighting Hoosiers*, p. 100.

46. Sgt. Irving Strobing's last message from Corregidor is so well known that it needs no citation. *Small Unit Action No. 7*, p. 81. Wecter, *When Johnny Comes Marching Home*, p. 482. Maule, *op. cit.*, p. 259.

47. *Ibid.*, pp. 218–219. Dos Passos, *Tour of Duty*, p. 55. The little

poem about the dead Marine has obscure origins, and goes back far into Marine tradition.

48. Higgins, *op. cit.,* p. 83, pp. 188–189. Fehrenbach, *op. cit.,* p. 364.

49. Don Marshall to his parents, Oct. 17, 1951, by permission.

50. The Chicago *Tribune,* Sept. 18, 1966. Associated Press, Sept. 21, 1966. See also: The Chicago *Tribune,* July 20, 1966, for fine tribute to helicopter pilots.

51. Bolton, *The Private Soldier Under Washington,* p. 40.

52. Ira Blanchard, "Recollections of Civil War Service with the 20th Illinois Infantry." Typed manuscript, Illinois Historical Library.

53. *Illinois in the World War,* I, pp. 281–282. *Candid Comment on the American Soldier, 1917–1918.*

54. Schott, *Above and Beyond,* p. 97. Arch Whitehouse, *Heroes and Legends of World War I* (Garden City, N. Y.: Doubleday & Company, Inc., 1964), pp. 201–202.

55. Potter, *Yamamoto,* pp. 215–217. Edward Jablonski, *Flying Fortresses; The Illustrated Biography of the B-17's and the Men Who Flew Them* (Garden City, N. Y., Doubleday & Company, Inc., 1965), p. 123.

56. *U. S. Sub Losses,* p. 1, p. 124, p. 71.

57. Leigh, *48 Million Tons,* pp. 135–137. *Small Unit Action No. 7,* pp. 84–88. "Evaluation of American Troops and Tactics," D384, translated German document obtained from Chief of Military History, Department of the Army.

58. Wright, *1st Cavalry Division,* p. 22, pp. 141–143, p. 131, p. 96. The 1st Cavalry was only one of several excellent Army divisions in the Pacific area. Its divisional history, a well written one, allows for better citation, however.

59. Scott, *Above and Beyond,* p. 168. *Letters from Fighting Hoosiers,* p. 246. Sherrod, *op. cit.,* p. 96. Howard M. Conner, *The Spearhead: The World War II History of the 5th Marine Division* (Washington, D. C.: Infantry Journal Press, 1950), p. 181, p. 179.

60. *Ibid.,* p. 59, p. 64, p. 67. The first flag on Suribachi came from the transport *Missoula.*

61. *Letters from Fighting Hoosiers,* p. 361.

62. Robert Leckie, *Conflict* (New York: G. P. Putnam's Sons, 1962), pp. 425–428. Schott, *Above and Beyond,* p. 246, says 42 of these were won by Marines. For Clark's story, see Montross, *U. S. Marine Corps Operations in Korea,* II, pp. 61–62.

63. St. Louis *Post-Dispatch,* Aug. 5, 1966.

64. Letter of John Baylor, Mar. 11, 1861. David Givler, "Intimate Glimpses of Army Life During the Civil War," (typed transcript).

Fred C. Butler to friend, Oct. 31, 1918. H. Landes to mother, July 10, 1943. All of the preceding are from the Illinois Historical Library. The last two quotes come from Maule, *op. cit.,* p. 181, and Wecter, *op. cit.,* p. 494.

65. *Fighting for America,* ed. by Nathan C. Balth, p. 38, p. 40. Don Marshall to parents, Dec. 22, 1951, by permission. "War Diary of Thaddeus H. Capron, 1861–1865," *Journal of the Illinois State Historical Society,* XII, No. 3 (Oct., 1919), p. 332. H. Landes to mother, July 20, 1943, Illinois Historical Library. The Chicago *Tribune,* Dec. 31, 1861.

66. W. H. L. Wallace to wife, Mar. 25, 1862, Wallace-Dickey Collection; Payson Shumway to wife, April 1, 1862, Shumway Collection; H. Landes to parents, Jan. 3, 1942; Capt. Joe Shamel to Mary Miles, Mar. 21, 1944, Miles Collection. All of these are in the Illinois Historical Library.

67. Priv. Arthur Ragan to mother, Dec., 1918 Priv. Leo Provart to home. April 26, 1919: Illinois Historical Library. Don Marshall to parents, Aug. 14, 1945, by permission.

68. *Literary Digest,* Mar. 8, 1919. Wector, *op. cit.,* p. 320, p. 518. Don Marshall to parents, Aug. 12, 1945, by permission.

69. Stillwell, *Story of a Common Soldier,* pp. 275–279.

Bibliography

PAPERS, DIARIES, SCRAPBOOKS, AND COLLECTIONS

The American Revolution:

Armand Tuffin Papers (Armand Tuffin, Charles, The Marquis de la Rouène), Columbia University, New York.
Letterbook of General Samuel Smith, Columbia University, New York.

The War of 1812:

Journal of Sir John Maxwell Tylden, New York Public Library, New York.

The Civil War:

Newton Bateman Papers, Illinois State Historical Library, Springfield.
John C. Black Papers, Illinois State Historical Library, Springfield.
Ira Blanchard, typed manuscript, "Recollections of Civil War Services," Illinois State Historical Library, Springfield.
Civil War Diaries of James Howlett, Illinois State Historical Library, Springfield.
Edward H. Ingraham Papers, Illinois State Historical Library, Springfield.
David McFarland Papers, Illinois State Historical Library, Springfield.
Lyman K. Needham Papers, Illinois State Historical Library, Springfield.
Richard J. Oglesby Papers, Illinois State Historical Library, Springfield.
Ira A. Payne Papers, Illinois State Historical Library, Springfield.
Reuben T. Prentice Papers, Illinois State Historical Library, Springfield.
Payson Z. Shumway Papers, Illinois State Historical Library, Springfield.
D. C. Smith Papers, Illinois State Historical Library, Springfield.
Philip Welshimer Papers, Illinois State Historical Library, Springfield.
Civil War Diaries of Charles W. Wills, Illinois State Historical Library, Springfield.

John Wilcox Papers, Illinois State Historical Library, Springfield.
Richard Yates Papers, Illinois State Historical Library, Springfield.

Spanish-American War:

Scrapbook of A. L. Davis, Illinois State Historical Library, Springfield.

World War I:

The World War I Collections, Illinois State Historical Library, Springfield, which include originals or transcripts of clippings, letters or diaries by: Elden S. Betts, W. L. Buckner, Ralph Capes, Matthew I. Daniels, R. E. Farmer, Ted Fatanyaro, Frank Gippernick, Pearl Harlow, Sarah Harley, Clarence Hart, Herbert Hessel, M. S. Jones, Wiliam Jones, Emmett Kent, Fred Knipping, Oscar Lampley, Cecil R. Lee, Fred Long, A. H. Mauley, Verne Miller, John A. Modglin, George Nevill, E. C. O'Brien, Ed Radley, John Schell, Leo A. Schopp, J. Fair Smith, Clyde Sisson, Pierre Turch, Harry Turner.

World War II:

Herbert R. Landes Collection, Illinois State Historical Library, Springfield.
Sante Pasquesi Collection, Illinois State Historical Library, Springfield.

Korean War:

Donald Marshall Letters, Macomb, Illinois, by permission.

General:

C. Greenwell Diaries, 1911–1913, New York Public Library, New York.
L. S. Alexander Gumby's Scrapbook, Columbia University, New York.
Mary D. Miles Collection, 1918–1945, Illinois State Historical Library, Springfield.

DECLASSIFIED MILITARY INTELLIGENCE

Candid Comment on the American Soldier, 1917–1918 . . . by the Germans (AEF, 1919) Records of the War Department, General Staff Record Group 165 (The National Archives, National Archives and Records Service, General Services Administration, Washington, D. C.: 1967).
Interviews with German General Officers After World War II: Informa-

tion Compiled by Office of Chief of Military History, Department of the Army (National Archives, National Archives and Records Service, General Services Administration, Washington, D. C.).

B-490: "An Estimate of the Situation with a Concluding Description about the Fighting on the Invasion Front up to 31 July, 1944."

B-809: "Hitler's Evaluation of American War Potential and Strength."

D-381: "Evaluation of Both Sides, etc." Statement by former German General who fought in Italy, Greece, Romania.

D-382: "Operations Against American Army Troops." Statement stressing Normandy operations.

D-384: "Operations Against American Troops in France." Statement translated from Russian.

D-385: "Military Operations Against American Troops in Africa." Translated from Russian and German.

BOOKS

A Book of War Letters. Ed. Harry E. Maule. New York: Random House, Inc., 1943.

A Brief History of the King's Royal Rifle Corps: 1755–1948. Aldershot, U.K.: Gale & Polden, Ltd., 1948.

A Collection of Civil War Writings. Ed. Jay Luvaas. Chicago: University of Chicago Press, 1958.

Adleman, Robert H., and George Walton. *The Devil's Brigade.* Philadelphia: Chilton Company, 1966.

Alexander, Robert. *Memories of the World War, 1917–1918.* New York: The Macmillan Company, 1931.

Allen, Frederick L. *The Big Change.* New York: Harper & Brothers, 1952.

American Archives: Fourth Series, Containing a Documentary History of the English Colonies in North America from the King's Message to Parliament of March 7, 1774, to the Declaration of Independence by the United States. 9 vols. Ed. Peter Force. Washington, D.C.: M. St. Clair Clarke and Peter Force, 1837–1846.

American Archives: Fifth Series, Containing a Documentary History of the United States of America from the Declaration of Independence, July 4, 1776, to the Definitive Treaty of Peace with Great Britain, September 3, 1783. 3 vols. Washington, D.C.: M. St. Clair Clarke and Peter Force, 1848–1853.

An Army Doctor's Wife on the Frontier: Letters from Alaska and the

Far West, 1874–1878. Ed. Abe Laufe. Pittsburgh: University of Pittsburgh Press, 1962.

As They Saw Us: Foch, Ludendorff and Other Leaders Write Our War History. Ed. George S. Viereck. Garden City, N. Y.: Doubleday, Doran & Company, Inc., 1929.

Aston, Major-General Sir George. *The Biography of the Late Marshal Foch.* New York: The Macmillan Company, 1929.

Bach, Julian, Jr. *America's Germany: An Account of the Occupation.* New York: Random House, Inc., 1946.

Bandel, Eugene. *Frontier Life in the Army, 1854–1861.* Ed. Ralph Bieber. Glendale, Cal.: Arthur H. Clark Company, 1932.

Banning, Kendall. *Our Army Today.* New York: Funk & Wagnalls Company, 1943.

Battalion and Small Unit Studies: American Forces in Action Series, II, V, VII. Washington, D.C.: Historical Division, War Department, 1946.

Biderman, Albert D. *March to Calumny; the Story of the American POW's in the Korean War.* New York: The Macmillan Company, 1963.

Blond, Georges. *The Death of Hitler's Germany.* Trans. by Frances Frenaye. New York: Pyramid Books, 1958.

Bolton, Charles Knowles. *The Private Soldier Under Washington.* Port Washington, N. Y.: Kennikat Press, Inc., 1964.

Bonsal, Stephen. *The Fight for Santiago: The Story of the Soldier in the Cuban Campaign from Tampa to the Surrender.* New York: Doubleday & McClure Co., 1899.

Bowman, Allen. *The Morale of the American Revolutionary Army.* Washington, D.C.: American Council on Public Affairs, 1943.

Boyd, Mrs. Orsemus B. *Cavalry Life in Tent and Field.* New York: J. Selwin Tait, 1894.

Boyle, Martin. *Yanks Don't Cry.* New York: Bernard Geis Associates, 1963.

Bradley, Omar N. *A Soldier's Story.* New York: Henry Holt and Company, Inc., 1951.

Brininstool, E. A. *Troopers with Custer: Historic Incidents of the Battle of the Little Big Horn.* Harrisburg, Pa.: The Stackpole Company, 1952.

Brown, D. Alexander. *The Galvanized Yankees.* Urbana: The University of Illinois Press, 1963.

Burgoyne, John. *State of the Expedition from Canada.* London: Almon, 1780.

Butler, Lewis. *The Royal Americans: Vol. I, The Annals of the King's Royal Rifle Corps.* London: Smith Elder and Co., 1913.

Butow, Robert J. C. *Tojo and the Coming of the War*. Princeton, N. J.: Princeton University Press, 1961.

Carter, William Harding. *The American Army*. Indianapolis: The Bobbs-Merrill Company, Inc., 1915.

Churchill, Winston S. *The Second World War: Closing the Ring*. Boston: Houghton Mifflin Company, 1950.

Churchill, Winston S. *The Second World War: The Hinge of Fate*. Boston: Houghton Mifflin Company, 1950.

Clark, General Mark W. *From the Danube to the Yalu*. New York: Harper & Brothers, 1954.

Clews, John C. *Communist Propaganda Techniques*. New York: Frederick A. Praeger, Inc., 1965.

Collins, James. *Autobiography of a Revolutionary Soldier*. Ed. John Roberts. Clinton, La.: Feliciana [La.] *Democrat*, 1859.

Conner, Howard M. *The Spearhead: The World War II History of the 5th Marine Division*. Washington, D.C.: Infantry Journal Press, 1950.

Coles, Harry and Albert K. Weinberg. *Civil Affairs: Soldiers Become Governors. United States Army in World War II: Special Studies*. Washington, D.C.: Office of Chief of Military History, Department of the Army, 1964.

Cook, Fred J. *What Manner of Men: Forgotten Heroes of the American Revolution*. New York: William Morrow & Company, Inc., 1959.

Correspondence Relating to the War with Spain, Including the Insurrection in the Philippine Islands, and the China Relief Expedition. Washington, D. C.: U. S. Government Printing Office, 1902.

Crowell, Benedict and Robert F. Wilson. *Demobilization: Our Industrial and Military Demobilization After the Armistice, 1918–1920*. New Haven, Conn.: Yale University Press, 1921.

Cunningham, W. Scott. *Wake Island Command*. New York: Popular Library, 1962.

Cushing, Harvey. *From a Surgeon's Journal, 1915–1918*. Boston: Little, Brown & Company, 1936.

Cutler, Robert. *No Time for Rest*. Boston: Little, Brown & Company, 1965.

De Chambrun, Colonel, and Captain De Marenches. *The American Army in the European Conflict*. New York: The Macmillan Company, 1919.

Decisive Battle of World War II: The German View. Ed. by H. A. Jacobsen and J. Rohwer. Trans. by Edward Fitzgerald. New York: G. P. Putnam's Sons, 1965.

Dennett, Carl P. *Prisoners in the Great War*. Boston: Houghton Mifflin Company, 1919.

De Trobriand, Phillippe R. Dennis de Keredern. *Army Life in Dakota*. Ed. Milo M. Quaife. Chicago: The Lakeside Press, 1941.

Dew, Gwen. *Prisoner of the Japs*. New York: Alfred A. Knopf, Inc., 1943.

Dewar, George A. B. and Lieut. Col. J. A. Boraston. *Sir Douglas Haig's Command: Dec. 19, 1915 to Nov. 11, 1918*. 2 vols. Boston: Houghton Mifflin Company, 1923.

Dickinson, John. *The Building of an Army*. New York: Century Company, 1922.

Dietrich, Otto. *Hitler*. Trans. by Richard and Clara Winston. Chicago: Henry Regnery Company, 1955.

Documents of the German Revolution. Fall of the German Empire, 1914–1918. 2 vols. Ed. Ralph Lutz. Palo Alto, Cal.: Stanford University Press, 1932.

Dos Passos, John. *Tour of Duty*. Boston: Houghton Mifflin Company, 1946.

Dupuy, R. Ernest and Trevor N. Dupuy. *Military Heritage of America*. New York: McGraw-Hill Book Company, Inc., 1956.

Eby, Henry H. *Observations of an Illinois Boy in Battle, Camp and Prisons. 1861–1865*. Mendota, Ill.: by the author, 1910.

Ellsworth, Captain Harry A. *One Hundred and Eighty Landings of U. S. Marines, 1800–1934*. Washington, D.C.: Historical Section, Marine Corps, 1934.

Ewert, Earl C. *The United States Army*. Foreword by Hanson W. Baldwin. Boston: Little, Brown & Company, 1941.

Falls, Cyril. *The Second World War*. London: Methuen & Company, Ltd., 1948.

Familiar Letters of John Adams to His Wife, Abigail Adams. Ed. Chas. F. Adams. New York: no pub. listed, 1876.

Farago, Ladislas. *Patton: Ordeal and Triumph*. New York: Ivan Obolensky, Inc., 1964.

Fehrenbach, R. T. *This Kind of War: A Study in Unpreparedness*. New York: The Macmillan Company, 1963.

Fifty Years in Camp and Field: Diary of Major-General Ethan A. Hitchcock, Ed. W. A. Croffut. New York: G. P. Putnam's Sons, 1909.

Fighting For America. Ed. Nathan Balth. New York: National Jewish Welfare Board, 1944.

Forsyth, Gen. George A. *The Story of the Soldier*. New York: D. Appleton & Company, Inc., 1909.

Fredman, J. George and Louis A. Falk. *Jews in American Wars.* Washington, D. C.: Jewish War Veterans of the U. S. A., 1954.

Freedom to Serve: Equality of Treatment and Opportunity in the Armed Services. A Report by the President's Committee. Washington, D. C.: U.S. Government Printing Office, 1950.

Friedel, Frank. *Our Country's Presidents.* Washington, D. C.: National Geographic Society, 1966.

Friedel, Frank. *The Splendid Little War.* New York: Bramhall House, 1958.

Fuchida, Mitsuo and Masatake Okumiza. *Midway: The Battle That Doomed Japan.* New York: Ballantine Books, Inc., 1955.

Fuehrer Conferences: on Matters Dealing with the Germany Navy. Washington, D. C.: Office of Naval Intelligence, 1947.

Fuller, Maj. Gen. J. F. C. *Grant and Lee; A Study in Personality and Generalship.* Bloomington: Indiana University Press, 1957.

Galland, Adolf. *The First and the Last.* New York: Ballantine Books, Inc., 1948.

Gayn, Mark. *Japan Diary.* New York: William Sloane Associates, Inc., 1948.

Geer, Andrew. *The New Breed: The Story of the U. S. Marines in Korea.* New York: Harper & Brothers, 1952.

Gibbons, Floyd. *And They Thought We Wouldn't Fight!* New York: George H. Doran Company, 1918.

Glisan, R. *Journal of Army Life.* San Francisco: A. L. Bancroft, 1874.

Goebbels Diaries. Ed. Louis P. Lochner. New York: The Fireside Press, 1948.

Gould, Benjamin J. *Investigations in the Military and Anthropological Statistics of American Soldiers.* New York: U. S. Sanitary Commission, 1869.

Gulick, Luther H., *From Morals to Morale.* New York: Association Press, 1919.

Harbord, James G., *Leaves from a War Diary.* New York: Dodd, Mead & Company, Inc., 1925.

Heinl, Robert D. *Soldiers of the Sea: The United States Marine Corps, 1775–1962.* Annapolis, Md.: U. S. Naval Institute, 1962.

Hicken, Victor. *Illinois in the Civil War.* Urbana: University of Illinois Press, 1966.

Higgins, Marguerite. *War in Korea: The Report of a Woman Combat Correspondent.* Garden City, N. Y.: Doubleday & Company, Inc., 1951.

Historical Statistics of the U. S., Colonial Times to 1957. Washington, D. C.: U. S. Bureau of the Census, 1960.

History of the First Division During the World War, 1917–1919. Philadelphia: John C. Winston Company, 1922.

Hoffman, Conrad. *In the Prison Camps of Germany*. New York: Association Press, 1920.

Hough, Frank O., and Major John A. Crown. *The Campaign in New Britain*.

Huie, William B. *The Execution of Private Slovik: The Hitherto Secret Story of the Only American Soldier Since 1864 to Be Shot for Desertion*. New York: Duell, Sloan & Pearce, 1954.

Hunt, Frazier. *Blown in by the Draft*. Garden City, N. Y.: Doubleday, Page & Company, 1918.

Hunter, Col. Charles N. *Galahad*. San Antonio: Naylor Company, 1963.

Illinois in the World War. 3 vols., Chicago: States Publication Society, 1920.

Jablonski, Edward. *Flying Fortresses: The Illustrated Biography of the B-17's and the Men Who Flew Them*. Garden City, N. Y.: Doubleday & Company, Inc., 1965.

Jacobs, James Ripley. *The Beginning of the U. S. Army, 1783–1812*. Princeton, N. J.: Princeton University Press, 1947.

Jamison, Matthew U. *Recollections of Pioneer and Army Life*. Kansas City, Kan.: Hudson Press, 1911.

Janowitz, Morris. *The Professional Soldier: A Social and Political Portrait*. Glencoe, Ill.: The Free Press, 1960.

Johnson, Robert. *Thence Round Cape Horn: The Story of the United States Naval Forces on Pacific Station, 1818–1923*. Annapolis, Md.: U. S. Naval Institute, 1963.

Johnson, Robert S., with Martin Caidin. *Thunderbolt!* New York: Ballantine Books, Inc., 1963.

Kase, Toshikazu. *Journey to the Missouri*. Ed. by David Nelson Rowe. New Haven, Conn.: Yale University Press, 1950.

Kinkead, Eugene. *In Every War but One*. New York: W.W. Norton & Company, Inc., 1959.

Kirke, Edmund. *Rear-Guard of the Revolution*. New York: D. Appleton & Company, Inc., 1888.

Kris, Ernst and Hans Speier. *German Radio Propaganda: Report on Home Broadcasts During the War*. New York: Oxford University Press, Inc., 1944.

Lafayette, Marquis de. *Memoirs: Correspondence and Manuscripts of General Lafayette*. New York: Saunders and Otley, 1837.

Leckie, Robert. *Conflict*. New York: G. P. Putnam's Sons, 1962.

Leigh, Liet. Col. Randolph. *48 Million Tons to Eisenhower: The Role of the SOS in the Defeat of Germany.* Washington, D.C.: The Infantry Journal, 1945.

Letters from America, 1776–1779, Being Letters of Brunswick, Hessian, and Waldeck Officers with the British Armies During the Revolution. Trans. by Ray Pettengill. Port Washington, N. Y.: Kennikat Press, Inc., 1964.

Letters from America, 1773 to 1780, Being the Letters of a Scots Officer, Sir James Murray, to His Home During the War of American Independence. Ed. Eric Robson. Manchester, Eng.: Manchester University Press, 1951.

Letters from Fighting Hoosiers. Ed. by Howard H. Peckham and Shirley A. Snyder. Bloomington: Indiana War History Commission, 1948.

Letters from Libby Prison: Being the Authentic Letters Written While in Confederate Captivity in the Notorious Libby Prison in Richmond. Ed. Margaret W. Peelle. New York: Greenwich Book Publishers, 1956.

Livermore, Mary. *My Story of the War.* Hartford, Conn.: A. D. Worthington, 1889.

Lonn, Ella. *Foreigners in the Union Army and Navy.* Baton Rouge: Louisiana State University Press, 1951.

Lossing, Benson J., *The Pictorial Field Book of the War of 1812.* New York: Harper & Brothers, Pub., 1869.

Lowe, Percival G. *Five Years a Dragoon ('49 to '54): And Other Adventures on the Great Plains.* Norman: University of Oklahoma Press, 1965.

Luvaas, Jay. *The Military Legacy of the Civil War: The European Inheritance.* Chicago: University of Chicago Press, 1959.

Lyonn, C. C., *Experience of a Recruit in the United States Army.* Washington, D. C.: U. S. War Department, 1916.

Marcus, Jacob Rader. *Memoirs of American Jews: 1775–1865.* Vol. I. Philadelphia: The Jewish Publication Society of America, 1955.

Marder, Arthur J. *The Anatomy of British Sea Power: A History of British Naval Policy in the Pre-Dreadnought Era, 1880–1905.* Hamden, Conn.: Archon Books, 1964.

Masters, John. *The Road Past Mandalay.* New York: Harper & Brothers, 1961.

McGrath, John. *War Diary of 354th Infantry, 89th Division.* Trier, Germany: J. Lintz, n.d.

Merrill's Marauders. American Forces in Action Series. Washington, D. C.: U. S. War Department, 1945.

Millis, Walter. *The Martial Spirit.* Cambridge, Mass.: The Literary Guild of America, 1931.

Military Affairs in North America, 1748–1765. Ed. Stanley Pargellis. New York: Appleton-Century Company, Inc., 1936.

Mitchell, Donald W. *History of the Modern American Navy: from 1883 Through Pearl Harbor.* New York: Alfred A. Knopf, Inc., 1946.

Montgomery, Gen. Bernard. *Normandy to the Baltic.* London: Hutchinson & Co., 1946.

Montross, Lynn. *Rag, Tag and Bobtail.* New York: Harper & Brothers, 1952.

Montross, Lynn, and Nicholas A. Canzona. *U. S. Marine Operations in Korea, 1950–1953.* Vols. II and III. Washington, D. C.: Historical Branch, U. S. Marine Corps, 1955–1957.

Morison, Samuel E. *The Oxford History of the American People.* New York: Oxford University Press, Inc., 1965.

Newsome, Edmund. *Experience in the War of the Great Rebellion by a Soldier of the 81st Regiment Illinois Volunteer Infantry.* Carbondale, Ill.: by the author, 1880.

Nichols, Major Chas. S., and Henry I. Shaw., Jr. *Okinawa: Victory in the Pacific.* Washington, D. C.: Historical Branch, U. S. Marine Corps, 1955.

Nichols, Edward J. *Zach Taylor's Little Army.* Garden City, N. Y.: Doubleday & Company, Inc., 1963.

Odell, Joseph H. *The New Spirit in the Old Army.* New York: Fleming H. Revell Company, 1918.

Ogburn, Charlton. *The Marauders.* New York: Harper & Brothers, 1956.

Okumiya, Masatake, and Jiro Horikoshi. *Zero!* New York: Ballantine Books, Inc., 1966.

Omaha Beachhead. American Forces in Action Series. Washington, D. C.: Historical Division, U. S. War Department, 1945.

Palmer, Frederick. *Our Greatest Battle (The Meuse-Argonne).* New York: Dodd, Mead & Company, Inc., 1924.

Palmer, John A. *Life of Steuben.* New Haven, Conn.: Yale University Press, 1937.

Palmer, John McAuley. *America in Arms: The Experience of the United States with Military Organization.* New Haven, Conn.: Yale University Press, 1941.

Palmer, R. R., B. I. Wiley and William Keast. *The Procurement and Training of Ground Combat Troops. United States Army in World War II.* Washington, D. C.: Department of the Army, 1948.

Pargellis, Stanley M. *Lord Loudoun in North America.* New Haven, Conn.: Yale University Press, 1933.

Patton, Gen. George S. *War as I Knew It*. Boston: Houghton Mifflin Company, 1947.

Pelzer, Louis. *Marches of the Dragoons in the Mississippi Valley*. Iowa City: State Historical Society of Iowa, 1917.

Percy, Earl. *Letters. Comments on Battles from Lexington to Long Island by a British Leader*. Ed. Charles K. Bolton. Boston: Goodspeed, 1902.

Pershing, John J. *My Experiences in the World War*. 2 vols. New York: Frederick A. Stokes Company, 1931.

Physical Examination of the First Million Draft Recruits: Methods and Results. Washington, D. C.: U. S. Army Medical Department, 1919.

Post, Charles Johnson. *The Little War of Private Post*. Boston: Little, Brown & Company, 1960.

Potter, John Deane. *Yamamoto*. New York: The Viking Press, Inc., 1965.

Pyle, Ernie. *Brave Men*. New York: Henry Holt and Company, Inc., 1944.

Pyle, Ernie. *Here is Your War*. Cleveland: The World Publishing Company, 1945.

Reed, William B. *Life and Correspondence of Joseph Reed, Military Secretary of Washington*. 2 vols. Philadelphia: Lindsay and Blakiston, 1847.

Rees, David. *Korea: The Limited War*. New York: St. Martin's Press, 1964.

Reischauer, Edwin O. *The United States and Japan*. Cambridge, Mass.: Harvard University Press, 1965.

Reminiscences of the Old Navy: from the Journals and Private Papers of Captain Edward Trenchard, and Rear-Admiral Stephen Decatur Trenchard. Ed. Edgar S. Maclay. New York: G. P. Putnam's Sons, 1898.

Repington, Lieut. Col. Charles À Court. *The First World War, 1914–1918*. 2 vols. London: Constable & Company, Ltd., 1921.

Rickey, Don. *Forty Miles a Day on Beans and Hay: The Enlisted Soldier Fighting the Indian Wars*. Norman: University of Oklahoma Press, 1963.

Rodnick, David. *Postwar Germans: An Anthropologist's Account*. New Haven, Conn.: Yale University Press, 1948.

Sassé, Fred A. *Rookie Days of a Soldier*. St. Paul, Minn.: W. G. Green, 1924.

Schott, Joseph L. *Above and Beyond: The Story of the Congressional Medal of Honor*. New York: G. P. Putnam's Sons, 1963.

Sherrod, Robert. *Tarawa: The Story of a Battle.* New York: Duell, Sloan & Pearce, 1954.

Sherwood, Robert E. *Roosevelt and Hopkins: An Intimate History.* New York: Harper & Brothers, 1948.

Shirer, William L. *The Rise and Fall of the Third Reich: A History of Nazi Germany.* New York: Simon and Schuster, Inc., 1960.

Simmons, Kenneth W. *Kriegie.* New York: Thomas Nelson & Sons, 1960.

Simonson, Sigurd J. *Soldier Bill.* New York: Fortuny's Pub., 1938.

Smith, Justin H. *The War with Mexico.* 2 vols. Gloucester, Mass.: Peter Smith, 1963.

St. Lo. American Forces in Action Series. Washington, D. C.: Historical Division, U. S. War Department, 1946.

Stallings, Laurence. *The Doughboys: The Story of the A. E. F., 1917–1918.* New York: Harper and Row, Publishers, 1963.

Statistical Abstract of the United States, 1965. Washington, D. C.: U. S. Bureau of the Census, 1965.

Stevens, W. O., and A. Westcott. *A History of Sea Power.* New York: Doubleday, Doran & Company, Inc., 1920.

Stillwell, Leander. *The Story of a Common Soldier of Army Life in the Civil War.* Kansas City, Mo.: Franklin Hudson Co., 1920.

Stouffer, Samuel A., and associates. *The American Soldier.* 2 vols. Princeton, N. J.: Princeton University Press, 1949.

Straub, Elmer F. *A Sergeant's Diary in the World War.* Indianapolis: Indiana Historical Commission, 1923.

Stromberg, Roland N. *Readings and Study Guide in American History.* New York: McGraw-Hill Book Company, 1960.

Strong, Robert H. *A Yankee Private's Civil War.* Chicago: Henry Regnery Company, 1961.

Sullivan, Mark. *Over Here, 1914–1918.* Vol. V of: *Our Times, The United States, 1900–1925.* New York: Charles Scribner's Sons, 1933.

Swetland, Maurice J. *These Men. For Conspicuous Bravery Above and Beyond the Call of Duty.* Harrisburg, Pa.: The Military Service Publishing Co., 1940.

The American Negro Reference Book. Ed. John P. Davis. Englewood Cliffs, N. J.: Prentice-Hall, Inc., 1966.

The Best from Yank, the Army Weekly. Cleveland: The World Publishing Company, 1945.

The Civil War Letters of Henry C. Bear: A Soldier of the 116th Illinois Volunteer Infantry. Ed. Wayne C. Temple. Harrogate, Tenn.: Lincoln Memorial University Press, 1961.

The Civil War Letters of Sergeant Onley Andrus. Ed. Fred Shannon. Urbana: University of Illinois Press, 1947.

The Fremantle Diary: Being the Journal of Lieut. Col. Arthur James Lyon Fremantle. Ed. Walter Lord. New York: Capricorn, 1954.

The Hebrew Impact on Western Civilization. Ed. Dagobert D. Runes. New York: Philosophical Library, 1951.

The Japanese Story of Midway. Trans. Washington, D. C.: Office of Naval Intelligence, 1947.

The Private Papers of Douglas Haig, 1914–1919. Ed. Robert Blake. London: Eyre & Spottiswoode, Ltd., 1952.

The Spanish-American War. War Notes. Washington, D. C.: Office of Naval Intelligence, 1899.

The Rommel Papers. Ed. B. H. Liddell Hart. Trans. by Paul Findlay. New York: Harcourt, Brace and Company, Inc., 1953.

The Stilwell Papers. Ed. T. H. White. New York: William Sloane Associates, 1948.

The Times History of the War. 21 vols. London: *The Times,* 1919.

The Uncensored Letters of a Canteen Girl. No author listed. New York: Henry Holt and Company, Inc., 1920.

The United States Navy in Peace Time: The Navy in Its Relation to the Industrial, Scientific, Economic, and Political Development of the Nation. Washington, D. C.: Navy Department, 1931.

The United States Navy in World War II. Ed. S. E. Smith. New York: William Morrow & Company, Inc., 1966.

The War Reports of General of the Army George C. Marshall, General of the Army H. H. Arnold, Fleet Admiral Ernest J. King. New York: J. B. Lippincott Company, 1947.

The Writings of George Washington. Ed. John C. Fitzgerald. 37 vols. Washington, D. C.: George Washington Bi-Centennial Commission, 1931–1940.

The Writings of George Washington. Ed. Worthington C. Ford. 14 vols. New York: G. P. Putnam's Sons, 1890.

This Was Andersonville Military Prison as Told in the Personal Recollections of John McElroy. Ed. Roy Meredity. New York: McDowell, Obolensky, 1957.

Thoumin, General Richard. *The First World War.* Trans. by Martin Kieffer. New York: G. P. Putnam's Sons, 1964.

Three Years in the Army of the Cumberland: The Letters and Diary of Major James A. Connolly. Ed. Paul M. Angle. Bloomington: Indiana University Press, 1959.

To Bigotry No Sanction. Philadelphia: Anti-Defamation Council and The American Jewish Committee, 1941.

Tolischus, Otto D. *Through Japanese Eyes.* New York: Reynal & Hitchcock, Inc. 1945.

Tolischus, Otto D. *Tokyo Record.* New York: Reynal & Hitchcock, Inc. 1943.

Tompkins, R. S. *The Story of the Rainbow Division.* New York: Boni ··and Liveright, 1919.

Tregaskis, Richard. *Vietnam Diary.* New York: Holt, Rinehart and Winston, Inc., 1963.

Trevelyan, Sir George O. T. *The American Revolution.* 3 vols. London: Longmans, Green and Co., Ltd., 1905.

United States Submarine Losses, World War II. Washington, D. C.: Chief of Naval Operations, 1963.

Upton, Gen. Emory. *The Military Policy of the United States.* Washington, D. C.: U. S. Government Printing Office, 1912.

Van Doren, Carl. *Mutiny in January.* New York: The Viking Press, Inc., 1943.

Walker, Harriet J. *Revolutionary Soldiers Buried in Illinois.* Los Angeles: Standard Printing Co., 1917.

Warfare Along the Mississippi: The Letters of Lieutenant-Col. George E. Currie. Mt. Pleasant, Mich.: Central Michigan University Press, 1961.

War Notes. Nos. I, II, III. Washington, D. C.: U. S. Government Printing Office, 1899.

Way, Virgil. *History of the Thirty-Third Regiment Illinois Veteran Volunteer Infantry.* Gibson City, Ill.: Regimental Association, 1902.

Wecter, Dixon. *When Johnny Comes Marching Home.* Cambridge, Mass.: Houghton Mifflin Company, 1944.

Welding of the Nation, 1845–1900. Vol. IV, American History Told by Contemporaries. New York: The Macmillan Company, 1910.

Westover, John. *Combat Support in Korea.* Washington, D. C.: Combat Forces Press, 1955.

What Europe Thinks of America. Ed. James Burnham. New York: The John Day Co., Inc., 1953.

What Happened at Pearl Harbor? Documents Pertaining to the Japanese Attack of December 7, 1941, and Its Background. Ed. Hans Louis Trefousse. New York: Twayne Publishers, Inc., 1958.

While Berlin Burns: The Diary of Jans-Georg von Studnitz. Englewood Cliffs, N. J.: Prentice-Hall, Inc., 1963.

White, William L. *Report on the Germans.* New York: Harcourt, Brace and Company, Inc., 1947.

Whitehair, Charles W. *Out There.* New York: D. Appleton & Company, Inc., 1918.

Whitehouse, Arch. *Heroes and Legends of World War I.* Garden City, N. Y.: Doubleday & Company, Inc., 1964.

Wiley, Bell I. *The Common Soldier in the Civil War.* New York: Grosset & Dunlap, Inc., n.d.

William, Crown Prince of Germany. *My War Experiences.* London: Hurst and Blackett, Ltd., 1922.

Williams, T. Harry. *Americans at War.* Baton Rouge: Louisiana University Press, 1960.

Wilson, Herbert W. *The Downfall of Spain: Naval History of the Spanish-American War.* London: Low, Marston & Co., Ltd. 1902.

World War Records: First Division, A. E. F. Washington, D. C.: The Army War College, 1920.

World War Records: Second Division, A. E. F. Washington, D. C.: The Army War College, 1918.

Wright, Maj. B. C. *The 1st Cavalry Division in World War II.* Tokyo: Toppan Printing Co., 1947.

Wright, Quincy. *A Study of War.* Chicago: University of Chicago Press, 1964.

ARTICLES OF SPECIAL SIGNIFICANCE

"A Sunday With Westmoreland, The General Who Runs Our War in Vietnam," *Look* (Oct. 18, 1966) 27–31.

Baldwin, Hanson W., "Our Fighting Men Have Gone Soft," *Saturday Evening Post* (Aug. 8, 1959) 13–15, 82–84.

Baldwin, Hanson W., "What's Wrong with the Regulars," *Saturday Evening Post* (Oct. 31, 1953) 19–21, 104–110.

Bonsal, Stephen, "The Negro Soldier in War and Peace," *The North American Review* V. 185 (1907) 321–327.

Buaken, Pfc. Manuel, "Life in the Armed Forces," *The New Republic* (Aug. 31, 1943) 279–280.

Buaken, Manuel, "Our Fighting Love of Freedom," *Asia* (June, 1943) 357–359.

Clark, Blake, and Russell, Oland D., "Japanese-American Soldiers Make Good," *The American Mercury* (June, 1945) 698–703.

Clausius, Gerhard P., "The Little Soldier of the 95th: Albert D. J. Cashier," *Journal of the Illinois Historical Society,* LI, No. 4.

Dempsey, Sgt. David, USMC, "Fear in Battle," *The American Mercury* (June, 1945) 677–683.

Deverall, Richard L. G., "Wild GI's: Our Black Eye in Japan," *America* (Mar. 6, 1954) 597–598.

Farnsworth, Amos, "Journal," A Massachusetts Corporal's Experiences, 1775–1779. *Massachusetts Historical Society Proceedings* (2nd Series) XII, 74–107.

Foraker, Joseph Benson, "A Review of the Testimony in the Browns-ville Investigation," *The North American Review*, V. 187 (1908) 550–558.

Hale, Edward E., "Naval History of the Revolution," *Proceedings of the American Antiquarian Society*, New Series, Vol. 5 (Oct., 1887–1888).

Hill, Gladwin, "Brain-Washing: Time For a Policy," *Atlantic Monthly* (April, 1955).

"How British Soldiers Were Tortured by Red Chinese," *U. S. News and World Report* (Aug. 19, 1955) 94–100, 102.

"How Negro Americans Perform in Vietnam," *U. S. News and World Report* (Aug. 15, 1966) 60–63.

Jane, Frederick T., "The Maine Disaster and After," *Fortnightly Review* (April, 1898).

Karpinos, Bernard D., "Current Height and Weight of Youths of Military Age," reprint from *Human Biology* (Dec., 1961).

Lardner, John, "Those of the First Generation," *The New Yorker* (Mar. 31, 1945) 42–49.

"Leatherneck Salesmen," *Marine Corps Gazette* (Aug., 1955).

Lewis, Ralph, "Officer-Enlisted Men's Relationships," *The American Journal of Sociology*, Vol. LII, No. 4 (Jan., 1947) 410–419.

Marshall, S. L. A., "Men Facing Death: The Destruction of an American Platoon," *Harper's* magazine (Sept., 1966).

Marshall, S. L. A., "Our Army in Korea—The Best Yet," *Harper's* magazine (August, 1951) 21–27.

McLendon, Bart, "Teen G.I.'s Know Why They Fight," *Detroit Free-Press*, (Aug. 18, 1966).

Olsen, Arthur J., "Touchy Coexistence: G.I. and German," *The New York Times Magazine* (Sept. 9, 1956) 15, 56–62.

"Red Torture Broke Few GI's," *U. S. News and World Report*, (Aug. 26, 1955).

Seaton, John, "The Battle of Belmont," *War Talks in Kansas: A Series of Papers Read before the Kansas Commandery*, (Kansas City, Kans.: Hudson Publishing Co., 1906).

Sergeant, Elizabeth Shepley, "The Indian Goes to War," *The New Republic* (Nov. 31, 1942) 708–709.

Shearer, Lloyd, "Why the French Are Throwing Us Out," *Parade*, (Oct. 2, 1966) 6–7.

Sherrod, Robert, "Notes on a Monstrous War," *Life*, (Jan. 27, 1967).

Stillwell, Leander, "In the Ranks at Shiloh," *Journal of the Illinois Historical Society*, XV, Nos. 1–2.

Stouffer, Samuel A., "A Study of Attitudes," *Scientific American*, vol. 180, no. 5, (May, 1949) 11–15.

Taylor, Captain Henry, "The Indiana at Santiago," *Century* magazine (May, 1899).

"The True Story of Pearl Harbor," *U. S. News and World Report,* (Dec. 11, 1961) 56–57.

Villard, Oswald G., "Our Military Disgrace Abroad," *The Christian Century* (June 26, 1946).

Waldo, Albigence, "Journal," An American military surgeon at Valley Forge. *Pennsylvania Magazine of History,* XXI, 299–323.

"War Diary of Thaddeus H. Capron, 1861–1865, Extracts From Letters Written by Major Thaddeus H. Capron from September, 1861, to August, 1865, to His Father, Mother, Brother and Sisters, During His Service in the Fifty-fifth Illinois Infantry Volunteer Regiment in the Civil War," *Journal of the Illinois State Historical Society,* XII, No. 3 (Oct., 1919), 330–406.

"What Communists Did to Americans in Korea," *U. S. News and World Report,* (August 26, 1955), 40–47.

"What the Soldier Thinks," *Periodical Publication of the Research Branch,* Information and Education Division, U. S. War Department (Dec., 1942–Sept., 1945).

"What's Wrong in Korea? British Military Expert Answers." This is an interview with Maj. Gen. J. F. C. Fuller. *U. S. News and World Report* (Aug. 25, 1950) 14–17.

Wheatley, Austin, "The Asian Retreat We've All but Forgotten," *The Detroit News,* (Aug. 14, 1966).

White, William S., "The End of the Old Army," *Harper's* (June, 1959), 82–85.

"With Grant at Vicksburg: From the Civil War Diary of Captain Charles E. Wilcox," ed. by Edgar Erickson, *Journal of the Illinois State Historical Society,* XXX, No. 4 (Jan., 1938).

Wright, Aaron, "Journal of a Pennsylvania Rifleman at the Siege of Boston," *Boston Transcript* (April 11, 1862).

"Yanks Are in Britain to Stay," *U. S. News and World Report,* (Aug. 31, 1951) 27.

OTHER MAGAZINES OR PUBLICATIONS USED IN PREPARATION OF MANUSCRIPT

America, Mar. 6, April 17, 1954.
American Mercury, July, 1945.
Associated Press, Oct. 13, Dec. 3, 1966.
Atlas, April, September, 1966.
Current History, June 20, 1918.

Harper's Weekly, Jan. 7, 1865.

International Affairs, Moscow edition, Oct., 1965.

International Relations, Oct., 1965.

Japan Advertiser, Jan. 17, 1934.

Japan Times & Advertiser, Dec. 23, 1941, Jan. 9, 1942.

London Daily Telegraph, Sept. 1, 1950.

Look Magazine, May 28, 1957.

Newsweek, Feb. 19, Mar. 5, April 23, April 30, May, 7, May 28, June 4, June 11, 1945; July 30, Aug. 6, 1966; Feb. 19, 1967.

The Chicago *Tribune,* June 9, 1917; July 11, July 20, Sept. 1, Oct. 25, Oct. 27, Nov. 12, Dec. 4, 1966; Feb. 19, 1967.

The Commonwealth: Journal of the Commonwealth Club of California, XIX, No. 21.

The Current Digest of the Soviet Press, XVII, No. 15, XVI, No. 25, XVII, No. 2, June 29, July 21, 1965.

The New Republic, June 3, 1957.

The New York Times, March 9, 1927, July 1, July 5, 1942.

The Russian Review, July, 1966.

The Saturday Evening Post, Nov. 10, 1917.

The Saturday Review, Nov. 10, 1945.

The St. Louis *Post-Dispatch,* July 8, Aug. 7, Nov. 8, 1966.

The Scientific American, May, 1949.

Time, Jan. 1, 1951; July 16, July 30, 1956; Sept. 16, 1966.

U. S. News and World Report, June 1, Oct. 5, 1951; Jan. 23, Mar. 13, 1953; July 15, 1955; Aug. 22, Sept. 5, Nov. 28, 1966.

Index